FELLINI

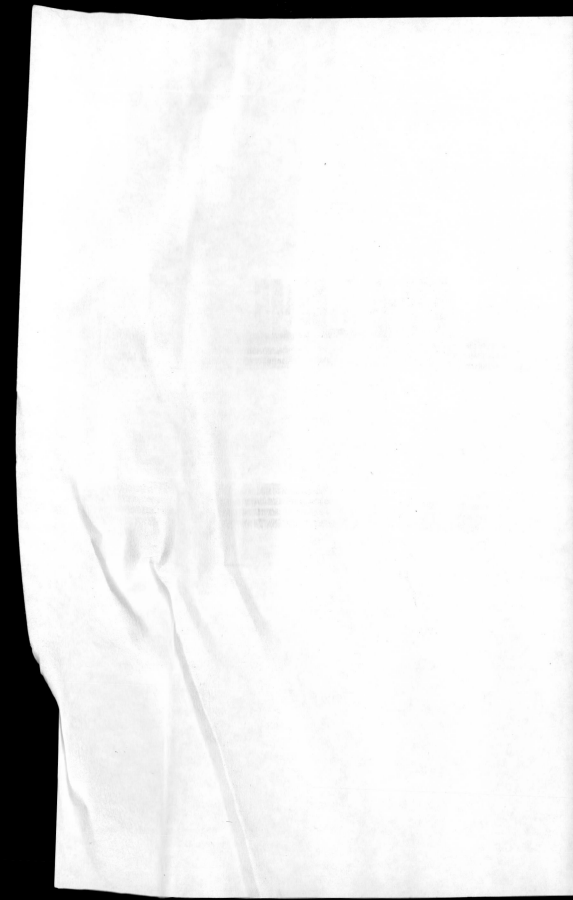

JOHN BAXTER

FELLINI

Monterey Public Library

ST. MARTIN'S PRESS
NEW YORK

921
FELLINI

The publishers acknowledge the following copyright holders for permission to reproduce the photographs in the plate sections: The British Film Institute: pages 2 (3), 4, 5 (2), 6, 7, 9 (2), 10 (2), 11, 12, 13, 14, 16, 17 (2), 18, 19 (2), 22; Deborah Imogen Beer: pages 20, 21 (2), 22 (2), 23, 24; Vera Fotographica Levibrom: page 1; Roger Viollet: page 8; Marika Rivera: page 19.

Library of Congress Cataloging-in-Publication Data

Baxter, John.
    Fellini : the biography / John Baxter.
      p.   cm.
    ISBN 0-312-11273-4
    1. Fellini, Federico.   2. Motion picture producers and directors—Italy—
Biography. I. Title.
PN1998.3.F45B38   1994
791.43′0233′092—dc20
   [B]   94-25341
                                            CIP

First published in Great Britain by Fourth Estate Limited.

First U.S. Edition: October 1994
10 9 8 7 6 5 4 3 2 1

For Marie-Dominique

Contents

'Se non e vero, e ben trovato'
'If it isn't true, at least it's well invented'

– Traditional Italian saying

1   'Signor Fellini is making a new film . . .'

'The movie business is macabre, grotesque. It is a
combination of a football game and a brothel'
Federico Fellini

In the summer of 1979 Federico Fellini and his entourage swept up via
Tuscolana from Rome and through the gates of Cinecittà studios to
start work on his new film, *La città delle donne/City of Women*. His
collaborators were already installed: cinematographer Giuseppe
Rotunno, editor Ruggero Mastroianni, long-time secretary, confidante
and now casting director Liliana Betti, all the way down to Ettore
Bevilacqua, for more than twenty years his chauffeur and masseur,
and probably the only person ever to receive on-screen credit in a film
as 'Director's Bodyguard'. All dutiful. All adoring. The *maestro* was in
residence again. '*Il poeta*', as the Romans called him, had come home.

Fellini was fifty-nine. People meeting him for the first time were
surprised by his height – 1.82 metres; almost six feet – and his light,
gentle, almost feminine voice. At least fifteen kilos of overweight sat
awkwardly on a thin frame, and swollen ankles betrayed the poor
circulation that often accompanies low blood pressure; but though,
like many big men who spend much time on their feet, he was a chronic
sufferer from lumbago and sciatica, he moved gracefully and fast. His
white sideburns were untrimmed and his kinky, greying hair, once
black, was receding. Vain about his baldness, Fellini for two decades
had never gone out in public without something on his head: first the
black stetson made famous by *Otto e mezzo/8½*, then a beret, and these
days the soft, tweedy, Irish walking hat popularised by Rex Harrison in
My Fair Lady. With a car coat and a patterned silk scarf draped over
the shoulders, the hat completed Fellini's official public image.

Though born on 20 January, on the cusp of Capricorn and Aquarius,
Fellini was a typical Aquarian, or so he believed. Famously superstitious, he'd always been a ready client of astrologers, psychics and

seers, many of whom were brought into his circle and cast in his films. Aquarians are 'inventive, mad and miracle-minded', says one text, and noted for vision, intolerance and delight in scandalising people. The description could have been tailored to Fellini. Even the swollen ankles are consistent. For Aquarians, they are the body's most significant zone.

His obsession with the occult was a clue that, behind the flamboyance, even arrogance, Fellini was anything but sure of himself. In particular he felt keenly his lack of education, having left school at eighteen with a dismal academic record. 'I have never read *Ulysses*,' he said, with his typical mixture of defiance and charm. 'I have never seen *Last Year in Marienbad*. I don't know anything about Proust and I have seen only one film by Ingmar Bergman.' Asked to name his twenty favourite movies, he confessed he'd hardly seen that many in a decade.*

What then was the origin of the vivid and intricate visions in *Giulietta degli spiriti/Juliet of the Spirits*, *Fellini–Satyricon* and *Il Casanova di Federico Fellini/Fellini's Casanova*? 'Dreams. The best part of the day is when I go to bed. I go to sleep and the *fête* begins.' For years he'd kept diaries in which, an accomplished sketch artist and caricaturist, he recorded each dream in detail. They were the source book and foundation of almost all his later films. But that made it worse. A gift so casually conferred by providence could be just as readily taken away.

Since 1943 Fellini had been married to Giulia Anna 'Giulietta' Masina, a diminutive actress he met on a radio serial he wrote called *Cico e Pallina*. He called her 'Ceccina' and she called him, as do his intimates, 'Fefé'. She had starred in his most famous early successes, *La strada/The Road* and *Le notti di Cabiria/Nights of Cabiria*, and in two later, and odder, films, *Giulietta degli spiriti* and *Ginger e Fred/ Ginger and Fred*, but these days she was little seen on his sets and for

---

*In a poll of major international directors held by *Sight and Sound* magazine in 1992, Fellini was selected as the world's greatest director. He was the only film-maker with two titles, *La strada* and *Otto e mezzo*, in the top-ten list. His own choice of ten favourites was eccentric: *Maciste all'inferno* (Guido Brignone), *City Lights* (Charlie Chaplin), *Fra' Diavolo* (Hal Roach, with Laurel and Hardy), *Frankenstein* (James Whale), *Stagecoach* (John Ford), *Paisà* (Roberto Rossellini), *2001: A Space Odyssey* (Stanley Kubrick), *Le Charme discret de la bourgeoisie* (Luis Buñuel), *Toto e Peppino divisi a Berlino* (Giorgio Bianchi) and *Intervista* (Federico Fellini). No other director included his own films.

some years the couple, though sharing an apartment on Rome's via Margutta, had led if not separate, then distant lives.

With Fellini's arrival, Cinecittà, built by Mussolini in the thirties to revitalise the Italian cinema, came to life. In some ways he had never left. Stage 5, cavernous as an aircraft hangar, was always the 'Fellini Stage'. Here he had re-created via Veneto for *La dolce vita*, eighteenth-century Venice for *Casanova* and his own home town of Rimini for *Amarcord*. Now it was being readied for another enormous set, an amphitheatre where Marcello Mastroianni goes on trial before a thousand feminists and from which he escapes in a balloon ten metres high, shaped like a beautiful half-naked girl.

Relics of previous Fellini films littered the back lot: a giant polystyrene head of Venus from *Casanova*, a pig's-foot sausage six metres long from *Ginger e Fred*, a jumble of rusted steel that had been the hydraulic jacks supporting the deck of a liner in *E la nave va/And the Ship Sails On*. In the prop department, surrounded by plaster models of a Greek Poseidon and the *David* of Michelangelo, a statue of Christ, twice life size, raised arms of dusty gilt over Cinecittà as it had once lifted them in mute reproach above modern Rome from beneath a helicopter in the opening image of *La dolce vita*.

Fellini's return to Cinecittà was always the occasion for celebration. It was as if a feudal lord had once again taken residence on his estate, promising excitement, beauty and fun. One no longer noticed the unused sound stages, the splintered floors and leaky roofs. Even the cats scavenging for scraps under the umbrella pines that shaded the studio's ochre walls looked more sleek, and the blank-faced apartment blocks surrounding the back lot, staring down into this aristocrats' playground like malevolent children, seemed to take a step or two back.

Word that Fellini was working drew the world to his set. In the sixties, he had been one of the first directors to surround himself with a 'court' of collaborators and sycophants. After *La dolce vita*, he had felt free to squabble with producers, walk out on productions and in general play the great artist. But such foibles had become so typical of star directors that he now appeared, by comparison with terrors like Michael Cimino, almost benign. He'd become an institution. Visitors to Rome wanted, it was said, to meet only three people – the Pope, President Alessandro Pertini and Fellini.

Cinecittà was happy to accommodate them. It provided a dining-room adjacent to every stage for his famous lunches. Over the next few months he'd entertain, among many others, Charlie Chaplin, Paul

Newman, Danny Kaye, painter Henry Balthus and Ingrid Bergman. Since the new film seemed to offer an affront to women, he was also visited by feminist writers Germaine Greer and Susan Sontag.

In one way he revelled in the attention. On the set of his next film, actor Freddie Jones told him: 'You should be Pope.' 'I was Pope two years ago,' Fellini informed him airily. 'It was very boring.' But in another sense he found it humiliating. There was little admiration in these visits. People didn't seek him out for his brilliant and erudite conversation, as they might have visited the late Pier Paolo Pasolini, or his good taste, as they had once come to call on his arch-rival Luchino Visconti. He'd become one of the sights of Rome, like the Fontana di Trevi and St Peter's; less a person than an event. What people most hoped for from a visit with Fellini was that he should behave outrageously. Usually he obliged.

Fellini's position in the Italian film industry had always been ambiguous. In November 1938, as foreign film imports dried up under Fascist censorship, the magazine *Il travaso delle idee* published a cover cartoon showing Italian film directors as knights in armour with their names and noble heredity emblazoned on their shields. At their head, Alessandro Blasetti calls: 'It's a good moment to fight, gentlemen. Nobody's here.' In this company, Fellini, the son of a provincial grocer, would have rated as little more than a foot-soldier. In a country addicted to casual honorifics like *'dottore'*, *'commendatore'* and *'professore'*, his *'maestro'* often seemed like an insult.

Not everyone involved with *La città delle donne* was as admiring of Fellini as his lunch guests. Its first producer, *Penthouse* magazine's publisher Bob Guccione, had pulled out a year before when the director wildly overspent. Daniel Toscan du Plantier, head of Italian operations for the French Gaumont company, was now in charge. He'd produced films by Fellini before, and he knew his cunning and stubbornness.

'Working with Fellini is extremely difficult, because he changes producers.' Toscan du Plantier laughs. 'On *La città delle donne* we had a particularly hard time. We had a terrible thing [happen] – which Fellini did not organise, though he was not so far from that.'

Fellini first thought of the film in 1968, when Ingmar Bergman came to Rome. During a night-time walk around the city with his star and companion Liv Ullmann, the two men had decided spontaneously to collaborate. Their film, to be called *Love Duet*, evaporated, along with the relationship, after Fellini and Bergman had an argument at dinner over which of them knew the most about death, but the plot

Fellini chose for his part of the movie survived and, ten years later, took root.

It was, however, a very sixties idea. Marcello Mastroianni, Italy's great lover, Fellini's close friend and *alter ego*, plays a philanderer trapped in a conference of feminists. He's forced to relive his childhood sexual experiments, his unhappy marriage, his countless conquests. A burning issue in 1968, feminism was less so in 1979. Fellini had rewritten the script with the author of the original story, Bernardino Zapponi, and called in Brunello Rondi for a final polish, but still the doubts persisted.

Casting wasn't difficult. It never was with a Fellini film. Liliana Betti simply inserted the usual ad in the personal columns of *Corriere della sera*: '*Signor Fellini sta preparando un nuovo film a gli piacerebbe incontrare chiunque lo vuole incontrare*' ('Signor Fellini is making a new film and will be happy to meet anyone who wants to meet him'), and within hours the casting office was overwhelmed. Women besieged the studio for the 170 roles. He could have chosen from a thousand.

For the main part he had Mastroianni, of course, *caro Marcellino*, old 'Snaporaz', as he'd christened him, the actor with whom he'd shared so much in the nineteen years since *La dolce vita*, the film that had made both of them stars. But there were some problems with the lesser roles. One in particular: Doctor Sante Katzone, based on Fellini's friend Georges Simenon. A seducer of ten thousand women, Katzone in a basement museum commemorates each conquest with a giant back-lit transparency and a taped gratified tribute. In one of the film's key sequences, Katzone, safe in his country villa, guarded by killer Dobermans from the feminist terrorists who want him dead, celebrates a lifetime of fornication with a party for a few old friends, after which he accompanies Mastroianni in a voyage of sexual discovery into his (but in fact Fellini's) childhood.

To play Katzone, Fellini had chosen, as often in the past, someone not unlike the character in real life. For Trimalchio, host of history's greatest banquet in *Fellini–Satyricon*, he had cast the owner of his favourite restaurant. Now, as the great lover, he wanted Ettore Manni. In his day, burly, theatrical Manni, star of a dozen sword-and-sandal epics whose harnesses and togas showed off his powerful torso, had been the groupies' darling. Women melted at the sight of his oiled deltoids gleaming in the Roman sun, and Ettore hadn't been slow to offer them a place to lie down in his trailer. But life had been unkind to Manni. He was fifty-two years old and running to fat. Epics were out of fashion and he'd been reduced to playing in spaghetti westerns.

Starlets no longer spread their legs quite so readily, but there were still plenty to be had, especially on a film with so many actresses.

'Manni was *so* happy to play in *La città della donne*,' says Toscan du Plantier. 'But week after week it became obvious that he was in bad shape. His agent started explaining he had a very bad feeling about himself because Fellini was working on his character and using some of him in the film in the worst way.'

Fellini, everyone agreed, could be a devil like that. Under the cheerful surface – the laughs, the hugs, the jokes – there was another Fefé: cruel and manipulative.

'The character was called in the movie a terrible name in Italian,' continues Toscan du Plantier, '*Katzone* – which means "big prick", but in an insulting way. To play a part as Katzone in a Fellini movie is difficult for a man.'

The agent complained that Fellini was asking Manni to do and say things that humiliated him – mostly because they were drawn from Manni's own life. He accused him of having women in his dressing-room. Well, of course he did. Ettore was, after all, only human. And if he did drink, it was largely because of the strain of the role. Was this any excuse for Fellini to embarrass everyone with a screaming abusive attack, calling him a drunk, a skirt-chaser and a ham, especially in front of the crew?

Yet though he complained, Manni stayed with the film. Fellini, in the end, could make an actor do anything, even, as he demanded of Manni, caper around a giant cake pissing on the candles to put them out. An actress named Betsy Langman had seen Fellini get his way in similar circumstances on *Satyricon*, coaxing a man in a bath scene crowded with extras. The actor was, Langman recalled, 'a short, fat man with a double chin and the look of a happy cardinal. Fellini told him to walk towards the pool, sit on its edge, and ease himself into it. As the man readied himself, the direction was modified: *nudo*.

'His face reddened; he looked down, obviously not just embarrassed but really hurt. He had an unusually gross, squat body, with short legs. Fellini went over to him, nudged him, and shrugged warmly, intimately, as if to say: "Really, between you and me it is nothing . . . " The man did as he was asked.'

On the morning of 28 July 1979, Toscan du Plantier had a phone call. Manni had been found dead at his apartment in the via Flaminia Vecchia. Everyone knew the actor carried a gun but they weren't aware that, each night, he dressed himself in a cowboy outfit from one of his westerns, complete with .45 Magnum revolvers. This was how they'd discovered him, still in his costume. He'd been shot through the genitals with his own gun and had bled to death. Accident or suicide? Nobody could tell.

'I'll never forget,' said Toscan du Plantier. 'They called me and said: "Ettore Manni is dead." I phoned Federico and said: "Federico, you know that Ettore Manni died?" and told him the circumstances. There was a long silence. Then Fellini said: "Well, it could be a problem. But you know, it goes to show – the screenplay *does* work."'

2   *'Alea jacta est!'*

'I don't know where I was born. Perhaps I was not born at all. Perhaps in a plane . . . '
Fellini to the author, 1992

In 1964, a German publisher asked critic Gideon Bachmann, then part of Fellini's circle in Rome and trying to write his biography, to interview him about his working methods.

'He was making *Giulietta degli spiriti* at the time,' Bachmann said, 'and it was the usual thing: "Tomorrow", "Tomorrow", "Tomorrow". In the end he said: "Look, you've watched me work on so many films, why don't you just write it, then let me read it and I'll see if I agree?" Faced with a deadline I sat down and did this, shaping it in the form of a question and answer session.

'I handed it to Fellini, who said: "OK", and put it in his pocket. And the days passed. Telegrams from the publishers increased in frequency, so I pressed him. "Oh, that stuff you gave me," he said. "I didn't read it. But does it contribute to the myth?" I said: "Yes, I'm afraid it does." And Fellini said: "Very well. You can print it then."'

Most great film-makers have had their myth, and many, like Hitchcock, have actively maintained and lived up to it, but it is rare for anyone to acknowledge its existence so openly. Fellini, however, has always felt that he needs his more than most artists. The arrogance and self-doubt that make up his character demand the catalyst of its evasion in order to find union. Without the myth, he feels, he is nothing more than the sum of some less than impressive parts.

The Fellini myth began at nine thirty pm on the night of 20 January 1920, in an apartment at viale Dardanelli 10, in Rimini, on the Adriatic coast of north-eastern Italy.

Federico's father, Urbano, was a twenty-six-year-old travelling salesman in coffee, confectionery and café supplies, working out of a grocery shop in Rimini owned by his elder brother, Alboino. He'd been raised on a farm in the village of Gambettola, a few kilometres inland, but his wife, Ida, née Barbiani, was Roman. They'd been married less than two years and this was their first child. Another, Riccardo, arrived the following February but the last of the Fellini children, christened Maria-Maddalena but usually called simply Maddalena, wasn't born until 1929.

Later, Federico did his best to obscure the circumstances of his birth, as he did most facts of his life. 'I don't remember my childhood. I invent it when I need it.' He has claimed, for instance, that he was born in a railway carriage, in (inevitably) a first-class compartment of a train travelling between Viserba and Riccione, not far from Rimini. This fantasy, unlike many others he spun about his life, was easy to rout: Italy's railways were paralysed that day by a strike.

At various times in his infancy the Fellinis occupied apartments at Palazzo Ripa, corso d'Augusto 115, then, from 1 April 1926, in the Palazzo Ceschina, at via Gambalunga 48. In February 1929 they moved to via Clementina 9, and in April 1931 to via Dante 9, where Fellini remained until he left Rimini. Typically he names none of these addresses in his reminiscences, though he does describe his father pointing to a house as the family drove past and telling Federico: 'That's where you were born.' It was on via Fumagelli, a street where the Fellinis never lived.

Why lie? Simply because the events of his birth were so prosaic. That his parents were conventional and middle-class rather than picturesquely poor, that no crone foretold his genius and only a simple thunderstorm raged outside when he was delivered rather than the rending of the heavens with attendant opening of graves and walking abroad of monsters which he felt he deserved, disappointed a man who would live and be guided in his career by omens, dreams and the counsel of mediums and clairvoyants. He hasn't so much lied about his life as rewritten it. Biographer Paul Ferris is right to say: 'People's memories are dramas as well as documentaries.'

Fellini's unremarkable birth was what might have been expected of Rimini. Tucked into the hollow behind the knee of Italy, the town has neither the glamour of Venice, to the north, nor the grubby enterprise of Ancona, its nearest neighbour to the south. This part of the northern Adriatic, shallowed by millennia of silt from the delta of the Po that separates it from Venice, isn't deep enough for large ships, which pass kilometres from the shore. Julius Caesar preferred to establish his naval headquarters at Ravenna, the next big town up the coast. When

Rome fell, Venice emerged as the centre of trade, condemning Rimini to be bypassed again. Its consolation prize was twenty-five kilometres of clean, sandy beaches, the best in Italy, which in summer drew tourists from the cold north, and in particular Germany, like flies.

In 1920, Rimini was a backwater in a country still mostly rural, a town of narrow cobbled streets and small piazzas puddled round a few Roman and medieval buildings. It straddled the inconsequential Marecchia a kilometre back from the coast. A wide avenue lined with plane trees and tall turn-of-the-century villas in their own grounds connected the railway station to the beach. Where it met the ocean, the Grand Hotel ruled over a sweep of white sand colonised by streets of wooden huts, connected by duckboard paths. A rococo wedding cake in pink stucco, the Grand symbolised a cityfied sophistication most Riminese would only know – or wish to know – at second hand.

The best-preserved of the Fellini houses still standing after Rimini's Second World War battering by the US Air Force is the one on corso d'Augusto. The street, Rimini's most popular evening promenade, is a narrow shop-lined avenue, closed to traffic. It crosses old Rimini from the Arch of Augustus to the Bridge of Tiberius over the Marecchia, intersecting Rimini's largest open spaces, piazza Giulio Cesare (now the piazza del Tre Martiri) and piazza Cavour.

Like most houses on corso d'Augusto, number 115, designed in 1849 by G. Benedettini, presents a three-storey frontage flat to the street. A carriageway leads through to a paved courtyard with an old well-head and a fountain, where a stone dolphin dribbles water into a pool filled with goldfish. It's an attractive, elegant place. 'The rags-to-riches aspect of the Fellini myth is a journalistic invention,' wrote Eugene Walter, *Vogue*'s Rome correspondent in the sixties and among the first journalists to question the myth. 'His family were always comfortably off and educated.'

For all this comfort, Fellini, like any child of Romagna, grew up with a sense of lost opportunities. 'The villages of the region are all on the banks of small rivers,' he says, 'and there are lots of small rivers. But nobody knew how to make something of the rivers, like they did in Venice. We don't have the souls of merchants.'

The coast here is flat, empty and desolate, sandy grassland cut by an occasional river, the horizon's monotony broken here and there by the square-sided *campanile* marking a village. The landscape most often associated with Fellini's films, a featureless riverine plain with an enigmatic tower of metal scaffolding, is its stylised reflection. One would be surprised if it were otherwise.

While Fellini agrees the Rimini coast shaped his life, the acknow-ledgement is grudging. Once he became an adoptive Roman, he seldom returned to the town, not even to shoot the sequences in *Roma*, *I Clowns/The Clowns* and *Amarcord* set there. He preferred the banks of the Tiber near Rome and the nearby Tyrrhenian coast at Ostia and Fregene. If he thinks of himself as a child of any place in Romagna it's his father's birthplace, Gambettola. There was nobility in the rural gentry, but much less in the life of a wholesale grocer. He even attributes his habit of rising at six am to 'some trace of my grandfather the farmer in my blood'.

Urbano didn't share Federico's enthusiasm. To him, having been born there marked him as a peasant. 'One time, on a Sunday,' recalled Riccardo, 'we were in a cakeshop, and my father was asked if he was from Rimini. He said he was from Cesena, and when I exclaimed: "But Papa, you were born in Gambettola!" I received a clip on the ear.'

The heritage of Rimini in Fellini's eyes is a vagueness of thought, a want of ambition and the physical softness which, troubled by poor health all his life, he especially resents. 'It's important to be born somewhere, in a place that is not like every other one. If I was from Geneva I would probably have become a banker and I would have a beautiful and comfortable bottom. If I was born in Seville I'd be a toreador and I'd spend my life dying of fear. But I was born in Rimini, so I don't understand anything about numbers; I don't like numbers at all. And my body is always disturbed. And bulls are animals I think of as soft and thoughtful. The idea of killing them seems really absurd.'

The low blue hills on the horizon twenty kilometres inland, domin-ated by the crag of the fortress state of San Marino, are the northern tip of the Apennines, the mountains that divide Italy north to south like a spine. In Roman times, Rimini marked the point at which the road out of Rome, the via Emilia, became the via Flaminia, the main route into the hostile north. The region was called Romagna because Rome's power began here. Everything beyond was technically Cisalpine Gaul.

So Rimini was on the way to everywhere without being much of a place itself. All the same, some distinguished people passed through. St Francis supposedly preached off the beach to an interested congrega-tion of fish after the locals proved inattentive, and when St Anthony of Padua, patron saint of animals, visited the town, his mule traditionally knelt as the sacrament was carried past on the piazza Giulio Cesare. A bus-shelter-sized temple immortalises the spot.

Caesar himself took his most crucial career decision just outside Rimini. In 49 BC, headed home after pacifying Gaul, with every prospect of a glittering political career, he was ordered by a nervous Senate to halt at the frontier. This point is now marked by the village of Savignano, sited, like most Romagnolo towns, beside a stream, in this case the Rubicone.

The legend of the Rubicone is bigger than the river itself, hardly more than a stony creek that dries up in summer. 'When I knew I was alone,' Fellini says, 'simply to show my spirit of revolt, I would jump head first into the historic trickle, screaming like a damned soul: "*Alea jacta est!*"'*

Romagna is a soft, moist country, a region of orchards, slow white long-horned cattle and slab-sided ochre farmhouses with doors and windows painted verdigris green. It shelves so imperceptibly into the Adriatic that the calm, milky water seems like an extension of the land.

'Last night,' Fellini wrote in 1967, after an illness that almost killed him, 'I dreamed of the port of Rimini opening on to a green, swelling sea, as threatening as a moving meadow.' Such a sea, sinister and seductive at the same time, preoccupied him all his life. He dislikes mountains and loves anything flat, yet the ocean, which he finds particularly calming, always carries a hint of threat. '[It is] an element I have never conquered, the place from which come our monsters and our ghosts.'

This ambivalence towards the sea permeates his films. *Lo sceicco bianco/The White Sheik, La strada, La dolce vita, Otto e mezzo, Satyricon* and *Amarcord* all end on the beach in moments of fulfilment, resignation or despair. But along the way that sea has also uttered monsters, as in *La dolce vita, Satyricon* and *Giulietta degli spiriti*. All his life, Fellini has elected to live by the sea, but he's never learned to swim.

In winter, fogs roll in moistly, hanging for days, immersing the town in dripping silence. Rimini traditionally celebrates spring with the *fogharezza*, a ritual whose centrepiece is a bonfire in which the Witch of Winter is incinerated along with her mists and damp. Fellini, however, was sorry when winter ended. From his films, mostly shot in landscapes seared to bleakness by wind and cold, one can see he likes its emptiness. The fecundity of summer carries for him a sense of decay. 'The country that surrounds Rimini is green, like country everywhere, but I don't like green too much. It's the favourite colour of

---

*'The die is cast!', traditionally the comment with which Julius Caesar crossed the river with his army and marched on Rome, to become Dictator and first of the Caesars.

death, the favourite colour of very old ladies and of jealous men. At the time when they put the stems of hemp into water to let them rot, the air of the whole country stinks with the smell of corruption mixed with the odour of beetroot.'

If Rimini (and Fellini) has a ruling spirit, it's not Anthony, Francis or Julius Caesar but Sigismondo Malatesta, the fifteenth-century warlord whose name translates variously as 'Wronghead' or 'Head-ache'. He hovers as a disagreeable presence over Rimini's history, having murdered three wives and committed repeated infidelities with various lovers, including his mistress Isotta degli Atti, but also his own daughters and even his son-in-law.

Malatesta's legacy to his home town is a forbidding castle on piazza Cavour and the Basilica of St Francis, which the church prefers to call the 'Tempio Malatestina', since he buried his mistress there and decreed the building, which looks more like a corn exchange than a church, to be 'sacred to the deified Isotta'. Crosses in the Tempio are outnumbered by the illicit couple's monogram, an entwined 'I S', interspersed with plump *putti* in white marble and hundreds of elephants, the Malatesta emblem.

Fellini admired the combative, creative, vicious and vengeful Sigismondo. 'Malatesta, that was my favourite name. One needed to be an extraordinary villain, an invincible warrior, a man who triumphed over innumerable women, to be called that. You know the arms of the Malatestas? An elephant and a rose. Perhaps because they were at the same time poets and soldiers, strong and fragile, rough and delicate.' As if acknowledging the inspiration, elephants appear repeatedly in Fellini's films, and the comparison most used in describing the society he created for himself in maturity is the medieval court.

Fellini's parents were ill matched and not especially happy. Urbano, conscripted as a miner by the Germans during the First World War and sent to Belgium, returned through Rome, where he found a job in the Panetone pasta factory and met Ida Barbiani. She came from a totally different background, with echoes, albeit distant, of aristocracy. Fellini claims references to the Barbianis go back to 1400. One relative was an apothecary attached to the pontifical court of Pope Martin V. Involved in a poisoning, he was jailed for thirty years – 'training mice and spiders: who knows?' Fellini speculates. 'Maybe a little of my desire to be a movie director can be traced back to that remote ancestor.'

The Barbianis opposed Ida's marrying a provincial nobody and the couple were forced to elope in 1918. Ostracised, Ida settled with her new husband in his mother's farmhouse, a jarring contrast to Rome. Federico saw nothing of his Roman relatives until he was ten.

'My mother was a severe woman and a religious one,' Fellini says. 'No meat on Fridays; that sort of thing. My father, a wise man, travelled a great deal.' In 1960, Fellini used Urbano as the basis of Marcello Mastroianni's father in *La dolce vita*, showing him as a typical travelling salesman, charming, clubbable, genially womanising, henpecked at home like many Italian men and, again conforming to the national stereotype, only truly comfortable in the all-male society of the cafés.

'My father had an eye for women, and this led to many bitter quarrels between him and my mother.' From time to time, he returned home loaded with gifts intended to soften Ida's heart. 'He would give her very gaudy dresses, *à la* Anna Fougez, sometimes with sequins, which irritated my mother because they betrayed his ideal of a music-hall singer.' Fellini was saddened to find, after the death of a father whom he'd felt had no interest in him, that Urbano took some of his son's first drawings with him on his trips and regarded them with pride. A photograph of him is always on Fellini's desk.

Ida hoped Federico would become a priest or, failing that, a lawyer. Asked by Eugene Walter if she liked his films, she said: 'Oh, I enjoyed them all, although I can't understand why he wanted to make *La dolce vita*. They are full of jokes and references which sometimes only his family can see. *Otto e mezzo* was the saddest. It made me cry, when the son says to the ghost of his father: "Please don't go, let's talk, we've never really had a talk,"* because, you see, Federico and I have never had a talk. Oh, he's played tricks on me and he's always made me laugh – we're good friends – but I don't feel as if I really know him.'

These cosy reminiscences put a cheerful face on a relationship that was strict and repressive. Ida even refused her sons their own keys, and until well into their teens demanded they be in by seven thirty each night. As an adult Fellini pointedly kept his distance from her. When, after Urbano's death, Ida came to Rome with her design for his mausoleum, she spent a week in his apartment without ever seeing him. It was only in the car on their way to Termini to catch her train back to Rimini that she got to show Fellini the plans. He agreed without looking at them.

Young Federico was closer to his paternal grandmother, Francesca, a classic rural widow who presided over a way of life not much

*This scene is actually in *La dolce vita*.

changed for three centuries. There was no running water and no electricity in the Gambettola house. Meals were taken communally at the huge kitchen table, and the children were bathed together in the same enormous wooden tub by a no-nonsense maid. Francesca always carried a cane, the symbol of her control over the day labourers who worked her farm. 'When she appeared, these violent men suddenly looked respectful, as if they were in church.' Her influence on Fellini was intense. 'There was a time in my life when my grandmother was the most important person in my life. I couldn't imagine life without her.'

Though the new family moved into Rimini after their first year in Romagna, Ida and the children always spent summers in Gambettola. Federico was mesmerised by the people who passed through the big farmhouse: black-faced mountain charcoal-sellers from the Abruzzo, a knife-grinder with his rickety portable whetstone, the castrator of pigs, a villainous figure out of Boccaccio in long black coat and wide-brimmed hat. Most visitors to the farmhouse had stories to tell and, then as now, Federico was an excellent audience. Whatever he might have learned later during his brief formal schooling, these nights around the kitchen fire in Gambettola listening to stories of the hinterland provided Fellini's real education. The characters of his films, from the show people of *Luci del varietà/Lights of Variety* through Gelsomina and Zampano, the clown and strong man of *La strada*, to Marcello in *La dolce vita* and Casanova, are often itinerants, plying their trades from town to town, at home nowhere, forever moving on.

Since there were few asylums or hospitals in rural Italy, the deformed, retarded and insane were often kept at home, the more grotesque among them locked in attics. Most people accepted them as a fact of life but, to Fellini, dwarves, giants, hunchbacks, the mal-formed and mutilated came to seem exotic, even attractive. He was fascinated by Nasi, a Riminese who'd broken both legs when a tree fell on him and now walked in 'lop-sided movements, like a frog', and by the amputees from the First World War who limped around Rimini or creaked in their wooden wheelchairs.

Fellini has always been defensive about his fascination with deform-ity, justifying it as simple realism. 'Have you ever really looked at the people at a press screening?' he demanded. 'You call *them* beautiful?' But the mask could slip. 'I had a dresser on *E la nave va*,' recalled Freddie Jones, 'ugly as a dog, with a glass eye to boot. But Fellini whispered to me one day: "Isn't she beautiful? A beautiful . . .

*manifestation.''' * Fellini often used such people in his films, employing casting director Pippo Spoletini to locate them. Over the years Spoletini found a 200 kilo woman for *Roma*, twenty hunchbacks, twenty midgets and a female giant for *Casanova*, and ten people who looked a hundred years old for *Ginger e Fred*. He established his credentials on *Satyricon* when Fellini asked for 'the most crippled cripple that existed'. Spoletini produced Antonio Moro, a middle-aged man with neither arms nor legs. 'Fellini was absolutely amazed. He said: "It's incredible. I really didn't believe you'd go that far."'

Many highly strung people flirt with the notion of madness, and Fellini is no exception. Exploring one of the farms around Gambettola in childhood, he had looked up to see the moonlike face of a Down's Syndrome child at a barred second-storey window. The experience, which he re-created in *La strada*, impressed him profoundly, seeding a life-long interest in insanity which he fed on visits to mental institutions. Rimini had its 'village idiot', an irascible old man nicknamed 'Giudizio' – Wisdom or Judgement – who was tolerated since he genially mocked everyone in town with equal obscenity. Fellini wrote him into all of his films about Rimini, an emblem of his belief that the wall between insight and madness is a thin one.

The Romagna of Fellini's childhood whispered with legends and superstitions. Every Romagnolo village had its clairvoyant, healer or witch. An old man down by the docks could put a hex on sheep and chickens, or remove one. Another woman given to trances had the ability to cure sickness. Angelina, who came to restuff the farm's mattresses, showed young Federico a small glass casket hanging round her neck. Inside, a lock of her hair was entwined with part of her lover's moustache, souvenired while he slept. By knotting the two together she ensured that, though he'd gone to Trieste to work, he would surely come back. Alboino Fellini also dabbled in the occult, and Federico never forgot dipping into some books on black magic which his uncle brought to the house when he was eight. If one can judge from a lifetime spent consulting astrologers, clairvoyants and mediums, Fellini believed it all.

Like every Romagnolo child, Fellini was sent to church from infancy and, at five, placed in the parish school system. Catholicism, with its vested interest in eradicating sexuality and creativity, was a stifling influence. 'I was taught "No", "You cannot", 'You ought to be ashamed." There were so many admonitions to remember it was a wonder after all that I was not too incapacitated to button my fly. I was filled by school and church with an overwhelming sense of guilt before

I had the faintest idea about what I was guilty of . . . Sex was something not spoken of. For a time I thought all women were aunts. I was overcome by excitement if I saw a woman in an evening dress.'

Fellini preferred what he later called Romagna's 'strange, arrogant, blasphemous psychology, mingling superstition and defiance of God'. His personal creed is that 'blasphemous psychology' writ large, a thicket of mysticism, astrology, antique Catholic dogma and Jungian psychoanalytic theory, rooted in the peasant's fear of the unknown.

But while Fellini abandoned Catholicism in adulthood (and is pointedly anti-clerical in his films), his awe of the Church and its trappings never disappeared. His resentment of the hierarchy was transferred to other authority figures, in particular producers, with all of whom, but especially Dino de Laurentiis, the financier involved in *La strada*, *Le notti di Cabiria*, *La dolce vita* and *Casanova*, he clashed spectacularly. 'I know it's a bit ridiculous to imagine de Laurentiis in a cardinal's vestments,' he mused, 'but I like to think that film producers, like publishers, have inherited without deserving it a kind of sacred regalia, since the fate of the artist is to live off the bread of the grand duke, the prince and the Pope.'

In 1983, Fellini was delighted when Daniel Toscan du Plantier lost his position as head of the distributor Gaumont, which backed many of his films. When Michel Drach arrived in Rome to deliver the French-dubbed version of *E la nave va*, Fellini told him gleefully: 'You know, Michel, Gaumont Italy is finished, but French Gaumont too. They've arrested Toscan du Plantier.' Drach, who knew this to be totally untrue, said: 'Not at all. I saw him yesterday,' but Fellini, drunk on his fantasy, insisted jubilantly: 'It's true! He was arrested this morning. Everything happens quickly in Italy. This morning I saw Toscan du Plantier and Woityla [Pope John Paul] in handcuffs, like this . . . ' He held up his wrists. 'Both under arrest.' Producers and popes were twin aspects of a single menace.

3   'A backside as big as the world'

'As a boy I wanted to impress my circle of young friends –
my schoolmates, many of whose names and faces I no
longer remember'
Fellini in *Lo mio Rimini*

Fellini tells us he was a remote and solitary child at school. 'I liked to be pitied, to appear unreadable, mysterious. I liked to be misunderstood, to feel myself a victim, unknowable. I lived a life apart, a lonely life in which I looked for famous models like the poet Leopardi to justify my fear of bathing suits and my incapacity to enjoy myself like the others who went splashing into the sea.'

This is simply more myth. Everyone agrees the young Fellini was impossible to overlook. Even for Italy he was striking, with enormous dark eyes and an electric personality. He'd been born with masses of black hair which became more abundant as he grew, giving him a dashing appearance. He became accustomed to being petted, cosseted, admired, confided in. Urbano was average in height but most of the Fellinis were tall, and by eight or nine Federico was already skinny and showing signs of his later size. His boniness won him the nickname 'Gandhi'.

Precocious, inventive, fanciful, he occasionally lost consciousness at moments of excitement, a physical weakness that survived into adulthood. In his early films, male characters often faint or pass out under stress: Checco in *Luci del varietà*, Ivan in *Lo sceicco bianco*, Alberto in *I vitelloni*. As the problem receded for Fellini, so did such scenes. In the forties, when he was trying to avoid being drafted into the army, he claimed to be suffering from Basedow's Disease, a hyperfunctioning of the thyroid gland. It is generally assumed this was invented to fool the examiners but its symptoms accord strikingly with his lifelong medical problems. They include 'an acceleration in cardiac rhythm accompanied by palpitations and breathlessness after physical effort, thinness, with, at the same time, retention or even increase of the appetite; an intolerance of heat with an elevation of skin temperature and an increase in perspiration, particularly of the hands; thirst which demands drinking at frequent intervals, especially at night; a loss of force in the muscles, especially in the thighs; problems of temper and character with emotionalism, aggression and agitation.' The parallels with Fellini's character and behaviour are obvious.

Fellini's best friend in school was the stocky, blond Luigi 'Titta' Benzi, called 'Grosso', not because he was fat but because he would eat anything. He particularly impressed Fellini by swallowing raw fish; not simply sardines but mullet, cod, even sole, which seemed far too large for his mouth. Benzi, knowing his friend's taste for grotesquerie, invited him to 'Come and see my crazy old Pop.' He led him into the kitchen where his senile grandfather sat in braces and hat, eating pasta. When Titta said: 'Look who's here,' the old man stopped chewing in mid-mouthful, stood up politely, took off his hat and remained immobile for as long as the visitor stayed. Titta's father, Ferruccio, a building contractor of volcanic temper and, like many in his trade, a man with a Socialist/Anarchist background which kept him at odds with the Fascists, also impressed Fellini. In *Amarcord* and *Roma* he co-opted the Benzis as representatives of family life in Rimini in preference to Urbano and Ida, dull by comparison.

Sexually more precocious, Titta was prepared to chance his arm with the town vamp, Gradisca, where Fellini only fantasised. Titta once, he claimed, felt her up in the balcony of the Fulgor Cinema, slipping his hand under her dress. She merely turned to him and asked: 'What are you trying to do?' Chilled by her *savoir-faire*, he retreated. Again Fellini adopted the story as his own, incorporating it into his memoir *Lo mio Rimini/My Rimini* and *Roma*.

The charismatic leader of a gang of fourteen, Fellini was always ready for some wild scheme. His acts of rebellion were seldom as elaborate as those shown in *Amarcord*, like funnelling urine from the back of the class down a series of paper tubes to deposit a puddle at the feet of an incredulous dunce, but they did include waking monks in the local monastery by turning a hose on their cell windows. From references in *Amarcord* and *La città delle donne*, one infers that their entertainments might have encompassed group masturbation, often while fantasising about movie stars.

Sex and the cinema are entwined in Fellini's mind, not only intellectually, as subjects for his films, but physically, the hypnotic flicker heightening the aphrodisiac effects of darkness, warmth and anonymity. Fellini first evoked this in a piece for *Marc'Aurelio* of October 1940. One of a series called *Come si comporta/How a Man Behaves*, this one eavesdrops on the thoughts of a man as he moves ever closer to a woman in a darkened cinema. The idea reappears in his films: Fausto flirting with the woman next to him in *I vitelloni*, Titta groping Gradisca in *Amarcord*, the pharmacist's wife of the same film attending the Fulgor to be fondled by other men, and the boys masturbating in a huge bed in *La città delle donne* while watching Mae West on screen.

Fellini won't say if these experiences have a basis in autobiography, though he has commented: 'I think the cinema is a woman, by virtue of its ritualistic nature. This uterus which is the theatre, the foetal darkness, the apparitions – all create a projected relationship. We project ourselves on to it. We become involved in a series of vicarious transpositions, and we make the screen assume the character of what we expect of it, just as we do with women, upon whom we impose ourselves, woman being a series of projections invented by man. In history, she became our dream image.'

Fellini's other sexual stimulus was the sea. By the time he was ten, the beach already held a special erotic significance. Not as a place to swim, since he was too embarrassed by his thinness ever to learn, but for the sense it provided of a free zone where no rules applied.

In school he fantasised about the town nymphomaniac, Volpina, who haunted the beach, coupling with sailors and fishermen. With his gang he prowled the wide, flat beaches at Lungomare and Miramare, opposite the Grand Hotel, whose bathing-huts provided cover, watching the women from Germany and Norway sunning themselves or wading in the swell. It was their pale, buxom images rather than those of the dark local girls that he installed in the pin-up gallery already decorating the inside of his skull.

The beach provided the setting for the most powerful erotic experiences of Fellini's adolescence. A popular joke at ten, at least among members of the gang less self-conscious than he, was to strip naked, stroll up to a couple necking in the sand dunes or behind a boat and ask the time. Occasionally their voyeurism backfired, as when a sun-bathing German woman saw the boys watching, chased them and, catching Fellini, carried him back bodily to her friends. He was mortified, but also aroused.

In adolescence Fellini began to dream, vividly and usually erotically. In one fantasy that recurred throughout his life he was swimming in dark water, out of his depth, until he was saved from drowning by a giant woman who crushed him to her breasts. This lady leviathan – in all the dreams Fellini barely reaches her knees – crops up repeatedly. Sometimes she's wading out of the ocean or walking on a beach at night under a full moon. At other times, deified as 'The Giant Fabricator and Dissolver of Clouds', she perches on a couch of cumulus, spouting moisture on the earth from her breasts.

Not all the giantesses of Fellini's childhood were fantasies. A fat prostitute lived in a hut on the beach. Since she sold herself to fishermen in return for their unsaleable sardines – *saraghine* in Romagnolo - the townspeople nicknamed her 'La Saraghina'. For a few coppers La Saraghina would pull up her dress to expose giant thighs and a bush of black pubic hair, a scene Fellini re-created in *Otto e mezzo*, where schoolboys pay her to perform a seismic shimmy.

After this first glimpse of carnality, Fellini went home to find that his uncle Alboino had called, bringing with him some books on the occult. Fellini opened one. 'At the foot of the page, drawn in tiny black strokes, I was stupefied to recognise La Saraghina. She had the body of a leopard, a backside as big as the world, and a crown glittering with precious stones arranged like human eyes.'

Like many Fellini stories, that of the occult text is dubious, though he returned often to the image of women, and this woman in particular, as fantastic and malevolent. In a 1962 letter to Brunello Rondi outlining his ideas for *Otto e mezzo*, he called La Saraghina 'a horrible and splendid dragon who represents the first traumatic view of sex in the life of the hero'. In the film, a group of priests demand of the young Guido: 'Don't you know Saraghina is the devil?' Later, Fellini commented significantly: 'Some people fear God. I fear women.'

Stranger beasts than La Saraghina ended up on the beach. In the summer of 1934 a 'sea monster' was netted at Miramare. The artist Beltrame painted the event for the *La domenica del corriere* and Fellini never forgot it, incorporating it repeatedly into scripts until it reached the screen as the end of *La dolce vita*. By that time it had been combined with another Fellini dream in which he and his mother encounter some fishermen hauling on a rope. The men refuse to let him help unless he dismisses Ida, so he does so with a hand-clap. As she disappears, he pulls the rope and his giantess begins to emerge from the water.

Fellini dates his sexual history from an experience in convent school. A novice with a shaved head who usually worked in the kitchens became fond of him. When she hugged him, he smelled potato skins on her habit, an odour that may have resonated with infantile memories of the kitchen at Gambettola. The effect was electric. 'Held like a little doll against that big, solid, warm body, I felt a giddiness, an early stirring, a tingling at the tip of my nose. I didn't know what it was, but it made me almost faint with pleasure. Even today the odour of potato skins makes me a little weak.'*

This scene of infantile sexuality never found its way into a Fellini film but his work contains plentiful testimony to a precocious sense of the erotic. *Roma* re-creates an incident from when he was twelve. The parish priest's slide show on St Francis was disrupted when a boy slipped in a transparency of a semi-nude woman, to the delight of the class. For the film, Fellini turns the show into a parade of Roman antiquities, so that the woman shows her ample rump among images of the Colosseum and the Castel Sant'Angelo, an implied erotic tribute to his spiritual and sentimental home, Rome.

La città delle donne offers a parade of sexually charged images from childhood, supposedly recalled by Marcello Mastroianni but many of them attributable to Fellini. A boy of five or six watches the sturdy legs of a servant girl ironing in front of an open fire. When he touches her calves the girl squats to chide him, then cuddles him to her breasts. In a fish market, a girl grins lasciviously as she runs her hands over wet fish and slick black eels. A husky masseuse slaps mud on the legs of an adult Mastroianni in a steamy room at a spa. Two Germanic blondes in black leather strut on stage as part of a fairground motorcycle show. Kids of eight or nine with shaven heads (a common summer precaution in Rimini against lice) peek through a hole in a bathing-hut, then watch the thirties-style woman in rubber cap and one-piece suit stroll towards the ocean.

This scene segues into a cinema, the seats replaced by a huge bed. Dozens of boys and a few older men pile in, and the sheets billow as they masturbate to movie scenes. An historical sequence with flames and a bare-thighed queen recalls the 1926 *Maciste all'inferno/Maciste in Hell*, one of the first films Fellini ever saw. Then some shots of a Garbo-like star in soft focus are followed by a pastiche of Mae West,

---

*In 1963, British critic Alexander Walker speculated that '8½' might refer not to the total of his films, as Fellini claimed, but to some other significant figure; perhaps the age of his first sexual experience? 'Are you trying to psychoanalyse me?' Fellini snapped. Walker had struck a nerve, since Fellini later told José Luis de Vilallonga that the first encounter with La Saraghina (of which there were three, the last two alone) took place in the summer of his eighth year.

who undulates away from the camera while a chorus of bare-chested
body-builders pose and preen.

To close, Fellini offers a later, adult reminiscence, this time of the
brothels of Rome, which he would also evoke in *Roma*. As the smoky
basement rocks with distant bombardment, a man climbs the stairs
behind a whore, almost naked in a net costume, whose voluptuousness
is undercut by her prim face, pinned-up hair and horn-rimmed
spectacles. In the room she crouches with her rump towards the
audience, Fellini using a prosthesis three times life size so that her
buttocks and thighs fill the screen and cast a massive shadow on the
wall.

Women in Fellini's films are uniform with this prostitute, with
exaggerated hips and breasts, and tiny heads, hands and feet –
infantile symbols of idealised motherhood. Many are associated with
memories of Gambettola and the markets of Rimini. They wallow in
milky baths, grapple with giant eels, lower buttocks on to bicycle seats
or wobble breasts in the audience's face. Equally common in his
early work is a beaming androgyne, clown-like and sexless, famously
embodied by Giulietta Masina in *La strada* and *Le notti di Cabiria*.
Just as much as the fertility figures of the later films, Gelsomina and
Cabiria are a child's vision of sexuality: half playmate, half puppet,
sexually neutral.

At the root of both characterisations lies a disquiet with physical sex.
'Do you notice?' points out a friend. 'There are no love scenes in
Fellini's films. He can't bring himself to show the sexual act on screen.
Instead his women stick out their tongues, show their tits and bums,
talk dirty, and the men drop their pants and run about. But loving sex?
Never.'

The combination of a repressive social milieu, a distant, absent
father, dominating female figures and a sensitive, creative disposition
is often associated with homosexuality, but while Fellini's deepest
friendships and professional relationships – usually, in his case,
interchangeable – have often been with homosexuals, there's no
evidence of physical affairs. Nor, despite a long and superficially
cordial marriage and occasional rumours of extramarital romances,
does Fellini appear to be actively heterosexual. 'There is also a legend I
am impotent,' he acknowledged in a 1972 interview, a rumour which
Gideon Bachmann, the critic with best access to Fellini throughout the
sixties and seventies, referred to discreetly when he commented to a
Harvard audience on Fellini's 'public self-criticism and psychological

auto-flagellation, to forestall disdain, which has led many a superficial biographer to surmise that he is masochistic and impotent'.

Fellini shares the Italian male's sensitivity to implications of unmanliness and a want of sexual potency. In 1968, Bachmann directed the documentary *Ciao Federico!* about the shooting of *Satyricon*. Hoping to convey the ambiguity of Fellini's effusive, affectionate temperament, he added a song to the end of the film, one line of which was 'Why can't you love?'

'Of course,' says Bachmann, '"Why can't you love?" in English is one thing, but in Italian it becomes *'Perchè non sai voler bene?'*, something very simplistic and physical. The woman who translated the song for me, an Italian writer, didn't make clear in the translation that this was not our intent. And so the version shown at Venice, which had the Italian track, really hit him hard. With all the rumours that have circulated around him, this really took root in that fertile mind. A lot of people in the audience mentioned it. Michelangelo Antonioni told him: *"Te lo ha messo nel culo"* – 'He's taken you from the ass-side."' Fellini was so angry that he broke with Bachmann. When the critic showed up during the shooting of *Amarcord*, he threw him off the set.

'Sexually, women aren't of much interest to Federico,' a veteran collaborator confirms. If one were to infer a sexual orientation from his work and writings, it would be bisexual, with an emphasis on the pleasures of manipulation and domination. One senses that nothing Fellini ever did in bed gave him the thrill he felt on a set.

Self-advértisement always came naturally to Fellini. He once, he claims, smeared his hands and face with red ink from his father's desk and lay down at the bottom of a staircase, hoping to send his parents wild with grief. Instead he was discovered by his uncle who poked him with his cane and told him to get up and wash his face.

There's also an alternative version in which Fellini, more prosaically, is surprised by his mother using her lipstick to make himself up like a Red Indian. 'I often locked myself into the toilet,' he said, 'where I could enjoy myself for hours powdering my face and dressing up in the craziest ways. I would tape a false beard to my chin, smear egg-white all over my hair to make it slick like a man's d.a. and paint a set of sideburns with burnt cork.'

Fellini offered critics the story of the fake fall like a piece of candy, as 'an episode which, in the hands of a psychoanalyst, could suggest character, vocation, and even a hint of destiny', but it tastes more like one of his inventions. Whatever else he might have been as a child,

Fellini was, as he remains, an inveterate and accomplished fantasist. It's a policy he pursues with dedication, systematically erasing and redrawing his past. 'I don't preserve anything. I like to be new-born each day.' There are no 'Fellini papers'; he throws out almost everything, keeps no letters or copies of his own correspondence. 'Antonioni has cassettes of every one of his films,' says Gerald Morin, Fellini's secretary and assistant director for some years, 'copies of every book ever written about him, but Fellini has nothing. If you wanted to find out what had been written about him, you had to come to me or to Liliana [Betti, Fellini's personal assistant from 1963 to 1980].'

In place of documentary evidence about his life Fellini offers elaborate accounts that may contain a germ of truth but are mostly fabrications, albeit amusing and plausible ones. He sees nothing dishonest in this. When three journalists complained that he'd given each of them a different version of the same event, he was geniunely aggrieved. 'All of you got an exclusive story. What's wrong with that?' As he puts it: 'I am a liar, but an honest one.'

One of the most persistent of Fellini's fantasies involves his first contact with the circus, later to become a motif in his work. For years, he insisted that, when the travelling circus of the clown Pierino visited Rimini, he ran away with the show, being retrieved by his father after a week on the road. These days, however, he acknowledges that 'the truth is I would have liked it very much to be true'. His sister Maddalena says: 'Those things they write about him, how he ran off with á circus, they're not true. He did follow a circus off when he was about twelve,* but a friend of his father's saw him and brought him home. It was no more than that.' His entire circus career consisted of helping someone wash a zebra.

Fellini has been slower to disclaim another episode when, at ten, he was supposedly sent away to a school run by the Salesian brothers at Fano, thirty kilometres down the coast. 'I spent a whole summer. I was half imprisoned. In the evening I was fetched away. I remember with a feeling of great gloom the wretched ditch of a yard with its two dreary goalposts and all round it a high wall with wire netting two yards high on top.' He continued at length about his brutal treatment, and incorporated a scene into *Otto e mezzo* in which the young Guido recalls an inquisition at the hands of priests. But he never attended the

---

*The Pierino circus came to Rimini in 1927. Her error is understandable, since she remembers little of Federico before he was eighteen: 'It's been a friendship of adults,' she says. Fellini agrees: 'I don't know her very well.'

Fano school. His brother Riccardo, however, did, and Fellini simply co-opted his experiences.

This casual annexation of Riccardo's history was typical of their relationship and others in Fellini's life. The most conspicuous characteristic of his career and personal life is competitiveness. Associates have been purged when they tried to build careers of their own and collaborators dropped if their reputations threatened Fellini's primacy. Nobody was immune, least of all his family. Neither as intelligent nor as creative as Federico but bearing a strong physical resemblance, Riccardo all his life lived in Federico's shadow and was, not surprisingly, resentful. Fellini rubbed it in by casting him in *I vitelloni* as, essentially, the adolescent Federico. He later gave him a small production job on *Le notti di Cabiria*, in part, it seems, to spite producer Dino de Laurentiis, who'd put his own brother Luigi on the crew. After Fellini launched his own production company, Federiz, Riccardo approached him for help in directing a feature. Instead, Fellini could only think of urging him to change his name.

Riccardo, who settled down as a TV producer, lived and died bitter. Asked if he resented the connection he said drily: 'I'm very happy to be recognised best as "Fellini's brother". In certain circumstances I volunteer the information – for example if I'm stopped by the police on the road. It always goes the same way. The police talk to me about all of his films that they've seen, and when I leave they tell me: "Say hello to your brother for us!" or ask for free tickets (who can say why?) . . .'

Fellini was no less competitive with Maddalena, who remained in Rimini and married a local paediatrician. Her occasional visits to Federico in Rome were anything but cordial. 'He's a holy pain in the ass,' she says. 'Eating with him is a nightmare. He can't stand anyone smoking, nor the rattle of plates. He speaks so softly one can hardly hear him – when he *does* talk, that is. Very quickly he's sick of you, and thinking about something else. He's so distracted. One night, he invited me to his apartment in Rome, then, after dinner, he asked me to go downstairs with him. I thought he had something important to tell me. Not at all. When the lift reached the ground floor he said goodbye to me as if he'd never seen me before! "Goodnight, signora". On top of that, he goes to bed early. It was all I could do that year to keep him up until midnight on New Year's Eve.'

In 1991, after decades as wife and mother, Maddalena, who shares Fellini's height and air of command, revealed considerable native acting ability when Tonino Guerra, Fellini's co-writer on *Amarcord* and *E la nave va*, cast her in a episode of the film he directed and wrote.

To promote it, she appeared on a Rome TV talk show featuring relatives of the famous. Federico was invited but declined. The host then put in a call to Fellini and, on air, asked if he'd seen Guerra's film. The reply was a classic of evasion. He'd meant to, he said. He'd even walked past the cinema where it was showing, but unfortunately not at convenient times. Finally he'd decided to go, but when he got there the film had been taken off. 'I sent you a cassette,' Maddalena said sharply, knowing that her brother almost never visits a cinema. 'Yes, that's right,' Fellini said hurriedly, 'and I'm going to look at it tonight. I really am . . . '

Maddalena, though resentful enough of the snub to show a tape of the show when visitors ask about her brother, retails these stories, as did Riccardo when he was alive, with rueful resignation. No matter how ruthlessly they may have been treated, most collaborators speak of their time at court as the most significant of their lives. 'He has, to an immense degree,' said journalist Thomas Meehan, 'the charm of a confidence man, having the knack of talking almost everyone into doing exactly what he wants him to do.'

Fellini's capacity for inspiring love is legendary. Freddie Jones, who starred in *E la nave va*, said frankly: 'I just loved him. At the end of the shoot, I cried.' On the last day of *Casanova*, a nightmare for the actor, Donald Sutherland embraced Fellini and said: 'I love you.' Countless women have invented or inflated some flirtation into a grand passion. His first teenage girlfriend wrote a novel about their relationship, as did Sandra Milo, star of *Otto e mezzo* and *Giulietta degli spiriti*, who detailed a largely imagined affair with him. Marika Rivera, a minor middle-aged actress in *Casanova*, also fell under his spell. Liliana Betti sacrificed her life and career for Fellini, and is now, since she broke away, in the words of one friend, 'a broken woman'.

Most of the people used by Fellini, especially if they are Italians, are delighted to be so. The pleasure of having been chosen for one of his films expunges the discomfort of the experience. Mario Romagnoli, the restaurateur cast as Trimalchio in *Satyricon*, complained ceaselessly of the inconvenience and embarrassment of playing the ancient world's most vulgar host, then hung a ten-times life size portrait of himself in the role in his restaurant. It's there still.

To those whom he wishes to win, Fellini is obsessively attentive. For as long as they are within the focus of his attention, their interests are his, as are their tastes, their enthusiasms, their enemies. When he cast Terence Stamp in *Toby Dammit*, the actor was still smarting from having been fired by Antonioni from *Blow-Up*. Fellini, meeting the

other director at his barber, raved about Stamp. 'This actor is incredible. I think he's a genius.' Later, with glee, he retailed the story to
Stamp, making another small deposit of goodwill.

His link to these people, his creatures, can seem almost telepathic.
'From time to time in my life,' said Magali Noël, 'when I'm particularly
worried or sad, or I have family problems, there will be a phone call,
and it is Federico. "Magalotte, how are you?" *How does he know?*'

The dark side of this protectiveness is his jealousy. 'He's like a big
mama,' says Noël. 'You must eat your soup the way he likes, go where
he likes to go. At one time my husband was quite sick with a heart
problem and I didn't have time to give Federico the attention he
wanted. And suddenly he was very cold, turning and walking away
from me.'

'Towards the end of shooting *Ciao Federico!*' says Gideon Bachmann, 'I realised he was really using people for his own purposes; very
nicely, but you know . . . people would get hung on him and would
stay around for ever, waiting to go into a second Fellini movie, and that
would never happen. And a lot of them would die waiting, including
some people I knew quite well. They'd say: "Oh, Federico told me he'd
take me in his next movie," but another three years would pass and
they'd still be sitting in some cheap *pensione* where they couldn't pay.
This happened to Edra Gale, who was La Saraghina in *Otto e mezzo*,
and Jean Rougeul, the French actor who played his conscience in the
same film; the scriptwriter. He died in his unpaid *pensione* in Rome,
waiting.'

Like Sigismondo Malatesta, Fellini doesn't lack apologists. Lina
Wertmuller, his assistant on *Otto e mezzo* and later a major director, is
devotedly uncritical. She compares him to Jesus Christ and claims that
their association was 'like a window opened on my life'. In a long
tribute written in 1985 when Fellini received an Honorary Leone
d'Oro at the Venice Film Festival, she took time out from an otherwise
specific memoir to generalise about 'The Artist'.

'An artist is marvellous,' she wrote, in a justification that might have
come from a hundred of his collaborators, 'because he thinks the way
he wants, he's anarchic and bisexual, careless and infantile, stupid and
well above caring for anything . . . he's an artist! As such, he has to
stay totally free, and his main struggle is to defend that freedom from
everyone else, like competent administrators or nice mothers, who
would like to bog it down in logical statements, economic outlines and
political speeches. The artist is the antibody of society, because he is
wonderfully mad . . .'

4   The Elephant and the Rose

'Do you know Rimini? No, you couldn't know Rimini.
Nobody could know Rimini if he hasn't been born there
and hasn't spent a whole childhood there, rummaging
around with the curiosity of a rat'
Fellini to José Luis de Vilallonga, 1972

By the time he was ten, Fellini lived more inside his fantasies than in
the real world. School was an irrelevance. He learned as much from
Rimini itself as from the nuns at San Vincenzo. 'Rimini, you see,' he
says, 'is a city of the old Italy, feudal. It's fabulous; it has always been,
still is and will always be.' He loafed around the eighteenth-century
colonnaded fish market, the beach or the little port on the Marecchia,
and learned to squeeze through a window high up on the walls of the
Tempio Malatestina to gain access to its chill marble interior.

More important, he encountered the popular culture of the twenties,
especially *Il corriere dei piccoli*, a weekly humour magazine that
reprinted American comic strips like *Happy Hooligan*, *The Katzen-
jammer Kids* and *Felix the Cat*. Though he never had much time for
high art, his lifelong fascination with graphics and caricature began
here.

Even more crucial was his discovery of the Fulgor, Rimini's most
popular cinema. It had opened in 1914, on the corso d'Augusto, a
block or two from where Fellini would live at number 115. A narrow
three-storey building, once a town house of the Romagnoli family, it
had become the Hotel Aquila d'Oro in the mid-nineteenth century
before being gutted for a cinema. With its minuscule foyer, and lacking
a marquee, the Fulgor hardly competed with Rome's picture palaces;
when Fellini re-created it at Cinecittà in 1973 for *Amarcord* he
discreetly widened and glamorised the frontage. The balcony offered
velour seats, but groundlings, admitted by a separate door round the
corner on via Verdi, sat either on straw-covered chairs or on benches in

the cheapest section, a fenced-off enclosure almost under the screen. In the interval a woman with an atomiser sprayed pungent scent, and a burly bouncer 'with arms like hams' prowled the rows. He was known, after the strong-man hero of silent epics, as 'Maciste'.

Fellini doesn't remember the first film he saw except as a confusion of melodramatic images. His earliest clear recollection is of Guido Brignone's 1926 *Maciste all'inferno*, in which Bartolomeo Pagano as Maciste rescues Cabiria, the Sicilian slave girl invented by Giovanni Pastrone for his 1914 epic. The standard victim of historic melodrama, Cabiria is stolen by slaves during the eruption of Mount Etna, herself enslaved in Carthage, then kidnapped back to Rome just in time to be sent into the arena. Brignone's film became the symbol to Fellini of everything grandiose and fantastic in cinema. He re-created scenes in *Roma, Block-notes di un regista/A Director's Notebook* and *La città delle donne*, evoking the ambiance of its production in *Intervista/ Interview*, and naming the Giulietta Masina character of *Lo sceicco bianco* and *Le notti di Cabiria* after its heroine. Sixty years later, he still nominated it among his favourite movies of all time.

When sound came, Fellini switched his allegiance. 'When I was twelve or thirteen,' he said, 'I went to the movies all the time. American movies.' He was bored by drama but fascinated by the Marx Brothers, Fred Astaire and Mae West.* He had a special enthusiasm for melo-dramas about private detectives and newspapermen which mirrored his own vision of his adult self. Working as a journalist in Rome in the early forties, he adopted the regulation *film noir* trench coat and what he called 'a Fred MacMurray hat'.

The Fulgor was owned and operated by Carlo Massa, a worldly figure christened 'Ronald Colman' by the Riminese in recognition of his fancied resemblance to the suave British star. Massa played up to the image by wearing a loosely belted white overcoat, a cream Borsa-lino and a hair-line moustache. An enlightened operator, Massa knew better than to turn away a kid because he couldn't afford a place on the cheap benches. Those without money paid for a spot at the back by selling sweets in the interval. Fellini had described the Fulgor's capacity as '200 sitting, 500 standing'.

Fellini was beginning to discover his creative instincts. When he became famous, his mother took credit for his creativity. Noting that

*Fellini tried repeatedly to coax Groucho Marx and West into his films. Both refused, though Marx became a friend, introducing him to, among other aspects of American popular culture, the one-reel porno film.

he could whistle 'with a certain genius', sufficiently skilfully to soothe the cattle on his grandmother's farm by whistling songs in their ears, she forced him to take mandolin lessons. She also claimed that he'd inherited her drawing talent, and made him a puppet theatre, buying the heads and arranging for her dressmaker to create costumes. In fact Fellini showed no aptitude for the mandolin and the lessons soured him on music for decades. As for the theatre, it was a gift from his uncle in Rome when Federico was ten, and he made his own puppets. 'First I'd draw [the characters] up, on cardboard. Then I would cut them out. Last came the heads, which I'd make out of clay or cotton wool soaked in glue. Across the street from us lived an energetic young man with a red beard, a sculptor.* One day, [he] noticed me fooling around in a corner and that's when he taught me what you can do with plaster of Paris and Play-Doh.' Fellini also ground up pieces of brick for pigments and begged scraps of leather and wood to extend his theatre. Having created a show, he'd put it on for his friends, playing all the parts – and demanding they pay a *soldo* (a fraction of a lira) to watch.

The earliest surviving Fellini document is an elaborate inscription in a schoolbook indicating that it is '*Libro di Fellini Federico Class III Scuola Tonini via Gambalunga Scolaro del maestro Giovannini*'. Fellini enrolled in the school on via Gambalunga when he was eight. Now Rimini's public library, it's a forbidding building of bare high-ceilinged rooms. The classrooms are on the first floor. Students entered through a courtyard, littered today with shattered statuary and frag-mented mosaics unearthed from the foundations.

By tradition, pupils presented their headmaster with tributes of food each Christmas and Easter. Fellini remembered the principal, Giovan-nini, disappearing behind 'a wall of gifts that we, like a conquered, servile people, brought in, kneeling before his altar of food, smirking like pimps'. The bigger the gift, the better the grade. An unteachable boy named Stacchiotti was promoted when he donated a piglet, and Urbano Fellini was well placed to ensure with gifts of prime Parmesan cheese that his son moved up each year.

Fellini grew up with Fascism, which was born in Italy almost at the same time as he was. After the First World War, the Italian government had promised land reform, but it was slow to legislate for it. Especially in the newly industrialised north, Socialists and Anarchists agitated for change. In September 1920, inspired by the Russian Revolution, unionists all over Italy occupied their factories. The action failed, but

*Presumably Demos Bonini, with whom Fellini would go into the caricature business.

from it emerged a charismatic ex-journalist named Benito Mussolini who became head of the tiny Italian Fascist Party.

Mussolini was a Romagnolo, born at Predappio, near Forli. His mother was a schoolteacher, and his card-carrying Socialist father a blacksmith. 'Either the government will be given to us,' he announced, 'or we shall seize it by marching on Rome.' In October, he led such a march,* 26,000 strong, a propaganda exercise that panicked the king and government. No putsch was necessary. In a legal election in April 1924 the Fascists took 64 per cent of the votes and Mussolini became head of government.

Shrewdly he won the Church by accepting Catholicism as the 'sole religion of state'. The Lateran Pact of 1929 with Pope Pius XI recognised the Vatican as a separate country, with the pope as its head, something preceding governments had refused. In return, the Vatican formally accepted that Italy now existed as one nation and not, as it had been before 1870, a group of independent principalities. Church and state became one. When Fellini was enrolled in the Asilo San Vincenzo in the autumn of 1925, he joined a school system that, although nuns did the teaching and priests ran the bureaucracy, was essentially Fascist.

Like Hitler and Roosevelt, Mussolini spent the country's way out of depression with make-work schemes. He drained the marshes of the Po river, reorganised the railways, reconstructed the aircraft industry, built the state-of-the-art ocean liner *Rex*, modernised Rome and launched scores of grandiose public works, including the Cinecittà film studios and EUR, the modern suburb intended to house the 1942 Esposizione Universale di Roma, which never took place.

The Rimini of Fellini's youth, despite its distance from Rome, was staunchly Fascist. Occasionally a dignitary paid a ritual visit, but for most of the year the faith was fed by propaganda newsreels and newspapers magnifying the myth of Il Duce. Bank managers, lawyers and schoolteachers put on the Sahariana, the standard black bush shirt of Fascism, and rose to become the most powerful men in town, their will enforced by local thugs.

Mussolini campaigned against regional dress, dialect and custom, all of which undermined national unity. Youth groups like the Balilla dressed everyone in the same uniform, a combination of Boy Scout regalia and the Sahariana. Most children joined as automatically as

*Led, but didn't participate in. Despite much heroic statuary of the Duce striding towards Rome, Mussolini arrived on 30 October by train.

they went to church. The Church reciprocated on every level, from supporting the local hierarchy to favouring members of the Fascist youth when handing out absolution at confession.

At the beginning of 1931 Fellini moved from parochial school to the Ginnasio/Liceo Giulio Cesare on corso d'Augusto, another large, though more modern, building, a few doors from the piazza Giulio Cesare. He must have learned to hate the flat, cracked chimes of its little church.

Urbano was casual about the education of Federico and Riccardo, but Ida made up for his lack of interest. It was she who sent Riccardo to the Salesian brothers at Fano and who insisted that Fellini apply himself at high school. Federico, however, was a poor pupil, 'hopeless at mathematics and barely mediocre at Italian'. It was more exciting to doodle caricatures or spin sexual fantasies about Volpina, or the erotic acts that might have taken place in those tantalising gaps in Petronius' incomplete Roman satire *The Satyricon*.

In his early pieces for humour magazines and, later, in *Amarcord*, Fellini gives a sarcastic but accurate picture of his secondary education. Below twin portraits of Mussolini and the Pope, bored teachers struggle to inculcate some sense of Italy's imperial past and Fascist future. At the school on corso d'Augusto Fellini was confronted for the first time by the male authority figures he would battle with all his life. In particular he feared and admired Olivero Arduino, the school director whose oratorical manner and flowing beard earned him the nickname 'Zeus'.

The patriotism whipped up by Mussolini provided useful opportunities for mischief. When schoolwork palled, Fellini and Benzi would approach the headmaster and announce that the armies invading Abyssinia, which included some local men, had just made a breakthrough. If the newspaper suggested no suitable battle they invented one. They then requested permission to parade the school banner through town. A bamboozled teacher agreed and the gang raced off to spread chaos through the rest of Rimini's schools.

Fellini's attitude to Fascism was, and is, ambivalent. He claims he wore his youth group uniform without conviction, always with his socks around his ankles or lacking a piece of regalia, but photographs show both him and Riccardo smartly turned out, with every toggle and cord in place. Fellini also signed his caricatures for the Fascist magazines 'Av.' (for '*Avanguardista*') Fellini. While he insisted that *Amarcord* was an attack on Fascism, its vision of the *Rex* returning from its 1935 maiden voyage, looming out of the night, festooned with lights, is suffused with wonder and delight, while his re-creation of the seventh *Mille Miglia* (Thousand Mile) car race which passed through Rimini in 1935 is ironic and funny without mockery. In adulthood, writing about the patriotic fervour of Fascism and his feelings at nineteen, Fellini admitted: 'Even I, very young indeed, believed in that empire.'

5   Flash Gordon and the Rimini Kid

'Our mind can shape the way a thing will be, because we act according to our expectations'
Fellini to Charlotte Chandler, 1984

Fellini liked Rimini but there was never much prospect that he'd spend his life there. Ida's roots were in Rome and, with Urbano on the road for long periods and the marriage deteriorating, it figured increasingly in her thoughts, and in those of her sons.

When Federico was ten, the Barbianis had relaxed their hostility and Ida's children began receiving Christmas gifts from her elder brother, including the puppet theatre which so occupied Federico. It was always assumed this reconciliation was a spontaneous act of generosity, but Fellini now admits he manipulated it. 'I wrote Christmas letters to this uncle I had never seen,' he says, 'full of reassurances; I was good and would become even better . . . As a result of these little letters, packages arrived promptly every Christmas covered with sealing wax and string and containing pine nuts, nougat and all sorts of good things. Thanks to this uncle, Rome [when I first visited it] was already a beneficent city, dispensing gifts. I was filled with a desire to go and see if it were true.'

Fellini had his wish in 1930 when a stroke paralysed the uncle, and Ida's sister-in-law urged her to visit him. The family went to Rome by train. For the first time Fellini was exposed to long-distance travel, which he loathed and would continue to dislike all his life, and, more seductively, to Rome, with which he would have a life-long love affair.

'As soon as I came to Rome,' Fellini said in 1965, 'I had the feeling that I was home. Now I consider Rome my private apartment. That is the seduction secret of Rome. It is not like being in a city, it is like being in an apartment. The streets are like corridors. Rome is still the mother. Rome is protective.'

His uncle lived in some comfort in the suburbs. When they arrived, his mother fell to her knees beside the bed and kissed his pale hand. Federico was dizzy with admiration. Garbo couldn't have done better. But he would never really know or talk to the man who rescued him from provincial isolation. The relationship with his uncle was like a reflection of the tenuous link between Federico and his own father.

Fellini never lost his awe of the capital, a fact his enemies, especially the more aristocratic of them, like Luchino Visconti, used against him for fifty years. Even Roberto Rossellini, Fellini's earliest mentor, scorned his naïve enthusiasm. Orson Welles said patronisingly: 'Fellini's limitation – which is also the source of his charm – is that he's fundamentally very provincial. His films are a small-town boy's dream of the big city. His sophistication works because it's the creation of someone who doesn't have it.'

Fellini returned to Rimini determined to live in Rome. Everything in the next five years of his life, including his patchy academic record, might have been intended to further that aim. Ida's hopes for Federico as a professional man declined by the month. Two of his friends, Titta Benzi and Mario Montanari, became lawyers, Benzi settling in Rimini. Quizzed years later as to whether she'd have liked Fellini to have stayed there as well, Ida said: 'Well, not right here in Rimini. Maybe in Bologna. With his office in Bologna and his house here in Rimini . . . not here with his mother, necessarily, but here in Rimini.'

But Fellini was following his own bent. Spending August 1936 in a summer camp at Verucchio with other members of Opera Balilla, he experimented with caricatures. Some heads were published as 'Campeggisti 1936' in the Riminese organisation's magazine, *La Diana*, his first appearance in print. Encouraged, he branched out, selling coloured sketches of his schoolmasters to his subjects, and persuading Carlo Massa to let him draw portraits of movie stars for the foyer of the Fulgor and for the Caffè Giovannini. To make these, he collaborated with Demos Bonini. The drawings Fellini did alone were signed 'Fellas', those with Bonini 'Febo'. They were paid in free admissions, a privilege Fellini managed to get extended to Titta Benzi by telling him to stand just behind him at the box office and assume a deprived expression.

In the summer of 1937 he and Bonini set up 'FEBO', a stall on via IV Novembre, opposite the Tempio Malatestina, selling caricatures and black paper silhouettes. Fellini did the drawing and Bonini the colouring. At five lire a picture for locals (more for tourists) they made a modest profit.

Fellini's grades didn't improve much, though they were never as bad as he later made out. His scores for 1936/7 show mostly sevens (out of ten), with two eights, and sixes only in Mathematics, Physics and Military Culture. It's possible, however, that the records were 'cooked'. 'Look, there's no point in pretending that Fellini was thrilled with high school,' says Titta Benzi. 'Even though he had an eight in Latin, a nine in Greek, he didn't know a word, and technically he deserved a zero. But perhaps through some premonitory sense his teachers realised he was a mature person, special, and they promoted him.' Fellini's artistic skill may have persuaded the staff to inflate his grades. There's always the possibility too that, as in primary school, Parmesan changed hands.

As a teenager Fellini became less awed by the Grand Hotel and more familiar with its interior. Sometimes he hung round the tennis courts, retrieving balls. Occasionally he braved the lobby, snatching an impression of giant couches and marble bannisters before being chased out by a black-coated *concierge*.

Rules at the Kursaal, a one-storey *art déco* pavilion across the road on the beach with an outdoor café sheltered by a concrete overhang, weren't so strict, and Fellini became a regular there. He also frequented the Caffè Commercio and Raoul's Bar on the corso d'Augusto, where he got drunk for the first (and almost last) time, and passed out. First time drunk – and first time in love. The girl was fourteen-year-old Bianca Soriani, the daughter of a typographer who lived opposite the house (rented from Ferruccio Benzi) on via Dante 9 where the Fellinis moved in 1931. Fellini has described first glimpsing 'Bianchina' through the window of her house, a fairy-like figure in pink, though his friends remember him comparing her to Kay Francis and Barbara Stanwyck, two of Hollywood's more mannish heroines. As Fellini recalled the meeting, he wrote a message, in reverse, on her window asking her to meet him at the Arch of Augustus, where he presented her with a bunch of flowers.

Even by the standards of 1936, the relationship was innocent. The two went on bicycle rides together and her brother carried a few illicit letters. It might have died naturally had Ida not found out and confronted Signora Soriani, accusing her daughter of leading Federico astray. Physically the love story ended there, in boxed ears and recriminations, but, like most of Fellini's sentimental attachments, it would take root and flourish in his imagination. As he embroidered it later, they fled to Bologna, en route to Rome, with nothing but pocket money and a bag of sandwiches. By accident, however, they caught the

Ravenna train and Bianca broke down in tears, so Fellini brought her back. In other versions they got as far as Bologna, only to be captured after a day on the loose and returned by the police.

Though the Sorianis moved to Milan soon after, Bianca, who became a journalist, cherished the romance for years, even writing a novel about it. She agreed she and Fellini walked in the country and went to the beach, though he was too embarrassed by his skinny build to wear a bathing-costume. He gave her a ring and talked of running away to America where he would buy her a hundred beautiful dresses, a reflection of his father's gifts to Ida. But she insists they never left Rimini.

There's some evidence that Fellini and Bianca kept in touch after both moved away from Rimini. In the suspect reminiscences of Titta Benzi, he and Fellini even visited her in Milan, the first, he says, of many reunions. Among Fellini's first magazine pieces, published in 1940, is 'Hello Bianchina', the sentimental description of a long-distance phone call to his girl back home that leaves Federico at the end standing disconsolate and lonely in the Roman rain. It sparked a series in which Bianchina and Federico marry and begin to grapple with married life. Indirectly they are the prototypes of Cico and Pallina, the characters of Fellini's first radio serial, the star of which, Giulietta Masina, he *would* marry.

In high school, the gang, which now included Mario Montanari and Luigi Dolci as well as Titta, went through a phase of petty criminality. Inspired by the novels of Edgar Wallace, they started calling one another by snappy English surnames* and visualising themselves as a gang. As a life of crime it was unglamorous. They pilfered money from coats hanging in the cloakroom of the Dramatic Society and looted local shops of chickens, salt cod and flour. Once, they stole a large clock which they tried vainly to sell, an incident which turns up, like other adolescent adventures, in *I vitelloni*.

This enthusiasm for Wallace and Simenon marked the limit of Fellini's interest in literature not only in adolescence but in life. He read Ariosto, Petronius and Dante in school, but outside the classroom preferred thrillers and – something new in staid Italy – humour magazines and comic books. Most of the latter simply copied American strips, giving them new Italian dialogue balloons or *fumetti* – 'little puffs of smoke'. The term soon expanded to cover comic strips

---

*Fellini clung to this habit. In the sixties he still called his editor Ruggero Mastroianni 'Donovan', and Mastroianni called him 'Kerrigan'.

themselves, though by the forties it applied mainly to *fotoromanzi*, a particularly Italian form that used posed photographs rather than drawings. Fellini would parody these photo strips, their actors and fans in *Lo sceicco bianco*.

420, edited in Florence, became Fellini's favourite, along with its sister magazine, *Avventuroso*, founded in 1934 to satisfy the national hunger for American comic strips. Like a lot of Italian kids he also read the Roman bi-weekly *Marc'Aurelio*, a more aggressive version of Britain's *Punch*. The Rimini parish priest disliked *Marc'Aurelio* and persuaded local shops not to stock it, but Fellini found copies at the railroad station or in resorts like Riccione.

The humour magazines invited cartoons and jokes from readers. Through their letter columns and the caricatures of the editors and contributors that they published, Fellini built up an almost personal relationship with the people who ran them. In the thirties, US graphic artists like Petty, Vargas, Robert Benchley and Peter Arno had the standing of TV stars. Fellini's hero was Giuseppe Zanini, who special- ised in drawings of film stars, especially German, which he signed 'Nino Za'.

In Fellini's imagination Zanini wintered at the Hotel Cristallo in Cortina, which gave him its best suite, spent Christmas in Berlin, February in London and the rest of the year in Honolulu. He felt confirmed in this vision of caricaturists as playboys when, looking for *Marc'Aurelio* in Riccione, he spotted one of its artists, Ferrante De Torres, on the beach, recognising him from a caricature. He hung around until De Torres asked him to fetch a basket of fruit – or maybe it was a box of matches. Fellini introduced himself and returned two days later with some of his work. De Torres was politely encouraging. It's an index of Fellini's ability to exploit his charm that before long he would be working with him, and with Nino Za.

In the summer of 1938 Fellini was a Rimini schoolboy about to graduate from high school and being bullied by his mother to study law. By January 1939 he was living in Rome and, all thought of law school forgotten, beginning to make a living as a journalist. This dramatic change is one of the worst-documented periods in Fellini's life, because that's how he prefers it. Successive biographers have given differing accounts, to which *I vitelloni* and *Roma* added a few more.

At the end of *I vitelloni*, Moraldo, most sensitive and intellectual of the aimless young men loafing round the seaside town where they were born, simply leaves, hopping the Rome train early one morning without telling anyone. *Roma* picks him up at Termini station in 1939, an innocent about to be sucked into a city where he feels instantly at home.

In between Rimini and Rome, Fellini, according to certain versions, some of them plausibly circumstantial, spent a few months in Florence, where he worked for *420*. Demos Bonini is supposed to have arranged this by sending Fellini's sketches to its editor, Giuseppe Nerbini, receiving in return a cheque and an offer of work which he handed to Federico with the comment: 'Here is your passport.'

Fellini himself described his job there in detail, as 'halfway between doorman and editorial secretary. I stuck stamps on envelopes.' He graduated to drawing, he says, when 'in 1938, Mussolini decided to kill off comic strips. Well, another artist, Giove Toppi, and myself, we continued to draw and write the stories. Those *fumetti*, they were my first work.' Among his creations, he claimed, was a totally new Flash Gordon story in which Flash, seduced by the high priestess of the planet Phoebus, is carried off to a planet inhabited by hawk-men.*

Old friends in Rimini have also been liberal with reminiscences of this period. Mario Montanari described seeing him off on the train to Rome in January 1938. 'Federico, Titta and I had our picture taken in a little garden near by. We were a little dazed. We couldn't believe what was happening. Federico, who wanted to leave, was actually leaving. We were very sad.' Benzi added another detail. The whole gang, he said, rode along with Fellini as far as Bologna to keep him company.

Almost all this is invention. The real story is at once less dramatic and more revealing of Fellini's ambition.

Ida's dissatisfaction and her son's increasingly stubborn insistence on moving to the capital combined to dictate a change. He refused to enrol in a university near Rimini but the law school of the University of Rome was even more prestigious. As a student, Federico would also be exempt from military service.

His taste for private enterprise whetted by his experience selling caricatures, Fellini had taken to sending gags and cartoons to the humour magazines and those newspapers which paid for contributions. He picked up an occasional twenty lire from *La domenica del corriere*. The first cartoon, published on 6 February 1938, showed a lion-tamer warning his aerialist wife not to hold hands so long with her

---

*In 1957 he told Gideon Bachmann he also redrew Lee Falk's *Mandrake*.

partner during the Somersault of Death – Fellini's circus interest appearing early.

420 in particular was bombarded with cartoons, gag lines and longer pieces, as well as caricatures of the editor. Like most editors of the time, Nerbini responded through the letter column. From a note published in September 1937 it's evident that Fellini asked how one got a job there, and that the editor wasn't entirely discouraging, telling him that people like him were the future of the magazine and that its door was always open. Some Fellini gags were published during March 1938, illustrated by staff artists, and Nerbini, again via the magazine letter column, praised his energy and enthusiasm, while urging him to slow down.

This is almost certainly as close as Fellini ever got to working for *420*. No bootleg *Flash Gordon* ever existed. When Mussolini did issue a decree against comics in November 1938 (not especially because they were American but because their plots seemed insufficiently patriotic and inspirational), Nerbini replaced Raymond's strip immediately with an optimistic Italian one affirming group effort and family ties.

Fellini, a natural caricaturist but a limited one, admits that he lacks the draughtsmanship to copy Raymond's distinctive and intricate style. 'That's not my talent,' he agrees. 'I just put down on paper some vague ideas that help me fix some visual ideas.' The plot he outlined is actually one of Raymond's most famous, the basis of the 1936 movie serial and its 1980 remake.

The legend had its beginning, Fellini admitted to two French comic-book scholars in 1965, when he tried inventing his own *Flash Gordon* stories after it was discontinued. 'I knew all the figures by heart, the planet Mongo and its emperor Ming. I knew intuitively which adventure [Flash] and his companions would encounter. I didn't have the feeling I was working. It was simply fun to invent even more daring adventures for the cartoonists. I didn't know what a script was yet. I made up a story, wrote the dialogue and divided it up among the eight or twelve pictures of each plate.' But it was never more than an adolescent exercise. Faced recently with the suggestion that the whole Florence episode was imaginary, Fellini conceded: 'It might be.'

All the same, the impact on Fellini of *Avventuroso* and the Fulgor was profound and long-lasting. 'American films and comic strips had shown me,' he says, 'that there was a place where you could grow up and become president without studying Latin and Greek.'

Early in 1939, Fellini moved permanently to Rome. Titta Benzi recalls he left on 4 January, which might well be correct, since he shows up officially on the capital's records in March. The gang could hardly have gone with him as far as Bologna, however, since Fellini was accompanied on the trip by his mother and little sister, who would stay with him for the first year. The house was closed and its furniture sent on to Rome in two vans. Urbano and Riccardo remained in Rimini, taking a room in town. This was no casual move for Ida but a major relocation. With the birth of Maddalena, her relationship with Urbano had declined still further. The sense of what she had lost by coming to Romagna became more poignant as Rome flourished under Fascism and gleaming marble buildings in what foreigners derisively called 'Mussolini Modern' mushroomed all over the capital.

Riccardo confirms that Federico left with his mother rather than, as Fellini always insisted, alone. 'When Federico decided to go to Rome, my mother settled there with my sister, in the city where she was born and where she went in the hope that sometime my father would rejoin them. Me, I stayed in Rimini with Papa. I was supposed to help him, waiting for him to liquidate his business in Romagna so we could all settle in Rome.'

Free of his censorious wife, Urbano settled comfortably into a life of billiards, café conversation and a free and easy life on the road. He visited Ida occasionally but had no intention of moving himself. Rimini suited him. When Fellini based a film on his teenage days he adopted a mild Romagnolo insult to describe the group, calling them '*vitelloni*': young calves, immature animals who blunder around, doing damage and getting in the way. Federico never quite fitted that model, but Riccardo called his father 'a real *vitellone*'.

Riccardo had been given a railway pass and put to work learning the wholesale grocery trade, but it was a role he loathed. The younger Fellini had a good tenor voice and ambitions to go on the stage. After only a few months he joined his mother, brother and sister in Rome.

6   The March on Rome

'What's good about Rome is, it's big. Nobody knows you.
You're free to come and go'
Traveller in a Rimini bar in *Roma*, 1972

Ida took a house at via Albalonga 13 and Federico enrolled in the
University of Rome. The registration was almost certainly to gain the
draft exemption since there's no record he ever attended classes.
Instead, a gawky figure in flapping white suit and worn-down canvas
shoes, he made the rounds of magazines. Riccardo went out too, to
study singing and audition as an actor.

In the screenplay *Moraldo in città/Moraldo in the City*, which he
wrote with Tullio Pinelli and Ennio Flaiano in 1954, Fellini describes
the period between 1939 and 1941 when, hovering somewhere
between fan and professional, he touted material among Rome's small
papers and humour weeklies and, with other freelance journalists and
artists, scavenged for work in the tightening economy of an Italy
isolating itself from democratic Europe and bracing for war. Blasi, a
journalist he meets in a restaurant, offers to show some pieces to his
editor. Waiting in his office for the reaction, Moraldo notices Gian
Antonio Gattone, an overweight red-faced man in his fifties whose
work he's read and enjoyed. While they're talking, Blasi arrives, hands
Fellini his crumpled contribution and tells him: 'The editor says it
won't do. I'm sorry.'

This parallels Fellini's account of how he looked up Ferrante De
Torres at *Marc'Aurelio*. Its offices were at the foot of via Veneto, a wide
avenue lined with plane trees that climbs in a steep curve from piazza
Barberini to the city's ancient walls. Lined with cafés and hotels,
including the Excelsior and the Grand, Rome's most sumptuous, it was
a street Fellini would soon know well.

The doorman redirected him to the nearby offices of the cheap daily
Il piccolo, another Rizzoli publication which De Torres now edited.

The artist vaguely remembered Fellini from Riccione but told him to come back later. When he did so, the office was crowded with people. Among them was Vitiliano Brancati, a journalist whose account of a visit with Mussolini Fellini had studied at school. Blasi's perfunctory rejection recalls Fellini's treatment by De Torres and Moraldo's ingratiating approach to Gattone is probably based on a conversation with Brancati. In character, however, Gattone is recognisably Luigi Garrone, a hard-drinking and broken-down journalist who became Fellini's first mentor in Rome before dying of cirrhosis.

Fellini kept returning to *Il piccolo* with more material. Eventually De Torres gave him the banal theme 'Welcome, Little Rain', telling him to go into the next room and come up with a sketch and four lines of text. The 'weather piece' is a standard practical joke, the journalists' equivalent of sending out the new apprentice for a tin of striped paint or a left-handed screwdriver, but Fellini did his best, handing his effort to an indifferent editor, who spiked it. In September 1941 the item, now called 'Welcome, Little Snow', appeared in *Marc'Aurelio*. Fellini seldom discarded a good idea.

Tougher now and more confident, he made another try at *Marc'Aurelio*. This time he was lucky. Stefano Vanzini, the magazine's deputy editor (and later, as 'Steno', a successful film director) liked his drawings. 'They looked as if they had been sketched by [George] Grosz,' he said. 'I therefore kept him there waiting for the director.' This suggests the benefit of hindsight, since Fellini's chunky figures owed less to Grosz's jagged Berlin caricatures than to Frederick Burt Opper's *Happy Hooligan*. Still, they got Fellini's foot in the door.

The same day, another ambitious young writer, Ruggero Maccari, visited the magazine. The two struck up a friendship and Vanzini, sensing a chemistry, told them to come back with some cartoon ideas. After a number of brainstorming sessions in bars and at Fellini's home, they delivered the gags, to ambivalent reactions from the staff. Cheekily, Fellini returned a few days later with an article, *'E Permesso?'*, describing the editors' response to his first attempts. Resignedly, Vanzini published it in March 1939. He'd begun to realise, as Nerbini had done, that Fellini wouldn't take no for an answer.

For the next year Fellini lived hand-to-mouth as a contributor to *Marc'Aurelio*, initially freelance but in time on the staff. Later he liked to dramatise himself as the lonely observer, tired and hungry, wandering Rome at night. When Gideon Bachmann pointed out how often dark city streets and a deserted piazza with a fountain appeared in his films, he said: 'Possibly what is in my mind when I shoot these scenes is the memory of my first impression of Rome . . . I was sixteen [*sic*]; I had no job, no idea of what I wanted to do. Often I was out of work, often I didn't have the money to stay in a hotel or eat properly. Or I would work at night. In any case, it is quite possible that the image of the town at night, empty and lonely, has remained in my soul from those days.' In fact, he seems to have enjoyed himself hugely, relishing his freedom and the figure he cut. Nor was it any hardship for him, a chronic insomniac, to stay up most of the night.

Fellini was enamoured of the reporter image he'd seen in American movies: 'I liked the coats they wore and the way they wore their hats on the back of their heads.' A 1942 caricature by Nino Za shows him as a gaunt figure with felt hat tilted well back, hands thrust in the pockets of a casually belted trench coat, eyes dark, mouth twisted in a John Garfield scowl at the futility of existence. It's a supremely melodramatic and self-regarding pose, the essence of the Fellini myth.

In some interviews, Fellini also describes three weeks spent as a hard-news reporter for a Roman tabloid, usually assumed to be *Il popolo di Roma*, which had offices in the same building as *Il piccolo*. In a favourite anecdote of these days, he told of how, sent to cover a girl's poisoning, he interviewed everyone in the building and wrote a detailed account which the editor reduced to a few lines, adding a headline which suggested kindly that her death was accidental. His career as an investigative journalist ended, he said, when the Fascists clamped down on crime stories. But no example of Fellini's hard journalism has ever turned up, and since Luigi Garrone was in reality blacklisted by the Fascists, Fellini may have borrowed some of his experiences.

Meanwhile, Ida was finding Rome less congenial than she'd hoped. In the winter of 1939/40 she returned to Rimini and Urbano. Her sister-in-law found a boarding house for Federico, who had always told his friends he lived alone, and another, in a different area, for Riccardo. The gap between Fellini and his family widened. It's only at this point that *Roma* becomes genuinely autobiographical. The rowdy *pensione* where Federico takes his first room next to broken-down actors and dubious ex-journalists, ruled over by an elephantine landlady, usually prostrate with heat, with an infantile adult son in a hair net cuddling up to her bolster-like frame, rings vividly true.

In *Moraldo in città*, Moraldo is chatting to Gattone in Blasi's office when another man walks in and embraces the writer. The script describes him as 'the painter Lange, a young man about thirty. He is tall and has a wolfish face with an enormous smile that flashes constantly.' After Blasi's rejection, Lange and Gattone take Moraldo for a consoling drink. They become friends over a large and drunken meal for which, it emerges, none of them has the money. Lange tries to bluff their way into a free dinner by offering the manager a cartoon but he throws them out. Lange is recognisably Rinaldo Geleng, the second of Fellini's new friends in Rome. Geleng himself recalls first meeting Fellini not in an editorial office but by chance while both were meditating hungrily on chickens roasting in a restaurant window. He and Garrone introduced Fellini to bohemian Rome: landladies who didn't press for rent, restaurants which gave credit, and the few that fed artists free in the hour before they closed, to clean up unsold food.* If the three were feeling brave they'd hire a car, drive around all night, abandon it in front of the rental office and run away without paying.

Before he won a foothold in the magazines, Fellini, with Geleng, revived his Rimini trade in sidewalk caricatures. Geleng did well, flattering people and making good sales, But Fellini couldn't control his satirical eye. His subjects emerged on paper as pigs, elephants and giraffes. Many refused to pay. Other money-making schemes also backfired. Spotting a football star in a restaurant, Geleng dashed off a caricature and took it to his table, hoping he'd buy it. But the man simply complimented him on a good likeness, signed the drawing and handed it back. A plan to paint advertising cartoons on shop windows flopped too when Fellini, unhappy with a first attempt, tried to wash it off and found that Lange had given him oil paint. Telling the irate shopkeeper he was going to buy turpentine, he fled.

Working often with Maccari, Fellini became a regular contributor to *Marc'Aurelio*. Both were invited to the five pm editorial meetings on Wednesday and Friday at which ideas were generated and commissions handed out. Fellini ingratiated himself with the editorial director, Vito de Bellis. Breezing into his office, he'd ask: 'Is there anything I can do for you?' De Bellis would respond: 'Don't you mean: "Is there anything *I* can do for *you*?"?'

But Fellini had already learned to deploy his charm and de Bellis was seduced. He not only gave Fellini work but took him to the press where *Marc'Aurelio* was printed, showed him how to read and correct proofs, bought him meals and even polished up his table manners. 'I was blissful,' Fellini said.

---

*Loyally, Fellini continued to patronise one of these, Da Cesarino, which became famous in the seventies as his unofficial headquarters.

Fellini had the flair of the natural freelance for maximising the profit from a good idea. His first series about his imaginary romance with Bianchina, *Primo amore/First Love*, ran to eighteen pieces between 9 November 1940 and 11 January 1942. He followed it with *Piccoli fidanzati/Little Fiancés* (six pieces between 19 March 1941 and 1 July 1942) and *Oggi sposi/Married People Today* (twelve pieces between 18 February and 22 April 1942). All these were in turn recycled as his radio series *Cico e Pallina/Cico and Pallina*, just as his reminiscences of school in *Secondo Liceo/Second Lycée*, which ran between 7 December 1940 and 4 October 1941, provided the foundation of *Amarcord*.

His most successful idea was *Ma tu mi stai a sentire?/But are You Listening to Me?*, a series of imaginary monologues which he claims, perhaps rightly, to have overhead in cafés: a variety star, a caricaturist, a waiter, friends of his father. It became a regular feature of the magazine between 1939 and 1941.

Apolitical then as always, Fellini was indifferent to the fact that many of *Marc'Aurelio*'s staff wore the Sahariana and that the magazine operated, like all of the Italian press, under censorship. De Bellis's friends included politically aware writers, but though Fellini met some of them, in particular a short, irascible and erudite man with a black moustache named Ennio Flaiano, when the conversation strayed into politics his attention wandered. If he'd heard of Cesare Zavattini, the left-wing critic and theorist who was agitating for a new cinema in the style of Soviet Socialist realism and British documentary, it didn't register. He preferred Hollywood.

For Fellini, politics and the war meant mostly arresting images. He left the office on 10 June 1940 to find via Veneto and piazza Barberini empty. As he stood on the kerb a cyclist came free-wheeling down the hill and called to him: 'Hey, war's been declared!' Hitler had defeated France and Mussolini sided with Germany against Britain and its allies.

Before it closed in 1943, *Marc'Aurelio* published 700 pieces by Fellini, 200 of them in 1940 alone. However, he soon saw that journalism offered a short-term career at best. He made his break late in 1940. Mussolini's push for an integrated Italian culture encouraged radio, and broadcasters were hungry for material. Taking a cue from the humour magazines, the stations stitched comedy sketches and monologues into vaguely defined '*rivisti*' – revues. Marcello Marchesi, a *Marc'Aurelio* colleague, suggested that he, Fellini and Maccari write some pieces for the radio company Ente Italiano Audizioni Radiofoniche (EIAR). On 24 December 1940, the first was broadcast as part of a *rivista di mezza stagione* – a mid-season revue. The three quickly became a gag-writing unit within *Marc'Aurelio*. 'We were a little office for comic pieces,' says Fellini. He continued until 1942, his radio work culminating in *The Adventures of the Newlyweds Cico and Pallina*, a serial based on the imaginary romance of Bianchina and Federico.

Radio was crucial to Fellini, giving him experience in writing spoken dialogue. It was also his introduction to collaboration. On *Marc'Aurelio*, he'd discovered his skill as a manipulator, someone who could coax and charm others into helping him. In radio, he found he could fit into a creative group without ceding to it any of his independence. People began by working with him and ended, without rancour and in fact gladly, working *for* him, or at least for the realisation of his ideas. Radio made Fellini what he would remain throughout his career, a skilful user of others. 'Co-operation' in his lexicon would always be defined as 'A lot of people doing what I say'.

Fellini always loved vaudeville, the more vulgar the better. A taste for clowns, slapstick and drag shows would remain with him all his life and suffuse his work. For *Roma*, he shot a long and affectionate re-creation of a visit to one of Rome's more raucous theatres. The Jovinelli was a bloodhouse near Termini station, close to where he then lived, in a district 'haunted by poverty-stricken provincials, prostitutes and Chinese necktie-hawkers'. Renaming it the Barafonda, Fellini shows it as the nadir of theatrical elegance, with audience members eating, sleeping, arguing, socialising, even, in the case of a small boy, pissing in the aisle during the show. Its fumble-footed dancers and dismal comics could expect to be shouted at, even pelted with dead cats.

Inept younger acts alternate with performers who've grown old and tired on the boards. Three ageing comics in white faces, wearing bowler hats and carrying candles, perform a traditional song, at the same time carrying on a sulphurous exchange with barrackers in the audience, and a trio of plump matrons in gingham harmonise, to enthusiastic applause, in the style of the Andrews Sisters. During the show the manager announces that the Allies have landed in Sicily, establishing the date as 10 July 1943. Shortly after, air-raid sirens drive everyone into the shelters.

Fellini's friends changed from journalists to vaudeville people. Among the new group was Alberto Sordi, a moon-faced comic of twenty with a skilled line in embarrassed, fumbling young men that he would turn into a successful movie career. He and Fellini shared a fascination for Oliver Hardy. At thirteen Sordi had won a competition for Hardy imitators sponsored by MGM, and now dubbed Hardy's voice in Italian versions of his films. He was then working in *avanspettacoli*, vaudeville interludes that introduced and separated movies, a hangover from the 'prologues' of Hollywood's silent and early sound cinema. 'We practically lived together,' says Sordi, somewhat fancifully, of his early relationship with Fellini. 'During the day we ate in a small dairy shop on via Frattina. He had a flat on via Nicotera and we were always together, dreaming.'

The most valuable friend Fellini made at this period, and in all of his early career, was the comedian Aldo Fabrizi. Effusive, ebullient, but capable of deep rages, Fabrizi was an archetypal Fellini character in life. In 1940 he was thirty-six years old, with a successful vaudeville career behind him based on his famous comic monologues. Fellini interviewed him, and the comic, as de Bellis had done, took Fellini under his wing, inviting him to restaurants and to his home. Since they then both lived near the piazza San Giovanni, they would often walk home together, Fabrizi spinning tales of life on the road with a touring variety show. Fellini even became the godfather of Fabrizi's son, and the comedian asked him to write material for some records.

Quickly capitalising on his new connection, Fellini devoted a *Ma tu mi stai a sentire?* piece in September 1939 to 'a music-hall star'. Other pieces refer knowledgeably to vaudeville dancers and comedians. Fabrizi's experiences on the road found their way into *Luci del varietà*, his first film as director. Fellini, however, couldn't help embroidering the connection. In the fifties he often described how 'one day, Fabrizi proposed to me that I leave with him on a tour. The revue was called *Sparks of Love*. I travelled with that company six or seven months through all Italy. I think that was the richest period of my life. I accumulated a heap of observations and human experiences.' He also claimed to have helped paint scenery and even to have performed a few times. Six of the eight dancers in the troupe, he said, fell in love with him. Despite the convincing detail, the trip was a total invention.

Through Fabrizi, Fellini met the sub-society of music-hall comics, some of whom had been clowns and still worked under their *noms de cirque*. Both Ferdinand Guillaume, called Polidor, and Luigi Visconti, called Fanfulla, appeared in his films, and though he worked only once – to help out Rossellini – with Antonio de Curtis Gagliardi Ducas Commeno di Bisanzio, as Toto liked to call himself, he met, interviewed and learned to dislike the self-important little man who was to become one of Italy's biggest post-war stars.

Fellini was particularly struck by the comic Peppino de Filippo, mostly because of the circumstances under which he saw him first. 'It was in 1937,' recalled Fellini (1939 is more likely), 'at the Argentina Theatre in Rome. He was on the stage. I was in the audience, an audience black with Fascist uniforms. There had been that day a triumphant Fascist ceremony. Rome was full of banners, of loud-speakers extolling our Empire . . . The people in the audience – or at least a great part of them – until a few hours before had paraded, marched, trooped, sung the hymns of the Fascist revolution . . . But on the stage there was another type of Italian – a man who, with his presence alone, belied any dream of greatness in the audience . . . His typical way of walking with his hands in his pockets was sufficient to make one realise at once that the parades of that morning, the triumphant goose-stepping, did not stand on solid foundations. That glance, full of biological, untameable scepticism, was sufficient to make one realise that our dreams were wrong, not even a laughing matter.'

Fellini was also having his first adult sexual adventures. Some, though he hesitates to particularise, were probably in brothels. In *Roma* he describes visits to three, of contrasting sophistication. The first two are cheap, patronised mostly by soldiers, raucous white-tiled meat-markets staffed by lumpy middle-aged whores. Fellini seems, however, to have a special affection for them, since they occur again in *La città delle donne*. Another is more elegant, with a lavishly furnished lounge and an elevator to the rooms. At one point, business is suspended and doors locked while an important client is discreetly accommodated. In *Roma* Fellini re-creates one intimate moment when Federico is smitten by a prostitute in this smart brothel who dresses like Messalina from *Maciste all'inferno*, and initiates a relationship with her, but it's not clear if this is more than a fantasy.

He's more forthcoming about a non-commercial liaison with a girl he calls Andreina. In *Moraldo in città* she's in the crowd watching Moraldo desperately trying to wipe away his window painting but, unlike everyone else, doesn't laugh at his failure. He meets her later by chance and, after she's seduced him, briefly becomes engaged, only to break it off once her family insist he take an office job. Both in films and in real life, Fellini's fear of demanding long-term relationships was already evident. In one of the *Oggi sposi* series, the fictional Federico confesses he feels nothing for his new bride Bianchina and is terrified by the realisation that they will be married 'for ever'.

Moraldo also describes a more glamorous affair with a Signora Contini, older than Moraldo and the publisher of a small literary magazine. She seduces him and installs him in her apartment until his toy-boy status drives him back into freelancing. She also reappears later in the story, at the culminating orgy, during which, though the script is vague, it seems he shares her with her new lover.

The balance of probabilities suggests that Andreina did exist but that Signora Contini, or at least Fellini's relationship with her, is invention. Tullio Pinelli says the real Andreina was the daughter of a guard at the Museo Valle Giulia, and recalls vaguely that Signora Contini was based on a Signora Lenticchi. By 1941, Fellini's relative indifference to women and his preference for male companionship were already established, and the fact that these two affairs are the only ones mentioned, even in passing, in any of his memoirs or those of his friends suggests their insignificance.

7   In the City of the Movies

'When I was a youngster, this word, Cinecittà, evoked a
kind of city in which I wanted to live'
Fellini, quoted by Jerome Charyn

There were glamorous people in the Italian show business of the early
forties – stars like Vittorio de Sica and Assia Noris, a team to whom
Fellini paid nostalgic tribute in *Roma* when young Federico, arriving
at the Termini station, sees a billboard for their 1939 romance, *Grandi
magazzini*. But Fellini, though he'd meet and even work with some of
them as a director, was seldom part of their world and never an equal.

John Coleman is right to define Fellini as 'a poet of the second-rate;
of the dancer stumbling through a routine, the itinerant strong-man
scowling for pennies, the vulnerable starlet playing cool and intellectual at a party'. With his provincial background and his roots in radio
and comics, he would always be seen professionally as associated with
the dirty end of show business – vaudeville, cheap movie comedy,
rivista sketches, the circus – and feel happiest and most confident
there. Far from hiding the facts that some of the men with whom he
took coffee at the Canova were petty swindlers or that his friend
Peppino de Filippo left school at the second grade and still had trouble
reading, Fellini relished and publicised them. They made his own low
status and lack of education less galling.

Through Vito de Bellis, Fellini could have made contact with Rome's
literary circle. Marchesi tried to introduce him to literature, encouraging him to read Kafka and Steinbeck, but he never became an
enthusiast for fiction. His preference for fables, fantasies, travellers'
tales and scraps of experience refracted through the imagination
emerges in his life-long embrace of comic strips, science fiction and, at
the more reputable end of his reading, his schoolboy texts. *The
Satyricon* of Petronius and Ariosto's *Orlando Furioso* were, aside from
Kafka's fragmentary, uncompleted *Amerika* and Giacomo Casanova's

plotless memoirs, almost the only literary works he ever contemplated adapting to film.

While he was becoming established at *Marc'Aurelio*, Fellini worked for *Cinemagazzino*. Run by a man named Cucciola, 'half tailor, half poet, who was mad for journalism', it was edited in the apartment behind his shop, where Fellini had to find space on the kitchen table next to cheeses and bottles of chianti. Fellini invented an Advice-to-the-Lovelorn column called *Piccola posta* for which he wrote both letters and answers. From time to time Cucciola would call him into the shop to reassure a client that his new trousers were a good fit. He was too innocent to be much of an Agony Aunt, he admits, but he did learn a lot about tailoring.

He soon persuaded Cucciola to let him write about film and theatre stars. It was a small step from interviewing actresses and watching films in production to the idea of a career in that world. Italy had dozens of film studios but the biggest was Cinecittà, a walled city of the movies fifteen kilometres from Rome. Mussolini had opened it on 27 April 1937 by 'assisting' with the sound mixing of *Scipio l'Africano*, the Roman epic designed to give historical justification to his invasion of Abyssinia.

'It sat on 149 acres of land,' Jerome Charyn wrote, 'with sixteen sound stages, including a special stage for miniatures, make-up and animation. It looked a little like the Vatican *and* MGM, with nine acres of gardens and flower beds, three restaurants, an electric power station, and a huge tank that could hold entire islands and a fleet of ships.' The national film school, the Centro Sperimentale, was also sited there. Outside Hollywood, only the UFA complex at Neu Babelsberg near Berlin could compare.

When Mussolini began censoring and banning foreign movies as 'immoral' or 'unsuitable', distributors cut off the flow, aiding Italian production. Twenty-seven features were produced at Cinecittà in 1941, thirty-three in 1942 and thirteen in 1943 before bombing closed it and the studios became a refugee camp.

In 1987, for *Intervista*, his fiftieth-anniversary tribute, Fellini re-created his first journey to Cinecittà, a trolley car ride through a green countryside that seems enchanted into an imitation of the movies. At the studio, Fellini's surrogate walks into a lavish outdoor production shot, the air filled with whirling scraps of coloured paper, in the midst of which a director leaps about, bawling at an army of dancers. Looking for the star he's supposed to interview Fellini enters a sound stage filled with the impedimenta of an Indian epic, complete with life-sized cut-out elephants. Behind the scenes the producer and writer bicker while the director goes crazy, shoving elephants angrily so that they topple like dominoes, at which everyone breaks for lunch.

Fellini recalls that *Corona di ferro/The Iron Crown* was shooting on that first occasion, and the bar was filled with 'gladiators, men in breastplates and togas all sitting there and drinking beer and fizzy lemonade', but he's mistaken. Alessandro Blasetti's film wasn't released until 1941. His first interview subject was Osvaldo Valenti, a handsome, brooding actor whom his editor admired, but in *Intervista* he becomes the more languorous 'Katia Devis', a sex queen, based on Greta Gonda, who invites him to her all-pink caravan, takes a shower that's a voyeur's delight, then curls up on the couch in a feathered peignoir and, surrounded by her retinue, feeds the young journalist *bons mots* as soft-centred as fondant chocolates.

Fellini already knew the reality of film-making to be more gritty and eccentric. In *Roma*, he draws some of the other lodgers in his *pensione* as the detritus of movies, old actors and journalists living on history and hopes. The stars were even less admirable. Valenti was a cocaine addict and Fascist who was executed by the same partisans who killed Mussolini. Fellini also got to know Anna Magnani, foul-mouthed and sexually outrageous, slick seducer Amadeo Nazzari, and Vittorio de Sica, whose ambitions to direct films about the working classes clashed with his taste for high living and especially roulette.

Also beginning his career at Cinecittà in 1940 was a man who would become Fellini's greatest rival. Fourteen years older, Luchino Visconti had the aquiline glare of the natural autocrat. Until he discovered film he spent his time in the cultivated pursuits suitable to a hereditary duke of Milan. He bred horses, dabbled in design, and lived in Paris, where he socialised with Cocteau and Coco Chanel and became friendly with Jean Renoir.

In 1940 Renoir was invited by Mussolini to make a film at the Centro Sperimentale. Visconti, by then his assistant, returned to Italy to work on Renoir's version of *Tosca*. He'd gone to Paris a dilettante, a ladies' man and a Fascist. He returned a film-maker, a bisexual moving towards full homosexuality but also, more improbably than either of these, given his heritage, a convinced Communist.

It would be hard to think of two men with less in common than Fellini and Visconti, and until the latter's death their rivalry, nourished by acolytes, would flourish. For all his success, Fellini never earned the respect Visconti accepted as his right. Marcello Mastroianni, who owed his career to Visconti's *Le notti bianche/White*

Nights and *La dolce vita*, acknowledged with some embarrassment the gap between them. 'When I was asked the difference between [Visconti] and Fellini, I always answered that Visconti was the teacher the pupils liked and Fellini was your neighbour in class.'

In public Fellini was always courteous, even deferential to Visconti, sending him flowers and cordial telegrams, but privately he was scornful. 'We were driving around once, discussing Visconti,' said his assistant in the late fifties and early sixties, Dominique Delouche, 'and I said I liked *Senso*. Fellini put his lips together and made a rude noise. "It's the film of a fag," he said.' Privately, Visconti was just as dismissive of Fellini, comparing him to a country boy with his eye forever glued to the Roman keyhole, spying on his betters. In 1974, Visconti made a widely reported gibe that all film-makers with surnames ending in the peasant-derived diminutive *-ini* 'had no talent'. Hearing this, Fellini snarled: 'Who told you that – Vicont*ini*?' It was a lame riposte, but typical. Helpless to unsettle Visconti, Fellini consistently hired technicians who'd worked with him, as if with them he'd acquire some of the other's effortless style.

Mussolini, convinced of his invincibility by his Abyssinian adventure, had sent an army to enlarge Italy's new empire. On 23 October 1942, it was decisively defeated at El Alamein by Montgomery. Newsreel films of hundreds of thousands of Italian soldiers, mostly conscripts, trudging into imprisonment never reached Italian screens, but there was no disguising that the Rome–Berlin Axis was not working as Il Duce had promised.

Through all this, Fellini remained as non-political as it was possible to be in a country at war. On the tenth anniversary of its foundation, *Marc'Aurelio* was visited by the Secretary General of the Fascist Party, Ettore Muti. Young, tanned, jingling with medals, Muti was introduced to each member of the staff. Standing in front of Fellini, he asked: 'Can you hear me?' Fellini, vague as ever, replied he could hear him very well. Muti repeated the question and Fellini, puzzled, his answer. It might have developed into something worse had de Bellis not hissed that he was being asked if he wrote *Ma tu mi stai a sentire?* As it was, Muti, leaving, told de Bellis to have Fellini get a haircut.

Under pressure from the Ministry of Popular Culture, *Marc'Aurelio* had become overtly propagandist. 'We had to reveal to the Italian public that Churchill was a schizophrenic,' Fellini said, 'that English women were nymphomaniacs, their offspring degenerates and their husbands alcoholics.' He drifted away during 1942, not out of moral outrage but because he was doing better elsewhere. (The magazine closed shortly afterwards.) His radio writing was prospering. Its mainstay was *Cico e Pallina*, which ran for twenty minutes each Sunday night. Fellini's name was literally all over the series, which was advertised in magazines as *Le avventure degli sposini Cico e Pallina di Federico/ The Adventures of the Young Marrieds Cico and Pallina by Federico*, with a cartoon boldly signed 'Federico' in a cartouche, the name under which he was also listed as writer. Only that of the sponsors, Niba, a perfume company, was larger.

There was plenty of work too as a film journalist and, increasingly, as a gag writer for movies. Fellini worked usually with Maccari, on commissions from Steno, who was moonlighting as assistant to director Mario Mattoli. 'We were asked to intervene in a scenario already written along general lines by some other journalists like Steno,' says Maccari, who went on to a major screenwriting career. Fellini contributed (uncredited) to *Imputato alzatevi/Defendant, On Your Feet* and *Lo vedi come sei?/Do You See How You Are?* in 1939, and in 1940 *Non me lo dire!/Don't Tell Me!* and *Il pirata sono io/The Pirate is Me*. All were directed by Mattoli for the Piedmontese comic Erminio Macario and written officially by Steno, Marchesi and Vittorio Metz, but actually by almost everyone on *Marc'Aurelio*. 'Some days, the entire editorial staff of the magazine would be inventing puns and new gags,' Maccari says.

Fellini is casual, even a little ashamed, about his first film work. 'I was a rewrite man. I used to add gags to the scripts of dull comedies.' Mostly he hung round the producers' offices, tossing out ideas, some of which might find their way, much altered, into the script. But it proved he could think on his feet and 'pitch' a plot to a star or producer, attributes easily as valuable in a film writer as imagination and originality.

In 1942 Fellini worked, again uncredited, on *Documento Z3/ Document Z3*, a spy thriller set in Yugoslavia. 'There were eight of us . . . We met in the beautiful home of producer Alfredo Guarini where all we did was drink whisky, eat ice-cream and smoke a lot. Sometimes Isa Miranda, the mistress of the house, would appear with a large cake.' Only Sandro de Feo, Ercole Patti and Guarini, who directed the film, are credited. Fellini's first official mention on a film (in the documentation, if not on screen) is for *Avanti c'e posto/Move Along Inside*, directed by Mario Bonnard and written by Piero Tellini, Cesare Zavattini and Aldo Fabrizi, who brought Fellini on to the production.

Avanti c'e posto's producer was Giuseppe Vasaturo, a flamboyant character who'd adopted the name 'Amato' and would become known as 'Don Peppino'. Famous for Sam Goldwyn-like malapropisms ('It's certain. It's *absolutely* certain. It could even happen'), Amato would later help finance *La dolce vita*. A comedy set on Rome's trolley-buses, *Avanti c'e posto* follows the rivalry of a driver and a ticket collector for a girl. Despairing of winning her, the driver enlists in the army, the girl realises it's he she loves and the loser loyally races across the city by trolley-bus to reunite them at Termini station before he leaves for Africa. The critics didn't care for it but the film was a popular success.

The turning-point for Fellini was *Campo de' fiori/Field of Flowers*, released in 1943. Bonnard directed again, with a script by Bonnard, Fabrizi, Piero Tellini and, receiving his first screen credit, Fellini, billed, in line with *Cico e Pallina*, as 'Federico'. Set on the Rome square of the same name where Anna Magnani has a fruit stall, the film featured, as well as Fabrizi, Caterina Boratto playing a snobbish and elegant Roman woman and Peppino de Filippo as a barber.

Magnani, then thirty-five, made as dramatic an impact on Fellini as on most men. Beginning as a cabaret singer of bawdy street songs, she graduated to variety and theatre. Her director husband, Goffredo Alessandrini, whom she flagrantly cuckolded, put her into films in the mid-thirties, where her almost ugly but earthily sensual face won an awed following. Magnani never lost her brutal slum sense of humour. She'd shove a bunch of grapes into her pants and dance about, saying: 'Look, I've got one too.' Writer Suso Cecchi d'Amico said: 'She was a little crazy, but what tremendous charm.' Visconti, never quite totally gay, had a tormented affair with her. 'She was jealous of everything she felt excluded from, of every intimacy she couldn't penetrate,' he said. But, besotted still, Visconti would ring her at night and ask her to masturbate while he listened.

Fellini's script work made him new and influential friends, some of them under contract to Il Duce's film-struck son Vittorio, who not only published the country's leading movie magazine, *Cinema*, but produced and directed films through his company Alleanza Cinematografica Italiana. Late in 1942, Fellini worked on and off for ACI. It might have been the launching of his career as a director had he not been preoccupied with surviving in wartime Rome and, more important, staying out of the front line.

8   'Sit down and tremble!'

'If we had even been able to get hold of those [American] cigarettes before the war, everyone would have understood we could never have won'
Fellini to Giovanni Grazzini, 1983

In mid-1942, as part of *Dear Bianchina*, Fellini had written a piece in the form of a letter from Bianchina to Federico at the front, complaining about shortages and the nightly blackout. The Ministry of Popular Culture banned it. Vito de Bellis headed off formal censure, but Fellini embroidered the incident, claiming he was directed to present himself at the Ministry. A sign at the foot of the stairs directed 'Mount Two Steps at a Time', the idea being to establish an air of urgency. As a sarcastic gesture, Fellini says he took them four steps at a time (hard to visualise). The bureaucrat who'd summoned him slated the defeatism of his piece and, as he dismissed him, asked: 'What is your military status?'

This question at least rings true, since evading the draft was the preoccupation of every young Italian male. Initially exempted as a university student, Fellini had enjoyed rolling three-monthly deferments while he worked at *Marc'Aurelio*, journalism being a reserved occupation. When he left, a friendly doctor certified he suffered from Basedow's Disease, the irregular heartbeat and fainting spells of which had made him medically unfit.

Fellini's health has always been a shadowy area and it's possible he was genuinely 4F, at least under the rules of 1941. Alberto Sordi, one year older, recalled that, on his own conscription, 'I was sent to the garrison band of the 81st Infantry to play the cymbals, and went on acting . . . But Federico was rejected, thanks to his big head and thin legs.'

In 1942, with the war going badly in north Africa and Allied invasion of the mainland imminent, Italy accelerated the draft and

Fellini faced a real risk of conscription. At first he prolonged his medical deferment. 'I succeeded by bribing doctors and simulating mysterious illnesses. I spent three days in a sanatorium wearing undershorts and with a towel wrapped around my head like a maharajah.' The reasons for this aren't clear, nor is whether 'sanatorium' in this sense means a specialised clinic or, as Francesco Tornabene translates it, 'insane asylum'.

He was sent to a military hospital for a second examination. In Hollis Alpert's version, 'each time, in the past, friends on the staff had helped him, but this time he saw only one familiar face, and he was given a shrug of resignation. The reason became clear when Fellini saw that German officers were observing the examination procedures.' A German doctor declared him fit (in some versions without even examining him) and gave him three documents: a clean bill of health, his induction notice and orders to join a regiment training in Puglia for posting to Greece. Fellini amplified this part of the story to Giovanni Grazzini. 'A German doctor with drunkard's eyes gave me a packet of frightening papers and told me I had to rejoin my regiment in Greece *unmittelbar unverzüglich* (I understood that meant I had to hurry).' In the most dramatic version of what followed, Fellini stormed on to the street and, watched by a surprised sentry, ripped up the papers. Friends then raced him to Bologna (or perhaps Forli) for a new and hopefully more sympathetic examination.

Fellini says he arrived at the hospital an hour early and spent the time running up and down the stairs to boost his pulse. He was just about to be examined when 'all hell broke loose. The Americans were bombing Bologna. Even the hospital I was in was hit, and there I was, all covered with plaster dust, running like a horse, minus one shoe, along hallways filled with people who were screaming, crying, falling to their knees while ambulance sirens howled and the earth shuddered and shook. From that day on I never heard any more about my military dossier.'

An even more catastrophic incident followed when Fellini, if one can believe some accounts, went to north Africa to work on an adventure film called *Gli ultimi Tuareg/The Last Tuaregs*. He has never denied this trip but is reticent about details. The little evidence that he was in Tripolitania in the autumn of 1942 comes from the actor Guido Celano, part of a cast that included Osvaldo Valenti and Luisa Ferida. Friends at ACI, hoping to put him beyond reach of the draft, are said to have sent Fellini to Tripoli to 'help out' on the film, which he'd partly scripted. In Celano's version, Fellini had been there only a few days when director Gino Talamo had a car accident. Ferida promptly announced she was pregnant, Valenti sought consolation in cocaine and, with the production in ruins, Fellini was pressed into taking over. Celano says Fellini directed a few scenes, which would have been the first of his career, but when the British broke through at El Alamein on 23 October it seemed prudent to flee. The last plane out of Tripoli had only twenty-six seats and, rather than bump more deserving cases, Fellini and two other crew members took a German transport flight, reaching Sicily after a wave-height race with Spitfires. From there, he made it back to Rome by train, car and on foot, sheltering periodically from air raids.

There's some circumstantial evidence to support this story. *Gli ultimi Tuareg*, also called *The Adventure of Captain Bottego* and *Cavalieri del deserto/Horsemen of the Desert*, did exist, though it was never finished. Roberto Rossellini, a wealthy young screenwriter friend of Vittorio Mussolini with ambitions to direct but a more pressing desire to sleep with stars, had been due to make it but preferred to stay in Rome. No script survives, but Fellini could have worked on it.

Newspapers reported the film's crew returning from Tripoli in November and *Marc'Aurelio* published a description of Fellini's ordeal on 14 November 1942, as *The First Flight*. However, since Tripoli wasn't evacuated until 23 January there can't have been a Last Plane Out in October. The tale of a journey across war-torn Italy also rings false, but more unlikely things would happen to Fellini in his career and one can't discount the story entirely. Tullio Kezich is inclined to believe he did pass through Sicily in 1942, since specific Sicilian locations turn up in *In nome delle legge/In the Name of the Law*, a script Fellini co-wrote for Pietro Germi in 1949. As six writers share the credit, however, the evidence is flimsy.

Fellini worked on two more films while the Italian film industry survived. On *L'ultima carrozzella/The Last Carriage* he got sole screen credit with Fabrizi, and on *Quarta pagina/The Quarter Page*, an omnibus of seven episodes by seven directors, he shared credit with ten others. He also worked on the 1944 *Apparition* for French director Jean de Limur, though credit goes to Piero Tellini, Lucio de Caro and producer Giuseppe Amato. By late 1943, however, Fellini was less concerned with his career. He'd decided to get married.

Like most radio plays, *Cico e Pallina* was cast with actors chosen more for cheapness than talent. One of them was Giulia Masina, a tiny girl a year younger than Fellini from near Bologna who was studying acting at the University of Rome and playing in the University Theatre

Group. By comparison with Fellini's louche crowd, Giulia's friends were highly reputable. Some found important places in the post-war scene, directors Turi Vasile and Gine Cervi as producers, Enrico Fulchignoni as head of Unesco's cultural arm.

Giulietta won some attention and began to get offers of work, including *Cico e Pallina*, which she says she took to correct her 'Nordic' pronunciation. Even the Fellinis themselves don't agree on how they met. In one version, Fellini saw Giulietta's picture in the magazine *Radiocorriere* and asked her to lunch. In another, he rang her up, not knowing what she looked like, and told her: 'My name is Fellini and I am fed up with life, but before I die I would like to see what my heroine looks like.'

A third story, more prosaic, has him calling to tell her that *Cico e Pallina* might be filmed, and asking for photographs. If only because it enshrines the oldest come-on in show business, this seems the most probable. It is, anyway, the one Masina prefers today. 'I'd sent him the photos and he asked to meet me. I saw coming towards me a thin boy, so thin, with a black hat and trousers that were too short. He'd invited me to a luxurious restaurant and I thought: "He won't be able to pay!" So I just had some minestrone. But he ordered ham, then ravioli, some roast meat, cakes – and at the end he took out a roll of money.' Giulietta concludes this story: 'Eight months later we were married,' which would place the meeting in February 1943.

In was an unpropitious time to marry. On 10 July 1943, the Allies landed in Sicily and began a steady advance up the Italian peninsula. At the same time the US Air Force, flying from north Africa, began bombing Italian cities. On 19 July, Rome's San Lorenzo district was battered. A hundred and sixty-six people died and historic buildings like the basilica of San Lorenzo Fuori le Mura were badly damaged. For the first time the reality of war was brought home to the Italian people and there was agitation to get rid of Mussolini. On 23 July he was legally deposed by the king and placed in custody. Control passed to Marshal Pietro Badoglio on 13 August. The reaction in Rome was delight. People danced in the streets. Fascist emblems and images of Mussolini were torn down and destroyed. It was assumed the war was over.

The Germans fumed, but Badoglio reassured them that, though Il Duce was gone, the Axis remained firm. Privately, however, he was suing for peace, and on 3 September, in a tent near Syracuse, Italy surrendered, almost at the same moment as Badoglio was swearing to the German ambassador in Rome that it would fight 'to the end'. Field Marshal Kesselring, German military commander in Rome, ordered

troops stationed around the city to seize it, Badoglio's government fled
and Mussolini, rescued from his mountaintop detention in a daring
airborne raid, was installed at the head of a puppet government in
Salo, in the north. Rome was declared an 'open city', but actually it
was under German martial law. A curfew was imposed and any Italian
of military age seen in public risked imprisonment. In addition to
specific arrests, the police closed off whole streets at random, rounded
up the men and sent them to forced labour.

With no medical deferment, Fellini became just another draft-
dodger. By mid-1943 Rome was full of them. Of its 1.5 million people,
200,000 were estimated to be in hiding, many in churches, convents
and monasteries. Plenty of priests supported Fascism, as Fellini had
seen in Rimini, but many others, especially those with Communist
sympathies, sheltered deserters and worked for the underground. On 4
April 1944, Father Giuseppe Morosini would be shot for such activities
by the Germans.

Fellini moved into his aunt's apartment. An alcove provided a tiny
hide-out if the Germans should come, but he refused to be a hermit. He
applied for membership of the Italian Society of Authors and Publishers, enclosing a letter from the Certa Company attesting that he'd
written the radio plays *Gossip*, *The First Job*, *Waiting Room*, *A
Mountain Lodge*, *Escapes*, *Centennials* and *The New House* – mostly
episodes of *Cico e Pallina*. He was officially registered as an author the
following February.

On 6 June Geleng got married. Fellini was there with Giulietta,
whom he introduced as his fiancée. He also drew the comic invitation
cards. Riccardo sang 'Ave Maria', as he would do at Fausto's wedding
in *I vitelloni*. Fellini, however, confided his depression to the groom.
'Rinaldo, it's the end of everything.'

The literal end almost came for Fellini on 29 October, when he was
arrested while walking across piazza di Spagna. Too late, he noticed
the sympathetic looks of passers-by too cautious to warn him the
Fascist Brigata Nera had closed off the square and were checking
papers. Fellini was loaded into a truck with other unfortunates. On via
del Babuino, which runs out of piazza di Spagna, he saw a German
officer on a corner. Jumping out of the truck he ran to him, calling:
'Fritz! Fritz!' and hugged him. Apparently fooled by this stratagem,
the Fascists drove on and Fellini bolted past the astonished Nazi and
into via Margutta, where he hid in a pharmacy. Years later, he moved
into an apartment on the street that had brought him luck. In 1993, he
still lived there.

If Fellini's memory of the date of his arrest is accurate, he married Giulietta the following day, on Saturday 30 October, in her aunt's apartment at via Lutezia 11. A priest who lived on the same floor had permission to say mass there and performed the service. Isolated in the north, neither set of parents knew of the wedding. The handful of guests included Geleng, his new wife, and the actor Vittorio Caprioli. The comic cards, again drawn by Fellini, included one with cartoons of a baby being thrown down from a cloud, indicating that the Fellinis planned a child.

After the wedding, Fellini and Giulietta went to the theatre where Sordi was playing. 'When I saw them come in,' Sordi says, 'I stopped the orchestra, had the lights turned on and said to the audience: "My best friend got married today. I couldn't go to the wedding and I couldn't buy him a nice gift because I don't have a penny. But I know what he wants from life . . . and the finest gift I can give him is to ask this audience to applaud him, with the hope it's the first applause in a long career." The spectators accepted my invitation and applauded him warmly.' It was a generous gesture, though perhaps not one that Fellini, as a fugitive, whole-heartedly welcomed.

This was the last bright spot in Fellini's life for some time. Shortly after their marriage Giulietta became pregnant, but lost the baby when she fell downstairs. She conceived again, and a son, Federico, was born in March 1945. He lived only two weeks, dying on 1 April. Giulietta suffered badly from a puerperal infection after the birth and the Fellinis would have no more children.

On 1 November American bombers began raids on northern Italy, softening up the area for a possible landing. Between November 1943 and September 1944 Rimini was bombed and shelled 396 times; 607 people were killed and the survivors, including Urbano, Ida and Maddalena Fellini, driven to become refugees in San Marino. 'Rimini in the summer of 1944 was a dead city,' wrote one historian.

The Italians had launched armed resistance to the Germans under a Committee of National Liberation made up of most non-Fascist parties, including the Communists. All over the country, dissidents and fugitives, armed and sometimes led by Allied agents, harried the occupiers. More people were killed in the resistance than in the Allied Fifth Army during its Italian campaign. At least three died in Rimini's piazza Giulio Cesare, hanged by the Germans. The Riminese changed the name to piazza del Tre Martiri – the Square of the Three Martyrs.

Conditions in Rome became more desperate as refugees swelled the population to 2.5 million. The USAF continued to bomb the city, levelling historic buildings and killing civilians as often as it damaged military targets. Among the innocent sites devastated was Cinecittà. On 22 January 1944 the Allies tried to bypass the German lines by landing south of Rome, at Anzio. They established a beach-head but the Germans prevented them from breaking out. In Rome, arrests, deportations, tortures and executions were stepped up. In March 1944 Teresa Gullace, a mother of five, ran after the German truck taking her husband away to forced labour and was machine-gunned.

Interrogation centres on via Tasso and in the Pensione Jaccarino in via Romagna operated non-stop under the head of the Gestapo, Colonel Kappler. His interrogator, an Italian officer of German descent, Pietro Koch, was a cocaine addict who tortured prisoners with the help of his two Italian mistresses. Koch lived in luxury at Pensione Jaccarino, surrounded by a garden, the carpeted, softly lit bedrooms isolated from the blood-splattered corridors and cells of a cubic metre in which prisoners squatted for days. Among those imprisoned and beaten there was Visconti. Now known as the 'Red Count', he'd thrown in with the Communists, helping stranded pilots and escaped prisoners of war, and was held for twelve days in April 1944 after having hidden with Magnani.

By May the Allies had slogged to within shooting distance of Rome. From Salo, Mussolini demanded the capital be defended to the death, street by street, but by now the Romans were exhausted. On 2 June the Pope proclaimed: 'Whoever raises a hand against Rome will be guilty of matricide to the whole civilised world and in the eternal judgement of God.' The same day Kesselring, after a night at the opera listening to Beniamino Gigli in Verdi's *Un ballo in maschera*, ordered Rome's evacuation. As staff cars outside the Excelsior and the Grand were loaded with officers' luggage and loot, the infantry started its long march back to Germany. By 5 June the Allies were in Rome.

It wasn't a civilised occupation. General Mark Clark's men took over more as medieval conquerors. Prostitution and the black economy were reorganised with American efficiency, the randy, drunken GIs providing a huge market for women and booze.

With radio, film and magazines dead, Fellini returned to caricaturing. A rich young man named Forges Davanzati opened the Funny Face Shop in via Santa Maria delle Fratte, where for $3 (usually rounded up to $5) Fellini and some other artists added cartoon portraits of GIs to standard scenes drawn up beforehand. A fishing soldier hooking a mermaid was a particular favourite. A shrewd merchandiser, Fellini took a leaf from the tattooist's book and appealed to the bravado of his customers. On the wall behind the artists was painted, in English: 'Look Out! The Most Ferocious and Amusing Caricaturists are Eyeing You. Sit Down and Tremble!'

As trade increased they installed painted backdrops of Rome against which the soldiers could be photographed, and a machine that produced small wax records. Pretty girls made sure that the soldiers spent to the maximum. As tips, the servicemen often left cans of beef, beer or especially cigarettes, the packaging of which mesmerised Fellini. 'In Italy, everything looked boring. A pack of cigarettes looked plain and grey and smelled terrible. Whenever we saw a pack of American cigarettes it had an attractive wrapper, full of colour, and it smelled good. If we had even been able to get hold of those cigarettes before the war, everyone would have understood we could never have won.'

With the first shop flourishing, others were opened on via della Vite, via Tomacelli, piazza San Silvestro, piazza Barberini and via Nazionale. Fellini says he has never in his life earned so much money in such a short time. Each was like 'a kind of casino. It had an atmosphere not unlike western movies, something halfway between an American saloon and a waiting room.' Brawls broke out often and the MPs, who had their headquarters opposite the via Nazionale shop, were frequent visitors.

Fellini was steeling himself for a brawl one day, having just used an unflattering yellow to draw a soldier with a sallow, Oriental complexion, when he looked up to see a man beckoning him through the window. It was Roberto Rossellini, the friend of Vittorio Mussolini who had decided not to direct *Gli ultimi Tuareg*. 'Extremely pale, with a pointed chin and soft floppy hat, he was easy, quiet, cool and pensive,' recalled Fellini. 'Maybe he was thinking it might be better for him to become my partner in the shop rather than stick to the proposal that had brought him to me: to invite me to write a scenario with Sergio Amidei – a tragi-comedy on the life of Don Morosini, the embryo of *Roma città aperta*.'

9　　Open City

'In those days we were excited by a flag flapping in the wind, by a cannon squarely hitting its target'
Luchino Visconti on *Roma città aperta*

By the time Fellini met Roberto Rossellini, the charismatic Roman was approaching forty and had already outgrown two or three personalities. His background was everything Fellini's was not. He'd been born rich. His father, a building contractor and property developer, dreamed of being a writer, and Sunday afternoon salons at the Rossellini home drew the intellectual élite of Rome between the wars.

Since their father had built Rome's biggest cinemas, the Corso and the Barberini, Roberto and his younger brother Renzo had automatic free admission, which they genially abused, turning up with thirty companions. By the mid-thirties Roberto was in the movies, laying sound effects and just as vigorously laying Assia Noris. His fascination with film survived that liaison, though with Rossellini film and sex would always be close.

Though Rossellini directed for Vittorio Mussolini he no more believed in Fascism than in the Communism and Catholicism he embraced later. He'd exploited it to build a career. He just as skilfully extricated himself as the war ended. By 1944, politically born again courtesy of Cesare Zavattini, the ideologue of film naturalism, he was a 'Neorealist,' committed to a vernacular cinema dealing with the living world.

Zavattini, with his imperious profile, the long nose seemingly ruled with the same straight edge as his impressively high forehead, was a forceful proselytiser, but drunk on generalities. 'The cinema should never turn back,' he proclaimed. 'It should accept, unconditionally, what is contemporary. Today, today, today. It must tell reality as if it were a story; there must be no gap between life and what is on the screen.' In his via Merici apartment that Visconti called an Aladdin's cave of ideas were hatched the plots of De Sica's *Sciuscia/Shoeshine* and *Ladri di biciclette/Bicycle Thieves* and Visconti's *Bellissima*.

Rossellini believed some of what Zavattini said but he was more interested in simply making movies. With few lights, no studios and almost no film stock, films were perforce shot in natural light on real locations. In the Italy of 1945 one had to be a Neorealist in order to work.

What he wanted to discuss with Fellini was *Storie di ieri/Stories of Yesterday*, a script about Giuseppe Morosini, the priest executed by the Germans, which Communist writer Sergio Amidei had written with contributions from Rossellini and others. A Countess Politi, who scorned cinema but liked Rossellini, had put up seed money for the film. Women were both the secret of his success and his downfall. Fellini, who was frankly jealous of Rossellini's love affairs, could still sneer fifty years later that the director rushed through a scene in *Paisà* shot on the Po marshes because he 'absolutely had to get back to Rome for who-knows-which of his preoccupations – perhaps a certificate of deposit had matured or he had an appointment with some old maid'.

Rossellini was the first man with whom Fellini fell in love. The relationship wasn't physical but the attachment was none the less passionate. Giulietta looked on helplessly as Rossellini's charm and glamour swept the naïve Federico into his circle. 'Rossellini was the father he never had,' says one friend of the time, but the relationship was deeper than that – so deep that Fellini replicated it again and again in his own life, long after Rossellini had left it.

Rossellini explained that the characters of the Morosini film would be Manfredi, a Communist organiser for Badoglio's banned Committee of National Liberation, Francesco, an underground printer, his pregnant fiancée Pina, her twelve-year-old son Marcello, member of a sabotage gang, and Don Pietro, who hides deserters and carries messages for the Resistance. Ranged against them are Bergmann, homosexual head of the SS in Rome, his lesbian helper Ingrid, and Manfredi's corrupt lover Marina, a showgirl seduced by Ingrid with cocaine. On the day before his wedding, the Germans arrest Francesco and, when Pina runs after the truck, shoot her. Manfredi and Don Pietro are caught, and Manfredi tortured to death while Don Pietro looks on. Neither talks, and the next morning a firing squad executes the priest, watched by Marcello's gang, which disperses to do more damage.

Fellini was flattered to be approached but disappointed when Rossellini turned out to have other motives. Could he use his friendship to persuade Aldo Fabrizi to play Don Pietro? Fellini asked the actor, who, though he'd actually witnessed the killing of Teresa Gullace, wasn't enthusiastic. 'What do I care about Don Morosini?' he said. The money was derisory too, and he demanded a million lire (which Rossellini would sell some of his family's antique furniture to raise). In fact Fabrizi was frightened, in part about playing drama after years of comedy, but mostly about the possible repercussions. 'What if the Germans come back?' he asked Fellini nervously.

For Pina, Amidei favoured Anna Magnani, but the producers preferred Clara Calamai, from *Ossessione/Obsession*. She refused because there was no script. By the time they had one she was working on another film, so Magnani got the role that made her a star. The remaining performers were also imposed to some extent by Amidei. Maria Michi (Marina) was his mistress, Harry Feist, a dancer friend, played Bergmann, and the saintly Manfredi, played by Marcello Pagliero, was written to promote his politics. Not that nepotism was confined to Amidei. Rossellini and Magnani began an affair during the film that was to continue until he met Ingrid Bergman.

Fabrizi brought Fellini with him on to the film. On 21 October 1944 Fellini signed a contract to collaborate on the screenplay for 25,000 lire. They wrote it 'in one week, working at my house, in the kitchen because there wasn't any heat, [but] frankly, without much conviction.' His sourness sprang from his minor role, which was to write gags for Fabrizi, though Rossellini also credited him as assistant director, with Amidei.

Shooting began on 19 January 1945, after Rossellini found a backer in a black-market fabric dealer named Venturini. Sympathisers in the US Signal Corps gave Rossellini 35mm raw stock. He bought more from street photographers, twenty or thirty metres at a time. The Germans had doled it out on the understanding that they saw the pictures. As Bergmann explains in the film, street photographs allow him to stroll around Rome without leaving his office.

Fellini's mark on *Roma città aperta/Rome, Open City* isn't large. One sees it best in the sequence where Morosini, waiting in a statuary shop above the secret printery, notices that a statue of St Rocco seems to be staring at a coy nude. He turns the nude away, realises that the saint is now contemplating her backside and turns *him* away. The gag betrays the fascination with the female buttocks that was to become a feature of Fellini's work. He also wrote the scene where the priest, on the pretext that a paralysed old man demands his attention, bluffs his way into a building being searched by the SS. The one invalid he finds is anything but co-operative when Morosini tries to hide a bomb and machine-gun under his bed, but by the time the Nazis arrive he's satisfyingly comatose. After they've gone, Fabrizi contemplates ruefully the frying-pan with which he's beaned him.

Since there was no footage for a work print, Rossellini never saw rushes, so shots were seldom redone, adding to the film's immediacy. With no recording equipment, sound and dialogue were dubbed later, along with a portentous music score by Renzo. For interiors he used the cellars of the Braschi and Tittoni palaces, but Don Pietro's sacristy and Bergmann's headquarters had to be built in a basement under numbers 7/8 via degli Avignonesi. This was among the biggest expenses of the film, though one that was to pay off unexpectedly.

Rossellini showed a rough cut to Zavattini, Visconti and others, who were admiring. But its first public screening on 24 September 1945 in a festival at the Teatro Quirino in Rome flopped. A number of films not seen in Italy had been imported. Unfortunately for Rossellini they were all masterpieces: Eisenstein's *Ivan the Terrible*, Carné's *Les Enfants du paradis*, Olivier's *Henry V*. By comparison *Roma città aperta* looked crude and naive, and the critics dismissed it. For years Renzo carried the more scornful reviews in his wallet.

Distributors Artistes Associés, who had signed a contract for 4 million lire for the film, refused to accept the deal. But Ubaldo Areta, the cameraman, arranged a screening for Mosco, head of the distributors Minerva Film, who offered 13 million for the Italian rights. 'Venturini couldn't believe his eyes,' says Amidei. On release, *Roma città aperta* immediately attracted the following that was to make it an international hit. Minerva Film cleared a huge profit, as did its American distributors. According to Amidei, Venturini, the major backer, was found dead on a camp bed in an empty apartment twenty years later. 'The tax people could never bring themselves to believe he'd sold the film for only 13 million.'

The American sale resulted from a chance meeting between Rossellini and US sergeant Rodney E. Geiger during the shooting. According to legend, Geiger, drunk, had just emerged from Tina Trabucchi's famous brothel at via degli Avignonesi 36 when he tripped over Rossellini's cables and followed them into the basement. Claiming he was a producer (only an advertising copywriter, insists Fellini), Geiger stopped to watch. Later Rossellini sold him the American rights for $20,000.

Geiger denies he was drunk or had just left the whorehouse but there's no doubt he bought the film, carrying a print back to America in his kit bag. He sold it to independent New York distributors Arthur Mayer and Joseph Burstyn, who opened it at New York's World Cinema, just off Broadway, in February 1946 as *Open City*. The lurid advertising ('Sexier Than Hollywood Ever Dared to Be') suited the theatre which, three decades later, would house the first run of *Deep Throat*. After a slow start James Agee praised it in the *Nation* and other critics followed suit. When Amidei and Fellini were nominated for an Academy Award for best screenplay, the film's success was assured.

Within the year, Geiger formed Foreign Film Productions and sailed for Europe with, he promised Rossellini, an all-star cast, ready to produce his next film. The reality, as Rossellini and Fellini discovered when they met him off the boat in Naples, was some seed money, lots of film stock and five unrecognisable Americans with, at best, minor movie careers behind them. Control of the film soon passed to Mario Conti, who raised most of the money.

This time, Rossellini made the episodic story he'd visualised at the time of *Roma città aperta*. *Paisà*, a corruption of *paesano* – neighbour or countryman – that Americans shortened into a greeting, has no continuing characters, though its six episodes all relate to problems of communication between Italians and the invading Americans.

The action moves north with the Allied advance. A peasant girl in Sicily, a street kid in Naples, a whore in Rome, the people of Florence, monks in an Apennine monastery and the partisans of the Po marshes all encounter the advancing Americans and are influenced for good or, mostly, for ill.

Paisà's script was written by Amidei, Fellini and Rossellini, from stories by all of them, plus Marcello Pagliero, American novelist Alfred Hayes, and, uncredited, Klaus Mann, son of novelist Thomas Mann, and Vasco Pratolini. Fellini helped fit them into a structure, wrote dialogue and, more important, genuinely acted as assistant director, for which he receives a separate credit, with Massimo Mida. He made his official directing début with a scene in the Florence sequence (mostly filmed in Rome, near his apartment). It simply showed a water container being hauled across a street under sniper fire. Otello Martelli proposed to shoot it from rooftop height, but Fellini argued for a low angle, suggesting that they might even dig a hole for the camera to impose a human perspective. They compromised by shooting from eye level but across the road.

Fellini also scripted the monastery episode. Mann had written about an American padré who, having killed two Germans at Anzio, deserts and hides out with the monks, from whom he gets the courage to return to the front, but Fellini suggested a different plot in which three American chaplains visiting a monastery scandalise their pious but simple hosts by revealing that only one is Catholic, the others being Protestant and Jewish. They politely chide the Catholic for having failed to convert his friends and, though they've starved through the war and the Americans have provided a sumptuous meal, elect to fast that night, hoping the pagans will be converted. Puzzlingly, the American priest announces that he's been given a lesson in 'humility, simplicity and pure faith' – when, if anything, the act seems emblematic of arrogance and bigotry. Fellini obviously liked the story, derived distantly from Boccaccio, but was unequal to providing the sting in the tail it demanded. As a result the episode falls flat. Despite this, Fellini and the other writers shared another Oscar nomination.

Until *Paisà* Fellini had always thought of himself solely as a writer but working with Rossellini changed all that. Part of it was the exhilaration of film-making itself, with Rossellini bawling at his recalcitrant amateur actors through his megaphone while war-surplus US Army trucks rumbled down the narrow streets and locals hung out the windows, screeching obscenities. Fellini recalls walking into a tiny editing room and seeing his friend hunched over the Moviola, 'pale, tearing his hair, staring at the first cut on the tiny screen. The images were shadowy; I could hear only the bobbin turning. But I was transfixed.' Long after Rossellini left Fellini's life, the love of cinema would survive, as it survived and transcended all his relationships.

Throughout the Rossellini years, Giulietta remained a dutiful if largely uncomprehending bystander. She and Federico still lived in her aunt's apartment where they'd been married. When the group went to Florence on location, she trailed along, cooking meals, then sitting in the kitchen or going to bed while the men noisily kicked ideas around through the night. Italian wives were expected to know their place, and while Giulietta did what was expected of her, the distance established between her and Fellini in these days would never be closed. In moments of stress he would cling to Giulietta, but as soon as the ties of marriage started to bite, Fellini retreated, as Urbano had done, into the comfort and warmth of male society. *Cico e Pallina*, with its implicit fears of entrapment, had become a self-fulfilling prophecy.

10 'A cigarette for Saint Joseph!': *Amore*

'I go to church only when I have to shoot a scene in church, or for an aesthetic or nostalgic reason. For faith, you can go to a woman. Maybe that is *more* religious'
Fellini in 1965

With the Americans going home, the Funny Face shops no longer did goldrush business. With time on their hands, the cartoonists played at catching flies and staining them with aniline dye. Fellini slipped back into the limbo from which Rossellini had rescued him, writing for the few magazines then struggling into print. Michelangelo Antonioni was on the staff of *Bis*, a film weekly to which Fellini contributed. Himself subdued by nature, Antonioni was put off by Fellini's even greater reserve. The ebullience of the *Marc'Aurelio* days had disappeared. Fellini seemed disoriented. And when he came in to deliver copy, Giulietta always accompanied him. They made Antonioni uncomfortable, a feeling Fellini reciprocated. The men were never friends.

Marriage, the death of his child, the collapse of the war and the strains of his relationship with Rossellini had combined to depress Fellini. He was also trying to make the difficult transition from gagman to scenarist, but it wasn't going well. Liliana Betti believes Fellini's greatest ambition was to be a writer, but that he realised in 1946/7 he would never have the vision and, more important, the concentration to become one. In the eighties he would begin to claim he could improvise a film as he went along, without a script, but it was an empty conceit. He would always rely on writers to put his dreams on to film, and resent them to exactly the extent he needed them.

In 1946, Aldo Fabrizi offered him a job helping to adapt *Il delitto di Giovanni Episcopo/The Crime of Giovanni Episcopo*, d'Annunzio's novel of a mild-mannered man who kills his wife's lover. He shared credit with Fabrizi, Suso Cecchi d'Amico, Piero Tellini and the director, Alberto Lattuada. He was also able to scrounge a small role for the struggling Alberto Sordi, the first time they worked together.

Meanwhile he'd met a puckish, alert, wry playwright named Tullio Pinelli. Twelve years older, considerably more mature and far better educated, Pinelli had worked exclusively since 1942 for Lux Film, one of Italy's most successful studios. Lux offered Fellini a job, and the two writers met finally at a news-stand outside the Lux offices on via Po. Pausing to read the open page of a magazine at a news-stand, Pinelli became aware of someone taller reading over his shoulder. 'I'm Fellini,' Federico said, 'and you're Pinelli.'

'From the moment we met,' Pinelli says, 'I regarded Fellini as a genius.· Even though he was only twenty-six, already, in whatever gathering he was part of, he would become the centre of attention. He has always had this ability to capture people. He had charm and a charismatic quality that made one feel somehow that he was import-ant. That impressed me very much because, you see, I am exactly the opposite.'

Pinelli's memories are characteristically generous. True, Fellini's personality had lost none of its adolescent magnetism. He was still the tall charmer with fire in his eyes who'd led the Miramare beach gangs. But he remained naïve and socially inept, with an inferiority complex about his provincial roots and lack of schooling that he would never quite lose. The polarisation that would divide colleagues and indeed the country into pro- and anti-Fellini was already evident. Gianfranco Corsini, a Communist partisan who advised on the Florence sequence of *Roma città aperta* and became influential in peace-time Italy, spotted Fellini's anti-intellectual bias and dismissed him as having 'no culture to speak of, and very little education'. He wasn't the only one.

Fellini and Pinelli began developing screenplay ideas. Collaboration was standard in European and especially Italian screenwriting, where the money was so poor that even the best writers worked on a score of scripts a year, usually with half a dozen others. Fellini doesn't rate his work highly. 'I had it very easy as a scriptwriter,' he says. 'I wasn't responsible for anything because everything I wrote was reworked several times by others. When there was a good passage in a film you could always say it was yours.'

They began with a Fellini dream about a man who discovers he can fly, but it was too much like de Sica's *Miracolo a Milano/Miracle in Milan* so they abandoned it. Pinelli brought Fellini on to a script from a Lattuada story called *Il bandito/The Bandit*, but their first joint sale was *Il passatore/A Bullet for Stefano*. The film that established them was *Senza pietà/Without Pity*, again for Lattuada, a crime story set in the black market around Tombolo, near Livorno. Black American actor John Kitzmiller played a GI deserter trying to escape the effeminate local crime lord. Fellini made some important connections on *Senza pietà*. Its production manager was Clemente Fracassi, who, after a brief directing career, became his production associate. Nino Rota, who would write the scores for all his films until *Prova d'orchestra/Orchestral Rehearsal*, composed the music, with a moving use of the spiritual 'Heav'n, Heav'n' as the lovers die together. Giulietta played, not for the last time, a prostitute, winning a Nastro d'Argento, Italian cinema's highest award.

Fellini and Pinelli joined six other writers on another Lattuada film, *Il mulino del Po/The Mill on the Po*, and went on to collaborate on a succession of increasingly prestigious projects: Germi's *In nome delle legge*, where a young policeman moves in on a Sicilian village and cleans out the new 'punk' Mafiosi with implicit help from the older 'Honoured Society'; *Il cammino della speranza/The Road of Hope*, about Sicilian sulphur miners migrating to France; *Il brigante di Tacca del Lupo/The bandit of Tacca del Lupo*, a melodrama about Garibaldi's troops fighting to depose the King of Naples.

They also outlined two projects never filmed. *Il diavolo in convento/The Devil in the Monastery* and *Paese felice/Happy Country* are both satires reflecting the new Italy, greedy and acquisitive, emerging under the Marshall Plan. In the first, a monk tries to block his monastery's conversion into a hotel in the face of resistance not only from the Church but also from the townspeople, who see themselves getting rich.

The idea for *Paese felice*, written with an eye to Hollywood, came from Luigi Barzini, the journalist who anatomised his countrymen in *The Italians*. An oil man sent to drill in Tuscany ends up besotted with Italy and its people. Mario Camerini would have directed, with finance from David Selznick and Cary Grant in the lead. Selznick flirted with Italy in the fifties, investing in de Sica's *Stazione Termini/Indiscretion of an American Wife* and a version of *A Farewell to Arms*, but always disastrously. He showed no interest in *Paese felice*; perhaps just as well for Fellini and Pinelli.

Another crucial catalyst entered Fellini's life when he met *Il bandito*'s producer, Dino de Laurentiis. The 1.62 metre Neapolitan barely came up to Fellini's chest but his effect on his life would be as far-ranging as his impact on European cinema, and just as turbulent. Fast-talking, cunning, confident, he'd graduated from the Centro Sperimentale at sixteen and by twenty had produced his first film. His Turin production company, Realcine, collapsed during the war, but Dino sprang back as an independent, working through Lux before going into partnership with another Lux producer, Carlo Ponti. In the next fifty years he helped finance more than 500 films. He built half a dozen empires and lost them, usually in catastrophe. The last, De Laurentiis Entertainment Group, collapsed in 1988 with debts of $200 million.

The Fellini–Pinelli team, joined later by Ennio Flaiano, the irascible, politically aware journalist from *Marc'Aurelio*, survived intact until 1965. Its durability was seen by many as proof of the loyalty Fellini inspired. The reality was very different, a shifting battleground of mutual respect, bullying, ambition, hero-worship, emotional blackmail and even love, in which Pinelli, courteous, reserved and diplomatic, held the balance between the mercurial Fellini and a no-less-volatile Flaiano. Pinelli called Flaiano 'The Demolisher'. Every time he and Fellini came up with a particularly sentimental or funny idea, it was Flaiano's role and pleasure to smash it flat. On occasion, Pinelli would point out that Flaiano's line would lead to an entirely different film. In the early films this persuaded Flaiano to change his approach, but by *Otto e mezzo* that amiability would wear thin and on *Giulietta degli spiriti* there would be an explosive parting.

On some of the films he wrote between 1948 and 1950, Fellini flirted with directing. *Persiane chiuse/Closed Shutters*, produced by Luigi Rovere for Lux, was supposed, he says, 'to have been directed by Gianni Puccini in Turin, but then he got cold feet and Rovere sent me up to encourage him. At the same time Luigi Comencini was being prepared to succeed him. I directed several short scenes but had never felt responsible, had always felt like a tourist. And after Comencini arrived I went my own way again.' The film was released under Comencini's name in 1951.

When Rossellini's professional relationship with Magnani became a full-blooded affair, it was his turn to endure her rages, her voracious sexuality, jealousy and ambition. Searching for a vehicle to convey these qualities he hit on Jean Cocteau's *La Voix humaine/The Human Voice*, a monologue in which a woman prowls her bedroom, talking to her lover on the phone, cajoling, chiding and spurning him, only to end by begging him to return. It was an ideal showcase, capturing Magnani's undisciplined, obsessive nature. In Paris, in 1947, Rossellini shot a forty-minute version of the piece, with Magnani behaving much as in real life. He thought her performance extraordinary. 'She is a genius,' he told American journalist Quentin Reynolds, 'the greatest since Duse.' Cocteau, however, detested the film. Magnani, instead of elegant lingerie, wears a shapeless nightdress and a shawl. Her bed is unmade and the baroque room chaotic. She also insisted on including her dog. The squalor offended Cocteau. So did what he perceived as malice towards the character. 'In twenty-five takes, amounting to 1,200 metres of film,' he wrote, 'he has shot a cruel documentary on a woman's suffering . . . This documentary might be entitled "Woman devoured by a girl" or "The telephone as an instrument of torture".'

Rossellini planned another short film to bring *La Voix humaine* to feature length. With Magnani badgering him to complete it for Venice in September, he called on Pinelli, Fellini and Amidei to come up with a story. Fellini and Pinelli suggested one about a prostitute who's picked up by a celebrity and enjoys a night of luxury, but at the idea of playing a whore, and a low-rent one, Magnani exploded. As the deadline approached, Rossellini would appear in the office, glare at the writers and announce with heavy emphasis: 'I must begin shooting in five days.'

According to Fellini, the team gathered for a last-ditch conference at Amidei's house. Pinelli leafed through some Pirandello stories. Rossellini sat stonily, speaking only to reject one idea after another. Suddenly, Fellini volunteered an anecdote about a retarded peasant girl who mistakes a stranger for St Joseph, sleeps with him and bears a child she believes to be sacred. Rossellini lifted his head and Amidei and Pinelli stopped in their tracks. They quizzed him. Where had he read it? When? In a book? A magazine? Fellini, flustered, lied at first that he'd seen the tale in some French or Soviet magazine, then confessed it was his idea, based on a legend from Gambettola. A man named Gaetanaccio, who travelled the forests of Romagna gelding pigs, got a gypsy girl pregnant. When the child arrived, the others drove her away, claiming the baby was a child of Satan. Rossellini immediately rang Magnani and retailed the story, telling her it was Russian. She loved it.

It would have made sense to shoot the film, now called *Il miracolo/ The Miracle*, in Romagna, but Rossellini remembered that Maiori, the town clinging to the cliffs over the sea near Amalfi where he'd shot parts of *Paisà*, had a history of religious processions, so the team was whisked to Naples for pre-production, where Fellini found himself cast as the spurious St Joseph.

As with most events in Fellini's life, stories differ on how this happened. Rossellini explained simply: 'Why search for another actor? When Federico described his character, he *was* the character. Also, he adores acting.' Rossellini might also have been moved, say cynics, by the fact that Fellini was available and cheap. Fellini's version shows him as more Machiavellian. 'I was going to write the scenario for *Il miracolo*, but, at the same time, I was supposed to return to Rome to write another script. During this time Rossellini was looking for someone who could play the vagabond, but as he became afraid that I wouldn't finish "his" scenario, he proposed that I should play the role, on the condition that I start immediately.

'But Rossellini wanted the vagabond to be blond. He was determined that I should change the colour of my hair. In Naples, the hairdresser I went to had been tipped off by the camera operator, who'd told him: "I have a friend who's suddenly become a pederast. Don't be panicked if he comes in and asks you to blond his hair."

'I was received in a very amiable way, with everyone laughing. The hairdresser told me it was absolutely normal, that it happened every day! Then he made me appallingly blond. There was no question of me returning to Rome. Rossellini had won.'*

Set in the present, *Il miracolo* hinges on Ninna, a mentally subnormal peasant, played by Magnani at her most dishevelled. In return for minding the convent goats, she gets her meals and sleeps on a pile of rags in front of the church. A stranger meets her on the hillside. Though he never speaks, Magnani imagines he's St Joseph. He gives her wine and, when she passes out, presumably rapes her. Pregnant, she gets no help from the townspeople, least of all when she talks of a child conceived with St Joseph. The nuns can only worry whether she's confessed her 'sin', her fellow derelicts drive her away, and the townspeople mock her, which culminates in a 'holy' parade with her as the saint.

Ninna hides in the mountains, but stumbles back towards town when labour begins. One of her goats leads her to an empty church where she's able to have her baby without hindrance. In agony, she pulls on the bell ropes. 'The big bell now begins to sway,' wrote Fellini and Pinelli in their treatment, 'moved by an exultant and desperate force. It swings back and forth, again and again, and more violently, until a deep, sonorous solemn note falls upon the valley . . . And other notes of the bell follow the first . . . more and more urgent, joyous,

---

*Rossellini could have had less devious reasons for changing the hair colour. While the real Joseph was probably swarthy and dark, a peasant would visualise him in terms of images in the local church, where he appeared, like Christ and all the saints, as northern European. (Fellini also wore a plaster saint's goatee beard for the role.)

triumphant, announcing to the world that the child of the miracle, a new saviour, is born.'

Fellini may have adored acting, as Rossellini claims, but he displays little aptitude for it, the mute role exposing an almost total lack of expression. He never performed again on screen (except briefly to play himself in documentary essays like *Roma*), but the experience was none the less pleasant.

'I believe that the job of an actor is the easiest in the world,' he announced with a typical airiness. 'It is extraordinary how the brain ceases to function when one finds oneself in front of the camera: one forgets every preoccupation; others think for you; you find your responsibilities reduced to a simple and modest effort of memory. And then, everyone looks at you, everyone takes care of you. During those few hours when I was a "star", I only had to gently raise my hand for twenty people to cry: "Cigarettes! Cigarettes! . . . A cigarette for St Joseph. Quickly!" . . . An agreeable life, really.'

Even more agreeable was his fee. In lieu of money, Rossellini presented him with a red Topolino, the first of many Fellini cars.

Hurriedly yoking together *La Voix humaine* and *Il miracolo* with a title dedicating the film 'To the Art of Anna Magnani', Rossellini added a melodramatic score by Renzo and screened it at Venice in September 1948 as *Amore/Love*. It was a personal success for Magnani, if a disappointment to left-wing critics who expected better from the leading light of Neorealism.

At Venice, the first mutterings of scandal were heard when Catholic critics suggested *Il miracolo* might be blasphemous. It's never been clear if Rossellini meant the film to be anti-religious. In the outline, Fellini and Pinelli say unequivocally that a miracle has taken place, but in the film it's just as likely that the bells are imagined – the interpretation Pinelli himself prefers today.

Rossellini almost certainly, in this Communist/atheist phase of his career, saw the story as ambiguous and ironic. All 'miracles', he implies, exist, just like Ninna's, only in deluded, childlike minds. In 1956, for the film's re-release in Paris, he cut its final shot so that the episode ends as Ninna grasps the bell rope. No responding chimes are heard and the film climaxes on a humanist note. Ninna has triumphed over the narrow-mindedness of her village and the Church, even delivering her baby on its premises, led there by that most pagan of animals, the goat. Fellini was certainly sympathetic to this view. In both *Le notti di Cabiria* and *La dolce vita* he would show miracles as fantasies generated by a cynical Church playing on public credulity.

The charge of blasphemy didn't take root in Europe, because Pius XII, unexpectedly, was reported in October as having found 'marvellous' this 'modern version of a miracle of the Virgin directed by a Communist'. Since it's hardly likely the Pope saw the film, the announcement probably came from the Church's censors, heartened to see even so vaguely spiritual a subject embraced by the godless Rossellini.

In the United States, however, *Amore* became enmeshed in one of the great scandals of post-war cinema. Rossellini sold the film to Burstyn and Mayer, who'd handled *Open City* and *Paisà*. They discovered almost immediately that *La Voix humaine* couldn't be shown. This may have been because Rossellini, not for the first time, had sold the rights to more than one company – both Burstyn/Mayer and Ilya Lopert claimed US rights to *Paisà* – but it's more probable that he'd failed to clear copyright on Cocteau's play, since *Il miracolo* was also shown without *La Voix humaine* in Britain. Resourcefully Burstyn and Mayer joined it with two more short films, Renoir's *Une partie de campagne* and Marcel Pagnol's *Joffroi*, and released the result as *Ways of Love*. (The British distributor followed suit, but with different short films.) The New York State Board of Regents passed the film and it opened to modest critical approval at the Paris Theater on 12 December 1950, but the next day Edward T. McCaffrey, Commissioner for Licenses (and a prominent Catholic) illegally over-rode the Board's decision and banned it, claiming to find the film 'personally and officially blasphemous'. To emphasise that the Paris risked losing its licence if it continued to show *Ways of Love*, fire inspectors pointedly visited the newly built cinema searching for infringements.

Burstyn had McCaffrey's decision reversed in court, but by now the hand of New York's Cardinal Francis Spellman was evident. Though Catholic influence in Hollywood was nearly absolute in 1950, the Church exercised little control over imported films. Spellman chose *Il miracolo* as a vehicle to correct that. At his urging the Catholic League of Decency condemned it. McCaffrey mobilised old friends in the Catholic War Veterans, of whose New York branch he'd been commander, and a thousand pickets descended on the Paris, where they denounced the film as 'Communist blasphemy'. Panicked, the Board of Regents reversed its decision and on 16 February 1951 revoked the licence of *Ways of Love*. Burstyn took the case to the Supreme Court, which ruled in May 1952 that 'sacrilegious' was a term unacceptable in law, and that *Il miracolo* was protected by First Amendment guarantees of free speech. A serious dent was put in film censorship, and especially that part of it exercised without legal mandate by the Catholic Church.

Heat was added to the battle by another scandal involving Rossellini. In May 1948 he'd received a letter from Ingrid Bergman. Though they'd never met, the star of *Casablanca* and *For Whom the Bell Tolls* had seen both *Open City* and *Paisà*, the latter in an almost empty cinema, and been impressed. 'Maybe if this man had somebody who was a *name* playing for him,' she mused, 'then maybe people would come to see his pictures.' She told Rossellini that if there was ever a role in one of his films for her, she was eager to work with him 'for the sheer pleasure of the experience'. He cabled back his enthusiastic agreement.

Shortly after, he wrote her a long letter in which he outlined the plot of *Volcano*. He'd planned it for Magnani, but its heroine, isolated on Stromboli, the volcanic island off Sicily, could easily become an East European refugee who'd married an Italian to escape from an internment camp.

Bergman was enchanted and Magnani furious at what she saw as betrayal. The relationship ended explosively even before Bergman arrived in Italy to start work on *Stromboli*. Famous for sleeping with her directors, Bergman quickly seduced Rossellini. 'When I was living at the Plaza,' Marlene Dietrich recalled, 'Rossellini came and told me that he did *not* want her in bed, only on film, but she forced herself on him.' As he succumbed, both left their spouses and children to live together.

The runaways arrived in Rome on 20 March 1949. His team had arranged a dinner in the tiny apartment he kept permanently in the Excelsior, the walls of which Fellini had decorated with caricatures of Bergman, Roberto and Stromboli. For the star-struck Fellini, Bergman belonged to a world he'd never really believed existed. 'Italy had just come out of the war. The people were starved. There were disasters. The figure of Ingrid was like an ambassador of well-being. She was very familiar, like Clark Gable, like Gary Cooper, like Mickey Mouse.'

Suppressing his jealousy, he tried to make Bergman feel at home. He and Giulietta took her to one of their favourite seafood restaurants at Santa Marinella, and Fellini (without Masina) was a guest at the dinner that preceded the couple's lightning wedding in 1950, when they raced around Rome, dodging reporters, looking for a priest who would marry them.

Fellini remained in Rossellini's orbit for another two years. He turned twenty-eight pages written by two priests into a script for

Francesco, giullare di dio/The Flowers of St Francis, and even coaxed Fabrizi into the film as the local tyrant, though the actor dismissed the saint as 'a madman'. In 1950 he and Pinelli were enlisted in Rossellini's campaign to relaunch Bergman with *Europa '51* where she played a saintly do-gooder. Giulietta was 'Passerotto' – 'Little Sparrow' – a factory girl whom she rescues.

Long after he'd moved on, Fellini found himself called back to salvage some troubled Rossellini project. In 1952 he directed a few shots on his Toto comedy *Dove la libertà?/Where is Liberty?*, when Rossellini fell ill. This pattern of sudden reconciliations after years of silence repeated itself in Fellini's own life, as did the stormy master–pupil relationship with its implicit resentments. In private, Rossellini was increasingly contemptuous and resentful of Fellini, calling *La dolce vita* 'the work of a provincial' and 'the lowest point of the Italian cinema'.

One of their last cheerful moments had been after *Il miracolo*, when they returned to Amalfi for some shots on *La macchina ammazzacattivi/The Machine That Kills People*. British critic Paul Rotha visited the location, and Sergio Amidei, pointing out Fellini, said: 'Behold that young man. He has far to go.' In 1948, nobody realised how far.

11 Milena Amour and the Passionate Doll: *Luci del varietà* and *Lo sceicco bianco*

'I invented Fellini'
Alberto Lattuada

The new influence on Fellini's life in 1949 and 1950, and a crucial one, was Alberto Lattuada. Another pushy Milanese, he'd grown up in comfort as the son of composer Felice Lattuada. Only six years older than Fellini, he was already a successful director, and married to the beautiful star of sex comedies, Carla del Poggio. Fellini fell into Lattuada's orbit as he had that of Rossellini. He would always be drawn to these slightly smarter, richer, more polished men, almost as if he perversely enjoyed seeing someone who, with less ability than he, was ahead of the game simply by the accidents of birth. An edge of resentment helped Fellini. It kept him sharp, alert to excel.

Lattuada and Fellini had little in common. Even their shared enthusiasm for Hollywood movies diverged. Lattuada admired *film noir* and its world of dark, wet streets and desperate men. Fellini preferred Laurel and Hardy, Fred Astaire and Mae West. But it was indisputably Lattuada who initiated Fellini's first feature, *Luci del varietà*, on which they take joint director credit.

Beauty contests were a phenomenon in the Italy of the early fifties. Half the new female stars had been Miss Italia or the equivalent: Silvana Mangano, Gina Lollobrigida, Sophia Loren, Silvana Pampanini, Fulvia Franco. Irwin Shaw called them 'glossy female brutes'; women who weren't afraid to display themselves in skin-tight dresses and net stockings or even, occasionally, nude. In 1953 Loren appeared boldly bare-chested in a film based on Verdi's *Aïda*, high point of the directorial career of Clemente Fracassi. Magnani's craggy, ravaged glare had been supplanted as an emblem of Italian cinema by Silvana Mangano in crotch-hugging shorts, a skin-tight sweater and hairy armpits, glamorous even standing knee-deep in the dirty water of the Po rice fields in the 1950 *Riso amaro/Bitter Rice*. No wonder Dino de

Laurentiis married the nineteen-year-old ex-Miss Italia. Embracing her, he embraced the whole post-war Italian cinema.

Lattuada suggested to Fellini that a film about competitors for Miss Italia would be a sure success, particularly if Carla del Poggio played the winner, but the focus moved quickly away from this simple idea. Where might such a girl go after winning? Show business, of course. What branch of show business? The first choice was films, but Visconti was already working on *Bellissima*, with Magnani as a stage mother pushing her tot into the movies. In terms of worlds about which Fellini knew anything, that left vaudeville.

This, at least, is the way Fellini and Lattuada describe the genesis of the film, but the real story shows both men in a less favourable light. A project about a cheap music-hall troupe had been in the air at Lux for some time. In his anecdotes about Aldo Fabrizi and his fantasies of having toured with him (which the star increasingly resented), Fellini almost seemed to be acting out such a story, and it's probable that he or Lattuada decided to make their own version.

Fellini and Pinelli wrote a screenplay called first *Figli d'arte/Sons of Art*, then *Piccole stelle/Little Stars*. After a number of drafts they brought in Flaiano. The fact that he'd just left his wife and was living in a hotel hadn't improved his temper and he was characteristically abrasive, demolishing the plot and suggesting something more cynical and realistic. In the end, the script, now called *Luci del varietà*, had only the most peripheral connection with beauty contests. The tenuous thread was the main character, Liliana Antonelli, a pretty girl from the provinces with little talent but a good body and no scruples, who runs off with the touring theatrical troupe of which the ageing, self-important Checco Dalmonte is the 'international comedian'.

'We were about to start making the film,' Lattuada said, 'when I had the idea of forming what might be termed a "family" group. I engaged my wife, Carla del Poggio, Giulietta Masina, my father for the music score, my sister for production manager, and I thought to myself: now we have to face the distribution block. Our best bet is to form a closely knit group, plus a few other young people, so that we can create a kind of avalanche and see if we can't break through somehow.'

This much rings true. The rest of his account, however, is hilariously biased. 'Somewhere along the line,' he claimed, 'I said to Fellini, an extraordinarily talented young man who was my assistant-director: "As our wives are working side by side and you are working so close to me, and as we've written two or three films together, why don't you sign as co-director?" And that was how his name appeared in the

1926

ABOVE: Federico, aged six, with his younger brother Riccardo.

LEFT: Riccardo *balilla*, and Federico *avanguardista*.

BELOW: The Rimini beachfront of Fellini's childhood, with the Kursall (centre). Vera Fotografica Levibrom – Milan.

Rimini – Lungomare e Spiaggia

ABOVE LEFT: Aldo Fabrizi (left). British Film Institute (BFI).
ABOVE RIGHT: Alberto Lattuada: 'I invented Fellini.' BFI.

BELOW LEFT: Anna Magnani in *Roma città aperta*, 1946.
BELOW RIGHT: Fellini, with blonde hair and a beard in *Il miracolo*, 1946. BFI.

Roberto Rosellini and Ingrid Bergman in 1950.

Fellini in the fifties; far to go. BFI.

Alberto Sordi as the secret homosexual in *I vitelloni*, 1953.

Riccardo Fellini in *I vitelloni*, 1953. BFI.

ABOVE LEFT: Broderick Crawford and his wife just before *Il bidone*.
ABOVE RIGHT: Dino de Laurentiis. BFI.

Giulietta and Richard Basehart as Gelsomina and Il Matto in *La strada*, 1954.

Zampano (Anthony Quinn) snaps his 'steel' chains in *La strada*, 1954. BFI

'Is neorealism dead or alive?' Sylvia Rank (Anita Ekberg), quizzed by the Roman press, including Walter Santesso as Paparazzo (far right) in *La dolce vita*, 1960.

Fellini with Georges Simenon at Cannes, 1960, after the writer had engineered the Palme d'Or for *La dolce vita*. Roger Viollet.

credits – after mine, of course. "In this way you will have your name on
the screen as a director, and this will open the way to your becoming
one. You will have your 'degree'."''

There are numerous examples of such fake credits but *Luci del
varietà* isn't one of them. Fellini was no sleeping partner. 'I wrote the
original story, wrote the screenplay and chose the actors,' he says
tersely. 'Moreover, the film recalls some worn-out routines I saw
presented by a vaudeville troupe with Aldo Fabrizi . . . I can't
remember what I directed or what Lattuada directed, but I regard the
film as one of mine.' Assistant-director Massimo Mida agrees. Though
Lattuada handled the technical details and worked with lighting
cameraman Otello Martelli, the acting and the film's mood were
entirely Fellini's.

And who can doubt it? The troupe of *Luci del varietà* are exactly the
sort of performers Fellini had seen at the Jovinelli. Aside from Checco
and Milena, there's an 'Indian' fakir who eats light-bulbs, a Neapolitan tenor, a soubrette and two dancing girls. Milena's father, Achille,
does the bookings and looks after the money. For years the company
has travelled round Italy much as Fabrizi did. They've settled into a
routine of third-class railway carriages, sleazy theatres and accommodating relationships, like that between Checco and the company's
impersonator and quick-change artist, Milena Amour.

No one can mistake Fellini's signature on the details of backstage
life. The name of the troupe's first show, *Polvere di stelle/Star Dust*,
has resonances of the imaginary *Sparks of Love*. Fellini cast Giulietta
as Milena, Checco is played by his old friend Peppino de Filippo, and
Vittorio Caprioli, who was at his wedding, appears briefly as a
nightclub comic. Nobody of Lattuada's city background would know
how performers cross themselves superstitiously before they go on,
how a fakir goes through his weary routine of chewing broken glass (a
foreshadowing of Zampano's tired act in *La strada*), or why the
heckling of a provincial audience for Milena's fumbling and not-very-
quick changes of character from Verdi to Napoleon might halt
abruptly when she re-emerges as Garibaldi: however bad the imitation, Italy's Great Emancipator, at least here in the sticks, still
warrants respect.

Lattuada's family and the Fellinis contributed 35 per cent of the
cost, not in money but by working for nothing. The rest was put up by
Mario Inghirami of Capitolium Films. But *Luci del varietà* wasn't a
success. It went over budget, and its small chance of profit was

destroyed by another and almost identical film, *Vita da cani/A Dog's Life*, produced by Lux.

Fabrizi, smarting over not having been invited to make *Luci del varietà*, starred in *Vita da cani* opposite Gina Lollobrigida. He wasn't the only old friend of Fellini's to be involved. Carlo Ponti produced, Steno and Mario Monicelli directed, Amidei, Steno and Maccari wrote the script and Rota the music. (A young Marcello Mastroianni also appeared.) Given its plot, almost a carbon of *Luci del varietà*, it's hard to believe *Vita da cani* wasn't produced simply to cut the arrogant runaways down to size. Whether or not this was the intention, it was the effect. *Vita da cani* rated thirty-fourth in that year's Italian grossers, as against *Luci del varietà*'s dismal sixty-fifth. (It was thin consolation that Visconti's *Bellissima* and de Sica's *Miracolo in Milano* did almost as badly.) The distributors went broke, leaving the partners stuck with its debts. The lawsuits weren't settled until the sixties, and *Luci del varietà* had no showings outside continental Europe until 1964, by which time Fellini's reputation ensured an interested, if far from ecstatic, reception.

Luci del varietà closes on the note of ironic endurance typical of Fellini endings. After having run away with Liliana (and Milena's money) and been totally unsuccessful at launching his own 'sophistic- ated' revue with her as its star, Checco has returned, humiliated and broke. As their train is about to leave Termini station on another tour, he's mortified to see Liliana also travelling, but north to Milan, in first class and wrapped in furs, as the star of a leg show. He spins her a tale about the company now being a big success, with a Viennese ballet and heavy bookings, when it's obvious they are again headed south, into the hinterland of one-night stands. The train pulls out. Milena goes to sleep and Checco dozes on her accommodating shoulder until a girl looks into the compartment. He lifts his head and, fixing his tie, is soon lying to Milena about her, claiming she started talking to him, and to the girl, telling her: 'I have a variety company. You're very pretty.'

It's not surprising that, after having ended his first film as director with the scene of a self-important middle-aged man in a moustache with a pretty but not very bright girl at Termini, he should begin his second with the same setting and physical types. The narrowness of Fellini's concerns was already evident. He would never adapt popular novels, create star vehicles, make historical melodramas, gangster films, musicals or even comedies in the accepted sense. His own world would be his subject, his friends the performers, his themes those that had preoccupied him in childhood: the circus, the cinema, vaudeville, sex, dreams, fate, failure, Rome. Every two or three years he shuffled these cards and dealt himself a hand that became his next film.

Though no more successful commercially than *Luci del varietà*, *Lo sceicco bianco* was the film that established Fellini as a serious talent. Its origin was a documentary by Michelangelo Antonioni about the *fotoromanzi* magazines. Called *L'amorosa menzogna/The Loving Lie*, it screened at Venice in 1948 and won a Nastro d'Argento. The idea of a feature satirising the romantic obsession of some women with *fumetti* heroes, as passionate and obsessive as the fad for Rudolph Valentino in the twenties or the Beatles in the sixties, had been kicking around ever since. Antonioni wrote an outline which reached Carlo Ponti at Lux. 'Then, while he was in Bomarzo working on the documentary *La villa dei mostri*,' says Fellini, 'Antonioni fell ill and Mambretti, the partner of Ponti, convinced him to sell the idea and give up the direction of the film in favour of Lattuada. The project wandered from one producer to another until it wound up with Luigi Rovere, a producer whose office was next to that of Ponti at Lux. Rovere offered the film to two or three directors. Then he thought of me.'

As usual, the real story is less simple. Rovere was the producer who'd sent Fellini to Turin to hold the fort on *Persiane chiuse*, and there's no doubt that, despite the failure of *Luci del varietà*, he saw the young director as promising. Antonioni, however, was still involved, and there was some thought that he might direct the *fumetti* story after *Cronaca di un amore/Chronicle of a Love Affair*, his first feature.

Fellini and Pinelli began work on a script. It went slowly until, one day in the Borghese Gardens, during a rambling café 'conference' of the sort Fellini enjoyed, Pinelli thought of a young provincial couple coming to Rome, the woman of which wants to meet her favourite *fotoromanzi* hero. Fellini was immediately hooked by an experience not too far from his own. 'Yes, and it all has to happen in one day,' he said, inspired. 'And she also wants to see the Pope.' Antonioni, not surprisingly, disliked what Fellini proposed to do with his idea, but as the project had acquired momentum he let him run with it, though retaining his screen credit for the original story.

The man in the moustache who arrives at Termini at the start of *Lo sceicco bianco* is Ivan Cavalli, on his honeymoon with his pretty, younger but obviously distracted wife, Wanda. The bullying Ivan has organised the holiday down to the last detail: first Wanda's ritual approval by his Roman relatives, then visits to patriotic and historical sites, a performance of *Don Giovanni* and finally a Holy Year blessing by the Pope in St Peter's.

Wanda, however, has other plans. As soon as they get to the hotel she asks the bellboy the way to the offices of the magazine *Incanto blu* (*Blue Romance*) which carries the country's most popular *fumetti, Lo sceicco bianco*. Wanda reveals to its editor that she's 'Bambola Appassionata' ('Passionate Doll'), who's been bombarding the strip's hero, Fernando Rivoli, with letters. The editor is sympathetic, reassuring Wanda 'dreams are our true lives', and arranges for her to meet the sheik, sending her out with the company that's just leaving for the location on the coast at Fregene.

Fellini's first day as a solo director, which began with these beach scenes, found him nervous to the point of distraction. 'I left the house at dawn, after having kissed Giulietta with feeling and having received rather sceptical good wishes from the housekeeper, who kept repeating from the doorway: "But you'll die of the heat that way!" Although it was already summer I had dressed up like a director: shirt, boots, leggings, sunglasses and a whistle hanging from my neck like a soccer referee. Rome was deserted. I searched the streets, the houses, the trees, looking for a propitious omen. There was a sacristan opening a church as though for me. I gave way to an ancient impulse, got out of the car and went in.'

Fellini found the church brightly lit with candles and a coffin standing in the middle of them. A man was weeping beside it. He retreated in alarm, 'making hand signs to ward off evil, from my feet to a metre above my head'.

The summer wardrobe is unlikely, since he began shooting in September 1951. In other respects, especially the search for a good omen, the account seems accurate, though in some versions he adds a flat tyre between Rome and the beach. He certainly had ill luck with the first day's shooting, which, as filming often does on water, went badly. The crew were also unsupportive − 'forty people looking on, that terrible Roman troupe, looking at their watches, and with faces that would happily end your career'. The first day didn't produce one metre of usable film.

On the second, weary of trying to second-guess the sea, Fellini bedded the boat in sand, dug a hole for the camera and got his shots. The tide, however, continued to come in during the afternoon and, when some scenes showed the breaking waves, he had to change the action and retake a few shots later at Cinecittà against backdrops. Enzo Provenzale, the production manager sent by Rovere to keep an eye on him, disapproved. A tough professional, he disliked Fellini's improvisatory approach and tendency to invent dialogue and 'business' on the set.

Like all the films to follow, *Lo sceicco bianco* is a series of long, deceptively casual sequences, enlivened with carefully staged fantasies whose imagination marks them as the work of a unique cinematic intelligence. In the first of these in Fellini's work, Wanda comes upon the white sheik in full Arabian costume on a swing strung high between two pine trees. It's not clear from what the ropes of the swing are suspended; it could be a cloud. He's an apparition at the same time specific and impossible, like the Cheshire Cat in *Alice in Wonderland*.

Fellini visualised this image in great detail, sketching it out beforehand and setting it up with some elaborate engineering. The swing would reappear often in his work. Richard Basehart is an acrobat in *La strada* and, in a scene cut from *Il Bidone/The Swindlers*, plays on a carnival ride; Christ's statue dangles below a helicopter in *La dolce vita*; Sandra Milo appears on a flowered swing in *Giulietta degli spiriti*; girls on swings feature in *Casanova* and *Satyricon*; and in *La città delle donne* Mastroianni hangs in the basket of a giant balloon in the shape of a woman. In each case, the swing represents dangerous infantilism.

Fellini had only one actor in mind for the sheik, Alberto Sordi. His large, mobile, utterly unreliable face was ideal for the dumb, dissembling Rivoli, but the actor had made five films, none of them hits, and Rovere was doubtful. After seeing him pendulating drowsily back and forth in the empty forest and crooning to himself, it's impossible to imagine the character played by anyone else.

Traditionally, Rovere is also supposed to have vetoed the first choice to play Ivan, Peppino de Filippo, as too obscure. Fellini is then said to have seen Leopoldo Trieste in a film being projected at Cinecittà and offered him the role. Aside from the obvious objection that if de Filippo was too obscure, an unknown like Trieste, who was mainly a screenwriter, was worse, all the evidence suggests that de Filippo, already cast, became unavailable and that Fellini, meeting Trieste with a friend by chance, asked him to test for the role.

Like most forced casting decisions in Fellini's career, this one was wrong. Trieste overplays in a role that, in any event, offers little but eye-rolling, panic and the occasional faint. Brunella Bovo as Wanda, on the other hand, is an ideal foil for both the overbearing Ivan and the oleaginous Sordi.

While Wanda flirts with Rivoli, who slips her into the *fumetti* as a harem girl, a distracted Ivan stalls his relatives. That night, he wanders the streets, where he meets two prostitutes on their way home. One of them, Cabiria (Giulietta Masina), comforts him, admires his family snapshots and, in an attempt to cheer him up, has a passing fire-eater put on an impromptu display. Ivan isn't amused. His carefully constructed life is in ruins and he goes off glumly with Cabiria's older, maternal companion, more his speed than the flighty Wanda.

Distraught by the revelation that her sheik is married, and henpecked at that, Wanda is rescued by the crew's camel handler, who finds her shivering under the pines, and brings her back to her hotel. Unable to face Ivan, she goes to the Tiber and, noting that angels on a nearby bridge seem symbolically to have turned their backs on her, proclaims: 'Dreams are our true life, but sometimes dreams plunge us into a fatal abyss,' and flings herself melodramatically into the river – only to land on her hands and knees in the mud.

The next morning, Ivan has a call to pick her up. Dodging squads of *bersaglieri*, the briskly trotting, cornet-blowing infantry who are assembling for the Papal blessing, he finds the mental hospital where she's been taken for observation. A doctor tells him that she has 'a headache that aspirin can't cure', implying that her obsession is permanent. But Wanda manages to accommodate both her fantasy and the reality of marriage. As she meets and charms the family at last just before they hurry into St Peter's, she murmurs that she remained faithful during her escapade and that Ivan is now her sheik. Uneasily remembering his own fall from virtue, Ivan wonders if she's telling the truth.

Shooting ended in December and Fellini edited through March. He showed his rough cut to Rossellini, who had mixed feelings, not so much about the film as about Fellini's obviously rising star. 'I felt old and disturbed because he seemed so young,' he admitted.

Lo sceicco bianco was short-listed as one of the official entries for Cannes. The panel of Italian critics were divided on whether it belonged with their other choices, all by established directors (including Lattuada), and in May they replaced it, to Fellini's acute disappointment, with *Guardie e ladri/Cops and Robbers*, the year's big box-office success, made by his old colleague Steno and Mario Monicelli.

The film was selected for Venice, and shown there on the afternoon of 6 September. The audience liked it well enough, but reviews were scathing. Desultorily distributed by Fincine, which went broke soon after, the film was taken off at many cinemas after a few days. Rovere decided that audiences had taken a particular dislike to Sordi, but it's more likely they distrusted the film's shifting sympathies. There was no obvious hero, no clear line. *Luci del varietà* had been too fantastic to be considered Neorealistic but at least it retained some of Neorealism's semi-documentary tone. The story of Checco and Liliana was easily read as an attack on pretension and disloyalty. Audiences knew where they were.

Lo sceicco bianco, however, was more complex, without an obvious moral. Fellini seemed to be exposing the dangers of a life nourished by fantasies, even those of the Church. 'While Wanda follows the White Sheik as her dream romantic hero,' he says, 'Ivan follows his own mythology, consisting of the Pope, *bersaglieri*, the nation, the king.' As Pierre Kast pointed out mischievously in *Cahiers du cinéma*, Ivan at the end of the film takes Wanda to 'meet a new White Sheik, who will tell new and equally imaginative stories; in other words the Pope himself'. In the Italy of 1952, ruled in effect by Pius XII, these were unpalatable ideas, and the audience viewed them with suspicion.

On the other hand, to attack fantasy he used a technique and story which were themselves fantastic. Paul Rotha, one of the few critics writing about Italian cinema in English at the time, summed up the prevailing ambivalence well. Fellini, he said, 'has created an intangible half-world, somewhere between realism and fantasy, which some call poetry and others surrealism. It is . . . equally repellent to the routine filmgoer and critic because it is elusive in meaning, not crystal-clear to grasp.'

12 'Down with fantasy! Punish the author': *I vitelloni* and *Un'agenzia matrimoniale*

Critic (to Sylvia Rank): 'Is Neorealism dead or alive?'
Translator (without translating): 'Say: "Alive"'
Dialogue from the press conference in *La dolce vita*

By 1952 Neorealism was dead and all but buried. Younger filmgoers, to whom the war, the motor of the movement, was a memory, wanted glamour, romance and high living. In the new climate of national greed, stories of partisans, bootblacks and stolen bicycles were old hat.

With his religious films, Rossellini had served notice of his interest in the heightened realism of drama and a dwindling desire to work with amateurs on authentic locations. The Marxists branded him a traitor, especially after the start of his liaison with Ingrid Bergman, as symbolic as Dino's marriage to Mangano. His defection placed the whole intellectual basis of the movement in doubt. Perhaps, joked critic Franco Venturini in 1951, there had never been any Neorealism at all; just *realismo* with a *neo* – a mole.

Fellini, more cartoonist than portraitist, more journalist than novelist, more fantasist than documentarist, and the exact opposite of a Marxist, never truly embraced Neorealism. The knee-jerk appropriation into the movement of anything remotely squalid irritated him. 'When people saw a badly made shack, they mistook it for Neorealism. When they saw two tramps, they said: "Neorealism".' Pressed to define his personal concept of Neorealism, Fellini insisted it should include 'not just Neorealist truth but spiritual reality, metaphysical reality, all that there is within man . . . In a certain sense, everything is realistic. I see no dividing line between imagination and reality.' So broad a definition was no definition at all.

Fellini had lately become preoccupied with the itinerants who wandered the roads of Italy. He passed them all the time around Rome, and noticed more when he and Giulietta took a holiday after *Lo sceicco bianco*. Masina remembers: 'In the south of Tuscany, as night was falling, we met two travelling acrobats. [One] was a big woman, already aged, but she had a rough kindness.' The other was a hulking brute. In Fellini's memory, the woman squatted by a tiny fire, cooking. Her companion stood near by, silent, uninterested, waiting to be fed. They had nothing to say to one another.

The same sorts of people used to pass through Gambettola and warm themselves in his grandmother's kitchen, paying for shelter with anecdotes and gossip. They seemed eternal, an underclass of knife grinders, clothes-peg and toy vendors, pot menders and entertainers that provided a living link with Collodi, even Boccaccio.

For once, Pinelli and Fellini agree on how a project was conceived. Moved by nothing more than 'a confused sensation . . . a feeling of indefinable melancholy, a pervasive sense of guilt hanging over me like a shadow' – guilt about what? A sense that, in abandoning Neorealism, he was betraying his roots and class? If so, it was a remorse that, typically, he quickly recovered from – Fellini sketched out an idea about a roving clown and 'a dark, towering shadow' who was her master. He took it to Pinelli, only to find that, during the summer on his farm in Tuscany, Pinelli had made notes for a similar story about travelling circus people.

With Luigi Giacosi, his production manager, Fellini tried to raise money for the project, and even shot some test footage to attract a producer. None was tempted, but incidents and images began to collect in Fellini's mind and sketch books. Moraldo Rossi, his continuity man, recalls them driving one evening when Fellini suddenly stopped and reversed the car. He'd seen a horse with a hide oddly spotted, as if from some disease. They never found the horse but, when they at last shot the film two years later, a lone horse, appearing when Gelsomina has been abandoned by Zampano in a miserable village all night, provided an emblem of isolation and despair.

Even with *Lo sceicco bianco*'s poor reviews, Fellini didn't lack offers. Ponti suggested a police story for Lux, another producer wanted to film Diego Fabbri's *Il seduttore* with Giulietta and Leopoldo Trieste, and the beauty contest project surfaced again as a vehicle for ex-Miss Italia Fulvia Franco and her husband, the boxer Tiberio Mitri. Only one producer, however, was ready to let Fellini choose his own subject. Lorenzo Pegoraro was an unknown quantity, but he claimed to have seen *Lo sceicco bianco* six times and was prepared to offer a two-film contract with his Peg Films, backed by a consortium of Florentine businessmen. Fellini accepted. Pegoraro, however, was anything but enthusiastic about the clown script, now called *La strada*. Perhaps, he suggested, if Gelsomina was played by someone glamorous, like Silvana Pampanini? Fellini was scornful, but agreed to shelve it for the moment.

Chatting about adolescence in a café with Flaiano (who shared Pegoraro's doubts about *La strada*), Fellini had told him some anecdotes about his Rimini gang. Flaiano, too, was raised in a dead-and-alive seaside town, Pescara, and had his own tales. With Pinelli, they fleshed out their memories into a script. Though some of the stories have an autobiographical thread, they are more like projections of the life Fellini might have lived had he stayed in Rimini.

The main characters are five young men, all in their early twenties, all living at home and all unemployed. Fellini and Flaiano christened them *vitelloni*, from *vaudellone*, a slang word for 'big gut', signifying someone who'd rather eat than work. It also has overtones of *vitello* – calf. Arthur Knight summed them up well as 'the sons of lower middle-class families who feel that they are too good for manual labour. Not rich enough to be called wastrels or poor enough to be bums, they drift along aimlessly, hoping for the break that will give them a definite status in society.'

I vitelloni is a group portrait, symbolised in the opening image of their interlocked shadows spilling across a wall as they march, singing, through the empty night-time town, but its focus is Fausto, tall and blond, a tireless womaniser whom the omniscient, anonymous commentary introduces as 'our chief and moral guide'. His ragtag gang includes Alberto, a suppressed homosexual obsessively attached to the sister whose secretarial work supports them and their mother; Leopoldo, the intellectual who lives with doting maiden aunts, forever writing unperformable plays; and Riccardo, played by Riccardo Fellini, who is, as in life, a nonentity with a pleasant singing voice.

Only Moraldo, the youngest, neat and thoughtful, who says little and spends many nights walking alone, occasionally chatting with a boy who works at the railway station, has any promise of a life beyond the nameless town. He represents Fellini, who attaches to him a number of autobiographical traits, including his own taste for long walks. When Federico was finally allowed out after eight thirty pm by a censorious Ida, he took advantage of his freedom. 'He never slept,' recalls Maddalena. 'He'd go out walking after supper, and walk God knows how many kilometres to some fishermen's bar or a workmen's tavern, and sit there drinking wine and talking. Or he'd go to the railroad station and wait all night to see the train come in, and the mail bags unloaded.'

Moraldo, however, isn't completely Fellini, nor is the town, except in a general geographical sense, Rimini. The beach, the huts, the flimsy pier could be anywhere on the Italian coast, and in fact he shot it in Viterbo and Ostia, carefully avoiding Rimini. If the film does reveal Fellini it's in its psychology. Three of the five represent aspects of his personality — womaniser, homophile, intellectual — with Riccardo supplying the physical resemblance and Moraldo the professional.

The opening sequence is set on the terrace of what is obviously meant to be the Kursaal opposite the Grand Hotel. Riccardo croons a song out front, while backstage Fausto puts his moves on a finalist in the Miss Sirene contest. When the winner's announced, it's Fausto's girlfriend (and Moraldo's sister) Sandra. She promptly faints, and is found to be pregnant. Fausto tries to leave town that night, but his father thrashes him like a child in front of an embarrassed Moraldo and forces him to marry the girl. At the wedding Riccardo sings his real-life party piece, 'Ave Maria'.

After the honeymoon, Fausto seems resigned to, even contented with, married life. His father-in-law gets him a humiliating job in a religious supplies store. With the honeymoon magic wearing off, he flirts with a woman sitting in the darkened cinema and, leaving Sandra on a pretext, follows her home.

Leopoldo Trieste was an obvious choice for Leopoldo and Riccardo Fellini for Riccardo, but casting Moraldo and Fausto posed problems which Fellini, never comfortable when interviewing actors, found almost insurmountable. With his limited experience of watching film and theatre, Fellini has never felt competent to assess performances. 'When he is casting,' said Elia Kazan, who (not always approvingly) has watched Fellini work, 'what he looks for is not a good reading but an eloquent face . . . A face, he believes, is a piece of sculpture that has taken a lifetime to mould, so it tells more than any actor's technique possibly could.'

For his interview, Franco Interlenghi, who would play Moraldo, was called to a Rome apartment and told to wait in a room lined with heavy red curtains. After a few minutes he realised someone was spying from behind the curtains. It was Fellini — and that, it turned out, was the audition.

Destined to be cast as Fausto, Franco Fabrizi was summoned to the Capitani Studios in via degli Avignonesi but, finding that he was head of the line, pleaded nausea and hid in the toilet to spy on the first interview through a window. Seeing from Fellini's fumbling technique that he had nothing to fear, he walked in confidently when it was his turn. After their talk, Fellini gratefully stopped auditioning.

I vitelloni was almost the last film on which Fellini followed convention in choosing actors. He began to collect photographic portraits that would expand into an archive of thousands. They included every interesting face from his auditions, plus those of friends. He augmented these with snapshots taken in the street and pictures of interesting performers, often in other countries, shot at his direction. Actors on the other side of Europe who had long forgotten their meeting would get a call demanding their presence in Rome to play a role in which they'd been cast without knowing it.

Under a deal with Cité Films in Paris, Pegoraro agreed to fill three roles with French actors. Jean Brochard plays Fausto's father, Arlette Sauvage the woman he picks up in the cinema, and Claude Farell is Olga, Alberto's sister. For Alberto himself, Fellini demanded Sordi – not a popular choice, least of all with Pegoraro, who concurred with the rest of the industry that the actor was box-office poison. To make things worse, Sordi was then touring with Wanda Osiris, whose lavish leg shows inspired the revue Liliana fronts at the end of *Luci del varietà*. Shooting had to be planned around his schedule, demanding expensive trips to Florence and Viterbo.

Life in the *vitellonis'* town is enlivened by spectacles like the carnival ball, for which the group dress up, revealingly in character: Moraldo in the sailor suit Fellini wore as a boy, the eternal sidekick Riccardo as a musketeer, Alberto as a woman. The ball is an opportunity for drunken sex. Alberto tangoes with a moustachioed man, gets drunk, becomes morbidly attached to a giant papier-mâché head and passes out in the dawn. Later, a theatrical troupe comes to town, including a distinguished old actor, Sergio Natali, who performs sentimental monologues. The gang go backstage and invite him to dinner. Leopoldo hopes to interest him in one of his plays, but the homosexual Natali, to Leopoldo's alarm, has other ideas. So does Fausto, who sleeps with one of the showgirls. His infidelity is the last straw for Sandra, who runs away from home with the baby. Her flight jolts Fausto and, after a frantic search, they're reunited. The incident also catalyses something for Moraldo and, without telling anyone, he takes the train for Rome, and a new future.

For Natali, Fellini wanted the man who had inspired the role, Achille Maieroni, whom he would show stumbling through *Julius Caesar* in *Roma* and later fastidiously sipping Mandarin Punch at the

Caffè Commercio. Pegoraro disagreed. Since this was just a cameo, they could have a big name in the role; why not Vittorio de Sica?

Somewhat in awe, Fellini went over to Termini station, where de Sica was directing the ill-fated *Stazione Termini*. They met late at night in the private car he'd co-opted as his caravan. Not being friendly with Italy's most famous leading man, Fellini was diffident as he described the character. De Sica understood immediately that he was being asked to play an old homosexual. 'But is he . . . human?' he asked. Fellini assured him Natali was drawn sympathetically. 'Because', de Sica told him patronisingly, 'it is possible that there is a great deal of humanity in such people' – no news to Fellini. De Sica agreed to do it but, sensing his phoniness, Fellini persuaded Pegoraro to use Maieroni after all. Having set his heart on a performer, Fellini was adamant.

Intransigence like this took its toll on Pegoraro, and by the time they reached Viterbo in December to start shooting, the producer was losing his grip. According to Pinelli, he locked himself in a bathroom on the first day and refused to come out. Many producers were to feel the same urge on a Fellini film. From Pegoraro onwards, he fought with them all. Almost no Fellini film has been shot within its budget. Most have gone catastrophically over, some to the extent that they were shut down. *Casanova* and *La città delle donne* changed producers during production, in *Casanova*'s case twice. *Roma* bankrupted its producer and the aborted *Il viaggio di G. Mastorna/The Voyage of G. Mastorna* cost Dino de Laurentiis millions.

The reasons were more often cultural and personal than artistic. With the Torinese Franco Cristaldi, the Milanese Rizzolis, the Neapolitan de Laurentiis and Grimaldi, and especially the Frenchman Daniel Toscan du Plantier of Gaumont, Fellini always felt like a country boy. His resentment ripened into loathing of producers as a class. In *Satyricon*, when Eumolpo bequeaths his estate to those friends ready to devour his corpse, we're meant to equate the dourly munching oldsters with movie moneymen.

Fellini developed techniques to keep producers at a distance: refusing to show them a script, closing the set and promoting the myth that he improvised his films. In this way he avoided having to agree on a budget or a schedule. Even when he did, he had his escape hatches. Toscan du Plantier came to know them well. 'In the beginning, everything works. He's nice. He's kissing you. But you start to understand, at the end of the first two months, that something doesn't work. It takes time to know what. For example, he doesn't start the movie the day you think. Apparently you pay for the shooting but you don't shoot. They "prepare". They prepare for weeks and weeks and *weeks*, which looks like a shooting, costs the price of a shooting. A large part of the budget is spent before you start the movie, so you know you are going to spend a lot of extra money.'

Second assistant Gerald Morin kept a diary of *Casanova*, and was able to analyse one of Fellini's strategies in detail. Twice a week, the production team toured the sets being built at Cinecittà, after which Fellini issued orders for further construction. Over the first month, Morin noticed that, for certain sequences around the lake, Fellini ordered sets twelve metres high for scene A, the final carnival, but for scene B, a less lavish sequence, only seven metres. In choosing extras, Fellini also allocated 130 to scene A and only seventy to scene B, for which only seven days were set aside, as against twelve for A. With each decision, B was subtly short-changed. As the time approached to shoot B, Morin wrote in his diary: 'I'm sure we will cut this scene.' It was, as he foretold, shot, then deleted from the film.

Why? Morin realised this was part of Fellini's method for dealing with producers. 'If he said to the producer [before shooting the scene]: "I'm not using this scene," they would say: "You're crazy! We've opened up the studio lake. We've spent 50 million lire." If, instead, he shot the scene in only seven days and not twelve, used sets seven metres high and not twelve, only thirty or forty extras and not 150, they'd say: "Thank you, Fellini." And afterwards, he can cut it and nobody will mind.' (Nor, it goes without saying, will they complain at the cost of the more lavish and important carnival.) 'And that is a pity,' Morin concludes, 'because sometimes a director is a prisoner of his producers.' One might equally remark that the producers were victims of Fellini.

I vitelloni finished shooting on 15 January. By then it was clear that it was a film of unusual merit. Performances had meshed with setting to create a portrait not only of five men but of a generation. The film was filled with vivid images caught by Otello Martelli, of the group standing phlegmatically on a sketchy pier in identical dark overcoats watching the waves, or lounging in a scrap of sun, drifting between morning coffee and the first billiard game of the day.

Distributors didn't agree, however, and Pegoraro and Fellini hawked the film from company to company. Most found it down-beat, lacking in the comedy and glamour that typified Italian cinema of the early fifties. One suggested they shoot a new ending in which oil is discovered in the town and the five become rich, which sounds like a borrowing from the unproduced *Paese felice*. Everyone hated Sordi, to the extent that, when the film was finally bought, his name was omitted from the posters and from the first fifty prints of the film. Ironically, when he became Italy's top film comedian, his presence was its greatest selling-point.

I vitelloni won a Silver Lion at Venice in 1953, which attracted enough attention for ENIC to offer distribution, though only after Pegoraro threw in two other films. The title would always be a problem. The French just called it *Les 'Vitelloni'*, the British *The Spivs*, but in America, where it was released in 1956, after the success of *La strada*, it was embarrassingly, not to say misleadingly, called *The Young and the Passionate*.

As the tide for Neorealism ran out, its supporters were left intellectually high and dry, none more so than Cesare Zavattini. Hoping to retrieve some part of the movement's reputation, he persuaded old friends and acolytes to collaborate on an anthology film that would sum up its achievements. The theme, and the title, was *Amore in città/ Love in the City*.

Fellini, Carlo Lizzani, Dino Risi, Antonioni, Francesco Maselli and Lattuada (though, significantly, not Rossellini) all said yes, though Fellini did so grudgingly. 'I agreed to participate . . . with all the competitive spirit of a young student grumpily accepting the professor's jokes. *I vitelloni* had had a great success but left the left-wing critics cold and distant. Though the consensus was positive, they were critical about my locating the film in a nameless province and accused me of over-emphasising poetic memory and not knowing how to give the film a clear political meaning. I thought I'd take a little revenge.'

Fellini's twenty-minute sketch, scripted with Pinelli, was *Un'agenzia matrimoniale/A Matrimonial Agency*. A reporter is sent to investigate the agencies that find brides. At the office of Agenzia Cibele in a run-down palazzo, he tells the sinister owner, a burly woman in mannish suit and dark glasses with an ex-cop for a partner, that he's a doctor looking for a wife on behalf of a patient, a rich young man who turns into a werewolf on moonlit nights. The reporter assumes that only a swindler would accept such an impossible task, but the woman duly introduces him to Rosanna. Driving back to Rome with her, he realises that Rosanna is sincere. A nice girl from a poor family, she has little chance of marrying and looks on the fictitious friend, for all his problems, as a genuine prospect. With his story dead and his embarrassment growing, he tells her curtly to forget the whole thing and drops her off in the middle of Rome.

With its credits lettered on the pages of a magazine and a message insisting that everything in the film was true, narrated and played by the people to whom it happened, *Amore in città* aimed to make fiction pass as fact. Zavattini insisted on non-professional actors, so Fellini took drama students from the Centro Sperimentale, though the voice-over is by Enrico Maria Salerno. Shooting the film was the young Gianni di Venanzo, who would become Fellini's lighting cameraman on some of his best films.

Amore in città was shown at Venice in September 1953, to generally good reactions. Fellini lied to Zavattini and his left-wing supporters that during his research he'd found the equivalent of Agenzia Cibele in his own apartment building. To his secret glee, the pope of Neorealism counselled him complacently that reality was always more fantastic than the most outrageous invention.

13 A Strongman and a Half-Witted Girl: *La strada*

> 'Life . . . is so vastly and so delightfully more rich,
> magical and supernatural when it accepts in an easy and
> simple rhythm the miracle of every day'
> From Fellini's summary of the Giulietta Masina character in *Giulietta*
> *degli spiriti*

Writing *La strada* took more of Fellini's time and effort than any film until then; more, in fact, than he would spend on almost any film of his career. The need to reconcile a mystical vision with the vestigial demands of Neorealism threw all manner of barriers in the way of himself and Pinelli. More were erected by Flaiano, who never liked the idea. '[He] was saying that it was nonsense, that it was sentimental, woolly, not real,' says Pinelli, 'so much so that we were on the point of abandoning it.' Pinelli asked him to suspend judgement until he read the first sequence. After that, Flaiano grudgingly agreed that the script might just work.

The new version began with Gelsomina di Castanzo trudging over the dunes near the sea with a load of firewood. Her five young brothers and sisters run to her, saying that a man has come to tell them their sister Rosa is dead. The man is Zampano, named after the *zampano di maiale*, a pork sausage shaped like a pig's foot. He's a sullen carnival strongman who travels Italy in a tiny caravan balanced on a motorbike. Some time before, he'd taken Rosa as his assistant. Now he wants a replacement. Her mother, destitute and calculating, sells him Gelsomina ('Jasmine'), though warning she isn't smart like Rosa. Gelsomina kneels facing the sea and her face lights briefly in a grin. Show business!

The reality is different. At their first stop, Zampano beats her until she learns to roll the drum and announce his arrival in town. Afterwards, he rapes her. Thereafter, on a succession of vacant lots and town squares, Zampano lights a smoky fire, sends Gelsomina to drum

up an audience, and does his one trick, wrapping a 'steel' chain —
actually brittle cast iron — around his chest and snapping it by
expanding his muscles. Gelsomina's pale and funny face allows him
to swell his repertoire. He gives her a broken-backed hat (she's
delighted) and teaches her a comic act in which, for the first time, she
understands the pleasure of performing. She remains, however, no
more than his slave.

Pinelli and Fellini spent four months in writing, and more time in
travelling around Lazio, visiting small circuses, talking to itinerants
and petty tricksters. The figures of Zampano and Gelsomina were
already established, but now they were joined by Il Matto ('The
Madman'), a prototypical 'Fool for God' whose highwire walking and
clowning in paper angel's wings recalls the medieval *jongleur*, whose
juggling was a form of worship, but who manifests as well the
malicious character of the *commedia dell'arte*'s Arlecchino.

Whenever mysticism threatened to overwhelm the story, Flaiano
wrenched it back on to the track. Gelsomina, conceived initially as a
Pierrot Lunaire-like innocent, became shrewd and observant, with a
quality of remote dignity. Emerging from Zampano's shadow, she
evolved into the film's tragic heroine, an emblem of man's inhumanity
to women. As she sits disconsolate in the gutter, abandoned by
Zampano for a tart, a riderless horse clops by, an enigmatic symbol,
here and elsewhere in Fellini, of isolation. The surrealism of *Lo sceicco
bianco* gave way to the mixture of the poetic and playful, touching
and grotesque, that would come to be recognised as distinctively
'Fellinian'.

Gelsomina is protected from the worst of Zampano's cruelty by a
natural resilience, fuelled by a sense of wonder that reflects Fellini's
own childhood fascination with the strange and mysterious. When
they're invited to perform at a wedding on a mountain farm, a craggy
woman feeds them and gives Zampano the pick of her late husband's
clothes. While Zampano is paying for her gift in bed, the farm's
children lead Gelsomina to Osvaldo, a boy with a pale, slack face,
sequestered in an upper room, guarded by nuns. The sense of strange-
ness and awe persists when they move on to a religious festival. The
town is taken over by a procession which, in the eyes of an awed
Gelsomina, looks barbaric, pre-Christian. That night, Il Matto wire-
walks high above the square, a fantastic figure in angel's wings.

Since she had little dialogue, none of it profound, Masina worked
extensively on Gelsomina's movement. 'She has a very unusual walk.
All the agility is in the feet. On the other hand, an enormous weight

presses on the shoulders, which gives the impression that she drags her life behind her. Why? Because before she was a performer she carried bundles of wood on her shoulders. Everything is rigid with Gelsomina except the feet.' Fellini told her always to smile with her mouth closed, an expression he'd noticed in her childhood photographs. Other emotional clues also came from childhood. A photograph she'd seen when she was ten of a woman looking at her dead child gave her the pose, mouth part open, fingers on chin, for the moment when she realises Il Matto is dead.

The Gelsomina face wasn't, she insists, that of a clown. 'Fellini didn't at all want me to have the clown mask. It would simply be my face, with the addition of some small signs.' The 'signs' were the startled commas of eyebrows, sunrise marks above the eyes, themselves heavily outlined, a dot on the end of the nose and a heavily lipsticked rosebud mouth. After make-up, Fellini flicked talc into her face to give it the pallor of a kabuki performer. Her hair was made even more blonde, almost white. Then Fellini, like any peasant, upended a bowl on her head and trimmed around it. After that, he plastered it with soap to give it a spiky, untidy look. Her costumes came from Porta Portese, Rome's flea market, though her cape, a piece of First World War surplus, was bought from a shepherd. Its collar was so frayed that it cut into Masina's neck, but that was a small detail.

After their first encounter, Zampano, Gelsomina and Il Matto seem bound by a single fate. All three end up at a small circus. Il Matto mocks Zampano's stupidity and his one feeble trick. Gelsomina and Il Matto, on the other hand, are mutually fascinated, recognising the same affinity as Arlecchino has to Columbina, Pierrot to Pierrette. He plays tunes to her on a tiny violin, teaches her a new routine, even introduces her to philosophy by explaining that the existence of a simple pebble (or person) proves that the universe has meaning.

Il Matto's goading drives Zampano to fury. He tries to knife him and ends up under arrest. Gelsomina could leave with Il Matto and the circus but instead dutifully waits for her tormentor. In the mountains they stop at a convent, where the nuns also invite Gelsomina to stay on, but her loyalty to, even love for, Zampano demands that she remain, even when he scandalises her by trying to steal some of the poor place's treasures.

They run into Il Matto again. His car has broken down and he's alone, so Zampano beats him up and accidentally kills him. Watched by a horrified Gelsomina he dumps the body in a ravine and pushes the car on top. Thereafter Gelsomina languishes, and Zampano abandons her on a mountain road with a blanket and the trumpet she's come to love, and on which she has improvised her doleful song. Years later, in a seaside town where he's still performing his tired routine in a little circus, he hears a woman singing Gelsomina's song. She explains she learned it from a girl who came to town some time back. When he asks where she is, the woman says she died. Later that night, drunk, he goes to the beach and, looking up at the starry sky, senses for the first time his insignificance – an ironic reversal of Il Matto's philosophy.

In 1950 Carlo Ponti and Dino de Laurentiis had left Lux and set up independently – a logical step, since between them they'd produced a good share of the country's most successful films: *Senza pietà, Il mulino del Po, Riso amaro, Guardie e ladri.* Their headquarters was typical of the relationship, with offices at opposite ends of a corridor, the doors always open, allowing them freely to shout comments and abuse. The partnership never looked like lasting long. 'Dino likes quantity,' said Ponti. 'I like quality.' But both welcomed Fellini when he brought in the script. Dino urged him to star Burt Lancaster and Silvana Mangano, but Fellini resisted. The last people he wanted were Lancaster, who'd been a professional acrobat before becoming an actor, or Dino's glamorous wife. Giulietta must and would be Gelsomina. As for Zampano, he needed an actor expert enough to convey both brutish strength and childish simplicity.

He found him in Anthony Quinn. Since 1936 the Mexican-born star had impersonated Arab chieftains, Indian braves, Chinese gunmen, Filipino partisans and assorted ethnic heavies before settling down as a journeyman second lead. Neither marriage to Katherine, adopted daughter of Cecil B. DeMille, nor Broadway success as Stanley Kowalski in *A Streetcar Named Desire* raised his status. Even his 1952 Oscar for *Viva Zapata!* served to confirm his subsidiary role, since it was won for Best Supporting Actor.

In the early fifties there was an exodus towards Europe of actors who saw little hope of becoming leading men under the studio system. Richard Basehart, Kirk Douglas, Steve Cochran and Farley Granger all made profitable trips to Italy, and in 1953 Quinn followed, appearing in support (inevitably) to Douglas in *Ulysses* and going on to make three more Italian films. One of these was *Donne perdute/ Angels of Darkness*, a contemporary drama with Linda Darnell, Valentina Cortese and Basehart, soon to be Cortese's husband. Giuseppe Amato, Fellini's old colleague, produced and directed. Giulietta had a small role and Fellini, ever possessive, loitered around the set whenever she was working. (Persistent rumours that linked Masina and Basehart romantically began here.)

Giulietta introduced Fellini to both Basehart and Quinn. He'd seen and admired Basehart in *Fourteen Hours*, where he played a potential suicide on the ledge of a building. After casting him as Il Matto, he told the actor: 'If you did what you did in *Fourteen Hours*, you can do anything.' With the arrogant Quinn, however, there was no rapport. Today, Quinn claims that, after *Donne perdute*, Fellini pestered him to appear in 'something about a strongman and a half-witted girl', but in fact Fellini still leaned towards casting an unknown. He tested some real strongmen, but none was convincing. Meanwhile, Quinn had accepted the title role – his first – in *Attila*, with Sophia Loren. Just before shooting, Ingrid Bergman invited him to dinner, after which she and Rossellini screened *I vitelloni*. 'Thunderstruck', as he put it, Quinn immediately volunteered to play Zampano, and Fellini, convinced at last that the Neorealist road of non-professional actors led in this case only to disaster, and aware that the choice of a Hollywood star would mollify de Laurentiis and Ponti, accepted.

It was not a happy collaboration. No love is lost between Fellini and Quinn even today, and the director, whose remarks about him were never warm, has become increasingly dismissive. Today he'll only say, enigmatically, that he chose him 'for his shoes', and that Quinn is 'the kind of actor who enables a director to make a great picture' – placing any credit for *La strada*'s success where he feels it belongs. Quinn, however, rightly acknowledges that the film changed his career.

Production manager Luigi Giacosi calls it 'without any shadow of a doubt the most strenuous and troublesome film of my entire lengthy career in the cinema'. The first scenes were shot in a derelict convent of the Poor Clares at Bagnoregio. The weather was miserable and unreliable. At Ovindoli, where they went to shoot the snow scenes, the snow perversely failed to appear, so thirty sacks of plaster were laid down on borrowed bedsheets.

Fellini was ruthless in getting his shots, and manipulated people shamelessly to do so. The stunt man doubling Basehart on the high wire was expecting a telegram about his pregnant wife. Giacosi received one, advising she was in labour, but, following Fellini's lead, pocketed it, as he did the second, saying he had a son. When he delivered the cables after the stunt, the man wept – understandably. In the same scenes, Fellini needed the crowd to remain in place all day. When they became restive, he ordered Rossi to shout at an assistant:

'Get the rooms ready for Toto and Sophia Loren.' Eager to see the biggest stars of Italian cinema, nobody left.

Fellini's communication skills were tested severely on *La strada* since neither he nor Masina spoke much English and Basehart and Quinn no Italian. Everyone played in his or her own language and Fellini worked in gesture and mime. This was less of a drawback than it seemed since, by 1953, he had developed the technique that was to be his trademark.

Of his methods, Elia Kazan was both incredulous and disapproving. 'He did what would be intolerable for a stage director come to films (me). He talked through each take, in fact yelled at the actors. "No; there, stop, turn, look at her, *look* at her. See how sad she is, see her tears? Oh, the poor wretch! You want to comfort her? Don't turn away; go to her. Ah, she doesn't want you, does she? What? Go to her anyway!" And so on. That's how he's able . . . to use performers from many countries. He does part of the acting for the actors.'

Kazan didn't take into account the fact that Fellini had grown up with the dubbing system, a product of noisy Italian studios, polyglot casts and, during the war, bad sound-recording equipment or none at all. By *La strada*, talking through a take was integral to Fellini's method. 'My way of making a film prohibits my using even one metre of the original soundtrack,' he says. 'It's a Tower of Babel: voices of every nationality, dialects, prayers, voices which recite numbers instead of giving cues, voices which at my suggestion tell what they had eaten the night before.' He was derisive about Hollywood's obsession with authentic sound, typified by Stanley Kramer, who halted location shooting in an Italian village on *The Secret of Santa Vittoria* in 1968 while his crew located an extraneous noise – eggs frying in a nearby house. An army could march through a Fellini film and disturb no one.

Fellini lets actors say almost anything they like, provided their expression is convincing. He particularly favours counting out loud, since it helps pinpoint an instant in the speech where he wants a different reaction. 'Go back to "27",' he'll tell an actor, 'but this time, smile.'

The soundtrack is assembled later, at leisure, with new lines written to fit the final cut. In the sixties and seventies Rome-based writers like Anthony Burgess readily created English dialogue synchronisable to the lip movements of films whose principals spoke Italian, Spanish, French and German, often all on the same film, and faded stars like Edmund Purdom and Anthony Steel, retired in Rome, were happy to record it.

The track recorded during production was kept only as a guide to dubbing, but connoisseurs treasured the tapes. 'Fellini's guide tracks should be made public,' says John Francis Lane, 'as one conserves early sketches of paintings or drafts of novels.' Fellini himself speaks of them with equal lyricism. 'The answer print still has the flavour of the adventure of making the film – a train that passed, a baby that cried, a window that opened. I remember the people who were with me on location. I remember the trip. I would like to retain these memories. Once they put the clean, new track on it, it's like a father seeing his little girl wearing lipstick for the first time.'

Shortly after shooting began on *La strada*, Giulietta injured her ankle and the production was closed down. When it recommenced the schedule was totally dislocated. Otello Martelli had a prior commitment and was replaced on camera, uncredited, by Carlo Carlini. Worse, *Attila* was shooting by this time under Pietro Francisci and Quinn, who played the Hun chief in an elaborate fake beard and Oriental make-up, was forced to divide his time between the two films.

'I found myself getting up at three thirty am,' he says. 'In the dark of night I'd drive out from Rome . . . and at dawn we'd start shooting, getting precisely the bleak early morning light that, I soon discovered, Fellini had anyway planned to use in the film. At around ten thirty am I'd jump into my car and go tearing off to the *Attila* set, where I'd frequently work until ten or so at night. This schedule accounted for the haggard look I had in both films, a look that was perfect for Zampano but scarcely OK for Attila the Hun.'

As on every Fellini film, money ran out. Quinn, not above inflating his importance to the films in which he plays – he also claims to have discovered Sophia Loren – says it was he who asked de Laurentiis, also *Attila*'s producer, to advance enough to finish the film. Fellini recalls that *he* went to Dino and Ponti, and was told that he had nothing to worry about – provided he agreed to direct some pick-ups on *Attila* which Francisci had neglected to shoot. By all accounts, he did so.

Toto and Sophia Loren may not have visited the set of *La strada*, but Fellini did have guests who would prove more important than either to his career. One was Brunello Rondi, a writer and critic who immediately impressed Fellini with his sympathy and intellect. Rondi gets a credit as 'Artistic Collaborator', an acknowledgement he was to receive on a number of Fellini films for services as script doctor, on-set dialogue writer, confidant and friend. Fellini was in awe of Rondi's intelligence. In November 1961 he recorded a dream in which he and Rondi are taking an examination at night in a de Chirico-like square in front of a church. Federico doesn't know his subject and sweats like a comic-book character with embarrassment at his ignorance while Rondi sits complacently under a street light, having breezed through the questions.

With him, Rondi brought a filmstruck Jesuit priest, Angelo Arpa, destined to become the Church's unofficial ambassador to the film business. Already friendly with Rossellini, for whom he would produce the 1960 *Era notte a Roma/A Night in Rome*, Arpa had Vatican connections which Fellini could, and would, use, though he always found him slightly pompous, and parodied him in *Toby Dammit* as the priest/producer of the 'first Catholic western'.

Shooting finished in May 1954 and *La strada* was edited and scored during the summer. Fellini suggested a theme of Corelli for the tune Il Matto plays to Gelsomina and which she adopts as her own but, during editing, Rota gave Fellini a few sheets of hand-ruled music paper with a tune marked simply with the direction '*Tranquillo*', and said off-handedly: 'Do you want this?' It was Gelsomina's theme, soon to become one of the most famous of all film themes. The first recording alone sold two million copies.

De Laurentiis and Ponti entered *La strada* in the Venice festival, where it was screened on 11 September to an indifferent, even hostile reception. The most eagerly awaited film that year was *Senso*, Visconti's love story of a nineteenth-century Venetian countess and a young officer, starring Farley Granger and Alida Valli. At Italian festivals, it was usual for a claque of the director's friends and colleagues to barrack other films and applaud their own. Fellini's people had been vociferous at Visconti's screening and the rival group reciprocated at the awards ceremony that ended the festival.

It was already obvious that the jury wasn't disposed that year to honour anything radical or inventive. Although entries included Kurosawa's *Seven Samurai*, Mizoguchi's *Sansho Dayu* and Kazan's *On the Waterfront*, not to mention the Visconti and Fellini films, the Golden Lion went to a lavishly over-produced version of *Romeo and Juliet* by Renato Castellani with an all-British cast led by Laurence Harvey.

Next, four Silver Lions were awarded to, with diminishing degrees of enthusiasm from the audience, the Kurosawa, Mizoguchi and Kazan films, and finally, to *La strada*, with nothing for *Senso* at all. While Fellini was accepting his award, Visconti's assistant Franco Zeffirelli began blowing a whistle, which Moraldo Rossi took away from him after a struggle. The Fellini party stormed out of the Palazzo del Cinema. A young Parisian critic with ambitions to direct, Dominique

Delouche, who was covering the festival for a small French magazine, left in their wake. 'Fellini looked pale,' he recalled, 'and Giulietta was in tears.' Delouche approached them as they walked towards the Excelsior Hotel just opposite the Palazzo and, in faltering Italian, praised *La strada* and deplored the Visconti group's outburst. An appreciative Fellini told him to stay in touch.

14   A Bitter Harvest: *Il bidone*

'Reality distorts!'
Fellini in 1970

In the summer of 1955, Nastri d'Argento were awarded to *Romeo and Juliet* and *La strada* (Best Film, Best Director), but also to *Senso*. Visconti wasn't mollified. He wrote to Maria Callas that 'the satisfaction . . . has been compromised somewhat by the hypocrisy of the jury which assigned [the Best Director prize] also to Fellini and Renato Castellani'.

By then, *La strada* had already begun to win the fame that would make Fellini's – and Giulietta's – reputation. It was Gelsomina, however, whom most people talked about. A Gelsomina Club was started in Naples and Giulietta was bombarded with letters. Women wrote to say their husbands were as cruel as Zampano but that she had persuaded them to look for the good inside. Children quoted the parable of the stone as if it were a well-loved fairy story.

La strada was sold to America, the first Fellini film to be so. Its success meant the Fellinis could spend some money. Among the new suburbs mushrooming around Rome, the most fashionable was Parioli, and they bought a modern apartment on the fifth floor of a new building at via Archimede 141. Though the address marked Fellini as a material success, the apartment with its marble floors and *faux*-antique furniture was dull, even bourgeois. He imposed his visual signature with upholstery in sea-green, now a favourite colour (despite his complaints that it reminded him of the spring around Rimini), but only its bookshelves, where works on theatre jostled with travellers' tales and books on the occult, hinted at the complexities of his character.

Shrewdly, de Laurentiis, like Rossellini, saw that the way to Fellini's heart was through a car, and offered him a new one as a gift. After he made his choice, Fellini rang Richard Basehart to invite him for a drive. 'I expected to see him in a Ferrari, or Mercedes. But when I looked out the window he was sitting in a Chevrolet convertible.' Even more than the modern apartment, the slick black imported gas-guzzler signified that Fellini had arrived.

De Laurentiis pressured Fellini to capitalise on *La strada*'s success with something similar, ideally with Giulietta reprising Gelsomina: 'Gelsomina on a Bicycle', for example. 'I had scores of offers,' Fellini complained. 'To make *Il bidone*, which I was then planning? No. They didn't realise that in *La strada* I had already said all I wanted to say about Gelsomina. They all wanted Gelsomina. I could have earned a fortune selling her name to doll manufacturers, to sweet firms; even Walt Disney wanted to make an animated cartoon about her. I could have lived on Gelsomina for twenty years! Why this insistence on sequels? Have they so little imagination?'

What Fellini didn't articulate was his dismay and jealousy over Giulietta's success. The familiar competitiveness reappeared and he distanced himself both from Masina, professionally, and from the idea of a sequel. Instead he began planning an autobiographical story, picking up the life of Moraldo Rubini after *I vitelloni*.

With Pinelli and Flaiano, he spent the early months of 1954 working on an extended treatment. *Moraldo in città/Moraldo in the City* was the fullest expression yet of Fellini's desire, even need, to turn his own life into film. Virtually plotless, it's a thinly fictionalised retelling of his adventures with Garrone and Geleng, the abortive attempts at caricaturing and window decoration, encounters with a con man, here called Ricci, his affair with and engagement to Andreina, and the second affair, harder to substantiate, with Signora Contini. The climax is a wild party that develops into a sort of orgy, after which Moraldo considers returning home. He goes to the edge of Rome, but is persuaded to return by the smile of a beautiful girl which carries the promise of his later success.

Fellini had every intention of shooting *Moraldo* and even agreed to the magazine *Cinema* publishing the treatment in four parts from August to December 1954, a promotional device he'd used before, but the film was never made. Though he could hardly anticipate the acclaim *La strada* would earn him the following year, culminating in an Academy Award, nor its astounding commercial success – in New York alone it would run for three years – Fellini could see that his career had taken a new direction.

In the light of these changes, *Moraldo* looked parochial, thin and, worse, derivative. As well, it lacked the mysticism, eccentricity and fantasy that had driven *La strada*. It was too Neorealist, celebrating Little People, emphasising struggle and disappointment, and ending on a note of socialist hope. And, above all, Fellini had no desire to return to Neorealism.

Fellini has described how he was sitting in a café in the village of Ovindoli, where he shot the snow scenes of *La strada*, when he noticed a man in his fifties staring at him as he ate his soup. Sensing that he wanted to talk, he invited him over. The man confided that he was a swindler, travelling around remote villages selling worthless fabric as 'pure English wool'. Fellini said this incident inspired *Il bidone*, but the fact that such a hawker appears briefly in a café in *La strada*, trying to sell clothes from a suitcase to the tart Rosa before Zampano calls her to his table – 'Such wool!' she says, fingering a coat. 'That's what I'd like' – hints that he might once again, as he would do with Cabiria from *Lo sceicco bianco*, have seen that a minor character in one film could be recycled as the star of a later one.

Fellini had met plenty of doubtful salesmen and outright con men, both in Rimini and in his early days in Rome. One of them, nicknamed 'Lupaccio', had tried to enlist him in a scheme to sell fake diamonds to the film stars he interviewed. In Lombardy slang, such cheap crooks are *bidonisti*, from *bidone*, an empty can or drum. The script Fellini wrote with Pinelli to replace *Moraldo* focused on three such lovable rogues, swindling the rich, pompous and greedy while remaining decent and good-hearted. A sub-plot involved a wife who, having lost her husband, travelled around country fairs with her children, selling suspect goods.

This conception didn't outlive a few meetings with typical thieves at the Canova. Clearly these were not Robin Hoods but cynical villains who cheated one another as readily as they did their victims. Fellini and Pinelli were close to dropping the project altogether but, with some help from Flaiano and Brunello Rondi, they revised the script until it matched more closely the real Italy of 1954.

As the new story opens, Carlo, Roberto and Augusto are about to pull a con they've worked a score of times. Dressed as 'Monsignor de Filippi', his priest secretary and their chauffeur, they sweep up to a remote farmhouse and announce to a pair of beady-eyed sisters that they're seeking the body of a murdered man buried on the farm during the war. Almost in passing, Augusto drops the information that the man, a thief killed by his confederate, was interred with a substantial treasure. This, of course, belongs to the sisters, though it can't be handed over immediately because, on his deathbed, the murderer asked that 500 masses be said for his soul, and masses cost money. The sisters eagerly sell their cows for 425,000 lire, and receive in return a box of worthless trinkets.

The rest of the film trod the same line between scorn of the marks' stupidity and half-admiration of the con men's skill, with the final come-uppance of their leader, Augusto, offering the cathartic satisfaction of true tragedy. Fellini submitted the script to de Laurentiis at the end of 1954 and was astonished when he turned it down. Dino, as usual, had shrewd commercial reasons. The story was cynical and depressing when the prevailing mood in Italy was optimistic, humourless when people needed laughs, and almost entirely male at a time when everyone demanded beautiful women. As well, it set out to be a crime film but deepened and darkened into something far less trivial. In Dino's experience, audiences cheated of their expectations tended to be resentful. Also, *La strada* had done well in the suburbs and the country but relatively less well in the cities. If, as he suspected, Fellini was a director for ordinary people rather than, like Visconti, for the carriage trade, they wouldn't welcome a film about three city wiseguys who travelled the country swindling honest farmers.

Other companies were no more enthusiastic, though Goffredo Lombardo of Titanus finally put up the funding, with help from French Pathé. The price was a two-film contract.

By this time, Giulietta had been cast as Carlo's wife, Iris. The circumstances under which this happened are shadowy. Masina will say only: 'I asked Federico to let me make it; he didn't want to.' The commercial value of her name may have outweighed Fellini's resistance, though his resentment was to surface again later.

Franco Fabrizi was excellent casting for the flashy Roberto, a failed crooner, always coming on to showgirls and prostitutes, and Richard Basehart for Carlo, nicknamed 'Picasso' because of his artistic pretensions. Roberto is conscienceless, but Carlo is troubled by guilt and increasingly unable to hide the reality of his work from Iris, while Augusto, who has a grown-up daughter he seldom sees, hangs on mainly in the hope of a major score that will get him into the big time.

To play Augusto, Lombardo, with an eye on his Pathé partners, recommended a French star. He urged Fellini to see Jules Dassin's edgy crime drama *Du rififi chez les hommes/Rififi*. Both Pierre Fresnay and Jean Servais, who played tough old crooks, would, he felt, be ideal. When *Il bidone* had been a comedy, Fellini visualised Sordi, Aldo Fabrizi and Peppino de Filippo as the swindlers. Now his mind ran towards someone more dangerous, and, according to the legend, he suggested Humphrey Bogart, whose wolfish face reminded him, he said, of Lupaccio.

The story that Bogart was asked to play Augusto but couldn't do so because of illness has passed unexamined into the record, even though his cancer of the oesophagus wasn't diagnosed until early in 1956, by which time the film was finished. Tullio Pinelli doesn't remember that he was ever approached and Fellini has since said a number of times that he disliked Bogart, who looks 'pissed off from the beginning of the film to the end'.

Instead, Fellini hired Broderick Crawford. The burly actor had served his time in vaudeville and in supporting roles before winning fame on Broadway as the retarded Lenny in the play of Steinbeck's *Of Mice and Men*, then taking a Best Actor Oscar for his role as political demagogue Willie Stark in *All the King's Men*. Since then, he'd had a success as a millionaire junkman lobbying Congress in *Born Yesterday*, the high point of a career about to plunge downhill. Traditionally Fellini chose him on the basis of a poster for *All the King's Men* which he'd noticed, half torn down, in piazza Mazzini. At the time, he hadn't seen Elia Kazan's movie nor, it seems, any film of Crawford. The poster was enough. 'What a huge, magnificent face Broderick Crawford had! Those little eyes sunk in those fat cheeks seemed to be looking at you from behind a wall, like two holes in a partition. He had the same dry, wolfish face as Lupaccio, a face desperate with the knowledge that he would end badly.' Fellini was supposedly unaware that Crawford, then forty-four, was just emerging from hospital after one of many cures for alcoholism, but since Lombardo wrote into the contract elaborate directions on what the actor could and couldn't drink, it's clear that the matter was discussed.

After the 'buried treasure' score, the gang's backer, 'Baron' Vargas, conceives another con, this time trading on the post-war housing shortage. Claiming to be bureaucrats allocating new apartments, the trio visit a shanty town in the shadow of the Felice aqueduct. The locals, including a husky, moustached man named Ettore Bevilacqua, who would become Fellini's driver, masseur and bodyguard for the next thirty years, jostle to hand over their savings as down payments.

Augusto takes his gang to a New Year's Eve party thrown by Rinaldo, a slick drug dealer who drives a Cadillac and lives in Parioli. (Fellini gave him a modern apartment in via Archimede not far from his own.) The party, in which Fellini cast real *bidonisti*, including the originals of Augusto and Vargas, features an amateur strip-tease and a dance by a voluptuous girl in a strapless black evening dress – both to appear later in *La dolce vita*.

Augusto vainly begs Rinaldo to help him, asking to be set up in a loan office or even to become his secretary. The more successful man is contemptuous, and when Augusto is humiliated by Roberto, who's caught pocketing a gold cigarette lighter, and Picasso, who tries to sell Rinaldo a fake painting, he resignedly leads them back on the road again, this time working a scam with some trashy overcoats.

Crossing piazza del Popolo, Augusto runs into his daughter Patrizia. They meet the next day but the reconciliation ends in disaster when he's spotted at a cinema by one of his victims and dragged away humiliatingly by police while Patrizia looks on. A year later, he gets out of jail and goes straight to the Canova. Everyone he knows has disappeared. A stranger says Roberto is in Milan, and when he calls on Picasso, Iris sends him away. He's forced to don his monsignor outfit once more and go out with the buried treasure scam, this time with three strangers. They successfully con a farmer who's been saving to buy an ox for his two daughters, one of whom can't walk. As they leave, the paralysed girl asks Augusto for a blessing. He mouths his usual platitudes but the girl brushes them aside. She has no complaints. She feels like a queen, she says, able to work on her embroidery while the rest of the family slave. Shamed by her intelligence and lack of self-pity, Augusto tries to cheat his confederates and hold back the money for Patrizia. Enraged, the three beat him up and shove him over a cliff.

Crawford stuck to mineral water for a day or two after his arrival in Rome but when the crew moved in April 1955 to the town of Marino for the start of shooting, he stumbled on a wine festival in Castelli Romani and gloriously slaked his thirst. Searchers found him two days later, sleeping it off under a tree. After this, 'Brod' was never sober. Fellini was thrown back on techniques used by Rossellini to extract performances from amateurs. Dialogue was written on cards and pinned to furniture or trees. When the star was too drunk to take his cue, an assistant out of frame prodded him with a stick, just as Rossellini had cued actors on *Stromboli* with strings tied to their toes.

Like most alcoholics, Brod existed for part of the time in a private world, chatting with unseen companions, lapsing into sudden depressions. Forgetting where he was, he'd order a production assistant to go out for Turkish cigarettes, directing her to a shop on Manhattan's 14th Street. On one occasion, with Giulietta within hearing, the recently divorced actor advised Fellini loudly and at length never to get married. On another, Fellini, who still spoke almost no English, tried to convey in French that he wanted him to get out of the car and smoke – *fumer*. Instead Crawford alighted, lay down under a tree and began to cry – *pleurer*. But however much he raged, Fellini was filing away all of his behaviour, some of which would surface in the role played by Terence Stamp as the burned-out star in *Toby Dammit*.

Among the new additions to Fellini's team on *Il bidone* was Dominique Delouche. A friendship had developed since the young critic approached him after *La strada*'s hostile reception at Venice. For months he angled for a job but it wasn't until 15 May that he received a cable: '*Carissimo* excuse long silence but I waited until I had the news that you desire. I started the film fifteen days ago and invite you to come to Rome Monday 23rd. I await you and as soon as you arrive ring me at home after nine pm . . . I embrace you and wait with joy . . . ' There was no contract. Fellini simply told him to turn up. When he did so, Delouche, who had little film experience, found himself cast less as assistant-director than as companion and confidant.

'In France the role of assistant is very precise. You know exactly what you're supposed to do. And I was in an odd position. I spoke very little Italian and though everyone was very kind I sensed they didn't know what I was doing there either. Gradually I became aware that Fellini saw me as a sort of medium, a kind of lucky charm. I was well educated – better educated than him – and I came from a different social class. I was very timid, very well brought up – too well brought up. I worked – of course I worked – but I spent more time driving with Fellini in his car, discussing the film, discussing all sorts of things.'

The possibility that he might be both more and less than a helper was telegraphed on the first day. As Fellini, unshaven but tanned, elegantly dressed in a tartan waistcoat with gold buttons, drove him to Marino in his Chevrolet, Delouche noticed an object dangling above the windscreen. An ear of wheat had been bound up with a doll of pink felt and a chilli pepper. 'Don't touch that,' Fellini warned. 'It's a fetish.' A breath of wind from Gambettola blew through the car.

Delouche's confusion grew as he met the crew. 'My position was astonishing to the rest of the group. I was very privileged. On the first day, Fellini told me to use *voi* with him, addressing him in the intimate voice. In France at the time this was almost unheard of with one's master. Everyone on his team was nice to me. They invited me out and were very kind. I'm not saying there was no natural friendliness in this but I came to see a lot of them did so because they thought I had some power.'

The possibility that Fellini might be sexually drawn to him was clearly in Delouche's mind. 'We made an odd couple. Some people said we were like Hadrian and Antinous,* though it wasn't like that. If you want to ask the question, there was nothing homosexual between us. But there was a mutual fascination that was very strange.'

The friendship between Fellini and Delouche was the first of a series of 'white marriages' the director contracted with attractive, sensitive, younger men, often – though not always – homosexuals. He would court them, charm them, dazzle them with his connections and his reputation. Significantly, the Delouche relationship follows the definitive separation from Rossellini, who, Fellini told the American press in his limping English, was making a film in India 'alone . . . I think he most full of life,' he went on dolefully, 'of human feeling; we have right to expect wonderful things.'

One of the best descriptions of Fellini's methods of emotional seduction is by Terence Stamp. In 1967, after being summoned to Rome for costume fittings with Piero Tosi for *Toby Dammit*, Stamp, a famous tearaway even in the laid-back sixties, told Fellini he wanted to go to London for a few days.

'"I needa you here, Terencino Francobollo," the great maestro from Rimini wailed. "Why dis off back in Londra? You 'ave a mistress that cannot wait, hot for your body? Why you must be a *piccione*, everything is 'ere. This is Roma, the Eternal City. You stay. What you need? Piero buy you clothes. I buy you pasta. *Calma, stai qui.* I get to know you. You getta to know me – *Conosci? Va bene?*" . . .'* Stamp concluded: 'What Fellini actually meant when he said: "You get to know me" was: "You get to fall in love with me", which is tantamount to what he demands of his actors. It wasn't hard. I caved in.'

When shooting on *Il bidone* finished on 16 July, Crawford had confounded everyone by staying upright and almost lucid. Equally astonishing, he was to work in films and even on stage for another thirty years.

Lombardo, certain that the film was a prizewinner, was eager to get it into competition at the 16th Venice Festival, which closed in forty days. Fellini moved into the Titanus studios, still known under the name of their pre-war owner, Michele Scalera, and with two teams of

*Antinous was the emperor's handsome young lover. Fellini later cast English actor Martin Potter in *Satyricon* because of his resemblance to statues of Antinous.

*The addition of the diminutive *-ino* is typical of Fellini. *Francobollo* = stamp, as in postage stamp. *Piccione* = pigeon.

editors, one under Giuseppe Vari, the other led by his confidant, the intellectual Mario Serandrei, got to work editing the interlocking stories of Augusto, Picasso and Roberto into shape.

Nobody is more skilful than Fellini in closing his films on an ambiguous, evocative note, and the ending of *Il bidone* which, like that of *Il miracolo*, needed to suggest a moral change in a character's nature, was the first film to show this skill. As Augusto claws his way to the road, two women and three children are walking past, loaded with brush. One of the women sings a plaintive, wordless song. Augusto calls after them: 'Stop. I'm coming with you', but they don't hear him. He bows his head and dies.

Fellini agonised over his choices, and finally shot three versions. In the first, the screen simply faded to black on the corpse; the Neorealists would, he knew, love it. In the second, a surrealistic coda worthy of Buñuel (and the one favoured by the intellectual Serandrei – which counted for a lot, since he'd worked with Visconti and was credited by some with having coined the term 'Neorealist'), a peasant child stops by Augusto and tells him: 'I can't do anything for you now, but nothing is lost. Who knows if in millions of years we won't meet again?'

It was the third Fellini elected to use, a scene that frankly defies analysis, and represents the first unequivocal sign that Fellini had transcended Neorealism. The camera backs away from the brink, and a breeze out of nowhere blows leaves over Augusto's body. Their rustle and the sound of the wind blend into a lonely flute picking up the peasant woman's song as she and the others disappear around a bend in the road. Life goes on. And perhaps Augusto has somehow found absolution. The shots are orchestrated movingly with the overall imagery of the film. The Italy roamed by the *bidonisti* is barren. Its bare earth produces nothing except the fake treasure and the bones of the supposedly murdered thief. In this context the sheaves of brush cut by the women suggest a harvest, thin and bitter but better than nothing.

The first cut of *Il bidone* ran over two and a half hours, and Fellini, in tribute to Crawford's performance, truncated the roles of Picasso and Roberto, losing them after the second act to concentrate on Augusto. The version hurriedly mixed on 5 September and delivered to Venice in time for screening on 9 September, the penultimate day of the festival, ran 113 minutes.

Fellini had trimmed the party, removing scenes outside in via Archimede at midnight on New Year's Eve, when Italians traditionally toss debris out the window. More ruthless had been his cuts to the secondary roles, especially those of the women. The conclusion of Irene Cefaro's much-publicised strip-tease at the party was gone, a sop to the censors. So had most of Mara Werlen's appearance as the English dancer Maggie, Augusto's mistress. Nobody suffered more in the editing than Giulietta, whose role was reduced to a couple of minor scenes. Those who knew of Fellini's rivalry with collaborators, even his own wife, were unsurprised.

Lombardo and Fellini retained their enthusiasm for the film even in its shorter version, which, by emphasising the rural winter setting and the world of low-life itinerants, underlined its resemblances to *La strada*. Neither, however, had taken into account the reservoir of hostility stored up since Fellini's skirmish with Visconti the previous year. The Venice screening was a disaster, among the worst in Fellini's career. Throughout the second part, people trickled out. Those who stayed were restive. Fellini had been seated next to a minister more impressed with the film's flashy cars than the plot. From time to time he whispered questions: Wasn't Valentina Cortese the wife of Basehart? Why hadn't he used her instead of Masina? Could Fellini introduce him to Cortese?

Outside, a storm raged across the Lido di Venezia, but its fury was nothing to the anger of Fellini and Pinelli. When Dreyer's *Ordet* won the Golden Lion and *Il bidone* received not even a consolation prize, both swore never to show another film in competition at Venice, a vow they kept for twenty years.

The critical reaction in Italy was mixed, but nowhere more hostile than among the Neorealists. Predictably, Guido Aristarco, the movement's most committed left-wing critic, spared it least. 'The *crepuscolismo* of Fellini, the recurrent themes of his philosophy and symbolism, his occasional step into reality (only in part nourished by realistic elements and attitudes), once again hint at insincerity,' he raged. 'The film seems almost prefabricated, containing exactly the same components as other films . . . '

Worse than the bad reviews, however, from Lombardo's viewpoint, was the lack of foreign interest. No American distributor was interested, and though it did show in France and briefly in Britain (as *The Swindlers*), *Il bidone* would remain unreleased in the US until 1964.*

**Il bidone has become one of the most elusive of Fellini's films, and the one with most alternative versions. The shortest is that released in the US, which runs for 92 minutes. In Britain it was seen at 113 minutes, Pathé's French cut runs for 108 minutes and Italian versions vary from 96 to 102 minutes.

15   Gelsomina's Fallen Sister: *Le notti di Cabiria*

'Fellini loves squalor. It never ages'
Bernardino Zapponi

When Fellini offered *Le notti di Cabiria* to Goffredo Lombardo, the producer is said to have whined: 'First a film about layabouts and fags. Then the story of a crooked gypsy and a half-wit. Then some swindlers. You wanted to make a film about mad women, and now it's prostitutes. Who's next?' To which Fellini replied: 'Producers.'

It's a good story, but probably apocryphal. A meeting did take place at Titanus's via Margutta office in the wake of *Il bidone*'s disastrous release but the conversation was more prosaic. Lombardo greeted him with the film's balance sheet on his desk, then reviewed the whole history of Titanus, implying that Fellini had personally set out to destroy the company. The upshot was that they tore up their two-film contract, leaving Fellini once again without a backer.

At the end of *Il bidone*, Fellini had four projects in development. He described them to Dominique Delouche during one of his wild drives to Ostia. One was a script about the efforts of a bigamist to keep all of his fifteen families content. He wanted Gérard Philipe to star. The second, *The Little Sister*, was based on the life of a nineteenth-century nun named Serenella who'd earned a reputation as a miracle-worker. After she'd miraculously kept herself and four sisters alive without food throughout a snowbound winter, she was summoned to Rome. 'We see her tiny in St Peter's,' explained Fellini, at his most anti-clerical, 'a contrast between the two faces of the Church, the majestic columns of the temple and the little wildflower of grace. After some days in Rome the flower is crushed; she is murdered.'

The third, and most promising, project was the 'film about a mad woman' he'd tried to sell Lombardo. *Le libere donne di Magliano/The Free Women of Magliano* was adapted from the diary of Mario Tobino about his experiences as a young doctor in a mental hospital near

Viareggio between 1949 and 1951. Insanity always fascinated Fellini. He'd never forgotten his boyhood glimpse of the Down's Syndrome child staring down from a farm window. 'I have often been called mad,' he says. 'Madness is an abnormality, so I don't take that as an insult. There is a kind of individuality in insanity that is rare in the so-called sane world.'

In the seventies Fellini took Liliana Betti on a tour of the Monte Mario mental hospital, telling her that, for him, the place confirmed the essential logic of existence; if even the insane lived by a set of natural rules, then there was hope for us all. *Le libere donne di Magliano* would have explored this concept, as a sensation-seeking young doctor, Roberto, exiled to the hospital, is won over to the magic reality of the patients' lives.

Fellini visited Magliano, still run by Tobino and, passing as a doctor, spent two weeks exploring. He never forgot the cells where patients who refused clothes were confined naked with only piles of seaweed to cover themselves. The image resonated with his childhood memory of the girl in Rimini's fish market handling eels, which he recalls in *Intervista*, and is probably the basis of the fantasy in *Giulietta degli spiriti* of a voluptuous woman entwined with a slick black python-like serpent. In particular a girl with Down's Syndrome caught his attention. Though she'd been born deaf and blind, she somehow sensed him and began to 'yelp with joy, almost like a little dog's cry of welcome. My presence, my "shadow", my warmth, were able to communicate something to her.'

After three months, however, Fellini abandoned the Magliano project. At the time he didn't explain, but later he admitted: 'I sensed the danger. It is very difficult to remain on one side of the border when you have once come so close to it.'

His fourth proposal was for a vehicle for Giulietta, a film about the life of a Roman prostitute. *Le notti di Cabiria* had existed since Fellini cast her as Cabiria in *Lo sceicco bianco*, but the character came more clearly into focus during *Il bidone*. Filming the apartment swindle near the Felice aqueduct, the crew encountered a prostitute named Wanda who lived in a water cistern. Martelli laid camera tracks right up to her door and she angrily ordered them away. Fellini won her with one of the box lunches provided for the crew. Through her, he came to know something of a prostitute's life.

Meanwhile, Pinelli read a newspaper story about the discovery of a woman's head in Lake Albano, and took the clipping to Fellini. 'We imagined the story of a prostitute full of human warmth who had a need for love,' Pinelli says, 'but who always fell in love with pimps who try to kill her. The film starts with an individual who throws her in the Tiber and ends with a type who wants to throw her in the lake at Castel Gandolfo.'

Flaiano was brought in, and the three went off for a two-week stay in a hotel. Remembering the idea rejected by Magnani for *Amore* of a star who takes home a street hooker, only to abandon her when his girlfriend returns, Pinelli suggested they insert it here. Fellini resisted, though the episode would become one of the most memorable in the film.

Even though Fellini interviewed prostitutes and threw what one report called 'a wine and pasta dinner' for 'former owners of brothels', who told 'tragic tales of prostitutes' ('Many wept like babies,' he recalled, presumably tongue in cheek), the script which he began to circulate early in 1956 had only the most general relationship to realism. Tracing Masina's character back to the fantasy of *La strada*, he called her 'Gelsomina's fallen sister'.

After *Il bidone*, finding money for *Le notti di Cabiria* proved almost impossible. Fellini contemplated setting up his own company, but found no banks willing to invest. In his embroidered retelling, the search for a financier was nightmarish. The first they saw was about to be jailed, the second was broke. Two more thought the subject too risky. Another was a horse-owner on a losing streak. Richard Basehart tried to interest a rich American in the film but the man's references to his pal 'Lucky' Luciano caused a certain disquiet. Fellini borrowed from banks but the sums became dangerously large without any sign of serious interest from a producer. He was forced, against Giulietta's advice and that of many friends, into the all-too-welcoming arms of de Laurentiis, who was about to break with Ponti and wanted to stock his stable. Dino read a few pages of the treatment by the light of passing cars as he and Fellini drove in the countryside outside Rome and announced that he would make it, even if he had to invest his own money. The best way to overturn Fellini's doubts has always been to mirror his own enthusiasm for a project, and he succumbed. The deal was signed in April 1956, by which time Dino and his brother Luigi were independent. It gave Fellini 25 per cent of the profits – if he agreed to make five films. For the second his share rose to 50 per cent, but the small print disclosed that the gains of one could be wiped out by the losses of another. Given that fewer than two films out of ten make a substantial profit, this almost guaranteed that Fellini would never earn real money.

The Fellini who believed in omens might have seen this contract as a bad one, since almost immediately he was plagued by disasters. In May, the face of Montgomery Clift, whom he had planned to cast as Roberto in *Le libere donne di Magliano*, was mutilated in a car accident. Then, on 31 May, Urbano Fellini died of a heart attack.

Fellini has always been reticent about his father's death, but the following year, with Pinelli, he wrote an extended treatment called *Viaggio con Anita/Journey with Anita* which hints broadly at reportage. Its hero is Guido, a successful writer living in Rome with his wife Gianna. The marriage isn't going well. Gianna – rightly – suspects Guido of infidelity. 'After seven years of marriage, this concealed suspiciousness of Gianna has become a continuing part of their relationship. Young still and without children, they live together in a conventionally formal way. Their love has become tired.' Guido's sister rings from his home town, Fano, with news of their father's heart attack. Not imagining it is serious, Guido decides to drive home for a few days, taking his mistress Anita, 'a young woman with a rich, full body', whom he easily persuades to join him in his Cadillac.

Uniquely among Fellini's projects, *Viaggio con Anita* is highly sensual. Guido and Anita make love along the way, and participate in a peasant ritual where young girls roll naked in the dewy grass on the night of St Giovanni (Midsummer Night). Anita also shows off her body to some roadworkers, who stop dynamiting to watch. Disturbed by her sensuality, Guido starts pointless arguments. After one, he abandons her by the side of the road, only to return and find her unconcernedly waiting for him, an incident he'd recycle in *La dolce vita*.

They arrive in Fano to find Guido's father much worse, though strong enough to chide his son for making the long trip. 'Now why did you go to all the trouble of coming?' he frets. This is Guido's opportunity to make contact with the father he hasn't seen for years, but he's too shy to do so in the presence of the doctor and other members of the family. Upset, he goes to a café, where news is brought to him of his father's sudden death after another attack.

Parking Anita in a hotel, Guido concentrates on arrangements for the funeral. Afterwards, embarrassed by his neglect, he offers a tour of the town. He tries to show her a secret entrance to the cathedral he used as a boy, but the door has been bricked up. Next day, he finds she's left her hotel. A letter explains she's leaving him because their love won't work. Disconsolate, Guido goes to visit his father's grave, and finds Anita kneeling in front of it. Both are glad of a chance to talk once more, but it's clear the relationship is finished.

Guido gives up Anita for the same reason that he leaves his roots. Both are 'sterile', stifling his development as an artist. 'Guido has a marital commitment', explains the treatment in justification, 'that he cannot throw over for Anita, just as he has a world of culture, art, consciousness and even anguish that he can't abandon for a world, however marvellous, that must now be left behind.' His sadness as he leaves Anita waving at the entrance of the cemetery and drives away 'is not without a shimmer of joy'.

Fellini made no serious attempt to disguise the real setting of *Viaggio con Anita*, just as its jaded marriage reflected his relationship with Giulietta. So violent were their disagreements during the filming of *Cabiria* that Giulietta decided the only way their marriage could be preserved was never to work with Fellini again, and the Venice screening of *Il bidone* in September 1955 was disrupted by stories that she had run off with Richard Basehart, with whose name hers had been romantically linked. While Fellini was occupied shooting *La dolce vita* in 1959, Masina went to Germany and Poland to make a film for Victor Vicas, *Jons und Erdme*. Basehart, who would leave Cortese in June 1960, after nine years of marriage, was again her co-star.

After his father's funeral, Fellini returned to Rome and assembled a crew for *Cabiria*. Some were old friends, like Nino Rota and Dominique Delouche. As cameraman, Fellini chose Aldo Tonti, who'd shot *Il miracolo* and Visconti's *Ossessione*. He knew Tonti worked quickly, which put less strain on the actors. As production secretary Fellini hired Riccardo, who'd spent some time at the Centro Sperimentale and was hoping to move from acting into direction. Since Dino had installed Luigi as executive producer, one suspects Fellini took on Riccardo as a joke on de Laurentiis.

Another and more important newcomer to the court was Pier Paolo Pasolini, a young poet from Friuli whose first novel, *Ragazzi di vita*, about the street kids of Rome, had been a scandalous success. They met by chance at the Canova and the two became good friends. Pasolini was typical of the new collaborators Fellini collected as he moved away from realism, men who could remedy his lack of visual and intellectual sophistication. Because of his homosexuality and his taste for the 'rough trade' who cruised the Termini station, Pasolini and his companion, the craggy young Sergio Citti, could introduce Fellini to the sort of arrogant street-wise Rome Cabiria would know. Fellini hired them to give the dialogue of *Cabiria* an authentic flavour.

Maria Cecciara is a cheap and victimised Roman street whore

nicknamed 'Cabiria' by her friends after the hapless Sicilian maiden of Pastrone's 1913 drama, harried from the eruption of Etna to Carthaginian slavery, only to end up in the arena before being rescued by her patrician lover Fulvio. In an ironic nod to this genealogy, the modern Cabiria works among the ruins of ancient Rome, on its Passeggiata Archeologica, the Archaeological Walk near the Baths of Caracalla.* That Maria accepts this nickname says a lot about Fellini's conception of her character. Driven by hope, she prides herself most on her ability to survive. 'She resembles me very much,' Masina says. 'Naïve, aggressive and finally very strong.'

Visually, *Cabiria* was the joint creation of Fellini and another new collaborator, Piero Gherardi. Eleven years older than Fellini, self-taught in painting as well as in architecture, which he'd practised in Rome during the war, Gherardi, equally expert in décor and costumes, had an encyclopedic knowledge of both, and of Rome. They were improbable colleagues. Gherardi, elegant and vague (he'd been known to get out of his morning bath and absent-mindedly return to bed), belonged to the Florentine aristocracy and was, properly, a count. At any one time during the seventies he owned seven or eight houses, including two in his native Tuscany and another in Bangkok. His squirearchical roots were never far from the surface. Interviewed in London in 1969 while he was designing *The White Devil* for the National Theatre, Gherardi startled critic Eric Rhode by suggesting they hire horses and go riding in Regent's Park.

In character, however, Fellini and Gherardi were well matched. Both enjoyed late-night walks around Rome. They researched *Cabiria* on a series of such strolls, Gherardi leading Fellini to exactly the building or background he wanted. 'Even before a film has taken complete form in my head,' Fellini said, 'he has understood what it's about, the atmosphere, and comes up with ideas and sketches which clarify things for me.' Between them they built a 'look' for Cabiria, a queasy combination of the coquettish and practical that reflected her character and improved on that created for *Lo sceicco bianco*. To a ratty fur jacket and a collapsible umbrella from which she's inseparable, they added a black skirt and striped T-shirt, bobby-socks and a plastic rain hat. For the rest of the prostitutes, Gherardi simply borrowed clothes from the whores who acted as 'technical advisers'.

---

*Mayor Salvatore Rebecchini protested about Fellini using an area whose image he'd been trying to improve.

Cabiria lives on the desolate outskirts of Rome. The lover with whom she's seen romping along the uninviting edge of the Tiber at the opening (played by Franco Fabrizi, in a cameo) steals her purse and shoves her in the river. None of the people who see her drowning feel like risking their lives or ruining their clothes. Only some boys who swim like seals and enjoy defying the river can be bothered to fish her out. When she's revived, Cabiria is less grateful than humiliated and angry. The incident triggers intimations of mortality. 'What if I'd died?' she muses.

Ever hopeful, she's soon back at her pitch. Marisa, who's bought a car, takes her downtown to the via Veneto, where the local whores scorn her frowsy outfit. She's wandering past the Kit Kat Club when film-star Alberto Lazzari comes out, arguing with his beautiful blonde girlfriend Jessy. (Dipping into his Cinecittà days and hoping to bolster the cast with some stars, Fellini cast ageing matinée idol Amadeo Nazzari as the star.) As Jessy storms away in a jealous rage, he quixotically invites Cabiria into his big De Soto and on to the next club, after which he takes her home to his luxury villa. The butler dishes up lobster and champagne, but before she can eat anything a contrite Jessy arrives and Cabiria is locked in the bathroom with a whimpering puppy until morning, when Lazzari sneaks her out.

A group of the girls plan to visit a famous shrine, where the uncle of one, a crippled pimp and drug dealer, hopes to be cured. Cabiria accompanies them, but the church is a circus, with people selling food and candles outside, and banks of priests dispensing instant absolution from improvised confessionals. When the uncle tries to walk at the height of the ceremony he simply collapses.

Disconsolate, she drifts into a music hall where a magician-hypnotist has convinced a group of men they're shipwrecked – a favourite Fellini metaphor. He lures her up as a subject. Under hypnosis she confesses her ambition to marry and have children. He introduces her to an imaginary lover, Oscar, and Cabiria is so girlishly struck with this fantasy that the audience roars in derision. When she wakes up she remembers nothing. After the show she's accosted by a man who says his name is Oscar. A number of dates convince an incredulous Cabiria that he wants to marry her and open a shop. Dazed, she sells her house and withdraws her savings from the bank.

For Oscar, Fellini had wanted Leopoldo Trieste, but Marceau Film, the Parisian company on which Dino had laid off part of his investment, demanded one of the stars be French. Dominique Delouche went through a casting directory with Fellini. 'When he saw the picture of

François Périer, he simply said "Voilà!", scribbled a moustache on the photograph, ripped the page out of the book and pinned it on the wall.'

Périer, whose career included Cocteau's *Orphée*, was not everyone's idea of a Roman con man. Later, Fellini rationalised his decision by insisting his flabby neck, reminiscent of Robespierre's, shrieked unreliability, but as with all casting choices made against his instinctive judgement, this one was wrong. Périer is the film's major disappointment. Since the actor didn't project ingratiating menace, Fellini had to impose it. He had him wait for his first date with Cabiria while chewing a toothpick, and, in a much-quoted example of subliminal characterisation, instructed him during their last meal to put on a pair of dark glasses; since these are associated in all Fellini's films with unreliability, the sense of betrayal is instant and pointed.

Oscar takes Cabiria to Castel Gandolfo to celebrate their engagement. She shows him the 400,000 lire, everything she owns. But as they walk through woods to the cliff overlooking the sea and watch the sunset, she understands at last that Oscar has lured her there to kill her. Her despair is more crushing than any violence. She drops the money, falls on the ground and shrieks hopelessly: 'Kill me. I don't want to live.' Shamed and disconcerted, Oscar grabs the purse and flees. When night comes, Cabiria picks herself up and walks back to the road. A group of young tourists are singing to an accordion as they walk and cycle home. One of them says: 'Good evening.' Looking out at the audience – an effect Fellini uses more than any other director except Chaplin – Cabiria smiles through her tears.

Though de Laurentiis was preoccupied with his first big production, *War and Peace*, with its international cast of Henry Fonda, Audrey Hepburn and Anita Ekberg, he made frequent visits to Fellini's set. Delouche recalls him as 'Napoleonic': short, silk-suited, slick-haired, magnetic, the eyes behind his glinting spectacles fixed, like the emperor's, on world domination, at least of the cinema.

On their nocturnal walks Fellini and Gherardi often met Mario Tirabassi, an ascetic ex-nurse from Orvieto who'd devoted himself to Rome's poor. Fellini was astonished when Tirabassi lifted a sewer grating to reveal an old woman sheltering under it, or introduced him to derelicts who slept in the corridors of a palace on the elegant via del Corso, sneaking out before the tenants arrived. A new sequence was written in, featuring a character called only The Man with the Sack. Cabiria, wandering across waste ground near the via Appia Antica in another disconsolate dawn, meets him handing out food to people living in pits where old quarries have caved in. She recognises one of them, an ex-prostitute nicknamed 'The Atomic Bomb', whose fate is a reminder of the need to provide for her own future. The man drives Cabiria back into the city and she shyly reveals to him what she's told to nobody else — her real name.

Fellini started shooting on 9 July 1956, but didn't finish until 1 October, with a long delay, as on *La strada*, after Giulietta suffered a fall, this time fracturing her knee. Even more punishing were their arguments as he bullied her into what he was determined would be a major performance. As the schedule lengthened, Tonti had to leave, and Otello Martelli shot the last three weeks, without credit.

The film was ready for screening in March. Meanwhile, *La strada*, bought by Trans-Lux for US distribution for $65,000, had been nominated for an Oscar, so in April Fellini, with Giulietta, Pinelli and de Laurentiis, made his first visit to the United States. He'd never liked travelling and this journey reminded him why. The size and stridency of American life, and especially of its film industry, muted for all time his Hollywood-founded enthusiasm.

In 1956, for the first time the Oscar for Best Foreign Film was voted by members rather than being bestowed as an Honorary Award. On 26 March, *La strada* received it at the Pantages Theater in Hollywood. Dino accepted the statuette from Academy president George Seaton. Fellini may have 'smiled from the audience', as some reports claim, but in later accounts he never mentioned the presence of de Laurentiis.

After the Oscars the Fellinis were subjected to the nine days' celebrity reserved for overnight successes. Fellini fanned it by being offhand about the awards in general and his own in particular. 'Nice show, a big show,' he said, 'but I don't know if the prizes are right.' De Laurentiis's PR man quickly exploited their fame. The press were given a fabricated story that Giulietta wanted only one thing in Hollywood: Clark Gable's autograph. The day after the ceremony, he told Fellini he'd managed to get him on TV. The programme would have an Italian theme. Someone would show the right way to boil spaghetti. Fellini was then to demonstrate how to kiss a lady's hand.

Some of the interest was, however, professional. One producer approached Fellini to direct a western with an Italian star,* for which he was supposedly prepared to pay $250,000 on signature. He left

---

*This is not as improbable as it sounds. English director Silvio Narizzano made the western *Blue* after his success with *Georgy Girl*, and Serge Bourguignon, most languid of New Wave directors, directed a Buñuel-esque horse opera called *The Reward*. Least likely of all, Akira Kurosawa was signed for *The Day Custer Fell*, with Toshiro Mifune as Chief Crazy Horse.

Fellini alone with contract, cheque and pen, like a disgraced subaltern offered the Only Honourable Way Out, but he resisted temptation. Later, Fellini liked to claim he'd slipped out of it by stipulating that all the horses in the film must be of the wooden rocking variety. This is obviously an invention, though no more so than the fee: in 1957 even Hollywood's top directors got less than £100,000. That he declined the deal is undoubted. The publicist was aghast. 'Maybe in Italy it's being a poet to turn down this sort of money,' he said, 'but if you do it in the states you're a — .' (Fellini deleted the expletive.)

He was more attracted by an offer from the production group of Burt Lancaster, Harold Hecht and James Hill. Hecht/Hill/Lancaster, which would make *The Bachelor Party* and *Sweet Smell of Success*, both unfashionably cynical films in the Neorealist style, offered Fellini a three-month contract to travel America and find a subject. He'd then be free to go home – a possibility they hardly contemplated – or shoot a film. Fellini paints Hecht/Hill/Lancaster as parodies of American prodigality. When he bumped his knee on the corner of a desk, they tried to take him to hospital. When he complained that his liver was reacting badly to the food, he was offered a private plane to fly to Texas for treatment.

Ideas for films, including one about American women, weren't hard to find, and they were warm to all of them, but after four weeks Fellini fell prey to terminal homesickness. He spent hours on the phone to Rome, just chatting. America had dramatised how little he knew about the life of Americans, and if he didn't understand the minutiae of daily existence he couldn't film there. 'How would I know what a Boston taxi driver would wear at home on Sunday afternoon? How does a cashier from a Bronx drugstore dress, smile, or react to a man insulting her? I'd be lost a thousand times a day, and that would be fatal, because cinematography . . . needs an absolute mastery, complete control of everything and everyone – the female star's underwear, the leading man's moustache, the way matches are placed on the left side of the table.'

Less apparent in his resistance, however, was his dwindling enthusiasm for Neorealism. His interest lay in a new and more fantastic cinema, and no American producer was likely to let him experiment with his money. Fellini went home early. He was seen off by a producer he called 'Serenella' (the same name as the simple nun of *The Little Sister*), whom he'd identified, from the fact that he owned two Las Vegas hotels, as a Mafioso, but who would start to cry when he hummed Gelsomina's theme. Serenella gave him the name and address of a certain deported Sicilian-American. Should Fellini ever have problems, he had merely to visit this man, kiss him on his behalf and whisper his request. Fellini never took him up on the invitation – but 'a couple of times, in the face of great difficulty getting a film started, I found myself looking at the note that the worthy, sinister old man gave me.'

With Fellini now an Oscar-winner, de Laurentiis delayed releasing *Cabiria* until after May 1957, by which time it would have been screened at Cannes. François Truffaut, then a critic, called it 'the most eagerly awaited film of the festival' and 'the only one to arouse much comment at the exits'. Until three in the morning, he said, Giulietta's role was 'the subject of violent argument'. She duly won the Palme d'Or for best actress, for the second time.

Many at Cannes thought the film, at 110 minutes, too long by half an hour. It would be cut soon after, but not for reasons of length. For general release, it needed an Italian censorship certificate. That this was not immediately issued came as no surprise. Before filming was finished, the authorities had voiced doubts, and demanded – in vain – that Fellini agree in writing to alter anything they might find offensive. Ostensibly the problem was the theme of prostitution. Fellini argued, rightly, that, except for a few references to 'customers' by the girls and one shot where a truckdriver picks up Cabiria, their job is never mentioned, nor is there either sex or nudity in the film. When the cloud refused to disappear, it became clear the real problem was the Church. Priests in *Cabiria* are shown either as greedy, like the merchandisers of spurious cures at the shrine, or holy fools, like Brother Giovanni, a beaming simpleton who meets Cabiria in the wasteland near her home, dispenses homilies about the holiness of matrimony, then wanders away.

The film was saved with the help of the Jesuit Angelo Arpa. Fellini took a print to Genoa, where Arpa had arranged a screening for Giuseppe Siri, the Church's youngest cardinal. The only private screening-room Fellini could find was in the city's seedy dockland. Anxious to create the right impression, he arrived the day before, scoured antique shops for a chair appropriate for a prince of the Church and found a sort of throne, almost a couch, with gold piping and a large red cushion. Siri and Arpa arrived in a chauffeured Mercedes after midnight, entered the cinema and closed the door. Fellini remained outside. For all he knew, he said later, Siri slept through the whole thing, waking only when Arpa pointed out a troublesome scene. When they emerged, the cardinal said simply: 'Poor Cabiria, we ought to do something for her.' A phone call was made and all objections, secular and religious, evaporated; all, that is, save one. Fellini was asked to drop The Man with the Sack.

Asked by whom is not clear; nor is the reason. Charity in Italy is traditionally the Church's prerogative and it was assumed that some Vatican bureaucrat was galled to see a layman doing its job. Tirabassi, however, was recognised as a unique case. The Pope had even offered him a car to help him in his work. Might the whole story then be an invention by the Machiavellian de Laurentiis, who, with or without Fellini's collusion, shortened the film for purely commercial reasons?

In October 1957 Fellini went on a second trip to America, this time to promote *Cabiria*. Arriving in New York, he was met by a friend (probably the producer Ilya Lopert, who had bought the US rights). Remembering Fellini's enthusiasm for shows, he'd acquired two rare tickets for *My Fair Lady*. They went to the theatre but the director impulsively gave the seats to a couple on the street and demanded a tour of midtown Manhattan instead. They spent four hours exploring the then relatively innocent Times Square and West 42nd Street. The place and its inhabitants fascinated Fellini, but by midnight he'd had enough.

The friend had meanwhile noticed that an East Side cinema was showing a double bill of *Lo sceicco bianco* and *I vitelloni*, and Fellini demanded they take a cab there immediately. The last screening was over, but Fellini gave the projectionist $40 to run the films again. 'So, on Federico's first night in the United States, he sat up until nearly five am in an empty theatre watching, in utter rapture, two of his own movies.'

One of the few people who knew of Fellini's visit was the critic Gideon Bachmann, who interviewed him on his programme on WBAI radio. Fascinated by the flamboyant Bachmann, who drove a Jeep and was usually accompanied by a beautiful girl, Fellini asked to meet some young film-makers. Bachmann drove him all over the Bronx and Brooklyn, introducing him to the New York underground. What Fellini learned is doubtful, since he knew, by his own admission, only two phrases in English, one of which, 'Follow that cab!', he used every time Bachmann took off in his Jeep.

Critic and director established an instant rapport. They shared an enthusiasm for comic strips, and when Fellini mentioned Lee Falk's *Mandrake* (which, he claimed, in the first appearance of the *Flash Gordon* myth, to have redrawn for *420* in 1938), Bachmann borrowed some rare and valuable early *Mandrake* panels from dealer Mark Ricci. When Bachmann asked for them back, Fellini said carelessly that he'd thrown them out.

As promotion for *Cabiria*, the visit was a flop. Nobody knew who Fellini was, and Bachmann's interview is almost the sole evidence that it took place, though their friendship would lead to Bachmann becoming part of his circle in the sixties. Fellini had no desire to prolong his visit, but the previous June the Directors' Guild of America, through some string-pulling by Sicilian-born Frank Capra, Hollywood's mouthpiece in appeals for Italo-American friendship, had voted him an award for special artistic merit. He flew to Los Angeles for the dinner, where John Ford presented the statuette after a speech of which the guest of honour, since Ford tended to mumble, understood almost nothing. The event was to become a metaphor for Fellini's troubled relationship with Hollywood.

16   'You come, you shoot everyone, you run away': *La dolce vita*

'When Fellini was once asked if he cared to make a jungle documentary, he replied "Yes, but in Rome"'
Robert Neville

On a trip to Padua in the summer of 1960, Fellini missed his train. There wasn't another until late afternoon so he took a stroll round the old city. The sun was hot, the streets empty. Even the dogs were asleep. Finding himself in a square, Fellini strolled towards the shadowed interior of a church. At the door, he stopped, chilled. Pinned there was a version of the black-edged poster-like notice used in Italy to announce a death. It urged: 'Pray for the salvation of the soul of public sinner Federico Fellini'. 'I felt as if I had died,' he said.

Twentieth Century–Fox's 1954 decision to shoot *Three Coins in the Fountain* in Rome turned the Italian capital, with its reliable weather, cheap facilities and cheaper labour, into Hollywood on the Tiber. It also put it on the tourist map. Egged on by Frank Sinatra crooning the film's theme, Americans flocked to toss coins into the ornate Fontana di Trevi, supposedly guaranteeing they'd return. *Cleopatra* and *Ben-Hur* soon took the road to Rome pioneered by *Quo Vadis?* a decade before. MGM boasted: '1960 is the Year of *Ben-Hur*', but 1960, in Europe at least, was really the year of *La dolce vita*. It thrust every other film into the shade. Fellini became at the same time a household name and a public enemy. 'Everywhere in Italy,' he said, shaken, '*La dolce vita* was like a bomb.'

After his return from America at the end of 1957, Fellini was pressed by de Laurentiis to name the second film of their five-picture deal. The public which, following *La strada*, clamoured for more of Gelsomina now demanded the return of Cabiria. Pinelli, Flaiano and Fellini had already written such a screenplay, *Fortunella*, about a waif who lives with a junk dealer on the banks of the Tiber while flirting with a protective intellectual called the Professor and harbouring fantasies of aristocratic ancestry. It might easily be seen as the continuation of Cabiria's story, or even a remake of *La strada*.

Fellini, however, was in no hurry to plunge into another film with Giulietta. He was even less happy about her *Cabiria* success than he had been about the acclaim she won for *La strada*. In a self-protective coup that satisfied Dino, the public and Giulietta, while keeping the Masina phenomenon at arm's length, he sold *Fortunella* to de Laurentiis as a vehicle for her on the understanding that someone else would direct it.

Released in 1958, *Fortunella* should have had all the qualities of a Fellini film. It was shot by Tonti, with a score by Rota, and Sordi played the junkman. Dino, however, made the mistake of choosing Neapolitan playwright Eduardo de Filippo to direct it. A disciplinarian with a penchant for realism and a writer's reverence for the text, de Filippo, the cast complained, stifled them. They were used to Fellini's flexible methods, evoked well by American critic Stanley Kaufmann at the time of *Il bidone*. 'The crowd of waiting extras, playing cards, chatting, drinking wine, staring into space, is a gallery of faces chosen with a Daumier eye. In the midst of the early morning hubbub, as carpenters hammer, electricians yell, lights glare on and off, trucks rumble, Fellini calls for a chair and a small table. With chaos eddying around him, the huge man hunches over a typewriter, rewriting the pages that he plans to shoot today . . . He rehearses and shoots a short scene over and over. One can see that he is not only refining the performances and camera movement, he is also refining his ideas of what it is that he wants from a scene.' By contrast, de Filippo's pacing is deliberate, the playing leaden and, without Fellini's light touch, Giulietta's mannerisms appear trite and contrived.

Persuaded now that Fellini deserved better than remakes, Dino offered him his most prestigious properties. These included Pär Lagerkvist's novel *Barabbas*, with Anthony Quinn as the thief pardoned by the mob so that Christ could die. Fellini wasn't enthusiastic, least of all about Quinn. Boccaccio's *Decameron*, *Don Quixote* with Jacques Tati, *Casanova's Memoirs* with Orson Welles as the great lover in old age, and Flaiano's original screenplay *A Martian in Rome* were all discussed. Some newspapers announced that Fellini was preparing the Casanova story but in fact he finally decided against all Dino's ideas. He preferred, he said, something autobiographical. Perhaps, he thought, he'd been hasty in discarding *Moraldo in città*. In the spring he met Pinelli and Flaiano at Caffè Rosati on the via Veneto to talk the project through again.

Moraldo as it stood, they agreed, was still too old-fashioned, and too much like a sequel to *I vitelloni*. Also, the culture Fellini had known in the late thirties, a *vie de bohème* with penniless artists starving in garrets, no longer existed. They contemplated showing Moraldo's life from eighteen to forty, but couldn't think of an actor with the emotional range to play it. Anyway, Fellini preferred that the Moraldo of the new film should reflect modern Italy, a nation rushing from post-war poverty to sixties greed.

These were the *anni caldi*, the hot years. The centrist Christian Democrats were under siege from the Communists, and Italian society bubbled yeastily in the burgeoning economy. To represent this Italy, amoral and greedy, he needed a cynical middle-aged version of Moraldo, 'already a little hardened, already at the edge of shipwreck' – like Fellini himself.

Emotional problems preoccupied Fellini. Urbano's death had dramatised how poorly he communicated with those close to him. 'One of the most pressing problems,' he confided to Gideon Bachmann, '[is] the terrible difficulty people have in talking to each other – the old problem of communication, the desperate anguish to be *with*, the desire to have a real, authentic relationship with another person . . . It may be that I'll change, but for now I'm completely absorbed in this problem – maybe because I have not yet solved it in my private life.'

These considerations dictated what was taken from *Moraldo in città* and *Viaggio con Anita* for the new script. Salvaged from the latter were the character of a Rome-based writer trapped in an unhappy relationship who's attracted to a sensual, flamboyant woman, and incidents like Guido abandoning Anita on the road. From *Moraldo* he kept the visit by his father, the wild party and the final affirmation of life in the smile of a beautiful girl. Recycled scripts, however, made up only half of the new film. The rest was headlines. 'Every episode in the film was suggested by a Roman scandal of the last ten years,' wrote *Time* magazine, 'and Fellini has somehow persuaded hundreds of Roman whores, faggots, screen queens, press agents, newsmen, artists, lawyers and even some authentic aristocrats to play themselves – or revolting caricatures of themselves.'

Rome buzzed with such scandals in 1958. Eugenio Pacelli, Pope Pius XII, a desiccated snob from the Roman 'black aristocracy', as Italy called those whose titles were conferred not by the crown but the Church, died in October. The capital's night life, limited for decades on the grounds that '*Il Papa* doesn't like it', reappeared. Rome loosened its belt and let down its hair, helped by an influx of American film people. US tax laws allowed US citizens to earn up to $20,000 a year overseas tax-free. Those who relocated permanently in Italy found the situation even sweeter. 'The highest [tax] anyone pays there is 25 per cent,' gloated Dick Basehart. 'A lot of people don't pay any tax at all.' Scores of dubious producers, second-rate directors, blacklisted writers and has-been actors moved to Rome, among them falling stars Rory Calhoun, George Nader, Edmund Purdom, Anthony Steel and Lex Barker. Barker, who went there in 1958 and built a modest career in European westerns, was typical. In *La dolce vita* he played, effectively, himself. 'Just think,' muses a cameraman, adjusting the actor's head the better to shoot his softening chin line as he sleeps off a binge in his sports car, 'he used to play Tarzan' – which Barker did, five times.

Government support for any film industry invariably attracts swindlers, and the Italian system of 'prizes' to encourage local producers was no different. 'Shady characters in small offices speculate on big names, counting on the prize money,' wrote William Weaver. 'They plan super-colossal productions; some of them are really made, others end only in a rain of unpaid bills and drawn-out Italian lawsuits.' These operators preyed on investors drawn by the glamour of the movies, and were exploited in turn by starlets on the make, journalists, hoteliers and nightclub owners, a decayed aristocracy, a venal Church, graduates of the Centro Sperimentale eager for their chance to direct, and an underclass of waiters, servants, gigolos and whores.

Life in the Rome of 1958 was one long manoeuvre. Gossip, the principal currency, was traded on via Veneto, the reef where the bottom-feeders of the Roman night browsed. At the outdoor tables of the Café de Paris, Rosati, the Strega-Zeppa and (a favourite of film people) the Doney, conveniently next door to the Excelsior, journalists and photographers swapped notes and reported the news, or created it. Any fast-breaking story could be delivered by Vespa to scandal sheets like *Lo specchio* and *L'espresso*, close by. When his father comes to visit him on the Veneto in *La dolce vita*, Marcello points out his magazine's office, almost overhead.

During the summer of 1958 Fellini was often seen at the Doney, sipping espresso and taking notes as he watched photographers like Pierluigi Praturlon, Uberto Guidotti, Giancarlo Bonora and in particular Tazio Secchiaroli stalk their prey. Magazines offered only 3,000 lire for a straight shot, whereas famous pictures like that of an enraged Walter Chiari chasing Secchiaroli or the series shot on 15 August 1958 of a white-faced and furious Anthony Steel storming towards him were worth 200,000 lire. If no celebrity fist-fights occurred spontaneously, these men engineered them. Fellini was present at the supposed birth of this tradition on 14 August when, working for the first time in a pack, they ambushed ex-King Farouk of Egypt slouched in dark glasses and a camelhair overcoat outside the Café de Paris, flanked by beautiful girls. A couple of photographers provoked Farouk by exploding their flashes closer and closer. As he lost his temper, overturned the table and charged, the rest got their shots.

Flattered by Fellini's interest, the photographers described how they tracked, stalked and goaded their victims. 'We work like commandos,' Croscenko explained. 'You come, you shoot everyone, you run away.' And Secchiaroli boasted: 'I'm like a paratrooper. I don't take pictures – I make war.' The tales became more fanciful until even Secchiaroli was embarrassed. 'Stop inventing, you idiots,' he shouted. 'You're talking to an old hand at the game.' Fellini didn't know whether to be complimented or insulted. (Both Secchiaroli and Praturlon left journalism shortly after to become movie stills photographers for, among other directors, Fellini.)

Fellini didn't have to look far beyond tabloid headlines for the plot of *La dolce vita*. Pictures of a Christ statue being carried across Rome by helicopter had appeared in most papers on 1 May 1950. In June 1958, Secchiaroli grabbed the front pages with pictures of two teenage girls from Terni who claimed to have seen the Madonna. Fellini co-opted both incidents. So blatant was this poaching that when the Albergo Ambasciatori burned down that summer and four chambermaids leapt for their lives into via Liguria, newspapers announced that Fellini was already writing the incident into his film.

The most shrill of all headlines, however, were provided by the Montesi Case. In April 1953 the body of twenty-one-year-old Wilma Montesi was found on the beach near Ostia. She wore no shoes, stockings or underwear, and it was rumoured she'd overdosed at an orgy on the nearby Capocotta estate and been dumped on the beach, to drown in the incoming tide. The prime suspect was Piero Piccioni, son of Italy's then Foreign Minister. He was said to have tearfully confessed to Rome's Chief of Police, Francesco Polito, offering Wilma's underwear as evidence, but millionaire businessman Marchese Ugo Montagna allegedly persuaded Polito to burn the lingerie and forget the case.

No one denied Montesi's murder was eccentrically investigated. On the grounds that 1953 was an election year, Polito handed the case to the Political Department, which buried it. The Communists, however, refused to let the story die. Montesi, daughter of a carpenter and, according to the forensic evidence, a virgin, was portrayed as a working-class flower crushed beneath the decadent capitalist heel.

The case belatedly came to trial in 1957. Piccioni was charged with manslaughter, Montagna and Polito with aiding and abetting, and eight others with perjury, withholding evidence or perverting the course of justice. The press gave lurid coverage to tales of wild parties with drugs and strip-tease. The movie connections were a tasty bonus to the press. Montagna was a friend of Sophia Loren, while Piero Piccioni, who later became one of Italy's better film composers, had spent the day before Montesi's death driving Alida Valli to Sorrento. The court acquitted everyone, but memories were still fresh when Fellini started *La dolce vita*.

By the June of 1958 Fellini, Pinelli and Flaiano were full of ideas for the screenplay. The structure was vague, but all agreed it would deal in part with the via Veneto, cover seven days and nights in the life of Rome, and end, like many Fellini films, at the sea. Pinelli, initially doubtful, warmed to the boldness of the conception after Fellini told him: 'we must make a film like a Picasso sculpture; break the story into pieces, then put it back together according to our whim.'

Weeks scanning the headlines and hanging out on the Veneto had given Fellini a new vision of Rome. The city seemed to him millennial, poised on the edge of enormous change. 'Rome was gradually becoming the navel of a world sated with living in a new jazz age, waiting for the third world war, or for a miracle, or for the Martians.' Why did he decide at that moment to abandon his attachment to fantasy and surrealism in favour of a sensational and scandalous piece of tabloid cinema? He gave a clue in a remark he made to Liliana Betti years later. In 1959 he was just about to turn forty. 'You become a little less generous after the age of forty,' he told her. 'You start to think about death, about the sunset. You have to think about someday if the energy goes away. If you become sick. Or if the young, new directors come, and what you are doing is stupid. So you prepare a little corner of your brain where you will not be wounded.'

By mid-summer the trio were ready to start writing. As scenes were completed Fellini submitted them to friends for their advice. Collecting them at night in his black Mercedes, almost a mobile office, he'd drive for hours, wrangling over fine points. Pier Paolo Pasolini became an important confidant, though he dreaded these excursions because of Fellini's driving. 'He is totally unaware of the most elementary needs of the motor,' Liliana Betti confirmed. 'He drives along for dozens of kilometres in second gear, or else he abruptly switches to low gear while doing fifty kilometres in a car with manual transmission.' Said a shaken Pasolini: 'I've never seen a style of driving so easy to recognise.' Gherardi too was often summoned for these nocturnal trips. Allegedly they were scouting locations but mostly they talked. After a long discussion while they auditioned twenty villas as possible sites for the orgy, Fellini said: 'Look, it's useless, Piero. By now we've invented everything. Let's invent this one as well.'

Late in August, as the heat became stifling, Fellini, Pinelli and Flaiano metaphorically completed the journey of *La dolce vita* at the sea, checking into a Fregene hotel for the final polish. By September a first draft was ready for de Laurentiis. But the producer wasn't impressed. Flaiano wrote in his diary: 'He finds the story incoherent, false and pessimistic. The public, he says, desires at least a little hope and some entertainment.' The most sophisticated of the team, Flaiano didn't hide his contempt for Dino's catchpenny ideas or the world of commercial cinema. While Fellini tended to agree, he wasn't anxious to break with the producer. Counselling Flaiano to control his tongue, he negotiated a compromise. Three outside experts would be asked for their dispassionate assessments.

Critics Ivo Perilli, Gino Visentini and Luigi Chiarini read the script. All found it badly structured and too complex, though Chiarini, who'd directed the Centro Sperimentale and now ran the Venice Festival, felt it might be saved by the introduction of a character who didn't expire in despair like the rest. Fellini insists that he ignored these criticisms but it's indisputable that two long sequences, comprising an entire additional day in the scheme of the film, were later discarded after having been shot. One was a boat party in which Marcello, the heiress Maddalena, her father and a rich older woman writer named Dolores see a pretty young swimmer incinerated when a match falls into floating gasoline. After the disaster Marcello seeks out Dolores in her medieval tower by the sea and confesses his doubts and fears. They spend the night together and the next morning, encouraged by her self-discipline, he goes to a nearby restaurant to work on his novel. The scene that follows, his meeting with the innocent Paola, is all that Fellini retained from this long episode. With these cuts the film was, albeit marginally, lightened and simplified.

The first image of *La dolce vita*, of two helicopters flying by the ruined Felice aqueduct, exploits both the timelessness of Rome and its gaudy journalistic present. A gilded statue of Christ, twice life size, dangles under the first. The second carries journalist Marcello

Rubini and his photographer, 'Paparazzo'. Swooping over the raw new suburban sprawl of Rome, pursued by kids and watched by construction workers, they hover to chat with some girls sunbathing in bikinis on a roof in Parioli, Fellini's home, then deliver the statue to St Peter's.

Fellini cuts from the Vatican to an Asian face, the mask of a Siamese nightclub dancer. Stalking a prince and his bimbo, Marcello runs into bored heiress Maddalena, an old friend. Thrown out of the club, they pick up a prostitute and drive her to her home, where Maddalena reveals the evening's hidden agenda: she wants to make love in a whore's bed. Marcello obliges.

Like W. H. Auden, who diagnosed baroque *couture* as a symptom of social decay in *The Fall of Rome* ('Fantastic grow the evening gowns . . . '), Fellini saw women's fashions and their appearance in magazines like *Oggi* and *Europeo* as symptomatic of Rome's decadence. 'For *La dolce vita*, the first thing that happened that indicated what the picture would be was when I was looking at costumes – a certain kind of clothes that were geometric in shape. The *moda a sacco*. The first meeting between me and the picture came through that sack.'

Inspired not so much by the sack dress – none appears in the film – as by clothes that extended, distorted or disguised the body shape, Fellini told Gherardi at their preliminary design conference in September to evoke the more outrageous examples of *haute couture* as they appeared in the news magazines, flash-photoed on the catwalk. His satin ruffs and wind-catching hats combined maximum self-advertisement with minimum practicality. The moment when a girl in a tight dress and a wide-brimmed hat with a big white bow minces on to the nightclub dance floor to 'Ma, He's Making Eyes at Me' is the true beginning of *La dolce vita*.

Fellini always wanted Marcello Mastroianni for Moraldo. He'd known him since 1948, when he acted with Giulietta. After *I vitelloni*, Mastroianni had cabled Fellini to tell him that the film was like 'an X-ray of my life', the sort of gesture guaranteed to win his heart.

In 1958, Mastroianni was thirty-five, an ageing *jeune premier* whose good looks had led to type-casting as a cab driver, chauffeur and latterly a young doctor in hospital romances. Famously addicted to women and food, Mastroianni had ambled through his career. Even Suso Cecchi d'Amico, an admirer, called him 'lazy'. Luchino Visconti concurred. 'Mastroianni is a fellow who sees tagliatelle or spaghetti and completely forgets he is doing [a role]. He eats, and then he picks up [his character] again . . . It's the Italian side, a bit frivolous.'

The actor had just earned his first serious credentials with Visconti's *Le notti bianche*, a Dostoevsky adaptation tailored to him by Cecchi d'Amico, but he seemed, especially to de Laurentiis, an improbable and uncommercial choice. Why not Paul Newman, for example, who had shown interest? Fellini rejected Newman outright, probably because the thought of working with a Hollywood star alarmed him. Anyway, Mastroianni's air of vanity, moral flaccidity, decaying intelligence and fading beauty fitted his protagonist like a tailored tuxedo. 'Moraldo' became 'Marcello' in the script and nobody else was ever seriously considered for the role.

After his night with Maddalena, Marcello returns to his bleak EUR apartment to find his suicidal mistress, Emma, comatose after a drug overdose. At the hospital he's cringingly affectionate while her stomach is pumped out, but by early afternoon he's back on the carousel, trailing Hollywood star Sylvia Rank from the airport to her press conference.

Sylvia was played by Swedish actress Anita Ekberg, who'd built a fourth place in the 1951 Miss Universe contest into a flimsy movie career, sustained by a 102cm bust, 58cm waist, 94cm hips and a well-coached line in hot chat: 'What do you sleep in?' asked columnist Sidney Skolsky. She replied: 'A warm room, for preference.' Only a fortuitous last-minute invitation to replace Marilyn Monroe on Bob Hope's 1954 tour of US bases had kept her in the headlines.

Fellini, however, was smitten. When he'd seen her picture in an American magazine, his reaction (which he'd give to an airline baggage handler in *La dolce vita*) was: 'My God, don't ever let me meet her.' In the ample flesh she was even more striking. For the first time he'd found a real-life equivalent of the female giants of his adolescent imagination. He sketched her repeatedly, stressing melon breasts and fried-egg nipples. Her eyelashes and eyebrows are drawn with such ferocity that they explode beyond the margins of the face. The drawings have an element of dread. She inspired in Fellini 'the incredulity one has before creatures of exceptional height, like the giraffe or the elephant'.

With their careers in terminal decline, Ekberg and her husband, Anthony Steel, arrived in Rome. She was to play an unlikely Zenobia, Queen of Palmyra, in a cheap Italian/French/West German peplum called *Nel segno di Roma/Sign of the Gladiator*. Forever flirting, drinking, dancing barefoot till dawn and skirmishing jealously with Steel, who would divorce her in 1959, Ekberg was the photographers' best subject since Ava Gardner had lit up Rome while making *The*

Barefoot Contessa in 1957. When Anita cut her foot during a night-time walk staged for a magazine and bathed it in the Fontana di Trevi, Praturlon's pictures were seen world-wide.

In November 1958 Ekberg, with Ingrid Bergman and the rest of Rome's glitterati, attended the party at Rugantino's for American millionaire P. H. Vanderbilt, where Turkish dancer Aichi Nana performed an impromptu strip, ending in a writhing climax on coats laid over the tiled floor. Inspired by the headline *'La Turca Nuda'* and Secchiaroli's images of Nana, naked but for black panties, sprawled at the feet of her chic, expressionless audience in the glare of the flashguns, Fellini added the strip-tease that became *La dolce vita*'s most controversial scene.

Fellini never imagined anyone but Ekberg as Sylvia, though initially she didn't return his admiration. His dithyrambs about having seen her zooming round Rome in her red Mercedes convertible convinced her only that he wanted to sleep with her. When she asked for a script and Fellini, as usual, told her none existed, her suspicions hardened. 'This Fellini is mad,' she told her agent. She signed the contract anyway, but remained sceptical right up to the start of shooting.

Mastroianni also demanded a script. Flaiano silently handed him a thick manuscript. Every page was blank except one, on which Fellini had sketched an image from one of his dreams. Adrift in shark-infested waters in a tiny boat without oars, he notices that his penis is as big as a tree and uses it to row himself to safety. Mastroianni contemplated the *maestro* waving a giant prick at fascinated mermaids and didn't ask again.

Mastroianni and Ekberg met for the first time in February 1959, at a dinner given by Fellini on the roof garden of the Hôtel de la Ville. The actor's reception was frosty, the more so because he spoke no English. Later he told Fellini she reminded him of a Nazi soldier who'd arrested him during the war. But Fellini was spellbound. 'The idea of the film is inseparable from the idea of Anita Ekberg,' he said.

After dancing at a club in the ruins of the Baths of Caracalla, Sylvia and Marcello take a stroll, culminating in the scene that became the motif of *La dolce vita*, Ekberg in a black evening-dress wading in the Fontana di Trevi. Returning Sylvia to her hotel, Marcello is beaten up by her actor boyfriend, Robert, an incident his cameraman colleagues record with relish.

By chance, Marcello meets his intellectual friend Steiner, who urges him to take up serious writing again. Fellini originally based Steiner on his first friend in Rome, the journalist Luigi Garrone. He intended he should die, like Garrone, of cirrhosis, but reconsidered when Pinelli showed him a French report about a professor who, apparently without motive, clubbed his children to death and leapt from a fourth-floor window. Passing the story to Brunello Rondi, who was generating screenplay ideas, Fellini amplified it in the telling. He visualised the academic as wealthy and elegant, with a 'gorgeous apartment' where one felt 'the deep calm of family feelings'.

Steiner is a crucial character, even though he has only three scenes, one of them as a corpse. In the first, Marcello is spending a hot afternoon in EUR supervising an inane publicity shot of a horse and a model (after the photographer shoots the girl on a café table and asks: 'What next?', Marcello looks up from his magazine long enough to suggest: 'Now put the horse on the table') when he sees Steiner going into a bleakly modern church and follows him.

Steiner has come to borrow a Sanskrit grammar from the priest. 'I'm rather at home here,' he says smugly. He asks about Marcello's work, urging him to take up fiction again. Sitting at the organ, he ponders rupturing the reverent atmosphere with some jazz and vamps a few notes of Europop, then launches primly into Bach's Toccata and Fugue in D Minor. Marcello leaves, guiltily determined to reform.

The second scene is a party at the apartment of Steiner and his pretty young wife. Guests include a talkative writer played by Irish poet Desmond O'Grady ('He's written many important books,' Steiner murmurs), an English artist (Margherita Russo) ('You know her abstract paintings'), the poet Iris Tree (who recites one of her own poems) and an Indian singer.

A guest tapes the highbrow conversation. Playing it back, he runs into the next part of the tape, where Steiner has recorded natural sounds: wind in a forest, birds, a thunderstorm. Woken by the noise, his two children come into the room. Steiner tenderly puts them back to bed. In the third sequence Marcello is called to the same apartment after Steiner has killed the children, then shot himself. With his role model dead, he abandons himself to hedonism.

Fellini dithered for months over the casting of Steiner until only two candidates remained: Enrico Maria Salerno, whose voice he'd used for the commentary of *Un'agenzia matrimoniale* and to dub Basehart in *Il bidone*, and a Delouche suggestion, French actor Alain Cuny.

Cuny, deep-voiced, imposingly tall and dignified, was screen-tested exhaustively in Paris, down to a recitation of the dialogue from all three scenes. He didn't know Salerno was doing the same in Rome. After seeing both tests, Pasolini urged Fellini to choose Cuny, in part because of his height, which suited both Gherardi's high-ceilinged set and Steiner's Olympian detachment. 'He looks like a Gothic cathedral,' Pasolini said. In typical fashion, Fellini kidnapped the line. 'You are the true primitive; primitive as a Gothic steeple,' Iris Tree tells Steiner. 'You are so high our faint voices scarcely reach you.'

Cuny found Fellini agreeably undemanding. Except for suggesting 'Smile a little' when he played the organ, he left him in control of his performance, even allowing script changes. 'A phrase from the great French surrealist writer André Breton came to mind,' Cuny says. 'Breton said: "I am an amateur among professionals and a professional among amateurs." I suggested it as the sort of thing the character might say. Fellini agreed immediately and put it into the script.' It appears in the party scene, paraphrased as: 'I'm too serious to be a dilettante and too much of a dabbler to be a professional.'

Cuny invented an elaborate subtext for Steiner. He is, he believes, a closet homosexual – an idea Fellini was happy to take on board. 'This is a man in tatters,' Cuny expounds, 'a man totally broken; a man who's lost. He plays on the organ because he's incapable of playing with a woman. He robs his wife of hope in the cruellest possible way, by taking the children which he never wanted to give her in the first place – which he gave her without pleasure. He kills them, then immediately kills himself. Steiner is a criminal, a monster. There are probably many people in universities and many intellectuals like that.'

Steiner is solemn, well-mannered, almost saintly. Most reviewers decided he was *La dolce vita*'s sole honest man, a Diogenes who fell tragic victim of the soft life. One praised his 'angelic sweetness'. But Fellini has never liked or admired intellectuals, and even Cuny was unaware, and apparently remains so today, that Steiner, with his Sanskrit, his pompous guests mouthing Artspeak at its most glib, his self-congratulatory smile while playing the classic organ repertoire's most clichéd piece, is meant as a parody. In casting so stiff an actor in the role, Fellini wasn't dignifying Steiner but ridiculing him. 'In Rome, there are many such theatrical intellectuals,' Fellini said later. 'And not only Italians are this way. Look at Norman Mailer.' When Charles Thomas Samuels suggested Steiner would like to be thought an intellectual but isn't one, Fellini said tersely: 'So much the better for him.'

While he wrestles with his conflicting ambitions as artist and hack, Marcello is sent to cover two children outside Rome who've announced they've seen the Virgin Mary. With Emma and Paparazzo, he drives to the site, already a circus of TV crews, gawkers and the dying, carried there in the hope of a miraculous cure. A thoughtful priest rejects the 'miracle' as a fake but the crowds increase. A rainstorm drives them away, leaving only the dead, but belief is stubborn. Onlookers, Emma included, battle for a twig of the tree over which the children claimed they saw the Virgin hovering.

Marcello tries to work in a seaside café but is distracted by Paola, a teenage waitress whose simple pleasure in life seems to mock Rome's pursuit of gratification. With some fanfare, a search was launched to find someone sufficiently virginal for Paola. Radio and TV appearances and a newspaper campaign failed to turn up a girl who displayed, as Fellini demanded, the purity of an angel in an Umbrian fresco. In the best traditions of such stunts, he found Valeria Ciangottini at the home of a friend who invited him to dinner. She was his fourteen-year-old daughter.

On the Veneto, Marcello unexpectedly encounters his father, a retired champagne salesman who's come to Rome ostensibly to see him but actually to taste a little of the soft life. To play him, Fellini bypassed big names in favour of Annibale Ninchi, star of Carmine Gallone's 1937 pro-Mussolini *Scipione l'Africano*. Ninchi resembled Urbano Fellini and would play the same father figure in *Otto e mezzo*. At a nightclub they pick up showgirl Fanny. Marcello's father goes to her apartment but suffers a mild heart attack in her bed. Humiliated, he hurries home on the morning train, deaf to Marcello's appeals that he stay longer so they can talk.

An increasingly dispirited Marcello joins Maddalena at a party in a country palace. Remnants of once noble families wander through the crumbling estate, clowning, holding mock seances, talking of ghosts. Maddalena demonstrates the odd acoustic properties of one room: you can eavesdrop on what is said elsewhere. On this ethereal long-distance line Marcello spontaneously confides his affection for her, unaware that she's listening with another man, with whom she makes love while Marcello wanders the palace in search of her. In time he gives up and couples with a predatory American painter.

Abandoning his literary ambitions, Marcello becomes press agent for a second-rate movie star (Jacques Sernas, Ekberg's co-star in *Nel segno di Roma*). With a gang of people they break into a villa and celebrate the marriage annulment of Nadia. Watched by her ex-husband and new lover, she performs a strip-tease, after which Marcello, drunk, urges the rest to wilder excesses. They're interrupted by the house's owner, who orders them out.

In the dawn they walk to the beach, where fishermen have just dredged up a bloated sea creature. As the others contemplate it with fascinated revulsion, Marcello hears someone calling over the noise of the surf. Paola, the innocent girl he met at the seaside café, is waving to him across a stream that divides the beach, but he can neither reach her nor understand what she's saying. With an ambiguous gesture, of resignation or unconcern, he turns away and rejoins the party.

In 1959 Fellini paid a visit to the Cinecittà set of *Ben-Hur*, where he met novelist, classical scholar and screenwriter Gore Vidal. Imported by producer Sam Zimbalist to answer such technical questions as 'When a Roman sits down, what does he loosen?', Vidal feels he rescued the film by inserting a homosexual subtext which made explicable the enmity between Charlton Heston's Ben-Hur and Stephen Boyd's Messala. Approving the changes, Zimbalist warned Vidal: 'Don't tell Chuck. He'll freak', but both Boyd, who was gay, and Fellini, whose fascination with homosexuality would emerge fully for the first time in *La dolce vita*, spotted the hints and relished them. Fellini and 'Gorino' became friends.

Engaging as he found Vidal, Fellini was more impressed by the CinemaScope camera. Twentieth Century–Fox had pioneered the new screen size six years before, but its main use until then had been on epics and westerns. Fellini saw that the narrow viewpoint of Marcello's story could be expanded if he discarded the standard 1.33:1 ratio for the 2.55:1 of CinemaScope. Discussing the film with the London *Times*'s correspondent, he said: 'I saw it in this shape', and 'His hands,' reported the writer, 'carved a CinemaScope screen out of the air.'*

With 'Scope, Fellini was able to embed the incidents of the film in its larger and more important subject, Rome itself. He told Otello Martelli to abandon his wide-angle lenses and use mainly the longer 75mm, 100mm and occasionally 150mm lenses normally reserved for close-ups. These gave a shallow depth of field, throwing foreground and background out of focus. *La dolce vita* has no panoramas. The characters seem to carry their own private Romes around with them. When Marcello and Maddalena park in her Cadillac and chat about the city, his comment that 'Rome is a sort of jungle: warm, quiet, where you can hide yourself' would lose its impact were they not surrounded by the impenetrable Roman night. Though the film used more than 800 performers, eighty-six of them with speaking roles, the overall

---

*Since Fox owned the patents on CinemaScope, Fellini used Totalscope, a local and almost identical knock-off.

impression is of lone figures in empty landscapes. 'Fellini said that we should have the air of castaways on a raft,' said Mastroianni, 'going where they were driven by any puff of wind, totally abandoned.'

As de Laurentiis tells it, his greatest objections to the first screenplay centred on the character of Steiner. As a Neapolitan family man to whom nepotism was almost a religion – his brothers Luigi and Alfredo were his assistants, his wife Silvana Mangano appeared in almost all his films, while his daughter became his producer – he found infanticide abhorrent. But Fellini challenges his memory. Steiner didn't really emerge as a character until the later drafts. The problem, in his recollection, was de Laurentiis's imperial ambition, manifested in his obsession with stars. Not only did he favour Newman as Marcello, but he also saw Maurice Chevalier as Marcello's father, Barbara Stanwyck as Dolores and, as Steiner, Henry Fonda, who'd played Pierre in his *War and Peace*. In this courting of Hollywood, Fellini glimpsed the *folie de grandeur* that would destroy de Laurentiis thirty years later. He accused him of fancying himself a big-time international producer, like Sam Spiegel, the man behind *Lawrence of Arabia*. What stung Dino about the gibe was its proximity to the truth.

To Fellini's relief Stanwyck was unavailable, Fonda declined and Chevalier, though he accepted the role, later reneged, but the problems of finding actors for such a dark story remained a headache. Among those in contention were Enrico Maria Salerno, Peter Ustinov, Walter Pidgeon and novelist Elio Vittorini for Steiner, and Madeleine Fischer and Silvana Mangano to play Maddalena. Edwige Feuillère and Greer Garson were considered for Dolores, but Fellini, after a chance meeting in Rome, quixotically offered this part to Luise Rainer, the frail, pop-eyed Viennese actress who'd won two Oscars in the thirties for *The Good Earth* and *The Great Ziegfeld* but hadn't worked in twenty years.

Many roles were still uncast when the film started shooting. The small ones were easy, Fellini filling them, as usual, on impulse. For Sylvia's press conference he recruited Roman critics and journalists, including long-time friend John Francis Lane, improvising their questions on the set. Visiting Milan in search of a Maddalena, he heard young Elvis Presley imitator Adriano Celentano and cast him as the rock singer in the Caracalla Club. Polidor, a friend from the Fabrizi days, was given a routine in the Kit Kat nightclub sequence.

Among the people Fellini consulted in the early stages was Paris-based critic Lo Duca. Duca condensed the plot into a page and showed it to Pathé, who offered to invest, provided Fellini used some French actors. Dominique Delouche suggested Anouk Aimée for Maddalena and Magali Noël to play the showgirl Fanny. For the thankless role of Emma, Marcello's whining mistress, he cast Yvonne Furneaux, who, despite her adopted name, was born of English parents. Fellini was developing a penchant for horror-film performers. Like clowns and music-hall comics, they were unlikely to patronise him or scorn his lack of sophistication. Furneaux's only featured role had been in Hammer's 1959 remake of *The Mummy*. She displayed a considerable ability to cringe, flinch and moan, which Fellini exploited.

The choice of Luise Rainer soon backfired as she started rewriting Dolores to make her more sympathetic. She barraged Fellini with letters and cables from New York for six months. He would parody her in *Otto e mezzo* as the ageing actress played by Madeleine Lebeau who swans around Guido proclaiming: 'I *am* this character. I'm like her in life . . . in love. And that's why I'm so alone.' He grudgingly agreed to some changes, but in June 1959, at a party on Gherardi's reconstruction of via Veneto, Fellini, with some satisfaction, told Rainer that her entire role had been cut from the script.

Advising on the French casting was Dominique Delouche's last task on a Fellini film. The young Frenchman had been his closest assistant and an intimate member of the court. 'But on *La dolce vita* everything changed,' he says. 'The climate of that film was very very different. *Il bidone* and *Le notti di Cabiria* were a little spiritual, more or less impregnated with Christianity, a little Dostoevskian, a little like Chekhov. And since I knew about this world I think Fellini was interested in whether I would approve or disapprove. But *La dolce vita* was like the entry into a sort of hell. And I was no longer useful to him. I was surplus, and his attitude started to change. We still talked, but there was a certain coolness there.'

Part of the coolness stemmed from Fellini's increasing closeness to Pasolini. The final break came when René Clément invited Delouche to work as his assistant on the thriller *Plein soleil* with Alain Delon, part of which would be shot on Ischia. 'My position with Fellini was very vague,' says Delouche. 'This job with Clément was far better paid and more official. I liked working with Fellini but I had to think about earning my living. I asked Fellini if he would mind me taking it. He said: "Go ahead", but I could tell he didn't like it. He felt I betrayed him. A Fellini production is a little like the court of Louis XIV at Versailles. A favourite could fall into disgrace. This happened to me. There was a period of crisis, of misunderstandings.' Though he receives a credit on the film as one of the three assistant-directors,

Delouche left part-way through. He wasn't the only person to resent Pasolini's growing importance to Fellini. Ennio Flaiano also made no secret of his dislike. It drove another wedge into the widening gap between Fellini and one of his oldest collaborators.

By the autumn of 1958, de Laurentiis had decided he couldn't afford a film with so little chance of profit and, after a shouting match with Fellini heard all over the production office, stormed off the project. If anyone wished to pick up *La dolce vita*, he announced, they could have it – if they first bought up Fellini's contract for 75 million lire. Humiliatingly, Fellini hawked himself – and the film – around Rome. Eleven producers turned him down, frightened off by the additional fee for his contract. They included Franco Cristaldi, young producer of *Le notti bianche*. Goffredo Lombardo of Titanus offered 400 million lire, but the combined price of film and contract was closer to 600 million. Finally Milanese publisher Angelo Rizzoli, then seventy and one of Italy's wealthiest men, emerged as the most serious bidder.

The classic self-made man, Rizzoli, who'd been born in an orphanage and worked his way up from a typographer to a publishing empire, typified the drive that is supposedly characteristic of Milan. 'In Milan they pay you with money,' runs a proverb, 'in Rome with promises.' His money had come mostly from books and magazines, including *Marc'Aurelio*, but he'd toyed with movies for decades.

With Rizzoli's involvement, Don Peppino Amato, now the publisher's adviser and partner in film projects, re-entered Fellini's life. Before Rizzoli could invest, Amato had to approve the script and the deal. He lived in the Excelsior and was delighted that someone might film 'his' street and 'his' hotel. In fact, why not call the film *Via Veneto*? Fellini declined, though Amato was to pester him with the suggestion.

Throughout September, discussions continued while other financiers, hearing rumours of the film, rang with offers. A German promised backing if the actress Lilli Palmer appeared in it. The Lombardy publishing empire of Tofanelli expressed an interest. Fellini claims he found himself committed to three producers while waiting for the fourth, Amato, to make up his mind.

Rizzoli was not particularly enthusiastic about *La dolce vita* but he trusted Amato and liked Fellini, a self-made provincial like himself. Unhappy with his own son and heir Andrea, a notorious gambler, he took to calling Fellini 'Dear Artist' and treating him like a favourite if wayward nephew. When Fellini showed him the rewritten Steiner episode, Rizzoli refused to believe he could have invented anything so terrible and blamed it on the more cynical Flaiano.

Amato, an old hand at doing a deal, was shameless in his manoeuvres. Clowning his way through meetings, he threatened to eat the blotting paper rather than concede an advantage, or drink the ink and poison himself if Fellini pressed his demands. At this he raised the inkwell flamboyantly to his lips, unaware that the top was loose. Ink spilled down his shirt. During the last conference, claiming Fellini was a robber, he offered him his trousers, dropping them to show he meant it. Fellini was perversely impressed by such grandstanding. If Amato would fight so hard for a deal, he'd fight just as hard for the film. A contract was signed with Amato and Rizzoli (as Riama Film) on 28 October. Rizzoli would back *La dolce vita* to 600 million lire, including buying up Fellini's contract. (The final combined cost would be closer to 750 million lire.) His Cineriz company would distribute the film. Fellini's fee would be the equivalent of $50,000, at the low end of the Hollywood scale, plus a share of the profits. The terms were not particularly advantageous to Fellini, but by then he thought only of starting work.

Anita Ekberg's scenes had to be shot first to free her for *Nel segno di Roma*. On the chilly morning of 16 March 1959, in Cinecittà's Studio 14 where Gherardi had re-created the curved staircase inside the shell of St Peter's dome, Otello Martelli's camera rolled for the first time as Sylvia, in a parody of clerical dress, sprints up the stairs with *paparazzi* in exhausted pursuit. Since their cool first meeting, Ekberg had warmed to both Fellini and Mastroianni, who christened her 'Anitona' – 'Big Anita'. Fellini had also convinced her, in the face of logic, that the fights with Robert in the film were not a caricature of her bouts with Steel but based on Ava Gardner's brawls with Tony Franciosa.

Next, she breezed through the sequence at the Caracalla Club, Gherardi's caricature of a Rome *boîte*, built against the ancient walls of the baths. In the Rome of *La dolce vita* everything is for sale, even the imperial past. Black musicians in ruffles and servile grins eagerly play whatever the guests demand, while bespectacled waiters dressed ludicrously in togas serve the new barbarians. A ruined fragment of one of Fellini's huge antique heads, not much more than a forehead and mute, imploring eyes, watches from the shadows. American actor Frankie Stout leads the dancing, a whooping satyr in a beard cultivated for a sword-and-sandal movie. Robert, whom Fellini portrays sympathetically as educated, artistic and sensitive, is unimpressed by the place and the people. He points out historical errors in the waiter's toga, asks Stout: 'When did you stop working with the wealthy widows, Frankie?', and, after the dancing, suggests Stout and Anita pass the hat.

Fellini set many scenes in or near fountains and running water, part of a motif that contrasts natural phenomena – water, wind, rain, animals – with Rome's sterile artificiality, and also acknowledges Fellini's superstitious regard for his astrological sign, Aquarius. Gherardi turned the Acque Albule, a sulphur spa at Bagni di Tivoli outside Rome, into the Kit Kat Club, which Marcello visits with his father, while its exterior became a poolside terrace at Maddalena's mansion. The miracle scenes were also shot near by, with Fellini's psychic adviser of the time, Marianna Leibl, playing a small role as the woman who befriends Emma.

Re-creating the tritons and mermaids of Niccolò Salvi's intricate Fontana di Trevi was, however, beyond even Gherardi's powers, so Fellini took it over for Sylvia's famous wade. People with roofs or balconies overlooking the tiny piazza charged extortionate prices for a view. The original paddle had taken place in August, with the actress wearing a modest belted cotton frock, hair demurely pinned up. This time Fellini put her in a low-cut evening-gown and set her hair free. Since the waters were icy, Ekberg's exposed shoulders and arms were rubbed down with alcohol after each of the fifteen takes to help circulation. Mastroianni took his alcohol more directly.

After the Trevi sequence, lavishly covered by the press, all Rome was eager to see Fellini at work. The procession of guests and gawkers swelled to a parade, most of them hungry for a glimpse of Ekberg. Her fame continued to complicate shooting long after she left to play Zenobia.*

Anouk Aimée joined the unit on 25 April, but the groupies persisted. Shooting the sequence outside the whore's apartment building, the crew had to deal with crowds who, hoping for Anitona, booed in disappointment when Mastroianni appeared with the frail Aimée. 'Be careful, Marcello,' they shouted. 'You will hurt yourself holding her! She has too many bones! Give her food, Marcello!' Fellini closed down the shoot until the crowd dispersed, but when the crew returned later that night so did the barrackers.

*In an oddity of fate, *Nel segno di Roma* was to have been directed by Guido Brignone, who made *Maciste all'inferno*, but he died during pre-production, and the film was completed anonymously by Antonioni.

Such reactions didn't help Aimée, nervous at the best of times. During the first meetings with Fellini, her murmured responses and nervous habit of speaking from behind her hand convinced Dominique Delouche that he'd erred in suggesting her. But the director was captivated. He would rhapsodise later about Aimée's lemur eyes, her high cheekbones and above all her sensuality. ('She isn't interested in a career,' said a later employer, producer Pandro Berman. 'All she is interested in is being with her lover of the moment.') The downside of this sex appeal was a high-strung thoroughbred distractibility. Fellini resorted to capering behind the camera, waving his arms and grimacing, while at the same time demanding that she keep a straight face. The technique put a hint of suppressed humour behind that mask-like beauty. Ekberg, who needed no such encouragement, had meanwhile succumbed so totally to Fellini's charm that, after her last shot, a car scene, she burst into tears. Fellini told Ingmar Bergman how she had to be disengaged gently from the wheel and helped from the set.

Crowd problems intensified when shooting moved to via Veneto. The city had reluctantly given permission to shoot from two am to six am but Rome's rowdies never slept. In addition to keeping a stream of cars flowing down the Veneto, into a side street and back on camera again, Fellini had to contend with insults from the crowd and Aimée's nervousness about driving the huge Cadillac. Unable to get the shots he needed, Fellini told Gherardi to re-create at Cinecittà the block of the Veneto in front of the Café de Paris. When Amato balked at the cost, he agreed to give up his profit participation.

The new set, christened on 6 June with a cocktail party, was convincing, even though Gherardi had to build it without the real Veneto's steep slope. Fellini insists he doesn't mind. It suited the CinemaScope frame, and Rome has always been to him, he says, 'a horizontal city'. In his imagination, if not in reality, the via Veneto *was* flat.* Shooting picked up as the weather improved, a consolation to Fellini, since Amato had taken to confronting him pointedly each morning with a summary of the previous day's costs.

Assistant-director Guidarino Guidi, familiar with Rome's dubious dukes and papal knights, organised the country-house party, shot in a sixteenth-century castle at Bassano di Sutri, half an hour outside Rome. He salted the extras with authentic counts and barons, includ-

---

*'Fellini likes everything that is flat,' says Liliana Betti. 'It's why he likes the sea. On the other hand, he finds insupportable anything vertical, like mountains.'

ing Prince Vadim Wolkonsky (whose role as the old prince launched a minor career as an actor), Prince Don Eugenio 'Dodo' Ruspoli di Poggi Sausa and Lady Rosemary Rennel 'Taffy' Rodd, who played the English medium (and provided her own pure-bred dogs as props). To create a sense of dreamlike timelessness in the exteriors, Fellini shot them 'day for night', filming in morning light but darkening the image with filters.

Gherardi, knowing Fellini's taste for caricature, mentioned that such parties were less formal around his native Florence, where the squirearchy (of which he was a somewhat disreputable member) were as likely to turn out in hunting gear as a dinner jacket. Inspired, Fellini dressed the son of the family in a droopy sweater. Beautiful blonde model Nico Otzak, a friend of Silvana Mangano, had dropped in to watch. When she casually picked up a candelabra, Fellini noticed her, added a borrowed helmet from a suit of armour to her slacks and sweater and put her into the scene. To emphasise the correct louche tone, Kurt Weill's 'Mack the Knife' was played on the set.

Fellini's story of how he filmed the climactic orgy has passed into movie mythology. Traditionally, he called in Pasolini to advise him as an expert on vice, only to be told he knew nothing of such 'bourgeois' diversions. As an alternative, Pasolini suggested Gualtiero Jacopetti, director of the sensational documentary *Mondo cane*, but since Jacopetti was in Africa an innocent Fellini had to fend for himself. After an hour of shooting, he claims to have overheard his Dutch assistant Lilli Veenman mutter in disillusion: 'He wants to play it dirty but he doesn't know how.'

There's little truth in any of this. Fellini well knew Pasolini was homosexual, and while he did hire him to work on the sequence, it was in that capacity. Pasolini and Franco Citti wrote the dialogue for the effeminate Pierroni and the two transvestite dancers, a task not unlike the one he performed on *Cabiria*, advising on Roman dialect.

There were plenty of better-qualified heterosexual experts on orgies closer at hand. Nico Otzak, later lead singer in the Velvet Underground and famously promiscuous, recalled: 'They wanted to do an orgy scene, but nobody knew how to do an orgy. Well, I thought, I can help them . . .' Fellini himself, while claiming he never goes to orgies, that he can 'do it better in dreams and fantasies', was perfectly able to stage a credible debauch. In 1967, Terence Stamp, playing a dissolute movie star in *Toby Dammit*, asked diffidently for 'a word of direction' before his first scene. 'Fellini didn't miss a beat,' Stamp says. 'He leaned his mouth seductively to my ear . . . "This night, last night, you was at a party. Big party, but really an h'orgy. You come late after your show. You drunk. You drink more, anything, but much whisky, lotta whisky. Also smoke hashish, marijuana, sniff cocaine and fuck, much fucking all night. Big woman with big breasts, you fucking her, somebody come fuck you. All night like this. This morning a *macchina* come take you to airport, put you on plane to Rome."'

La dolce vita's orgy, however, is mostly talk. Marcello accuses a lesbian painter of sleeping with her models and a singer of just getting off on her 'four little songs'. The ladylike strip by Nadia Gray, her private parts discreetly plastered with wax, reveals only that she is no threat to Aichi Nana. Possible reasons for his dishing up so tepid a scene range from nervousness about censorship to an implied criticism of Marcello as an impotent blowhard, but ignorance isn't among them. He hinted at his motives in a 1962 piece on the film. Researching contemporary Rome, he wrote, he offered a lift to 'a blond young man wearing eyeshadow, whom everyone called Chierichetta'. Strolling with Fellini along the via Appia Antica, the young homosexual 'burst out with his troubles, saying he wanted to change his life, that he could hear the voice of conscience. He wanted to set up with a lawyer, a serious person, and let all the rest go, all the more because there was going to be an apocalypse within the next few years and all the wicked would be swept away in a new Deluge.'

'What he said struck me profoundly,' Fellini said. It also inspired the dialogue of the two transvestites who flee from the party with the other guests. 'I've lost interest in all this,' says one, pulling off his drag costume. 'I want to go, to do penance. But others soon fill the places of those who do. Two go and ten fill their places. By 1965 there'll be total depravity. How squalid everything will be!' Since what apparently interested Fellini was a shift in Roman sexuality towards the homo-erotic, he hired Pasolini and Citti to give that theme the weight it deserved. The strip-tease, though demanded by the film's topical subtext, was irrelevant, and he treated it perfunctorily.

The crew moved to Passo Scuro, thirty kilometres north of Rome, for the final scene, where the partygoers stagger out into the seventh of *La dolce vita*'s dawns to find fishermen hauling a huge sea beast on to the beach. After the Montesi scandal, a sequence in which a monster appears from the sea to disconcert the guests at a sex party, and an innocent girl tries vainly to communicate from the far side of a river, might have been thought a barely disguised metaphor, but Fellini insists the scene came from his memories of Rimini rather than recent history.

Fellini had written the monster, which has its roots in one of his most familiar recurring dreams, into an early draft of *I vitelloni*, but later cut it. He seemed equally uncertain about using it in *La dolce vita*. Gherardi built a manta-like creature from plaster and draped it with tripe, but Fellini, who declined to see the model before shooting, was disappointed when he did so. He debated dropping it altogether, then shot a version of the scene in which the partygoers merely shudder over something grotesque which the audience doesn't see. Eventually he acquired a real giant ray whose watery eye and rubbery flesh he shot in close-up, using Gherardi's model only in brief long shot. Of the effect he hoped to achieve, he will say only that he aimed at 'an expression of absurdity, irrationality'.

Few images in Fellini's work have been more discussed than the last shots, where Paola waves and gestures to Marcello, trying to convey a message he can't or won't understand. In the furore after the film's release, one girl suggested Paola was asking to join the orgy, but most took the exchange as a sign of Marcello's determination to cut himself off from innocence and hope. Fellini isn't so doctrinaire. When an interviewer called Marcello's hand movements 'a gesture of resignation', he disagreed. 'No. He says: "I don't hear, I don't understand." It could also be considered a bantering gesture. "I don't hear you because I don't want to hear you."' Fellini may have seen Marcello's disillusion as just another phase in a varied life, one from which he'll recover and learn, as he himself did from *La dolce vita*. If there's a message to the film, it's the same as that of *Cabiria* – life, bitter or sweet, goes on.

When he finished shooting on 17 August, Fellini had exposed 92,000 metres of film – fifty-six hours – which would be cut to less than three. Mastroianni, who's in every sequence, remained enthusiastic to the end. 'It was an exceptional experience, marvellous; almost six months of joyful labour. One didn't really have the impression of making a film. We almost lived that "soft life".'

The first cut ran for three hours and twenty minutes. Fellini showed it to groups of friends with a guide track made during production, incorporating, as usual, fluffed lines, background music, extraneous noises, shouted directions and curses. Rota liked it so much he suggested he stitch an equivalent musical score together from natural sounds and pop songs, but copyright fees torpedoed the idea.

Rota's music is among the most distinctive of all film scores, mostly for its use of the Cordovox, an electric organ whose compressed, droning tone, combining harmonium, Hammond organ and a wooden street organ, became a Fellini trademark. Still keen to include as many pop tunes as possible, the aural equivalents of the newspaper photographs that inspired Gherardi, Rota reprised 'April in Portugal' from *Il bidone*. He added 'Arrivederci Roma' and in particular 'Patrizia', a Perez Prado's cha-cha-cha which Paola plays on the jukebox at Fregene and to which, in a neat inversion, Nadia also strips at the orgy. The remaining tunes are oldies like 'Yes Sir, That's My Baby' and 'Jingle Bells', newly arranged, or pastiches from Rota's skilful hand, like the replacement for 'Mack the Knife' in the Bassano di Sutri party, a doleful foxtrot whose middle eight reprises the *dolce vita* theme.

Those who saw the rough version were delighted. Nobody warned Fellini that it might give offence. Amato scheduled it to open in sixty-four theatres across Italy between 6 and 14 February, but in deference to Rizzoli a première was held in Milan on 5 February. The Milanese public was admitted free. That morning, at the Cinema Fiamma, Rome's blasé critics had given the film twenty seconds of applause, so Fellini was optimistic. Rizzoli was less so. His people had forecast that it would never recoup his investment.

The première seemed to confirm the gloomiest advice. The audience in Milan's Capitol Cinema guessed little of the explosion to come. The discreet credits promised only restraint, though Rota's theme music, with its brass flourishes and stuttering echo of a circus march, scored for chimes and gongs, subversively suggested parallels between modern Rome and its pagan past. Indignation grew as the film went on. People muttered during the screening. Gray's strip-tease drew cries of 'Ugly!', 'Enough!' and 'Shame!' As they left the theatre, Fellini, Giulietta and Mastroianni were jostled and someone spat on the director. Friends clustered round and hustled them out. In the next morning's papers, Milan police announced they'd broken a 100,000 lire a night call-girl ring. 'Do you know what the Milan upper bourgeoisie could not tolerate?' Fellini says. 'The orgy. It upset them; they were in agony at seeing themselves in the mirror.' The discontent, however, was not simply Milanese. Italians everywhere were shocked and offended.

Despite the enthusiasm of the Jesuit intellectuals of Catholic Action, who'd seen the film, Cardinal Siri, Fellini's champion on *Cabiria*, refused to give his seal of approval. The Church's old guard was under pressure from Pope John XXIII, whose Second Vatican Council was then busily reforming the Church, and Siri had been warned that, in this case, the hierarchy would make a stand. Any priest who reviewed the film favourably was disciplined, demoted or transferred to a new parish. *Il quotidiano*, the newspaper of Catholic Action, initially printed a good review, then recanted, deciding it was blasphemous, pornographic, bestial and un-Italian, opinions reinforced in two long articles in *La civiltà cattolica*. Milanese priest Nazzareno Taddei led the campaign, pointing out that Fellini had breached the Pope's guidelines on morality in cinema. The Vatican's *Osservatore romano* was quick to agree, condemning it as 'obscene' and 'disgusting' and demanding its withdrawal.

The Centro Cattolico Cinematografico, the Church's mouthpiece on movies, rated it E (for 'Escluso'), damning any Catholic who saw it. When an association of Rome's parish priests called for a ban, novelist Alberto Moravia convened a public meeting of intellectuals to endorse Fellini and his film, but from pulpits all over Italy priests continued to condemn both.

Fellini's more pious supporters pointed out that the Church didn't lack pretexts for anger. To cut in the first few minutes from the face of Christ to a pagan mask looked gratuitously offensive. Fellini had gone on to mock miracles, condone promiscuity and, if not endorse suicide, at least show it with compassion. Anita Ekberg visiting St Peter's in a travesty of clerical uniform was all the more resented because the Vatican had approved the film in outline and given permission to shoot there, though Fellini never did so; the St Peter's on which Marcello looks down from the helicopter and which he views with Sylvia is back-projected.

Within twenty-four hours of the opening Fellini received 400 telegrams, mostly accusing him of treason, atheism and Communism. In scores of editorials the Montesi scandal was raked up, to the delight of the left, whose papers backed Fellini. Ironically, Communist critics who'd harried him for abandoning Neorealism found themselves forced to praise *La dolce vita* in the name of the party line. Faced with such solidarity on the left, some political journalists charged that Fellini had hastened the long-feared *apertura della sinistra*, the 'opening to the left' which would admit Communists to the government. There were calls to withdraw his passport.

On 9 February, right-wing deputies forced a debate in parliament. On 17 February, Domenico Magri, Under-Secretary for Entertainment, announced, for the record: 'The government is not disposed to accept the request of the many people who have asked that the film be withdrawn from circulation, since fears that it may harm the good name of our country and of Rome are quite unfounded.' Privately, however, Magri sympathised with the critics. Parliament had no statutory power of censorship, but he urged the speedy introduction of new laws which would protect the Italian people from films capable of 'arousing disgust by scenes of a raw and ruthless realism'.

For Fellini, the assaults were painfully personal. 'In Rimini, my mother is still known as the mother of the man who made *La dolce vita*.' When Maddalena gave birth to her daughter in April 1964, Fellini made a rare visit to his home town for the christening, only to have Ida chide him: 'Why did you make such a picture?' His decision to go on the road in March and April, screening the film to intellectuals and opinion-makers, looked less a promotional device than a penance for having offended, if not God, then at least his own family.

Neither Church nor state could, however, stem *La dolce vita*'s enormous success. Two big Roman cinemas ran four packed shows a day for months. Despite the extraordinary cost of 1,000 lire a seat, cars were parked three deep outside. So huge were the queues in both Rome and Milan that people drove hundreds of kilometres out of town to see it. Within three months it grossed $1.5 million, smashing records set by *The Ten Commandments* and *Gone with the Wind*. By the time it opened in New York in April 1961, the film had made $10 million. Two hundred prints were struck for the US and, though it played everywhere on that first release with subtitles, traditionally a turn-off for American audiences, *La dolce vita* took $8 million, outgrossing the two biggest foreign successes to that time, *Never on Sunday* and *Et Dieu créa la femme*. The world rights changed hands again in March 1962, when Astor Films bought them for $1.35 million.

It was one of the ironies of his break with de Laurentiis that Fellini got to see some of the profits of *Cabiria* which would otherwise have been eaten up by later losses. For *La dolce vita*, however, having renounced his percentage to rebuild via Veneto at Cinecittà, he received only his $50,000 fee, plus a gold watch from Rizzoli, the twin of the one the producer wore himself.

17   Fellini Dances: *Boccaccio '70:*
Le tentazioni del Dottore Antonio

Seminarian (to man erecting billboard): 'Cinema?'
Billboard man: 'No. Milk'
Dialogue from *Le tentazioni del Dottore Antonio*

For most of 1960, Federico and Giulietta existed in the genial shadow
of Angelo Rizzoli, though Fellini spent much of the time travelling,
often with Mastroianni. During *La dolce vita* the two men had become
close, even rooming together on location. Fellini took Mastroianni to
Rimini to meet his family. They walked the stormy beachfront at
Miramare, and Fellini was overheard repeating to Mastroianni the line
from *I vitelloni*: 'If someone came along and offered you 10,000 lire,
would you take a swim?'

In competition with one another they bought cars. Fellini became
attached to a white Jaguar and Mastroianni to a gun-metal Porsche,
though in time Fellini settled on a Mercedes and owned one for
as long as he drove. The two also chased women, some of whom they
caught, leading to reports in the scandal press – denied, as always, by
Fellini – that he and Giulietta were separating. Mastroianni had been
married since 1950, but his wife, Flora, was used to his immoderate
infidelities, during which he moved to New York to live with Faye
Dunaway and to Paris for a liaison with Catherine Deneuve which
produced a daughter.

What the fantasising Fellini and his womanising star had in common puzzled many people. Mastroianni defined their relationship as 'a
love affair without sex', analogous to Fellini's friendships with Rossellini, Delouche and Pasolini. 'Marcello has always lived a very intense
life,' says Daniel Toscan du Plantier, 'whereas that of Federico has
remained more in the domain of fantasy. The story of Marcello's life, of
that sexual life in its most technical details, is in some ways Federico's
life by proxy. On the set, both of them are like children in a universe
from which everyone else is totally excluded. Once, I asked an assistant

to walk by them and discover what they were talking about. Between shots Federico would take Marcello by the shoulder and both would become like kids in a schoolyard. Their conversation was always a little specialised, but she found it turned entirely on sex and what Marcello had done the previous night.'

Meanwhile, open warfare had broken out between two collaborators on *La dolce vita*. In the debate that followed the opening, Pasolini had been an active and often critical participant. Increasingly ambitious, he had plenty to say about how he would have handled the film. After one such statement, Flaiano wrote an angry response entitled '*La dolce vita* As Pasolini Would Have Made It', but Fellini persuaded him not to publish. Flaiano was incensed that his old friend would side with a relative newcomer to the team.

In May, *La dolce vita* was in competition at Cannes. Chairing the jury was Fellini's adolescent hero, Georges Simenon. Rigidly disciplined, the inventor of Maigret, who wrote each of his novels in exactly eleven days, locked alone in a tower – a regime the tensions of which he relieved with visits to prostitutes, of whom he was a habitual and vigorous client – took charge with typical firmness, even ejecting autocratic Festival secretary Robert Favre LeBret from his customary courtesy seat at the discussions.

The initial reaction to Fellini's film was poor, critics, especially the French, favouring Antonioni's cooler *L'avventura* or Buñuel's *The Young One*. Distributors were no keener. One was heard to say: 'I wouldn't give $50,000 for it.' Simenon, charmed by Giulietta and impressed by the film, took this as a challenge. Henry Miller, also on the jury, preferred playing table tennis to watching movies, and gave him his vote, as did the one female member. He also had a casting vote as Chairman. Ignoring French pressure, he secured the Palme d'Or for Fellini.

Giulietta was in the wings, waiting for the announcement, when he whispered the news. She kissed him so hard that her lipstick was visible on his cheek when he went on stage. The Antonioni claque booed and Giulietta, shocked, wept on Simenon's shoulder. Elsewhere, Peppino Amato, as unmoved by jeers as by acclaim, set the price of the US rights at $1 million.

Fellini and Giulietta were together again in Paris in June for the French première. Delouche turned up loyally to translate when they met the critics. Afterwards they retreated to Ischia, where they were Rizzoli's guests for the summer at his Regina Isabella Hotel.

At last Fellini could relax. He took medicinal baths for the back trouble that had plagued him throughout the production and wondered what to do next. He was European cinema's undoubted star and producers queued to offer him projects. Most, however, wanted another *Dolce vita* – *La dolce vita '70* was suggested – whereas the one thing of which he could be certain was that he didn't dare repeat himself. He hit on a formula for reporters who asked about his next film. 'It will be an attempt to study what the little girl says with her enigmatic smile to Marcello at the end of *La dolce vita*,' he told them. This was so quotable nobody cared that it said nothing.

The Italian government and the Church, having failed to ban Fellini's film, redoubled their efforts against other directors. *Rocco e i suoi fratelli/Rocco and His Brothers*, Visconti's drama of sexual violence and homosexuality in a poor Milanese family, was repeatedly attacked, though by now the storm was almost blown out and Visconti weathered it. The *Dolce vita* campaign had been the last gasp of repression before liberalism overwhelmed it.

Meanwhile, the phrase had passed into the language. In Britain and America, with the emphasis on the second word, it connoted mindless hedonism, but in Italy, with a stress on the adjective, it signified a sense of physical well-being. Italian restaurants of the same name popped up like mushrooms in a dozen capitals, and Fellini was particularly annoyed when Toto cashed in with a farce in the popular *Pane, amore e . . . /Bread, Love and . . .* series, *Pane, amore e la dolce vita*. Clothing manufacturers tried to launch a 'Dolce Vita Look', but Gherardi never intended his floppy hats, stiff skirts, ruffs, bows and capes for street wear and they transferred poorly to the mass market. The film gave only one legacy to fashion: Nico Otzak's polo-neck sweater became known in Italy as a Dolce Vita.

Among the film's most durable coinages was the nickname 'Paparazzo'. It belonged originally to a Riminese in Fellini's childhood who spoke very fast and who could imitate insects, especially big mosquitoes – *papataceo* in slang. Adopted by the press, it became the generic name for impudent photo-journalists.

After all the fuss, or perhaps because of it, nobody in the US could find much to object to in *La dolce vita*. Despite some heavy-breathing pre-publicity, it opened uncut with both the seal of the industry's own Production Code and a clearance from the Catholic Legion of Decency. Fellini was nominated for an Academy Award as Best Director, the first time a foreign film-maker had been so honoured. The story and screenplay also received nominations, as did Gherardi's art direction and set direction and, separately, his costumes, which were the only winner; otherwise, *West Side Story* made a nearly clean sweep.

During the summer Rizzoli offered what Fellini called 'a gift or bonus' that promised to solve his chronic problems with producers. He suggested they transfer the de Laurentiis contract to a new production company, half owned by Rizzoli, the other 50 per cent divided between Fellini and Clemente Fracassi. The company, Federiz, would produce Fellini's films and also allow him to back young directors unable to find money elsewhere. The arrangement offered what Fellini always claimed to want – autonomy, but with a solid financial base – and he signed willingly.

In September 1960 Federiz set up shop in via della Croce. Fellini ran around – 'like a little kid', he wrote to Pasolini – buying furniture, including a huge antique table on which to sort his now enormous collection of casting portraits. Gherardi decorated the offices with orange curtains, green lampshades and some oversized couches from *La dolce vita*. Large double-doors padded in the same green as the lampshades separated the general office from Fellini's sanctum, which he referred to grandly as 'The Poet's Retreat'. Pasolini, unimpressed, said the place reminded him of a tavern from *The Three Musketeers*. The comparison was shrewd. There was a flavour of regal patronage about Federiz that Fellini didn't even try to disguise. 'I want to surround myself with saltimbancos, story-tellers and jesters, as in a medieval court,' he told the press. 'But,' he insisted, 'there will be no despotism.' The offices were 'not intended to be just the headquarters of a production company. When we are working, be it on a film of mine or one of the young directors that I intend to help, there will be room for the production managers and assistant-directors. But all the year round it will be a "workshop" where my friends can gather to exchange ideas.'

Before the furniture was in place Federiz was besieged by old friends and new talents, all with film projects. Three emerged as front runners. Vittorio de Seta wanted to make *Banditi a Orgosolo/ Bandits of Orgosolo*, the story of a shepherd forced into crime. The ex-documentarist intended to shoot on location in Sardinia, with dialogue in dialect. Ermanno Olmi's low-key *Il Posto/The Job* showed the problems faced by a boy in his first job in a large office, while Pasolini had adapted his novel about street kids, *Una vita violenta/A Violent Life*, into a script called, after the main character's nickname, *Accattone*. As well, Giulietta wanted Federiz to produce Salvato

Cappelli's script *Madre Cabrini*, in which she would play Maria Cabrini, the patron saint of emigrants.

In retrospect, it seems inevitable that Fellini would make a terrible producer. The paternalism and autocracy of his personal relationships transferred to Federiz almost intact. Pasolini's experience was typical. Fellini told him he liked his script, but, unsure if he could direct, asked him in September to shoot some tests. For the young writer these were 'the most wonderful days of my life'. Behind the camera for the first time, he discovered an immediate affinity for it. Essentially a poet, he was drawn to the visual fluidity of silent film, in particular to Buñuel and the bleak piety of Carl Dreyer. Fracassi and Fellini anticipated a stark drama. Instead Pasolini created a poem to Franco Citti, younger brother of his friend Sergio, whom he showed as a street angel rising above the squalor of the slums to a score skimmed from J. S. Bach. His model wasn't Neorealism but Dreyer's *Passion of Joan of Arc*. With its mysticism and Catholic imagery, the film would resemble in some respects Fellini's early films, which may have contributed to the subsequent conflict between the two men, but anyone who knew Fellini's possessiveness for those he admitted to his court, and the fate of Delouche when he struck out on his own, could hardly have been surprised at what followed.

Fellini screened the tests but said nothing to Pasolini. Two friends, Bernardo Bertolucci and Franco Citti, tried unsuccessfully to discover his reaction. Pasolini set up a meeting at Federiz, but arrived early in case Fellini tried to slip away. 'As I go in,' Pasolini recorded, 'Fellini also comes in by chance through the inner door. The Great Mystifier is unable to conceal, in the expression of his dark-rimmed eyes, his awareness that I am arriving unexpectedly and rather too early, but he gives me a welcoming hug. He is clean, smooth, healthy as a wild beast in a cage. He takes me into his office. And as he sits down, he immediately tells me that he wants to be frank with me . . . that the tests haven't convinced him.' At Pasolini's protests, Fellini, 'like a grand and elegant bishop . . . shifts the question to another plane' – the cost. 'I realise that all this is a euphemism, a chess move,' says Pasolini. Federiz is not going to back *Accattone*.

This rejection ended Pasolini's relationship with Fellini but inaugurated his career as a director. By chance, director Mauro Bolognini saw some stills from the tests and recommended the project to producer Alfredo Bini. Fellini and his ex-protégé continued to snipe at one another for years. In 1962 in his *La ricotta* episode for the omnibus film *Rogopag* Pasolini cast Orson Welles as a moody, hectoring director shooting a film in the hills outside Rome. A journalist asks: 'What do you think of the great director Federico Fellini?' Welles looks bemused, then replies haltingly: 'He dances . . . Yes, he *dances*.' In 1968 Fellini returned the gibe in *Toby Dammit*. Arriving in Rome to make a western, Terence Stamp is told by the producer that the film will be 'situated between Pasolini and Dreyer, with a *soupçon* of Ford'.

Fellini also, after early enthusiasm, blew cool over the projects of de Seta and Olmi. Would anyone pay to see a film in Sardinian? As for *Il Posto*, on reflection it looked like the softer kind of Neorealism, a style which films like *La dolce vita* had rendered passé. On 16 October Pasolini wrote hotly in *Il giorno*: 'It seems likely that Federiz will produce films by nobody other than Fellini.'

Federiz's final and saddest casualty was Fellini's brother. After working as production secretary on *Cabiria*, Riccardo had resumed acting, but in 1962 a producer offered to finance him in directing a feature based on three short scripts he'd written about Riminese fishermen. He shot two episodes but the producer refused to fund the third, so Riccardo approached Rizzoli, who looked at what he'd done and picked up the bill.

Storie sulla sabbia/Stories on the Sand was invited to Venice in 1963 – 'in anticipation of which,' Riccardo said, 'Federico gave me some advice.' The main suggestion was that he should change his name, 'so as not to confuse the audience about the director's identity'. It was a shrewd though humiliating comment, but Riccardo, prepared to believe that Federico had his interests at heart, put the idea to his producer – who refused. Federico, he realised bitterly, had been right. His backer had banked on just such a confusion. The film was finished and had a minor release, but the relationship between the brothers never recovered. Riccardo later joined RAI, the state-run TV network, and became a successful producer of wild-life documentaries and variety shows. He died in 1991, still resentful.

Out of Fellini's apparently aimless travelling in 1960 came *Otto e mezzo*. 'I was in limbo,' he said, 'taking stock of myself. I needed to reconcile my fears . . . I felt I needed to find the answers to countless questions. And that is when the idea took root. It would be a summoning up of dreams, recollections, forgotten feelings, shadowy doubts, and a kind of eternal quest for self knowledge and acceptance . . . '

In 1960 Camilla Cederna, a Fellini pet and one of the few members of the press to be allowed on *Otto e mezzo*'s closed set, had caught him in a weak moment and he'd poured out stories of his childhood. She published them in the July issue of *L'espresso* as 'Fellini Confesses'.

Later, people pointed to the affinity between the article and the film. Gherardi, on the other hand, believed it began with a visit he and the director made to Urbano's grave in the autumn. Fellini preferred to date it from the summer and his stay at the baths on Ischia.

More important than any of these was Fellini's discovery late in 1960 of the work of Carl Gustav Jung, which was to have a profound effect, personally and professionally. A colleague of Freud, Jung had broken with him over a diverging vision of the imagination. Against Freud's mechanistic view of the mind, Jung erected a theory of race memory and the 'collective unconscious'. Dreams weren't simply, as Freud would have it, symbolic indicators of mental disturbance rooted in infantile sexuality but archetypal images surfacing from a reservoir of common experience.

Fellini loved this idea. Under Jung's theory, the dreams that were the cornerstone of his work were not aberrant but creative. It was as if he had been offered absolution for a life of psychic sin. At one swipe the guilt of his Catholic upbringing and his embarrassment at his poor education were wiped from the slate. 'I have always thought that I had one major shortcoming,' he said, 'that of not having general ideas about anything. The ability to organize my likes, tastes, desires in terms of genre or category has always been beyond me. But reading Jung I feel freed and liberated from the sense of guilt and the inferiority complex that the shortcoming I touched upon always gave me.' He was even more delighted with Jung's essay on *On Synchronicity*, which suggested a logical basis for the coincidences and omens that had always ruled his life.

Vittorio de Seta had given Fellini the number of Ernst Bernhard, Rome's leading Jungian analyst. 'I became curious to meet him,' Fellini said. 'One day I dialled a number that I thought belonged to a very beautiful lady. A man answered. "Who is speaking?" I asked him. "This is Bernhard," he answered . . . ' Some time later, in the street, Fellini met a friend looking pale and shaken. He confessed he'd just visited his analyst – Doctor Bernhard. Freud, who insisted that such chance meetings were really subconscious rendezvous, would have explained that Fellini simply confused phone numbers and that, since Bernhard lived on via Gregoriana, not far from Fellini's apartment, meetings with patients were to be expected, but to Fellini the encounters were more evidence that Jung was right. Though he claims he was never formally analysed by Bernhard or anyone else, Fellini did visit him weekly for some months, solicited his advice, was guided in his reading by him and, most important of all, began towards the end of 1960 to keep a dream diary.

One of his first recorded dreams, dated March 1961, is set in an airport of which Fellini is both administrator and head of Immigration. A mysterious, silent Asian in mouldering grey robes confronts him and, though a crowd is waiting, Fellini is unable to make a decision about him. The scene changes to a room flooded in grey water where Fellini, in a ringmaster's top hat and tail coat, is forcing a large rodent to swim in desperate circles, urging it on with a whip. Such images, of airports and mysterious Asians, of the circus, of costumes and whips, and of indecision, would figure increasingly in Fellini's films as the freedom conferred by Jung unlocked the combined zoo, attic and whorehouse of his unconscious.

The discovery of Jung made the process of refining his ideas for the new film even more tortuous. Taking Flaiano on one of his nocturnal drives, to Ostia and the sea, Fellini explained he had 'a confused desire to sketch out a man in a day out of his life, the picture of a man in his contradictory, unclear sum of diverse realities, in which you could see all the levels of his being, the planes superimposed on each other like a palace of which the facades have crumbled and which reveals its internal structure, still intact: stairways, hallways, rooms, the furniture'.

Still smarting from the Pasolini incident, Flaiano sneered at this soul-searching. Pinelli and Rondi were more supportive, though no clearer on what Fellini had in mind. Flaiano christened the project *La bella confusione/The Beautiful Confusion*, but a better title would have been *The Myth*. Convinced by his reading of Jung that he need apologise no longer for his imagination, Fellini intended to celebrate it in a film dedicated to the concept of the director as creator.

One constant in all discussions was the spa, so, at the suggestion of Gherardi, who'd piqued his interest by describing surprising experiences in Turkish baths going back to childhood, Fellini and Pinelli checked for ten days into the *terme* at Chianciano, a sleepy but fashionable watering-place in Tuscany for those suffering the effects of too much *dolce vita*.

By October they had an outline, or at least a collection of characters and scenes. That month, Fellini wrote a long letter to Rondi, detailing his conception. It was the story of a man – 'a writer? any kind of professional man? a theatrical producer?' – who visits Chianciano to recuperate. Back in Rome he has a mistress and a wife, not to mention other problems that weigh him down. At the spa he 'spends his days taking the water cure, sleeping a lot (and dreaming whenever we like) . . . His day passes on two levels: the real one composed of meetings in the hotel and at the spring, friends from Rome who come to see him, the mistress hidden away in a little hotel, and the wife who appears one fine day to keep him company; and a fantastic level of dreams, imaginings and memories that assail him, showing up whenever we decide it's useful.'

One scene would feature a magician who performs a mind-reading act. Another would be set in a sort of harem, a recycling of his earlier project about a man with fifteen wives. There would be a priest, based on Angelo Arpa, and a wealthy businessman with a young mistress for whom he's left his wife of forty years. Also a homosexual couple, at the spa to arrange a theatrical performance, who fight bitterly after visiting the mummified body of a saint at a nearby abbey. A sequence would be devoted to 'La Saraghina'. He also envisaged a perfect woman, representing purity and selfless love. Having told journalists after *La dolce vita* that the new film would be about the meaning of the smile on Paola's face, Fellini in a sense kept his promise with this character, essentially a grown-up Paola.

In December Fellini and Yvonne Furneaux flew to London for the British première of *La dolce vita*, only to be caught in a baggage handlers' strike and stranded for an hour inside Heathrow while Amato fumed on the other side of Customs. The incident fed Fellini's dislike of unions. He wouldn't be pinned down by the British press about his new film, though he did tell them the ideal casting would be Charlie Chaplin – though Chaplin at forty, he added hastily, in case the seventy-two-year-old comedian considered it an invitation.

His second choice, which he kept quiet about, was Laurence Olivier. Like many of his casting brainwaves, this one was to flourish without much intellectual soil in which to take root, though the character of Archie Rice in John Osborne's *The Entertainer*, which Olivier created on stage and had just re-created on film, an ageing music-hall artiste with an embittered wife, a younger mistress and a plunging career, had resonances with Fellini's evolving hero.

Back in Rome, Fellini told Fracassi to book a flight to New York, where Olivier was playing on Broadway in *Becket* and living at the Algonquin with wife-to-be Joan Plowright while his divorce from Vivien Leigh went through. Ironically, Mastroianni was also in New York, being courted to make his American stage début in Arthur Miller's *After the Fall*, directed by Franco Zeffirelli.

However, Fellini kept postponing the trip. In his mind, admiration for Olivier battled with a consciousness of his famous performances. How would Olivier play the harem scene, for instance, where, Fellini had decided, Guido would confront all the women in his life and bring them to heel with a whip? 'Olivier can do everything,' he mused, 'but what would I do to make him perform in the farm/harem? When he entered, it would be with a sense of intimidation, with none of the emotion and laughter Marcello would put there. I would seem to be seeing Hamlet, King Lear or Richard III among my odalisques; in any case a baronet, full of disdain.' Or, put more simply, he was frightened of working with an actor of training and reputation.

Abruptly he cancelled the flight, rang Mastroianni in New York and asked him to come home and talk about the new film. The actor had an appointment that day with Arthur Miller, then living at the Chelsea Hotel, to discuss *After the Fall*, but the visit became his formal withdrawal from the project. Fellini wanted him and, though he had no idea of the role, he would of course take it. 'An actor is an animal,' he told Miller. 'I am that or I am nothing, and I am happy to be so.' Nobody in Fellini's team was surprised at the casting. 'He always had Marcello in mind for the role,' Pinelli said. 'We knew it, even if he didn't.'

In January 1961 Fellini took a call from producer Antonio Cervi, who had sold Carlo Ponti on the idea of an anthology film attacking censorship. A group of major Italian directors would each make a short film with a sexual theme, establishing in public consciousness and official circles the cinema's right to deal with such material. Visconti, smarting from the attacks on *Rocco e i suoi fratelli*, had been among the first to sign up. Vittorio de Sica and Mario Monicelli were on board too. This being a Ponti film, Sophia Loren could also be counted on to take part, and the project would be 'supervised' – whatever this meant – by Cesare Zavattini. Ponti called the film *Boccaccio '70*, hoping it would still be circulating at the end of the decade, but except in the sense that the film was a collection of salacious tales, parallels with *The Decameron* were tenuous.

French producer Raoul Lévy had been trying to tempt Fellini to film Simenon's *Three Rooms in Manhattan* on location in New York. He was confident enough to announce the film in March 1961, but given Fellini's animosity towards America it's hardly credible that he took the project seriously. Cervi's invitation was, however, more interesting and, with no workable script for *La bella confusione* in sight, Fellini

began doodling an anecdote about a Doctor Antonio who is friendly
with the sort of clerical power-brokers who savaged *La dolce vita* in *La
civiltà cattolica*. Another attraction of Ponti's project was the fact that
it would be in colour. Fellini had never used colour but was ready to
experiment.

Meanwhile, he urged the inclusion of more film-makers: Antonioni
and Rossellini, for example, both of whom had had censorship problems. The two agreed to think about it and Ponti began to envision a
film with six or seven stories of twenty minutes each. De Sica's
contribution was to be *The Lottery*, with Loren as a girl who raffles
herself at country fairs. *Renzo e Luciana* by Mario Monicelli showed a
young Roman couple trying to hide their illegal marriage from the
giant corporation that employs them. Visconti's *The Job* traded on the
recent Milanese call-girl scandals. Romy Schneider played the wife
who rekindles the passion of her philandering husband by demanding
he pay her for sex, just as he does his whores.

Visconti furnished his set with real antiques, many from his own
home (though Sophia Loren lent him two marble busts of Sarah
Bernhardt). Friends provided Afghan hounds and Coco Chanel was
flown in to coach Romy Schneider in elegance. By contrast, Fellini's
contribution, *Le tentazioni del Dottore Antonio*, had been written in a
fortnight and was, he admitted, lightweight. Dr Antonio Mazzuolo,
pillar of the community, patron of the Boy Scouts, intimate of Church
dignitaries and government figures, is a self-appointed moral watch-
dog. He tears the covers off girlie magazines, rings down the curtain on
leg shows and scares away the lovers who gather in the large open
space in front of his modern suburban apartment. He's scandalised
when a billboard is erected there. On it, Anita Ekberg, twenty metres
long, breasts spilling from a low-cut dress, holds a large glass and
urges Romans to 'Drink more milk'.

Visconti's lavishness egged Fellini into competition. With only
twenty minutes to work in, he pointed out to Ponti, he could do little
more than show Ekberg on the billboard and describe Antonio's
attempts to cover her up. But what if he added a fantasy sequence in
which a gigantic Anita came to life and walked through Rome? Ponti
pondered. The chronically deliberate Antonioni had yet to come up
with an idea, while Rossellini was busy filming the life story of
Mussolini. Seeing the box-office possibilities of a film featuring
Ekberg, Loren *and* Romy Schneider, Ponti agreed to the extra expense.

Pinelli, Flaiano, Rondi and Goffredo Parise fitted out *Dottore Antonio* with supernatural elements, adding Antonio's sister, who has

religious visions, and an impish female Cupid, who prefigures a similar sinister child in *Toby Dammit*. In the augmented plot, Antonio tries to blot out Anita's cleavage with ink when the authorities don't respond fast enough to his complaints. As a compromise they cover the poster with sheets of white paper, but that night a rainstorm washes them away and Anita comes alive to hunt down her tormentor. Antonio imagines himself clad in medieval armour to battle this modern monster, but she brushes his puny efforts aside. They play hide-and-seek among the high-rises until Antonio surrenders and lets himself be cuddled on those vast breasts. Next morning he's found on top of the billboard, trouserless and raving, and is carted away in a straitjacket.

Incorporating Antonio's dream into the film represented a crucial development in Fellini's work. Before encountering Jung he'd never included a dream in any of his films; after the discovery he seldom made a film without one, and later productions like *La città delle donne* contain nothing else. In addition, the fantasy of the tiny man bewitched and overpowered by an enormous woman is one of his own, recorded in a score of variants in his diaries. For the first time, Fellini the film-maker celebrated Fellini the dreamer.

Rizzoli was exasperated that Fellini should work for Ponti. 'We've been in business for almost a year and we still can't announce a title. And now you do a film for someone else!' But he relented, and brought Cineriz into the project with Ponti, the latter's French subsidiaries and American distributor Joe Levine. Rizzoli even lent Fellini his lucky gold coins to bless the first day of shooting.

As Antonio, Fellini cast Peppino de Filippo, the role of neurasthenic moraliser the exact opposite of the womanising Checco in *Luci del varietà*. The background was EUR but, with Cinecittà jammed with peplums, Gherardi condensed Mussolini's model suburb into an anthology of stark, deserted de Chirico perspectives which Piero Zuffi built in miniature on waste ground between via Appia Antica and via Appia Pignatelli.

Fellini shot a series of colour camera tests and was surprised at how much colour widened the range of possibilities. Facial expressions became more subtle. Make-up assumed greater importance. The way light fell on a background could fundamentally alter the tone of a scene. Even buildings presented a new challenge. The models, painted white to imitate marble, perversely photographed blue, reflecting the sky. Since colour film is less sensitive to light, the camera also had to move more slowly. If it panned too sharply, a hedge would appear on screen not as green but alternately blue and yellow.

Because of its technical demands, the episode took almost six months to complete, longer than *La dolce vita*. Most scenes were shot at night, Fellini starting just after midnight and wrapping at dawn. Locals who'd been amused by the billboard became bored with it. Some, in a wry echo of the film, even protested that it was obscene.

Fellini tinkered with the film during the mix, enriching its satirical content. A murmuring commentary sets the tone of gossipy innuendo, some of it aimed at the film industry. When Antonio distributes prizes to the Boy Scouts, all those honoured are named for well-known Italian screenwriters. Most subversive of all, the advertising jingle, one of Rota's most demonic tunes, gnaws at the attention, reiterating maddeningly: 'Drink more milk', and promising: 'Every Italian can be a stallion.'

The cut Fellini delivered in December was almost ninety minutes long, but his suggestion that Ponti release it as a separate feature received no sympathy. *Boccaccio '70* was getting out of hand. Antonioni and Rossellini hadn't come through. De Sica's episode was lacklustre, a reworking of ideas from his *Oro di Napoli/Gold of Naples*. Monicelli's film was charming but undramatic and, worse, cast with unknowns. Visconti's sensual *The Job* relied on the steady accumulation of emotion over its forty-five minutes and was too subtle to anchor the film. For that, Ponti needed *Dottore Antonio*, but at ninety minutes it threatened to sink it. Fellini cut the episode back to fifty-four minutes – still too long, Ponti thought – and left him to pull the anthology together as best he could.

The project limped into 1961 as the producers struggled to cram 200 minutes of material into the feature film format. They discussed showing it with two intervals, and though the full version opened in Milan on 22 February 1962, by the time it arrived at Cannes Monicelli's episode had been cut. There was an instant scandal about the excision. It tainted *Boccaccio '70*'s image and the film was reviewed ungenerously almost everywhere, with a dampening effect on the box office. In the US a 'Condemned' rating from the Legion of Decency did nothing for sales. Critics selected Visconti's segment as the most successful, dismissing Fellini's as trivial.

Boccaccio '70 had the unintended side-effect of extinguishing Federiz. Resenting Fellini's disloyalty and sensing he would never produce any films but his own, Rizzoli mothballed the company. Pasolini's forecast had proved more accurate than even he expected. Federiz never produced a film. Though it technically remained in existence, its offices were closed amid mutual recriminations. Fellini accused Fracassi of timidity; Fracassi charged that at heart Fellini was happy only when he worked alone. Giulietta was also furious at the loss of her Mother Cabrini project. At the end of 1961, under a new arm's-length deal with Cineriz, Fellini started work on *Otto e mezzo*.

18   'A fuckin' *classic*': *Otto e mezzo*

'What a monstrous presumption to think that others
might enjoy the squalid catalogue of your mistakes'
Daumier to Guido in *Otto e mezzo*

Between the end of 1961 and March 1962, Fellini assembled a script
for the nameless film. Still lost for a structure, he employed the unusual
method of meeting Pinelli, Flaiano and Rondi in a trattoria, often late
at night, outlining a scene and asking each to create his own version,
without comparing notes. Then he and Pinelli retreated to Lake
Bracciano, north of Rome, to assemble the final draft.

By now, everyone in the court sensed a tension between the director
and his writers. Flaiano now felt Rondi was usurping his place.
Whether out of pique or from genuine scepticism, he suggested that all
this self-analysis and Pirandellian toying with reality was inappropriate to cinema. Wasn't that better left to literature?

During the winter, Fellini talked to actors, but in a desultory
fashion. They were told to turn up at the production office after six,
when he came in after a day with the writers. Among his visitors was
Salvador Dali's wife, Gala, who arrived with the latest of many husky
young protégés, William Rotlein, a street kid she'd spotted from her car
window on a visit to New York. She demanded Fellini screen-test him.
'He's a good-looking boy who looks like a bandit,' Fellini said afterwards. 'But Italy is full of good-looking boys who look like bandits.'
Even if Rotlein had talent, he would have been of little use, since
Fellini rejected almost everyone under fifty. 'This picture is full of old
people,' he told them. At this, said journalist Deena Boyer, 'he would
sigh, as if this were a penalty someone else had inflicted on him.' Those
he did choose were an odd group, made up, said one, of 'members of
Rome's threadbare aristocracy and internationally known drifters'.
They had little in common except their oddity. 'We're all either in the

Almanach de Gotha,' said the performer, 'or registered with the police.'

Fellini did have a few specific people in mind and was ready to travel a long way to meet them. The Orfei circus family were startled when he turned up in the middle of a performance to see the youngest daughter, Liana. She was on the trapeze and 'almost fell off from emotion . . . All the other circus people . . . were drawn to him like pins to a magnet. The emotion given off by that colourful crowd was so intense you could almost touch it with your hands.' Fellini didn't use Liana, but he kept up with the Orfeis. They appear in *I clowns*, and Nando Orfei plays the womanising Pataca in *Amarcord*.

Misinformation about the new film was rife, and encouraged. When he started shooting, Fellini barred the set to all but one or two trusted journalists, sworn to secrecy. Some strange rumours circulated. As late as February 1963, only a few days before the première, London's *Sunday Times* printed an anonymous and notably ill-informed report that Mastroianni wasn't the star at all. 'The chief player,' it said, 'is new to the cinema. He is the industrialist Guido Alberti, fifty-four-year-old owner of the Strega liquor concern and the café on the via Veneto of the same name. Creator too of the important Strega literary prize.' Alberti does have a role, but it's the modest one of Pace, Guido's producer.

There had never been any doubt that *La bella confusione* would be a film about an artist battling through his mid-life crisis. Nor did anyone seriously believe, least of all after Mastroianni took the central role of Guido Anselmi, that he represented anyone but Fellini. Fellini dressed him in his trademark black Stetson and dark suit, and even coached him in his habits of sitting backwards on chairs and nervously jiggling his foot. (Mastroianni never mastered either.) His hair was shaved back and whitened, while tiny gauze bags of sand under his eyes gave them a pouchy look. Mastroianni, who loved to eat, dieted throughout the film to make him resemble less the sleek Marcello of *La dolce vita* and more the harassed (and four years older) Fellini. Even so, it was only when the film was released that the director finally acknowledged: 'I am Guido.'

In all its essentials, the film's action parallels Fellini's life. Anselmi is a successful film-maker who has sequestered himself with his entourage in a remote spa to complete the script for his new film. He takes the waters, visits its steam rooms and is poked and prodded by doctors who don't enhance his state of mind. 'Well, what are you cooking up for us?' enquires one. 'Another film without hope?' Hoping to ameliorate his reputation as a moody moralist, Fellini, before shooting *Otto e mezzo*, stuck on the camera a small piece of brown paper on which he'd written: 'Remember, this is a comic film.'

With Guido in the hotel are his loyal but ageing assistant Conocchia and production men Cesarino and Agostini. He's also brought along a critic, Carini, to comment on the script. As the film starts Carini has just read the latest version, and adds to Guido's despair by scorning its 'impoverished poetic inspiration'. He goes on remorselessly: 'It may be the most pathetic demonstration that the cinema is irredeemably fifty years behind the other arts.' One recognises Flaiano's jaded voice.

There would be plenty of familiar faces on the new film. Annibale Ninchi again plays Guido's father. (His mother is Giuditta Rissone, one-time wife of Vittorio de Sica.) Prince Vadim Wolkonsky returns as the *concierge* of Guido's hotel. Polidor appears in the final parade, as do the entire crew of the film. Clemente Fracassi, attached to Cineriz since the suspension of Federiz, was production manager. Gherardi created its design, costumes and hairstyles, and Rota the music. Within the immediate team, Guidarino Guidi had been elevated to first assistant, replacing Dominique Delouche. Working with him were young Alessandro 'Sandi' von Normann and, though she's not credited in the final film, a terse, mannish woman in her middle thirties named Lina Wertmuller.

Ruthless, determined and apparently tireless, Wertmuller, who affected tight black outfits often topped with a black Stetson like Fellini's own, was his most devoted acolyte. When, three months into *Otto e mezzo*, she left to make *I basilischi/The Lizards*, the first film in a distinguished career, Fellini, instead of purging her as he had Delouche and Pasolini, helped find finance and even lent her some of his crew. She repaid him with adoration. 'To me you are like Jesus Christ,' she has said. 'I will never meet anyone like you in my life.'

Far from finding the spa's regime relaxing, Guido is racked by dreams. The film opens with one, Fellini launching us immediately, without music or sound effects, into his fantasy with only the most perfunctory opening titles. Trapped in a traffic jam beneath an underpass, Guido begins to choke as fumes fill the car. All around him, other drivers stare without interest (though in one car his mistress Carla is being fondled by another man). He shoves open the window with his foot and floats into the open air, where he finds himself weightless, tethered precariously by one leg. Abruptly his weight returns and he plunges towards a beach, only to wake in terror in his bed.

Otello Martelli had turned sixty in 1963 and virtually retired. Gianni di Venanzo, the unquestioned genius of sixties cinematography, replaced him. Fellini had told Rondi he visualised the look of the film as 'extremely neat, shiny and limpid. I was thinking of Botticelli', but having seen di Venanzo's inky blacks and chalk whites for Antonioni's *La notte* and *L'eclisse* and for Rosi's *Salvatore Giuliano*, he decided they matched to perfection his studiedly artificial vision. *La dolce vita* had been a film of cloudless nights and grey dawns, shot in sharp, high-contrast CinemaScope. For *Otto e mezzo*, di Venanzo uses the more manageable wide-screen format, while his people float in a diaphanous, blurred world. As the film is set in high summer, and often outdoors at midday, light spills into scenes through shutters, doors and half-open windows. Figures in the background are distorted, even blotted out by a glow of halation. Shots like that of Anouk Aimée in her pale jacket sitting on a white seat under a white umbrella against the background of a blazingly bright village square stretch the limits of the photographically permissible. Single-handed, di Venanzo propelled film lighting forward ten years.

At the spa, Guido is increasingly prey to his imagination. Maurice, a schoolfriend, is now a magician performing for the few inmates of the spa with the energy to stay awake past sundown. In the course of his mind-reading act, his assistant Maya dredges up the word 'Asanisimasa' from Guido's memory. This triggers another fantasy/flashback, in which young Guido is dunked with other children into a communal bath, then carried tenderly to bed. Covering the bedroom walls are family portraits whose eyes are said on certain nights to move, but the curse, explains a little girl, can be averted with the magic word 'Asanisimasa'. It comes from a childhood game, a version of 'Pig-Latin', in which each vowel of a word is repeated with an 's'. 'Asanisimasa' disguises 'anima' – Jung's term for the female aspect of the personality.

Guido's flashbacks become more frequent and disturbing as the hotel fills with people who demand his time and attention. One dream takes him to a ruined cemetery where, in school uniform, he speaks with his dead father. Pace, his producer, appears in the dream, and the father greets him as Urbano Fellini spoke to Federico on his death bed: 'He shouldn't have taken the trouble.' As Guido helps him re-enter his grave, the father tells his son and daughter-in-law: 'You two have been the joy of my life' – ironic, since they are chronically estranged.

In most of Guido's dreams, the vision of childhood is spacious and welcoming. Fellini re-creates a Tuscan ritual in which people bathed

Magali Noel with Annibale Ninchi, lookalike for Urbano Fellini, in *La dolce vita*, BFI.
Shooting the Trevi sequence on *La dolce vita*, February 1960. BFI.

Shooting the Trevi sequence on *La dolce vita*, February 1960. BFI.

Anita Ekberg realises Fellini's favourite fantasy in the *Le tentazioni del dottore Antonio* episode of *Boccaccio '70*, 1962.

BELOW LEFT: Fellini directs *Otto e mezzo*, 1963.
BELOW RIGHT: Pier Paolo Pasolini, protégé then rival. BFI.

La Saraghina (Edra Gale) dances for the schoolboys in *Otto e mezzo*, 1963. BFI.

Giulietta (centre) with her sister (Sylva Koscina, left) and mother (Caterina Boratto), overpowered by Piero Gherardi's obtrusive costumes in *Giulietta degli spiriti*, 1965.

Sensualist Susy (Sandra Milo) on the slide between bedroom and private pool in *Giulietta degli spiriti*, 1965. BFI.

Fellini recreates the ambiance of *Maciste all'inferno*, his first film memory, in *Roma*, 1965.

Terence Stamp as doomed film star Toby Dammit in *Tre passi nel deliro*, 1968. BFI.

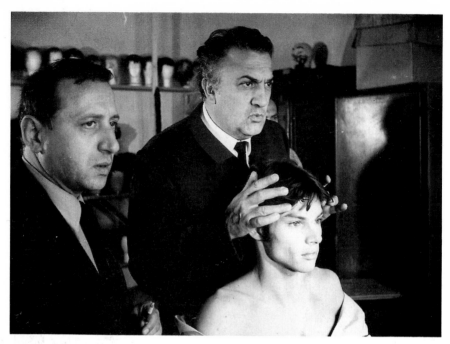

Fellini with long-time designer Danilo Donati. BFI.

Gideon Bachmann films Fellini during the editing of *Satyricon* for *Ciao Federico!*.

Martin Potter and Hiram Keller in *Satyricon*, 1969.

'A satiated look, as if no appetite went unsatisfied.' Restaurateur Mario Romagnoli as Trimalchio in *Satyricon*, 1969.

'A little whore with an angel's face'. London hippie Max Born as Giton in *Satyricon*, 1969. BFI.

their children in the lees of the new wine to make them strong. With its vast white-walled rooms, wide staircases and wooden floors, vats of milky water, soft towels and sheets warmed with the traditional *prete*, a wooden frame enclosing a pan of hot coals, the farm, an expanded version of Gambettola, with additions from Gherardi's own Tuscan farm and from Breughel, offers one of the most seductive of all idealised visions of country life.

Guido has invited his mistress, Carla, to visit him. 'Naturally [Carla] has a big fat ass,' he told Rondi, 'white skin and a small head. She's placid, good-natured, and seems to be the ideal mistress because she doesn't bug you, is very simple and submissive . . . The relationship that links him to this placid big-assed broad is based on a kind of dull physical well-being, as if he were sucking at a stupid and nourishing nurse, and then falling asleep, sated and spent.'

Initially Fellini saw Anita Ekberg as the voluptuous paramour who talks in *fumetti* dialogue, but the public search for a Paola on *La dolce vita* had been so successful (in publicity terms, if not in finding an actress) that he repeated it. Newspapers received a photograph of Mastroianni at eight years old, and lookalikes were invited to try out for the part of young Guido in the flashbacks, but the real search was for a Carla. From paintings by Rubens and Titian, Fellini assembled an Identikit portrait of this sexual paradigm and went on the road, auditioning (by his count) 5,000 voluptuous women.

He didn't find a Carla but he did meet Edra Gale, his Saraghina. The re-creation of his childhood encounter with the gigantic beach whore was to become one of *Otto e mezzo*'s most memorable scenes, and the Junoesque Gale, an American opera student, was perfect casting, though Fellini, not for the first time, misled her about what he had in mind. 'I was in Milan studying when Fellini came through and advertised for fat girls to try for the part of Mastroianni's mistress,' says Gale. 'He liked me, but before anything was done Sandra Milo became pregnant, gained weight and got the part. So Fellini invented the sequence of Saraghina dancing on the beach so as to use me in the film. I prayed my family in America wouldn't see me, but they did. My mother didn't speak to me for two years.'

Shooting had been due to begin in April, but Fellini temporised for weeks, filming tests and keeping his Carla candidates, among them Ekberg, Gale and singer Marcella Pobbe, on tenterhooks. Ekberg was particularly impatient, since she was expected in Hollywood, where she was to be married. She lost patience and left – to Fellini's relief, since he'd decided the role demanded an acting ability that Anitona, for all her physical attainments, simply didn't possess.

The part went to Sandra Milo, a bosomy Milanese who'd been launched as 'the Italian Judy Holliday' but who had little in common with her except a chronic weight problem. She had played in Rossellini's *Il Generale della Rovere* and *Vanina Vanini*, but something about her always carried an unignorable taint of the *déclassé*, and both films flopped. She went into semi-retirement, notorious as a trophy date among the Roman power élite. Fellini, who'd met her as a dinner guest at his home, was typically stubborn in wanting her for Carla, even when he found she'd dieted off her opulent curves. She asked for time to consider his offer, but next morning she and her husband were awakened by the arrival of Fellini, Gherardi, a make-up man, di Venanzo and two camera assistants, who began improvising a studio in her living-room to shoot tests. Stunned, Milo signed the contract and agreed to enter a clinic and put on five kilos – not a major problem, since she became pregnant soon after. Nevertheless, Fellini kept her gorging. 'Every time Federico sees me off the set he tells me to go eat something. I feel like a Strasbourg goose.'

Fellini's insistence on casting Milo is illuminated by her later claims that she and Fellini enjoyed a sexual relationship for some years during the seventies. In 1982 she published a scandalous 'faction' novel, *Caro Federico*, whose thinly disguised heroine, Serena, enjoys steamy interludes with one Federico. However, she later recanted and said the story was mostly invented, which, given Fellini's modest attainments as a Lothario and her flair for self-publicity, is probably true. Fellini said he never read the book. 'I don't even want to *smell* it.'

Guido parks Carla in a discreet hotel but has little time to enjoy her before his wife, Luisa, turns up. As Luisa, Anouk Aimée has none of the seductive *chic* of Maddalena in *La dolce vita*. Fellini trimmed her long eyelashes, cut her hair brutally short, made her up as if she had freckles, and dressed her in stern, black-rimmed glasses and an unflattering jacket with a high, tight collar. Seeing through the presence of Carla, who pointedly turns up wherever the group are eating and makes covert finger-wiggling gestures at Guido, Luisa berates him over the emptiness of their marriage. 'We've been stuck in the same place for years. You're the one who always wants to start over. You ask me to come back every time and you always think we can begin again.' Guido dreams of a world where all his women could accept one another. He imagines Luisa walking over to Carla as she sits alone in a restaurant and inviting her to join them.

From this spins off *Otto e mezzo*'s most beguiling fantasy. Its roots lie in Fellini's airport dream of the previous year, though the effect here is joyous, not sinister. Guido, arms loaded with gifts, bursts out of the snow to find the farmhouse crowded with the women he's loved or coveted: Carla, Luisa, transformed into the serene, loving chatelaine of his harem, a beautiful black girl, a Danish air hostess, a blonde model, Mezzabotta's Gloria, Luisa's friend Rossella, an ageing actress who hopes for a role in the film, another mysterious older woman noticed in anguished conversation on the phone in the hotel, a French showgirl in an abbreviated outfit of feathers and sequins, and La Saraghina. When the black girl, played by American dancer Hazel Rogers, leads a revolt against Guido's benign despotism, he quells them with a whip, like a lion tamer. 'What an extraordinary man,' Luisa says admiringly. One can almost hear Fellini murmur: 'If only . . . '

His interest in Jung had encouraged Fellini totally to abandon realism, and he kicked over the traces in his minor casting. After telling Rondi that 'actors dressed up as emperors, directors, magicians and priests fit in well with this story', he went in the opposite direction and dressed writers, restaurateurs, salesmen and businessmen as actors. Production men Cesarino and Agostini are played by restaurateur Cesare Miceli Picardi, a threatening nightclub patron in *La dolce vita*, and Bruno Agostini, a pharmaceutical salesman. As the octogenarian cardinal who's also taking the waters, Fellini cast Tito Masini, a retired tax official. Among the 'internationally known drifters' in minor roles was Mark Herron, who's Rossella Falk's lover. His show-business career culminated in a supporting role to the declining Judy Garland as her fourth husband.

The spa's guests are an anthology of coded personal references. Mezzabotta and his mistress, waiting out an annulment (since divorce was still illegal in 1963), are based on Carlo Ponti and Sophia Loren, often seen moping around Italy at the time while they struggled with the law and the Church to marry. Maurice the magician is Scottish playwright Ian Dallas. Another member of the court, *Vogue*'s Rome correspondent Eugene Walter, plays himself. His wife is Gilda Dahlberg, an ex-Ziegfeld girl and widow of an industrialist. After testing someone with a resemblance to Michelangelo Antonioni, his personal model of the bloodless intellectual, for Carini, Fellini chose French journalist Jean Rouguel, changing the character's name to Daumier to accommodate his accent.

Caterina Boratto, who'd played in *Campo de' fiori*, which Fellini co-scripted, came out of retirement to play the mysterious woman, in part because her daughter was Fellini's secretary. Madeleine Lebeau, who had the finest hour of a brief Hollywood career as the drunken mistress Humphrey Bogart discards for Ingrid Bergman in *Casablanca*, was brought from Paris to play the nameless actress (based on Luise Rainer) hoping for a part in Guido's film. She never left Rome again, becoming the lifelong companion of Tullio Pinelli.

After the main roles, Fellini's choices became more eccentric. 'All the servants and employees in the hotel were from aristocratic families of the *Almanach de Gotha*,' wrote a puzzled Eugene Walter. 'The guests were all people from the Rome asylum for the aged. They were given new hearing-aids, new teeth, or spectacles as needed; were permitted to take their finery home with them when work on the film was completed.' The priests of the tribunal that try a young Guido for consorting with Saraghina are played by women. One wouldn't get actors with interesting faces for such small roles, argued Fellini with his customary grand illogic. Besides, older women appeared 'ascetic, full of complexes, as a priest should look'.

The supernatural played its customary supporting role in the film. Yet again, Fellini followed his penchant for horror-film actors by choosing Barbara Steele, star of a dozen Italian vampire films, as Mezzabotta's spiky girlfriend Gloria. Mary Indovino, who played Maurice's clairvoyant assistant Maya, appealed to Fellini because 'Indovino' means 'clairvoyant' and the actress claimed some small talent in divination. Fred Hartig, a parapsychology buff with whom Fellini had fallen into a conversation at a party after *La dolce vita*, also has a small role.

At the spa, an audience is arranged for Guido with the old cardinal. In an oblique reminder of Fellini's skirmishes with the Vatican, his secretary expounds the Church's morality of movies, restating Pius XII's line: 'The cinema . . . does not lend itself very well to certain topics.' He chides Guido: 'You mix sacred love and profane love with too much nonchalance.' His staff envy him the meeting. Fellini had noticed that Italian film crews are, under their cynicism, intensely superstitious about religion. Agostini begs Guido simply to mention his name to the cardinal. Cesarino, whom Guido has caught in bed with two pretty 'nieces', is awed. 'He can authorise anything, even my Mexican divorce.' But the old man offers Guido only homilies from Origen (a eunuch, significantly), warning: 'He who is not in the City of God is in the City of the Devil.'

Meanwhile, Guido's film, a science fictional fantasy, is not going well. Towers of scaffolding have been built for a scene in which spaceships take off for Mars, but he has no idea how to use them. Pace arrives and begins harrying him to start shooting. They view some tests in which the roles being cast are recognisably those of Carla and Luisa. Humiliated, Luisa leaves the theatre. When Guido stops her in the lobby she berates him. 'What can you possibly have to say to others, you who have never been able to tell the truth to the person closest to you, to the woman who's grown old by your side?' This dialogue, like much between Guido and Luisa, rings authentically appropriate to Fellini's life with Giulietta.

While waiting for his daily ration of spa water in the garden and later drowsing in his room, Guido has a vision of a perfect and innocent young woman. She brings him his glass, turns down his bed and consoles him with her beaming smile. (In the script they also made love, but Fellini cut the scene.) While this role changed considerably in the writing, from the simple daughter of a watchman to a film actress, Fellini always visualised Claudia Cardinale in it. Twenty-four and married to producer Franco Cristaldi, she was waiting to star as the earthy peasant heiress in *Il gattopardo/The Leopard*, which Visconti would begin shooting in Sicily in the summer, a fact that made her even more attractive to Fellini.

Cardinale plays not only the beautiful innocent but also the actress Claudia, the film's voice of reason. She and Guido escape from the test cinema in Claudia's car (actually Mastroianni's own gun-metal Porsche) and drive to a half-ruined château. Guido tries to explain his film. Claudia isn't impressed and Guido finds he's talked himself out of the few ideas he did have. 'What a cheat you are,' she says. 'So there's no part in the film?' Guido agrees. 'There's no part in the film. There's not even a film. There's nothing at all, anywhere, as far as I'm concerned.'

Cardinale, initially anxious about her role, was calmed by Fellini's good humour, and also by the fact that he had cast her for beauty, youth and simplicity rather than her histrionic ability. 'I am the only actress Federico never modified,' she says. 'I remained myself, evidently because he liked me the way I was.' Despite a taxing schedule, Fellini was more relaxed with performers like Cardinale than he ever would be again. 'When we would go for a walk we'd talk a lot. He would take my hand and he'd say to me: "Tomorrow we'll go to Turkey." It wasn't true, but I believed it.'

During tense periods Fellini teased the cast into good humour with heavy-handed jokes, announcing, for instance, that the famous South American star Dolly Grandi was about to visit the set and, once maximum confusion had been achieved, unveiling his *dolly grande*, a mobile camera platform.

Gherardi's production design is a model of ingenuity. What appear as lavish sets are often real locations carefully lit to create the correct mood. The Italia cinema in Tivoli was used for the test-screening sequence. The ruined château where Guido and Claudia talk is the Palazzo Umberto I at Filacciano, 90 kilometres from Rome. The 'Mussolini Modern' frontage of an EUR building became the façade of Marcello's hotel. The station where Guido meets Carla is an old train cleaning shed on via Prenestina behind the Termini station, skilfully disguised and so brightly lit it dissolves in light.

As Cardinale and Guido stroll moodily around the abandoned castle, Pace and the production team appear. They've decided on a press launch of the film at the spaceship site. Guido has to be literally dragged there, past reporters demanding statements on divorce, atomic war, or whether he has ever fallen in love with an actress on one of his films. 'He's lost,' jeers an American woman. 'He hasn't got anything to say.' Out of control, with Pace threatening to ruin him, Guido crawls under the table to hide, and imagines shooting himself, only to be berated in fantasy by his mother.

When he reappears the press have gone and the crew is dismantling the towers. The film has been cancelled. The cynical Daumier approves. 'True perfection is in nothingness . . . What a monstrous presumption to think that others might enjoy the squalid catalogue of your mistakes.' No wonder that, in the middle of the screen-test sequence, Guido has a brief fantasy of the glib intellectual being led off and hanged.

But something in the chaos heartens Guido. 'All this confusion. It's me, myself. As I am, not as I would like to be. And it doesn't frighten me any more.' Assuming the role of ringmaster, he calls up everyone who has appeared in the film. Eighty people pour down the staircase from the towers, smiling and laughing together. Joined by Guido's ghosts, including his mother and father, they march round the ring to the sound of a clown band, led by a little boy in a white uniform with a piccolo. Guido and Luisa join the hand-holding ring. The last image is of the child still playing in the spotlight.

Serious shooting (as opposed to interminable tests) began in May, though not at Cinecittà. Fellini later filmed some pick-ups there, but Rizzoli preferred the Titanus/Appia 'Scalera' complex. Fellini moved in reluctantly. It was here that he'd edited the unfortunate *Il bidone*.

He also authorised the building at the beach near Rome of two sixty-metre towers of scaffolding, with little idea of how they might be used. 'Very often he starts building before he's ready,' says Gideon Bachmann, whom Fellini had invited to watch the shooting. 'That whole rocket launching thing at Ostia was just . . . *built*. I don't think he knew exactly what he was going to do with it. In fact he did very little.'

Throughout pre-production the team had continued to refer to the film under Flaiano's sarcastic title *La bella confusione*, though Fellini privately told Rondi: 'I don't like it much. Actually, I don't like it at all.' *Asanisimasa* was suggested, but Fellini didn't wish to be seen following the vogue for nonsense titles, like the 1962 sketch film *Rogopag*, named for the first letters of the names of its directors. Casually he'd begun calling it *Otto e mezzo*, since he would, he said, if one counted his shares of *Luci del varietà*, *Un'agenzia matrimoniale* and *Boccaccio '70* as halves, have made eight and a half films by the time he finished.

This reasoning is questionable. *Dottore Antonio* is only a quarter of the complete *Boccaccio '70* (or at most a third), while Fellini always insisted he directed most of *Luci del varietà*. Artistic licence then? Or could the title, like 'Asanisimasa' and the film itself, hide an obscurantist sub-text? Alexander Walker guessed, accurately, that Fellini had been eight and a half years old when he had his first sexual experience. Also, if one counts Carla as a half-share with her husband, the women in the farmhouse harem come to eight and a half. And, given the significance of dreams in Fellini's life and in the film, it's interesting that Tullio Kezich comments: 'The [Fellini] children were forced to go to bed every night at eight-thirty' – *otto e mezzo*.

The dimensions of the gamble he was about to take, basing an entire film on his own personality, struck Fellini in the days just before shooting commenced. He says he sat down the night (sometimes it's two days) before shooting and, 'desperate, confused', wrote Rizzoli a letter of resignation. In it, he confessed that 'the feeling, the essence, the flavour, the silhouette, the flash of light that had seduced and fascinated me had disappeared, dissolved'. However, he was interrupted by his workmen toasting him at the start of shooting. 'This will be a great film, *dottore*,' calls Gasparino, one of the machinists. 'Your health! Long live *Otto e mezzo*.' Loath to abandon his loyal crew, he tears up the letter and starts work. One can well believe in such a last-minute Gethsemane, since Fellini was to go through a similar travail on *Il viaggio di G. Mastorna* (though with disastrous results), but the story has been somewhat mythologised. Shooting began on 9 May, without, according to Deena Boyer's day-by-day report, the benefit of a champagne lunch. Champagne *was* served on 10 May, but at midday, and with Rizzoli – inconveniently for the legend – present on the set.

Until just before shooting, Guido had been a screenwriter working on a science fiction epic in which the whole population of the earth, led by the Church, boards a giant spaceship to flee from thermonuclear war. Vestiges of this idea survive in the model spaceship and the towers, and a large picture of a religious procession painted on glass to which Guido refers vaguely during the night-time visit to the set. Recognisably a special-effects glass painting, this would have been used to superimpose the exodus on a shot of the take-off. To offset the cost of the towers, Gherardi skimped ingeniously elsewhere. The spa gardens, based on those at Montecatini, were erected on an ex-Fascist barracks, military parade ground and rifle range at Cecchignola in the woods at EUR, where he also constructed the cemetery of Guido's dream. To manufacture forty art-nouveau chandeliers for the hotel lobby, he dipped holly leaves in gold paint and wired them to plywood frames which were then suspended from old toilet chains.

Making a virtue of necessity, Fellini let some of the ragged edges show. A corner of the hotel lobby set remained unfinished, so he incorporated the scaffolding and sandbags into the film. Why shouldn't the hotel be under repair? This effect was heightened in the sound mix by introducing the noises of production. We hear the hum of lights coming up to power, the buzzer warning that a take is in progress and the clatter of a projector. In the final scenes, light spills into the image from hidden lamps, giving flares along the edges of the frame. So influential was the film, however, that these and other eccentric effects would become commonplace, even clichéd within the next decade.

Throughout the film, Fellini struggled with the ending. He'd envisaged Guido boarding a dream train whose passengers were all the people in his life. Dressed entirely in white, they fill the dining-car. Though he shot this, he was never happy with it and, under the guise of producing a trailer, filmed the second ending as well, using the circus motif.

For a Fellini film the production was relatively free of disasters. 'Never have I had so easy a time with a picture,' he said, though, as on *La dolce vita*, sciatica troubled him towards the end of filming and he needed to support himself in a resting-frame. He finished shooting on 14 October. He could have stopped the previous day, but Sandra Milo reminded him it was the 13th, and unlucky. He dubbed through Christmas, observed with something between fascination and adoration by Liliana Betti, an unpretty but vivacious and persistent young woman from Brescia who'd written to him asking for a job and kept writing until he acquiesced. There was a vacancy at the Fellini court in the role of the loving confidant hitherto occupied by Delouche and Pasolini, and Betti filled it, becoming his secretary, chauffeur, straight-woman, Boswell, acolyte, collaborator and casting director for the next decade. Of the relationship, she says: 'It began as a continuous joke, and ended up in a kind of false love.' With Betti, physically and intellectually closer to his male homosexual colleagues than to the voluptuous mama-figures of his sexual fantasies (she's been accurately described as looking like 'a cheerful troll'), Fellini dropped his guard. 'Nobody understood Fellini better,' says Gerald Morin.

January 1963 was, even more than usual, a time of disaster for Italian film. Goffredo Lombardo had driven Titanus to the edge of bankruptcy with his investment in *Sodom and Gomorrah* and the de Sica/Ponti *The Condemned of Altona*. There were rumours – accurate for once – that Visconti had spent twice his budget on *Il gattopardo*, and de Laurentiis was pouring money into a new studio complex modestly christened 'Dinocittà'. Against this background the first screening of the complete *Otto e mezzo* took place on 21 January. Both endings were shown, but the second, more cheerful, version with the circus parade was unanimously preferred.

The same people at Cineriz who foretold – correctly – that Dinocittà would be a white elephant urged Fellini to make his film more accessible. They were alarmed by the audacity of its style and the way in which fantasies erupted unheralded into the action. The title galled them particularly. Mastroianni suggested *The Confessions of Snaporaz* and Fracassi *I Confess*, but Fellini was adamant in preferring his own. Alarmed that unsophisticated audiences wouldn't be able to differentiate between dreams and action, Cineriz made some prints for provincial areas in which the fantasies are tinted sepia. No amount of tinkering, however, could win *Otto e mezzo* the mass audience of *La dolce vita*. A German distributor left one preview growling: 'Fellini must be nuts. This is worse than *Marienbad*. I couldn't follow it at all. And I'm supposed to show that to my audience?'

At the première in Milan on 17 February there was scattered applause but no call for the director. Film-makers in the audience carped that Fellini had once again arrogated to himself the traditional sign of stardom by placing his name above the title in the final credits.

The slightly pompous logo of the film, '8½' in ornate Victorian script (suggested by posters for American westerns Fellini saw at the Fulgor), was more than matched by the credit '*Ideato e diretto par*' – 'Conceived and directed by' – which followed. (Fellini also took the usual credits for writing and directing.) Alberto Lattuada conceded, though with bad grace: 'It was a smart thing for him to do. It made him more important than the stars – it made *him* the star.'

Most reviews were enthusiastic, though novelist Dino Buzzati spoke for many when he called it 'the masturbation of a genius'. (Ironically, Fellini chose Buzzati to write the script for *Il viaggio di G. Mastorna*, his next project but one.) As with most Fellini films, public reaction was often hostile. An audience in Viterbo, where he filmed the school scenes, tore up a cinema after a screening.

Fellini took *Otto e mezzo* to Cannes in April 1963, where it was shown out of competition. The reaction was warmer than in Italy, especially among young directors, who were delighted at the way it celebrated and glamorised the film-making process. Roman Polanski, who was there with his first feature, *Knife in the Water*, recalled that it 'smote me like a revelation. It was all I'd ever dreamed of seeing on the screen, emotionally as well as visually.' François Truffaut concurred. 'Directors who have acted, or actors who have gone to the circus a lot, directors who have written scripts or know how to construct a set, almost always have something extra to offer. Fellini has been an actor, a screenwriter, a circus buff, a designer. His film is as whole, as simple, as beautiful, and as honest as the one that Guido in *Otto e mezzo* wants to make.'

At Cannes, Joseph E. Levine bought the British and North American rights, doing a deal with Columbia Pictures to distribute. For the film's New York opening in June, Levine threw a reception at New York's Four Seasons restaurant. It was attended by Fellini, Mastroianni and an entourage that included Pinelli, Flaiano, Guido Alberti and Gideon Bachmann.

The day before the launch, Levine screened the film with Fellini at his Festival cinema in Manhattan. From his confusion during the mute opening dream, it was immediately obvious that he had never seen it before. In his version of that first screening, Levine turned to Fellini and demanded of the sequence: 'Federico, what the hell does *that* mean? And he says: "*I* don't know,"' Levine went on. 'Now, I don't know whether he was putting me on or not, but *I* wasn't putting *him* on, and I think a lot of that shit he just put it in there, like he does now.

And the eggheads ate it up. Every egghead found something *different* – like looking at a painting.'

Levine had won a foothold in distribution by picking up the 1958 Steve Reeves peplum *Ercole e la regina di Lidia* for next to nothing, then promoting it furiously all over America as *Hercules Unchained*. He sold *Otto e mezzo* in much the same way. 'I did a helluva job with $8\frac{1}{2}$,' he boasted. 'Made a profit on it too, which was unusual for an art film – you better believe it! I had like a *hundred* screenings in New York. I showed it to every egghead professor school that I could find and it became what *I* call a cocktail picture. "Have you seen $8\frac{1}{2}$?" – you know. I don't think half of them understood it . . . Now it's become a picture you teach from, a fuckin' *classic*.' Levine was no admirer of the director. 'Fellini was as phony as a glass eye as far as I was concerned. I would never make another deal with him again. I didn't like the way he operated.'

Perhaps from marketing but probably from merit, *Otto e mezzo* appealed to American audiences as much as to those in Europe. The New York press, however, still harboured a vision of Fellini as a frisky Italian in love with life. Nobody this time asked him to demonstrate how to kiss a lady's hand, but when *Vogue* commissioned David Bailey, then married to top model Jean Shrimpton, to illustrate a feature on the friendship of Fellini and Mastroianni, the photographer suggested both men link arms with Shrimpton and skip towards the camera. Neither cared for this device, which Bailey had successfully used for other celebrity double-portraits, and nothing Bailey or Shrimpton could do induced the necessary spontaneity.

Fellini had asked Bachmann on the trip as his emissary. 'He wasn't sure of his English, and he thought I would be a wonderful connection with the American press,' he says. 'The first person who came up for an interview was Brendan Gill of the *New Yorker*, whom I knew from when I'd lived in New York. Brendan took one look at me and told Fellini politely: "I can't interview you with another film critic in the room." So Fellini realised that having brought me to New York would have the opposite result to what he intended. He immediately dropped me like a hot potato. I spent four days in New York, during which the only thing I did was to get him and Mastroianni into the Playboy Club, which they very much wanted. I left after that.'

On 18 July *Otto e mezzo* screened at the Moscow Film Festival, again with Fellini and Giulietta. The Palace of Congresses was filled with 8,000 people, most of whom followed the dialogue through French and English earphone translations. 'The whole place was crackling with metallic voices,' Fellini said. 'The atmosphere was that of Babel.' The Russian subtitles were few and inexpert. People laughed, if they laughed at all, in the wrong places, and incidents like La Saraghina's dance received applause for no apparent reason. Fellini had resigned himself to a flop but the film received a huge ovation.

It also became a political issue. Non-Soviet members of the fifteen-person jury, which included Sergio Amidei, were inclined to give Fellini first prize, but the Soviet bloc, on orders from the cultural *apparat*, protested at the film's lack of Socialist realism. Informally the Czech representative asked Fellini if he'd accept an award that praised *Otto e mezzo* but lamented that 'his film does not contribute to peace and friendship between peoples'. Fellini said he might do so if he wanted a story to dine out on for the rest of his life, and asked what he should say in his acceptance speech – that he wouldn't do it again? After threats to go public with the squabble, the film received the award with a citation praising it 'because it bears witness to the labour of an artist in search of the truth'.

Despite this, Cineriz assumed *Otto e mezzo* would never be generally shown in the USSR. A special screening was arranged for the censorious Nikita Khrushchev, who'd condemned decadent Western movies on a visit to Hollywood when dancers in the musical *Can-Can* exposed their frilly knickers for his benefit. Unexpectedly, however, he raised no objection to Fellini's film. The truth only emerged in 1992, when Khrushchev's projectionist revealed that the Chairman had dropped off in the first few minutes and slept until the end. When he woke he commented: 'Any film that gives me two hours of dreamless sleep in the middle of Moscow can't be dangerous,' and *Otto e mezzo* was approved for Soviet release.

19   The Maestro in Drag: *Giulietta degli spiriti*

José Luis de Vilallonga: 'Everything around me is fake.'
Fellini: 'Just like in life.'
On the set of *Giulietta degli spiriti*

Otto e mezzo was a modest success with the Italian public, taking 756 million lire, but a far greater one with film-makers everywhere. The influence of di Venanzo's lighting trickled down into every corner of the cinema, while Arthur Penn in *Mickey One*, Woody Allen in *Stardust Memories* and Paul Mazursky in *Alex in Wonderland* imitated Fellini's seamless alternation of reality and dream. François Truffaut was struck by the vision of the director as harassed artisan – 'a man whom everybody bothers morning, noon and night. They ask him questions he either doesn't know how to answer or doesn't want to answer.' He adopted it for *La Nuit américaine/Day for Night*, at the same time obliquely attacking Fellini's methods. Valentina Cortese plays an actress too drunk to remember dialogue. She suggests that he 'do it with numbers, the way I do with Federico'. 'Impossible,' Truffaut, playing the film's director, replies sternly, pulling down the boom mike to show they're recording live. 'In France we have to say the lines.'

In February 1964 *Otto e mezzo* won a nomination for the Best Foreign Film Oscar. Fellini was also nominated personally as Best Director, the writers for Best Original Story and Screenplay, and Gherardi for his art and set direction and, separately, his costumes. Fellini was at the peak of his reputation, one of a handful of directors, with Hitchcock and DeMille, whose names were known to the general public.

Among the producers pursuing him was de Laurentiis. Searching for a project equal to the swish new Dinocittà, he'd resolved to film the entire Old Testament as a fifteen-hour epic with segments directed by Bergman, Welles, Visconti, Robert Bresson – and Fellini. Welles visited the slopes of Vesuvius as a possible setting for the Sodom and Gomorrah episode, while Bresson went east, scouting Eves for his Garden of Eden. Dino offered Fellini what Liliana Betti called 'fabulous sums' to direct *Noah's Ark*. Fellini declined – wisely, since the project quickly fell apart. Bresson returned with footage of six possible stars, all, to Dino's alarm, black or brown. The Vatican ruled (in a belated endorsement of Rossellini's decision on *Il miracolo* to bleach Fellini's hair) that Eve must be white and, if possible, blonde and blue-eyed, and Bresson dropped out, followed by the other major names. The final film, called *The Bible: In the Beginning . . .*, was directed by John Huston, who also played Noah.

Since *Le notti di Cabiria*, Giulietta's career had languished. After their friction on the set and equally stormy marital relationship, the couple decided that they could either work or live together, but not both. While Fellini prepared *La dolce vita*, she acted independently in a few films, including *Fortunella* and *Jons und Erdme*. In Germany she starred in *Das kunstseidene Mädchen/La Grande Vie* for veteran French director Julien Duvivier, who had ideas of turning her into a sex star. He dressed her glamorously in tight blouses and had her hair teased into a Hollywood bouffant. When he asked her to play a nude bath scene, Giulietta called Fellini, then in the middle of shooting, for his advice. He ordered her to refuse.

On her return, Antonioni offered her the role of Mastroianni's estranged wife in *La notte* but she turned it down. Jeanne Moreau took the part – better casting, most people agreed. Masina also declined – 'by stupidity', she says – other plum roles, including another Mastroianni wife in Germi's *Divorzio all'italiana/Divorce Italian-style*, destined to be an Oscar-winning international hit. The refusals implied Giulietta would work only with Fellini, and though both denied this, incidents throughout the sixties gave credence to the idea. When, because of money troubles, she did return to film-making in the turbulent summer of 1968, opposite Katharine Hepburn in *The Madwoman of Chaillot*, Fellini, to the alarm of director Bryan Forbes, turned up uninvited on the French location and, silent and moody in his black Stetson, sat through every one of her scenes. After that, offers ceased altogether and Masina disappeared from the big screen for almost twenty years.

While shooting *Dottore Antonio*, Fellini told journalist Enzo Peri that Giulietta would star in *Otto e mezzo*, but apparently thought better of it. In 1963, however, the tensions of *Cabiria* were sufficiently remote and he began seriously to contemplate working with her again, perhaps to make amends for his neglect and the slurs, real and implied, of *Otto e mezzo*. But working on what?

Airing the fears of his mid-life crisis with *Otto e mezzo* had done little to ameliorate them, and, despite the film's relative ease of production, its completion had left Fellini as troubled as ever. Having embarked on a celebration and exploration of his own myth, he was helpless to return to the real. His disquiet is visible in *Otto e mezzo* itself. Even while praising its bravura, many noted its abnormal introspection. A psychiatrist assessing Fellini's mental health at the time and finding a man of ambivalent sexuality, morbidly fascinated by death, who liked to visit mental hospitals, who lived and worked in and for his dreams, who made films in which his *doppelgänger* confronted *his doppelgänger* and so on, into an infinity of mirror images offering no certainty, only sterile replication, might reasonably have inferred that he walked the lip of an emotional precipice. Fellini was as feebly tethered to reality as Guido in that opening nightmare.

In reaction, Fellini's obsession with the supernatural increased between 1963 and 1965. With Jung as his pretext and key, he admitted himself to a new world of sensory and mystical experiences. (In 1965 he even made a pilgrimage to Jung's Zurich home.) His interest was partly intellectual but it also disguised fundamental fears of death and of waning creativity.

Encouraged by 'an analyst friend', presumably Ernst Bernhard, he took LSD. As a leap into the unknown it was less than audacious, since he first submitted to an electrocardiogram, then had the drug injected under the scrutiny of a psychologist, a cardiologist, a chemist, a stenographer and two nurses. Everything he said was also taped. The 'trip' lasted seven or eight hours, much longer than expected, and during it Fellini walked and talked almost continuously. As a revelatory experience it was a disappointment. Fellini never listened to the tapes or read the stenographic record, and looks back on the event mostly with embarrassment.

He was happier with traditional mystic guides. In times of stress he made daily visits to the fashionable German-born astrologer of *Elle* and *Il messagero*, Francesco Waldner (and became enraged, Waldner recalled, when the omens were bad). Advised by occult writer Leo Talamonti, he called on healer Pasqualina Pezzola and a rural magician known simply as 'Uncle Nardu', who claimed to be able to turn himself into a horse. A visit to the Turin home of 'white' magician Gustavo Adolfo Rol was more fruitful. Rol was the undisputed psychic star of the sixties. Admirers like Tullio Pinelli claimed he could read closed books, paint in the dark, change the faces on playing cards, move objects from room to room without touching them and foretell the future. Rol and Fellini were walking in a Turin park when they saw a nurse asleep next to a baby being menaced by a hornet. 'At forty metres, simply with a gesture,' Fellini said, 'he blasted the hornet. I've *seen* it. It gave me goose-flesh.' He was sufficiently impressed to return frequently over the next decade.

Years later, journalist Sheilah Graham claimed that mediums told Fellini at this time that 'his next two films would die'. Word got around, she wrote, and actors refused to work with him. Fellini never confirmed this story, but, if true, it gives credence to his belief in the supernatural, since both films did 'die', one commercially and artistic-ally, the other literally, coming close to killing Fellini with it.

Ever since *La strada* Fellini had considered films about a woman with psychic powers. The first had been *The Little Sister*. This was supplanted by a biography of the clairvoyant Eileen Garrett, similar to the 1957 *The Three Faces of Eve*, which won Joanne Woodward an Oscar for her performance of a woman with multiple personalities.

The plot of what would become *Giulietta degli spiriti* developed from these. Fellini outlined it to Paul Gilles while it was in early production. 'Giulietta is the soul of my film; it's her film . . . Her character is a woman about thirty-five, a tranquil *petite bourgeoise*, calm, traditional and superstitious, full of prejudices, but all in all . . . good. Her husband, Giorgio, is a businessman, surrounded by bizarre people: painters, sculptors, actresses, mediums, fortune-tellers; in short, a gang of crazies. Giulietta, as a result of being around these people, falls into a sort of delirium. She's always being left alone and she feels herself completely lost in the *milieu* of her friends. They are intellectuals, and more or less depraved. There's one, for example, Val, who's a medium. She passes her days in spiritism seances. And outside of that, one could say she's a somnambulist. Another, Elena, is an obsessive voyeur: she photographs young couples when they are together, intimately; you see what I mean? There's another one, Alba, a nymphomaniac. Sandra [Milo] is a kept woman, the mistress of a Greek arms manufacturer, old and obviously a millionaire. She's called Susy. Despite the life she leads, she's perhaps the most human character and the most normal Giulietta meets. It's a cat that brings them together. Then Giulietta pays a visit to Susy in her solarium. But she sees her also in dreams, and in the course of seances with Val. Susy appears to her in the form of Iris, a mysterious presence of the *demi-monde*. It's thanks to her that Giulietta succeeds at the end of the film in chasing the phantoms and evil spirits and rediscovering peace and serenity.'

By mid-1964 Gherardi and di Venanzo were well advanced with plans for the film. The fact that it would be Fellini's first feature in colour, not to mention a supernatural fantasy, inspired them, and with his enthusiastic collaboration they developed the vision of a world as totally manufactured and peopled with phantoms as that of *The Wizard of Oz*. Colour would not be employed naturalistically but as a visual language, while the design would also echo and reinforce the sense of Giulietta's disturbed psyche.

Meanwhile, the writers wrestled with Fellini's ever-changing concept. 'This woman,' said Pinelli, 'was to have peculiar supernatural sensations, but in a realistic way. That is, she was disturbed by these strange capacities of hers. Then, we started to have problems.' The most common problem, familiar from all Fellini films, was the drift towards autobiography. He visualised opening with Giulietta sitting alone in a villa, waiting for Giorgio to return home on their wedding anniversary. Since Federico and Giulietta would be married for twenty years in October 1963, there was little doubt which couple he had in mind. Also, while the character of Giulietta was visibly Masina's, the dreams he planned for her, mostly fantasies of a repressive religious education, naked torsos in wardrobes, women semi-nude on horses or writhing with a slippery, black and python-thick eel, were all taken intact from his diaries.

Fellini wanted the film to end with Giulietta's rejection of the fears and phobias embodied in these dreams, symbolised by her walking out on the philandering Giorgio and burning down their villa. While this reflected his doubts about his marriage, it didn't necessarily square with Masina's, and she grew increasingly uncertain.

The psychic elements also disturbed her. Masina believes in the supernatural. She's been known to pause in the middle of a conversation and murmur: 'We are not alone.' Her belief was perhaps greater than that of Fellini, whose interest was mainly superstitious, an obeisance and sacrifice to his personal devils in return for an untroubled life. During pre-production, Fellini persuaded her to attend a seance in their Rome apartment, but she balked at holding others. 'I believe in it and am considered a good medium,' she said of spiritism, 'but that's why I don't want to do it. It reveals a fascinating world and a dangerous one.'

Though Fellini only occasionally dreamed about Masina, he did so at this time. She's isolated in the centre of a film studio while a camera dolly circles her, loaded with laughing clowns. Fellini tries to give directions, but the clowns drown out his orders until one by one they fall to the ground. He woke with a feeling of anxiety and a sense that the project was sinking. It's tempting to see the clowns as simple shorthand for his writers, resistant to the new film's ambivalence. 'We were thinking of one kind of woman,' Pinelli said, 'and Federico of another. His concern was less with human feelings than with images.'

By now, rifts were appearing in the Fellini team. Flaiano was convinced that Brunello Rondi was supplanting him and that the film anyway was out of control. Feeling he had little to lose, he became increasingly acid in his criticisms. Fellini complained that Flaiano wasn't contributing. Flaiano claimed he was never consulted. In April, when Rizzoli invited Fellini, Giulietta, Fracassi, Pinelli, Flaiano, Gherardi, Sandra Milo and her companion of the time, producer Maurice Ergas, to fly to Los Angeles at his expense for the Academy Awards, the relationship exploded.

Neither Gherardi nor Pinelli went, but Pinelli did see off the party at Fiumicino and witnessed the showdown. Everyone had been given first-class tickets – except Flaiano, who found himself in tourist. The slur infuriated him, all the more so when Fellini claimed, unconvincingly, that Cineriz had made the bookings and the exclusion wasn't his doing. Flaiano called him a liar, to which the director responded: 'Well, don't go then!'

Grudgingly Flaiano took the cheaper seat and during the flight Fellini sat with him for a while, but the damage was done. Though he receives a credit on *Giulietta degli spiriti*, Flaiano never saw it, never worked with Fellini again and abandoned the cinema almost entirely until his death in 1972.

The Hollywood visit was surrounded by the usual show-business circus. Foreign Oscar nominees, among them Roman Polanski, were treated to tours of Disneyland and Forest Lawn cemetery. Fellini, making his third visit, liked the former, calling it '*La dolce vita* for kids'. He confided to Polanski that he'd like to spend a week, and planned a documentary about it. At Forest Lawn, he was quoted $35,000 for a spot in its Columbarium, complete with an eternity of piped *muzak* – truly a vision of hell.

Fellini had another motive for visiting Los Angeles. He hoped to persuade two boyhood idols, Mae West and Groucho Marx, to appear in *Giulietta*. The fact that West was interested in spiritism had convinced him she'd accept, but she turned him down without seeing him. Marx, no more enthusiastic than Fellini about leaving home, also declined, though he and Fellini did meet in New York. Strolling down Broadway, Marx took him into a sex shop to show him some porn movies. 'He himself had seen an enormous quantity,' says Fellini. 'He said to me: "You're Italian, yes or no? Then you can't have not gone to see porno films." He was convinced that Italians spent their life going to see porno films and masturbating.' Fellini, who needed little convincing, admitted later that he has assembled 'a gigantic collection of photos and porno films'.

At the Oscar ceremony itself on 15 April, Polanski was seated with the Fellini party when the winner of Best Foreign Film was announced. He applauded with genuine enthusiasm as Fellini bounded on stage to receive his Oscar from Julie Andrews. Gherardi also won for best black and white costumes. Not everyone was so receptive. Columnist Hedda Hopper was scandalised that the pious *Lilies of the Field*, with nominations as Best Film and Best Actor, didn't also, as was traditional, earn a nomination for its director, Ralph Nelson, who 'stepped aside,' she wrote, 'for Italian Federico Fellini, whose $8\frac{1}{2}$ in my opinion was beneath contempt'. Equally contemptuous was Joseph E. Levine. 'That Fellini was selfish,' he whined. '[He] never mentioned *me*, never mentioned the poor bastard Rizzoli who put up the money, made it possible, *never* mentioned his name, got up there – they almost had to yank him off the podium.'

Fellini had hoped to finish writing *Giulietta* early in 1964 and begin shooting before the summer, but Rizzoli asked him to delay until November. The near-collapse of Titanus was on everyone's mind. Pondering Fellini's plans to shoot in colour and mostly on location at Fregene, where he proposed to burn a villa to the ground, Rizzoli wondered if Masina was popular enough to carry a \$2–3 million film, especially since this would be, technically, a production of Federiz, giving Fellini a slice of the profits. Wouldn't both their investments be safer with someone like Katharine Hepburn? But Fellini was adamant. Only Giulietta would do.

The decision, finally disastrous, to shoot in colour was consistent with the trend of the time. Europe's intense film-making style had usually dictated restraint in colour and design, but in 1964 rainbows seemed to mark the way of the future. In the United States psychedelia was the latest thing. DayGlo dyes and OpArt design were everywhere. In Britain Mary Quant and in France Pierre Courrèges and Paco Rabanne pioneered a garish and glittering *couture* of vinyl and metal.

Most major European directors were indulging themselves with impressionistic colour fantasies. Antonioni and Jacques Demy descended with paint pots on Ravenna and Cherbourg respectively for *Deserto rosso/The Red Desert* and *Les Parapluies de Cherbourg/The Umbrellas of Cherbourg*, daubing the old walls with gaudy primaries. Even Ingmar Bergman made his first colour film, the comedy *Now about All These Women*, using pastel costumes and a country-house setting not unlike *Giulietta*. It was cumbersome and unfunny, and he quickly reverted to subdued, realistic colour. Only the muted tones of Visconti's *Il gattopardo* reflected a truly modern colour sense, and significantly Giuseppe Rotunno, who lit it, would light Fellini's films for the second half of his career.

Originally, an existing house at Fregene was to have been used as a location but Fellini decided to build a new and larger, though fake, villa from scratch. Giulietta admired the design and spent some of *Otto e mezzo*'s profits on a scaled-down version as their private summer residence. It was completed during the production, a two-storey villa at the end of via Portovenere near a grove of the distinctive spreading umbrella pines, about ten minutes' drive from the ocean. Built of white stucco and red brick, it had a red tile roof, cherry-wood trim and windows outlined in green.

In the film, the villa, surrounded by formal gardens inside a white picket fence, is an island of calm in a disordered world, and Masina aimed for the same effect in real life. The garden, with its roses, gardenias and petunias, was her special pride, and a playground for their forty cats. For Fellini, its vegetables were of more interest, and invitations to meals at Fregene, cooked by Giulietta with the help of their long-time servant Fortunata, were sought after. Among the new acquisitions admired by the guests was a Renoir. Fellini was becoming rich, though – prudently, as it turned out – the house and most of its treasures were not in his name but Giulietta's.

Guests at a typical dinner during this period might have included Sandra Milo, Guidarino Guidi, Lina Wertmuller, Edra Gale, painter Anna Salvatore, Eugene Walter and a flock of bankers, writers and minor aristocrats. After dinner, charades were played. 'Who wouldn't pay,' recalled Walter, 'to see a pantomime of the election and ordination of Pope Joan with Lina Wertmuller in the title role, industrialist Albert Guidi playing the papal mule, and a college of cardinals composed of Fellini, several writers, a French princess, a prize-fighter and the delightful Edra Gale? Followed by a version of *La Maison de Madame Tellier* with Giulietta in the title role* and the "girls" played by a staggering variety of types, including a Milanese banker and a Roman count. Then *Carmen* as it might be performed in a Norwegian girls' school, and, to finish, Guidarino Guidi in *The Childhood of Mae West*.'

Under all this gaiety, however, was an increasing sense of stress and disturbance, both in the Fellini marriage and in the film-making team. When they had guests it was Giulietta who led the games and appeared in the charades. Fellini himself merely watched, or, more often, slipped away to read or watch TV.

As the deadline for the start of the new film approached, he worried increasingly about his team. Having broken with Flaiano, he next lost Leo Catozzo, who had edited every film since *La strada*. Catozzo's invention of a film splicer using Scotch tape rather than heat and glue revolutionised editing, and he retired on the profits. Though the parting was amicable and Ruggero Mastroianni, younger brother (and uncanny lookalike) of Marcello, replaced him, many felt that Fellini's work never regained its old pace.

Also on Fellini's mind were the insistent demands of Gherardi and di Venanzo. He'd given them their heads and they exercised an accelerating control over the film, setting its tone far more than the writers, or even, in a sense, Fellini himself. The court was cautious, as usual, about voicing its doubts, though Gideon Bachmann did complain that 'his films seem to be developing away from contact with humanity. What you see now is non-involvement and emphasis on spectacular visual effects. I don't think Fellini – or anyone else – realises how much he is influenced by . . . Gherardi and Gianni di Venanzo. I feel he is giving in, losing his drive.' As for the script, the few people who saw it were startled by its cynicism. 'All the defects of Federico's own marriage are in it,' someone on the set whispered to an American visitor. 'He hasn't left out a single bizarre and unhappy detail.'

Giulietta lurched into ungainly motion in the spring of 1965. Rizzoli had hoped to shoot in his own studios, the old Saffa-Palatino complex, but the film soon outgrew this modest setting and Fellini shot the interiors at Cinecittà, where Gherardi rebuilt Giulietta's garden, complete with plastic lawns.

---

*De Maupassant's story is about a brothel whose girls take a day off to attend a first communion. Masina's association in Fellini's mind with the role of prostitute seems indelible.

As Fellini had planned, it opened with Giulietta planning a dinner *à deux* with Giorgio to celebrate their anniversary.* But he has forgotten the date and blunders in with a group that includes their lawyer, an effeminate psychic, the middle-aged sculptress Dolores, her current young model/lover, and Val, Giulietta's friend, played by Valentina Cortese. Giorgio, a Fellini clone in well-cut houndstooth sports jacket and greying hair, is Mário Pisu, Mezzabotta from *Otto e mezzo*.

Later that night the guests hold a drunken seance. The medium contacts a spirit named Iris, who communicates by rapping the table. Her message, she says, is 'Love for everyone'. The group takes this as an excuse to flirt, but Giulietta, shy and sexually repressed, won't join in. 'Who do you think you are?' Iris raps at her. 'You're no one to anybody. You don't count, you poor thing.' Giulietta faints in shock.

Next day the table emits a confirmatory tap when she touches it, indicating that an open channel remains to the afterlife. A visit to the beach brings more visions. An old man tries to drag something from the water, and begs her for help. As she pulls, a raft with three horses, one apparently dead, drifts past, followed by a boat-load of armed warriors, then a barge that nuzzles up to the sand, threatening to disgorge its cargo of grotesque naked men and women. Everything disappears when Giulietta opens her eyes.

We're introduced to the women of Giulietta's family: her still-beautiful but censorious mother, who complains Giulietta doesn't wear enough make-up or dress with sufficient flair, and her sisters Sylva, a TV hostess, and Adèle, a doting mother, righteously pregnant, who wonders why Giulietta has no children. The obvious answer to Adèle's question is Giorgio, who habitually comes home late, watches TV, then goes to bed in earplugs and a mask. In his sleep, he murmurs 'Gabriella' but the next day denies knowing such a person.

Except for Giulietta's neat little mandarin jackets and straws, *fausse-naïve* and faintly Asian, which Fellini himself designed, Gherardi's costumes for the women, extending the vision of *La dolce vita*, are really giant sculptural hats and ruffs with dresses attached. Nobody can touch or kiss. Instead, ritual pecks are bestowed on the air half a metre from faces barricaded behind swooping starched brims, heavy veils, clouds of tulle and explosions of plumes. Cortese is such a slave to couture that she always wears the same dress, but in different fabrics and colours.

---

*Tactfully, Fellini changed their twentieth anniversary to the fifteenth for the forty-five-year-old Masina.

For Fellini and Gherardi, the film's design had become a malicious adolescent game. Gideon Bachmann recalls them 'sitting on one of the four-poster beds upholstered in silk and crowded with flimsy art nouveau paraphernalia, chuckling to each other in whispered tones behind cupped hands about the next joke they were going to play on Valentina Cortese by forcing her to wear a rebellious lock of hair purposely over her eye throughout the film, or adding and subtracting names from the list of extras through the sheer whim of visual conception.'

Giulietta, troubled by the possibility of a secret life for Giorgio, lets her friends lead her into their alternative existences. Valentina takes her to Bishma, a guru, ancient and androgynous, who tells her: 'Love is your religion. Your husband is your god', but rhapsodises about sex as a trade and an art. Giulietta scorns this as a kind of prostitution, but erotic visions pop unasked into her mind as the guru rambles about the wine and fruit-juice mixture *sangría*. 'They say it quenches all the thirsts of those who drink it,' Bishma murmurs, 'even those which are never confessed.' A different voice from the same mouth adds: 'They call it the drink of oblivion.'

In turning Giulietta from treatment into film, Fellini, as usual, removed most of its heterosexual eroticism. Dolores still has her male models but Elena is no longer a voyeur and the nymphomaniac Alba has disappeared completely. Replacing them is an anthology of sexual ambivalence. Unable to get Mae West as Bishma, Fellini replaced her with Valeska Gert, a famous lesbian actress of the surrealist period. Eugenio Mastropietro, aka 'Genius', camps up his role as the medium, Eugene Walter is pressed into drag as a nun, while the forty sisters of Giulietta's childhood, faceless in purple habits, are actually young boys recruited from the beach at Fregene. 'They walk more like nuns than nuns do,' Fellini insisted, a change of viewpoint from *Otto e mezzo*, where his priests were played by women. For Fellini the real fun lay increasingly in shuffling the cards, not winning the game.

Back home, Giulietta has more visions of herself as a little girl in a convent school, of her childhood friend Laura, who committed suicide, and of her grandfather, who ran off with an actress named Fanny but whom she thinks of as her spiritual protector. When she appeared at six in a school play, playing a martyr roasted by Romans on a grate, he interrupted the proceedings, indignantly dragging her away under the eyes of two rows of black-robed nuns.

That night Giorgio brings home another guest, a punctilious and aloof Spaniard named Luis who quotes Lorca and mixes some *sangría* for Giulietta, praising it in exactly the terms used by Bishma. She recognises his as the voice the guru produced. Overhearing Giorgio planning an assignation with Gabriella, Giulietta hires a private detective, whom she recognises as the old man she saw in the vision at the beach.

Sandra Milo had won a Nastro d'Argento for *Otto e mezzo* (one of a record seven earned by the film), so Fellini immediately cast her in the tripartite role of Iris, Fanny and Susy. It demanded, as before, major physical reconstruction. Milo checked into a clinic and lost sixteen kilos. She also took dance lessons – because 'Fellini wanted me to move in a certain way.' Gherardi, in charge of make-up as well as costumes, was even more exigent. 'He shaved my eyebrows completely. To me I was a ghastly ugliness, a monster, but Gherardi was blissful, as though now he had destroyed my face he could begin to rebuild. First came the blonde cotton-candy wig, then re-created eyebrows, red hair. Fellini said to me: "You must be absolutely pretty. Remember, inside of you – you must repeat it constantly – you say to yourself: 'I am beautiful, the most beautiful woman in the world.'"' Her bedroom boasts a mirrored ceiling and a slide down which she can slip after sex into an indoor swimming-pool. 'I accept everything. I deny myself nothing,' she purrs.

For Giulietta, meanwhile, the film had become a nightmare. Pasty-faced and nervous, she gave an increasingly unconvincing performance, though occasionally the *moues* and rueful grins of her usual screen persona, suppressed by Fellini, broke through unbidden, like bubbles in dough. 'Those who have seen *La strada* or *Le notti di Cabiria*,' Fellini explained expansively to the press when they queried the nature of their collaboration, 'know her as a poignant clown, a comedienne who can wrench the heart. But that engaging creature had to go. We worked endlessly. And all along I knew what I was losing – but not what I was gaining. She found a thousand objections. This or that did not "feel" right to her. And I became angrier and angrier. "But don't you understand?" I would tell her. "I want you to play *yourself*. What I'm asking you to do is what you *always* do – what I'm asking you to feel is what you *always* feel."'

Since it wasn't typical of Giulietta to fantasise about naked women wrestling with giant eels, or to contemplate fornicating with girlish Indian princes, these demands were doomed to fail. She'd expected a dispassionate, invented reality as an exercise for her talent. Instead she found herself cast as Fellini in drag. According to Thomas Meehan, 'Those who witnessed the shouting fights between Fellini and his wife

... feared that the film could even lead to the finish of the Fellini marriage.' After filming ended, Masina allowed herself the last bitter word. 'I hope I have a chance some day to play something near this character,' she said. 'I feel that this film doesn't permit me to arrive at the . . . high tide . . . of this character. But that's the way Federico wanted it . . . and he's a man.'

Gherardi had shown Fellini photographs of ornate tomb statuary in Genoa's Stagliano cemetery. Both were especially moved by one figure of a small boy with a carved butterfly on his shoulder. The naïvely sinister images reminded Gherardi of the Decadent and Symbolist art of late nineteenth-century Paris and Vienna, especially Klimt and Moreau, which influenced the design of Giulietta's beach dreams. Continuing the *fin de siècle* style, he gave Susy's villa art nouveau stained-glass windows in a peacock motif and staircases with looping vine-like balustrades. Di Venanzo's opulent lighting reinforced this vision. The interior of Giulietta's house was white, to convey — inevitably — purity but the villa was red, yellow and violet, fondant colours 'symbolising,' wrote designer Léon Barsacq, an enthusiast for the film, 'all the pleasure haunts of the world' but in practice evoking something between the *Playboy* mansion and a brothel.

In Susy's garden is a tree house, reached by a basket on a rope. She invites Giulietta up and the two have an intimate chat during which Giulietta confesses she's had no lover but Giorgio. Susy feels Giulietta should free herself sexually and lures two young men up to join them, but as they prepare to enter the basket Giulietta gets scared and flees. Susy invites her to a party, which Giulietta attends in an atypical crimson dress. The guests include a decadent Indian, a variety of pouchy, ageing and jaded aesthetes, and Susy's beautiful but androgynous half-Arab godson. The festivities become a limp and over-directed orgy like that in *La dolce vita*, with elaborate sex games in lieu of fornication. One casts the women as prostitutes, sex-slaves to the men. Giulietta almost succumbs to Susy's epicene godson. However, as she sinks back on her circular bed, staring up into the mirror, she has a vision of herself as the child martyr surrounded by flames, and once again runs away.

At her own garden party the next day, Giulietta does her best to ignore her intrusive visions. She dances with Luis, ridiculously tall and remote, a joke lover, like her Arab prince. He's played by the Spanish aristocrat and writer/journalist José Luis de Vilallonga, who was as discomfited as everyone else by the film's synthetic *milieu*, a 'nightmarish universe of plastic materials. Only the trees seem sincere. And not even them. The honeysuckle that climbs the walls of the villa is suspect. Even the rose I have to sniff at sunset, its feet in the mist, is artificial like the rest.' Gherardi's plastic lawns had to be watered continually to conserve their gleaming green. Since none of the vinyl, fibreglass or nylon settings absorbed water, the atmosphere became stiflingly hot and humid. De Vilallonga confided his disquiet to Fellini. 'Everything around me is fake,' he said. 'Just like in life,' Fellini murmured softly, 'Just like in life.'

Vilallonga's confusion increased as Fellini began to tinker with his character. Giulietta, dancing with him at the garden party, pointed out that she was talking to his neck. Fellini called for two 30cm blocks of wood. When they arrived, however, he ordered Vilallonga to stand on them, not Giulietta, who now found herself addressing his shirt buttons. Baffled at these changes to a character which made little sense to start with, he complained: 'I don't know any more who I am.' Fellini, he said, 'gave me a protective look. He enjoys other people's pain. "Don't worry," he said. "_I_ know. And you are getting better."' Vilallonga wasn't consoled. There was a growing sense that _Giulietta_ was not so much audacious and experimental as random. When Pasolini visited the garden-party shoot, Vilallonga noticed him smiling behind his hand. Another guest, French director Claude Sautet, 'had a good laugh'.

At her party, a woman psychiatrist, acting as another Fellini mouth-piece, counsels Giulietta: 'You're afraid of being alone, of being abandoned . . . and yet you want nothing more than to be left alone; you want your husband to go away.' Though she laughs scornfully at the thought of rejecting Giorgio, it nevertheless takes root.

Giorgio departs on his 'business trip'. Alone in the house, she gives in to her horrors, which invade the rooms. Laura, still in her white dress and frozen under the lily pond where she drowned, invites Giulietta to join her in 'a long sleep with no more pain'. Gabriella's sour-faced maid appears to finger her curtains. Two uniformed men pace past the window, raindrops tapping eerily on their slick black raincapes.

The phantoms become more flamboyant. A giant bearded figure of authority towers over her. Most daunting of all is her mother, a frozen-faced ghost driving Giulietta towards insanity. She's rescued by her grandfather, who appears again in his ancient plane. 'Don't hold on to me,' he tells her. 'You don't need me any more. I too am an invention of yours, but you are full of life.' Spontaneously, Giulietta tells her mother: 'I'm not afraid any more.' At this, a tiny door clicks open. Giulietta crawls through, to find her child self in a cramped attic-like space, still strapped to the grate of her martyrdom. She releases the bonds and immediately the phantoms disappear. Outside, Giulietta opens a gate in the white fence. She walks in the pine forest, alone but at the same time surrounded by invisible companions. According to Fellini's original outline, Giulietta is 'now in complete harmony with the fabulous spectacle of life which is so vastly and so delightfully more rich, magical and supernatural when it accepts in an easy and simple rhythm the miracle of every day'.

Almost from the moment shooting finished in June 1965, Rizzoli pressed to have the film entered at Venice, but, as usual, Fellini resisted. He disliked the festival as much as ever and he was also diffident about exposing his film to the critical wolves. Rizzoli persisted. 'He is a seventy-five-year-old man,' Fellini sighed to Lillian Ross, 'and he *likes* to go to film festivals. He tells me: "We will have a nice time on the yacht, we will see a lot of beautiful women, we will have good food." I tell him: "Film festivals are dangerous. This picture does not need publicity." But Rizzoli will do this we-have-to-defend-our-flag kind of talk, and sometimes I get so bored and tired of saying no that I might say yes.' But in the end Fellini said no, telling *Variety* on 22 June that he didn't feel 'in the right frame of mind to face the inevitable examination which a festival participation entails'.

Relations between Rizzoli and Fellini were deteriorating. Cineriz had allocated a full panel of the opening credits to the manufacturers of BriNylon, announcing that most of the materials in the film were made from its products. Though this was true enough and such quid pro quos are common in the cinema (if seldom so obtrusive), Fellini was furious at what seemed like a gesture of contempt for the film and for him. Rizzoli didn't help by telling Fellini he was disappointed in *Giulietta*. The criticism stung, all the more since it mirrored his own dissatisfaction. He knew the film was too long. Even after cutting the more gratuitous fantasies it ran for 148 minutes. (It showed at this length in Italy, shrinking to anything from 129 to 110 minutes elsewhere.) Nor did the first prints achieve the intensity of colour he hoped for.

Under continued insistence from Rizzoli that he promote the film more, Fellini's perverse streak emerged. In the autumn, Eugene Walter found him on a sound stage at Saffa-Palatino shooting Edra Gale dressed as D'Artagnan, with boots and a blonde moustache. On a papier-mâché rock a Brünnhilde drank from a flask, awaited by her horse. An Indian dance team, Asoka and Sujata, were rehearsing. There was a chorus of nuns, clowns and gypsies, and a Neapolitan tenor blared on the playback. Fellini explained he'd been asked for a scene from the new film for TV, so he was inventing one. He asked Walter: 'Do you know anyone with a Persian cat that can act?'

Late in the summer of 1965, rumours had circulated that upset Rizzoli. He confronted Fellini, who confirmed them. His next two films would be not for Cineriz but for Dino de Laurentiis. Since John Huston finished editing *The Bible: In the Beginning . . .* in March, Dino had no major project in production. He'd asked what Fellini wanted to do next. Fellini told him, as he'd told Eugene Walter during post-production of *Giulietta*, that 'my next film will probably be science fiction'. Where better to make such a labour-intensive project, coaxed Dino, than at Dinocittà?

Fellini had just read *Assurdo universo*, the Italian translation of *What Mad Universe?* by American sf and mystery writer Fredric Brown. Its hero, Keith Winton, editor of the magazine *Surprising Stories*, is jolted by a freak electrical explosion into an alternative universe based on the fantasies of its most obsessed teenage fan, Joe Doppelberg. In Doppelberg's ideal world, Earth is fighting an interstellar war with hideous Arcturian invaders. Only one man, the handsome, audacious adventurer and scientific genius Doppel, can save it.

Brown meant to satirise the garish covers and even gaudier plots of pulp sf magazines. Winton was based on Sam Merwin, editor of *Startling Stories*, in the September 1948 edition of which the novel first appeared, and Doppelberg parodies the adolescent fans whose letters Merwin published in his column 'The Ether Vibrates'. The pulp universe in which Winton finds himself has, like the settings of most Brown novels, the surrealist simplicity of a dream. Its handful of characters move through almost empty cityscapes from one nightmare situation to another. In the *pièce de résistance*, Winton is trapped at night in a New York City where, to fool the Arcturians, a black gas blots out all light. Mobs of murderous Nighters sweep the streets, linking arms and tapping canes in unison.

Such visions, plus the *doppelgänger* image and the resonances with his own early contact with *420*'s Giuseppe Nerbini through its letter columns, appealed to Fellini, and he persuaded de Laurentiis to buy the film rights. Dino and Fellini concluded a two-film contract, the first production to be *Assurdo universo*, for which the director would get $250,000, a fee more than comparable to the best Hollywood was then offering. For Fellini, over-extended after the modest returns of *Otto e mezzo* and irritated by Rizzoli's accusations of money wasted, Dino seemed for once more ministering angel than demon king. He signed and took a hefty advance.

Fellini quickly abandoned *What Mad Universe?* except as a hook for his fantasies. Tempting visions had been floating through his mind since 1964, when, as their plane nosed down towards a snow-covered and forbidding New York airport, Morris Ergas asked jokingly: 'How much would you want to make a film about the afterlife?' Fellini liked the idea of a story in which the main character apparently survives an accident in the first reel, to realise only later that he's dead. It wasn't an especially original concept, but Fellini saw it as an ideal focus for his ideas about death. After he and Dino signed their deal, Fellini wrote him a long letter outlining the film he called *Il viaggio/The Voyage*.

Giulietta opened in Rome in October, with a gala launching in New York two weeks later. The reaction in Italy was mixed, most people agreeing that the film's style swamped its content. It often seemed to be little more than what its glossy Hollywood colours promised, a psychoanalytical soap opera. Fellini had hoped to screen the film for Ernst Bernhard, who might have given it, like some Jungian Cardinal Siri, his *imprimatur* and *nihil obstat*, but the analyst died during the production, an incident Fellini claims to have foreseen in a dream.

The New York opening was as flamboyant as Rizzoli could have wished. Fellini, Giulietta and Milo arrived on 25 October and checked into the St Regis. A lavish but trashy two-week promotion was orchestrated by Bill Doll, publicist also for the Barnum and Bailey and Ringlings Circus. A Canadian TV crew followed Fellini for twenty-four hours for a documentary. He walked down Fifth Avenue while photographers shot pictures of him for a *paparazzo* competition. 58th Street was renamed 'Fellini 58th Street' for a night. The visitors had a party thrown in their honour by Jackie Kennedy, and Fellini and Giulietta hosted a dinner for thirty to celebrate their twentieth anniversary, for which Giulietta cooked spaghetti. Round the clock, all three did interviews, Giulietta modest in black lace and lacquered blonde hair, Milo, according to one reporter, in 'two baby-blue feather boas, a large smile and not much else – unless you count the shoes'.

Despite the hoopla, *Giulietta* was neither a critical nor a financial success. In Italy, it grossed only 770 million lire, about the same as *Otto e mezzo* and only a third of *La dolce vita*. American critics were lukewarm. The most common comparison was to glossy advertisements.

Fellini was, as usual, offhand about criticism, though he knew the film to be badly flawed. The best hedge against depression was work. A friend who dropped him off at Kennedy after the New York opening asked if he was taking a vacation. 'Making a movie *is* my vacation,' Fellini told him. 'All the rest – the travelling about to premières, the interviews, the social life, the endless arguments with producers who don't understand me – is the work.' He said he would sleep all the way back to Rome, and immediately start the new script. 'And when I sleep,' he said, 'I dream of my films.'

He could not – would not – deviate from the path to which his myth had committed him, even though he had begun to see that it led only to disaster.

20 The Mouth of Truth: *Il viaggio di G. Mastorna*

> Moraldo: 'At a certain point you get disgusted. I can't take it any more.'
> Leopoldo: 'You're right . . . disgusted . . . you've seen us in our true light . . . Yes! Yes! Escape . . . '
> Dialogue cut from *I vitelloni*

In a break during filming *Giulietta* at Fregene, Fellini drifted over to José Luis de Vilallonga.

'How do you write the word "death"?' he asked casually.

De Vilallonga replied : 'With a capital letter.'

'Ah. With a certain . . . apprehension?'

'No. Not at all. With friendship.'

Fellini sat in silence, softly rubbing the end of his nose with his index finger. Finally he said: 'I have often seen Death since I was a baby.'

'*Ah bon?* In what form?'

'A quite beautiful woman,' Fellini said, 'in her forties, dressed in red silk and black lace. Pearls at her throat; an air of calm; resigned, intelligent . . . '

Vilallonga responded with his own Top Person's vision of a Not Very Grim Reaper: a young woman, a little bitchy, in a white bikini, diving from too great a height into a round swimming-pool filled to the brim with Spanish champagne. At this, Fellini shivered – 'deliciously', Vilallonga said.

'I see . . . the Death of a sadist.' Fellini left quickly, crossing himself.

Looking at the history of *Il viaggio di G. Mastorna* it's difficult not to believe, as Fellini does, that it was cursed from the start. When he conceived it in 1964 he was one of the world's most famous and successful film-makers, on his way to Hollywood to receive an Academy Award. When he relinquished it two years later – though he has never totally abandoned the project – he was penniless, discredited and close to death.

On his return to Rome from America Fellini found himself embroiled in financial disaster. In the week after Christmas, self-employed Italians declared their income for the year. The Revenue Office then turned inspectors loose on the figures, paying special attention to colourful characters whose public inculpation might scare ordinary citizens into declaring every last lira. In the wake of the Italian government's shift to the left, the 1965 tax period was subject to special rigour. 'Out of Rome's cavernous municipal records building pour hundreds of taxmen to check on . . . Romans with fat wallets and poor mouths,' wrote *Time*. 'The taxmen peek into bank accounts, check salaries with employers, rummage in garbage cans counting the nightly output of liquor bottles, look into garages to see how many and what model cars are being driven, and pump the servants for juicy *dolce vita* details.'

Fellini had estimated his earnings for the previous year as $16,000 – low, but in line with claims by others in the film industry. Mastroianni, for example, declared only $48,000. However, the Revenue noted Fellini's new house in Fregene and other recent expenditure. In December, when its revised demands were displayed in front of the tax office, near the significantly named piazza della Bocca della Verità (Plaza of the Mouth of Truth),* Fellini's estimated taxable income had been multiplied by ten. So had Mastroianni's. Gina Lollobrigida and Sophia Loren would have been slammed even harder had they not prudently taken foreign citizenship.

. Since most of Fellini's money from *Otto e mezzo* was invested in the Fregene house, and *Giulietta* showed no signs of making a fortune, the assessment was catastrophic. The Fellinis sold their Parioli apartment and moved into a smaller one on via Margutta. The relocation marked the beginning of fiscal reverses that were to depress and hamper Fellini for the next decade.

If Fellini's finances were eroded, so was his popularity. *Giulietta* had made few friends, least of all among the young directors who'd adulated *Otto e mezzo*. 'Fellini is guilty of Fellini-ism,' snarled Marco Bellocchio, one of the most pugnacious new talents. 'He has rolled himself into a hermetic shell and has become repetitive and involuted, like the rings of a snail.' Fellini brushed this off. 'Out of Italy's chaos a few good directors always emerge, but I don't think Italy's young have

---

*The piazza is named for a stone face with a gaping mouth, immortalised in the film *Roman Holiday*. According to legend, the hand of a liar placed in the mouth will be bitten off.

lifted their voices high enough yet.' But there was no doubt he was stung.

Tight-lipped, he attended the French première of *Giulietta* in Paris with Sylva Koscina, an event for which Salvador Dali was coaxed out of seclusion. The arch-surrealist's opinion of the film isn't recorded but his old collaborator Luis Buñuel loathed it. Till *La dolce vita*, he said, Fellini had been 'one of the directors whom I found most interesting. Now he's always playing the genius. I saw *Giulietta*; it's worthless. Neither true nor false surrealism, nothing. Those hats . . . what's the point? Technical trickery, nothing but technical trickery.'

Fellini's sensitivity to criticism, always acute, increased as the dimensions of *Giulietta*'s failure became clear. He'd broken with Flaiano and alienated Rizzoli. Now a coolness appeared in his friendship with Tullio Pinelli, and even Gherardi, after a squabble over trivialities which some insiders feel had its roots in Fellini's resentment of the designer's Oscar for *Otto e mezzo*'s costumes, became an enemy. They never worked together again. 'He latches on to everyone, drains them dry, then throws them away,' Gherardi said bitterly. In Viterbo some months after the break, Gideon Bachmann met the designer by chance and they spent the evening together. 'He was destroyed by the fact that Fellini was no longer working with him, because that was his life.' Then, on 3 February, Gianni di Venanzo died suddenly in Venice of hepatitis while shooting *Anyone for Venice/The Honey Pot*. Fate had administered the *coup de grâce* to the *Otto e mezzo* team.

Late in the summer of 1965, Fellini wrote a long undated letter to de Laurentiis outlining *Il viaggio*. The main character, simply known as M, is a cellist (Fellini liked the instrument's female contours). Flying to a performance, he's involved in a risky but apparently successful emergency landing in a snowstorm. The plane halts in a large plaza not far from a Gothic cathedral, and M, with the rest of the passengers, is herded into a train and carried through what looks like a German city to a motel.

M explores the motel, including a peculiar cabaret in the basement, then finds that the street outside is filled with a huge festival. Lining the street are houses of worship: Catholic and Protestant churches, synagogues, mosques, all crowded and brilliantly lit. M, however, can't make it into any of them, on top of which he finds he's lost.

He's driven to the railway station but all the signs are illegible. The station is busy with massive trains as tall as office buildings and, as one of them leaves, M sees on it a friend he knows to be dead. It occurs to him that the landing may not have been successful at all and that he could be dead himself.

He goes to the police station, where they ask him for some proof of identity – not a paper but a moment of his life when he's been truly himself. M decides his best witness would be his wife, Luisa, but there's no way to make contact. He visits a medium, a trip that takes him through the city's metro and along a street of sex shops and strip-clubs like Paris's Pigalle. He also passes a procession led by the Pope on his ceremonial chair, surrounded by cardinals.

He sees a vast departure station of glass where one moves on to another level of consciousness in a huge white boat. He also finds himself in a theatre where prizes are being handed out. To win one, M must fight a white eagle.

Once it's clear that he has died, M is relieved. It was not as painful nor as frightening as he'd feared. He begins to explore. Fellini exploits Fredric Brown's idea of alternative universes by showing M moving through a succession of variant realities. There's a world of women, a promised land where one is reborn as a child, and another where he meets his own parents, grandparents and great-grandparents, all, of course, delighted to see him. He also sees Luisa, reconciled to his death and happy with a new man. (For those who find such sights disturbing, the world of the dead has a clinic where one can learn forgetfulness.)

At the end of his letter, Fellini listed the locations he'd need: the city square and its cathedral, an airport, train station, metro station, a harbour, the streets of a modern city and some others, more antique, plus the sea, and parts of Rome, New York, Amsterdam, Berlin, the Vatican and Venice. In case Dino panicked at such prodigality, Fellini assured him he had cheap ways of faking almost all these.

Disjointed and undisciplined as *Il viaggio* may have seemed in outline, de Laurentiis could see it was filmable. He was less sure that it was commercial, though his brother Luigi, an enthusiast for the supernatural, urged him to make it. Given Fellini's reputation, Dino decided to gamble, and put Luigi in charge. If the film didn't develop well, he consoled himself, he could always interfere. As he usually did anyway.

For the first time in his career as a director Fellini found himself without writers. The relationship with Pinelli was now so chill that he couldn't ask him to work on this film. He did outline the plot to Tonino Guerra on a drive to Ostia, but by the time they arrived Fellini had a raging headache, which both agreed was a bad omen. He also talked it over with Pier Luigi Rondi, but the writer he finally chose was the novelist Dino Buzzati.

Sixty years old, Buzzati, better known as a journalist for *Corriere della sera*, owed his literary reputation to some metaphysical fables with strong overtones – too strong, some critics felt – of Franz Kafka. He had never written a screenplay. He met Fellini when he interviewed him for a series of articles called *In Search of Mysterious Italy*. Fellini took him to visit some of his favourite mediums, including the healer Pasqualina Pezzola. In a confused audience, Pezzola suggested that Buzzati was dangerously ill. In fact this was true. He was already being treated for the disease that would kill him in January 1972. By the time the article appeared in August 1965 (without any reference to this revelation), Fellini felt sufficiently attuned to the novelist to invite him to collaborate.

But the partnership never caught fire. Buzzati lived in Milan and wasn't available for the spur-of-the-moment café conferences, late-night drives and long walks by the sea that characterised Fellini's writing methods. When they did meet, Fellini took immediate charge. Trying to invent a surname for the film's hero, Buzzati spun off some bizarre names from his imagination: 'Ermete Squoiato, with an "o" . . . Rondo, Tullio Rondo. Scidmeno. No, better Scimno. Paolo Scimno . . . ' Fellini listened for a while, then picked up the Milan phone book, opened it at random and said: 'His name's Mastorna; first name Giuseppe', and all discussion ended. Buzzati found himself increasingly shouldered aside as Fellini seized the reins and drove *Il viaggio* deeper into his private world, inventing major new sequences recalling his childhood and schooldays in Rimini. The completed script bore only Fellini's name.

Fellini and Liliana Betti relocated in the Dinocittà offices in via Pontina but spent little time there. In the sterile building he christened 'The Big Snake', Fellini drooped, says Betti, 'like a plant in a refrigerator'. At Cinecittà he was king. Here he was just another faceless foot-soldier of the Neapolitan Napoleon. No matter how large the monthly cheque, the fact that it bore the rubber stamp 'Waiting Artist' simply made him more angry and depressed. Arguing that casting would be easier nearer the centre of Rome, he took an office at via Nazionale 36 which became his de facto headquarters as he interviewed performers and took extended survey trips with Rotunno and Luigi de Laurentiis around Italy and to Cologne. As the sets progressed he also set up a production office at Vasca Navale.

Eager to break into the American market, Dino was negotiating with United Artists, which had made money backing Hollywood 'runaway' productions like *The Vikings, Solomon and Sheba* and *Around the World in 80 Days*, and picking up such European films as *Tom Jones* and the James Bond series. De Laurentiis argued that if UA would finance them, he could make films just as good. 'The presentation was so charming,' said UA executive Steven Bach of Dino, with whom he dealt in the eighties, 'that one assumed so skilful a stylist could not fail to deliver movies equally entertaining and convincing.'

In 1966, however, Dino wasn't producing the films UA wanted. Although Huston had finished editing *The Bible: In the Beginning . . .* in March, until it opened in October nobody would know if its huge investment would be repaid. Meanwhile, Dino had only *Il viaggio*. To protect his investment and to tempt United Artists, he demanded, as he had for *La dolce vita*, that Fellini cast an international star. Yet again, Laurence Olivier's name came up, but Fellini said no. Olivier had, he conceded, 'a stupendous face, but he would not be credible as Mastorna. His face has a peaceful spirituality, a deep, calm intelligence, the detachment of a man who has comprehended everything and grown familiar with the thought of death, overcoming it or merely giving it a suitable place inside himself. By the *end* of the film G. Mastorna could have Laurence Olivier's face, but not earlier. Prior to that, I would feel useless, listless with an actor like him.' And, it went without saying, threatened.

Mastroianni was the obvious casting, but though the actor was eager, Fellini resisted approaching him. As soon as the name of the new film was announced, Fellini-watchers had speculated that 'Mastorna' was shorthand for '*Mastroianni ritorna*' – Mastroianni returns. Resentful of the implication that he relied on him, Fellini told Mastroianni he wouldn't be needed, so the actor signed to appear in the stage musical *Ciao Rudy!*, playing Valentino. The run would extend well past 3 September, the scheduled start of shooting.

Fellini, meanwhile, sent out calls to some old friends, including Macario and Fanfulla, and even Toto. He also went through a half-hearted search for glamorous Anglo-Saxon faces. Steve McQueen was considered, but he held off contacting him. Vanessa Redgrave had just launched her film career with *Morgan*, and Fellini arranged to have her photographed in a London park, but she heard nothing more of it.

At Dinocittà the sets were going up. The largest was a scaled-down Gothic cathedral, based on Cologne's. Next to it was a DC8 airliner and the huge and sinister motel. Determined to distance himself as much as possible from the pastels of *Giulietta*, Fellini decided to shoot *Il viaggio* in as near to black and white as colour film would allow. After announcing Lili de Nobili as designer, he switched to Pier Luigi Pizzi, who worked almost exclusively in monochrome.

In 1956 John Huston had shot a version of *Moby-Dick* in which the film stock was pre-saturated by preliminary exposure to light. *Il viaggio* would go further, using colour only in smears and tones on an otherwise neutral image. Costumes, of which the film demanded more than 2,000, would be equally colourless, as if dusted with ashes, while the extras would be chosen from Slavic races to give the film an inscrutable other-worldly quality.

Meanwhile, Fellini had found a replacement for Gianni di Venanzo in Giuseppe Rotunno. As a member of Visconti's team, Peppino Rotunno was particularly attractive to Fellini. He'd begun as Visconti's operator on *Senso* and gone on to light *Le notti bianche, Rocco e i suoi fratelli*, Visconti's segment of *Boccaccio '70* and *Il gattopardo*. At a time when photography was becoming more casual under the influence of the French, Rotunno, though well up on new equipment and laboratory techniques, remained reassuringly formal. 'The test of a cameraman is how he handles the foreground,' Fellini said, 'just as the best test of a chef is how he cooks eggs.' Rotunno was also, unlike Venanzo, essentially a photographer of colour, though with a taste for Goyaesque gloom and rich colours thickened and diluted with black. From him Fellini learned how to show perspectives even in blackness. It helped refine the sense he pioneered in *La dolce vita* of people who carried a personal darkness around with them, one that would dominate *Satyricon, Roma* and *Casanova*.

Rotunno took the job with misgivings. 'Working with Federico is like working with four directors simultaneously. While you get one scene ready, he's one step ahead, preparing another one or trying to film something else. His idea of shooting a film is to do it as fast as possible; he starts work early in the morning and wants to start filming at once, anything at all, and bit by bit the whole day proceeds at that infernal pace. There are many shots, all of high quality, with special effects, characters, people moving around . . . Never anything simple, even though he keeps repeating: "This film is very simple, let's not touch a thing, we won't even move the camera."'

To preserve that spontaneity, Fellini even stood in front of the camera while scenes were blocked out, then stepped aside and called to Rotunno: 'Motor!' Rotunno would yell to his operator: 'Shoot!', hoping that they'd capture what Fellini wanted. 'The fact is,' Rotunno says, a little wearily, 'his creative instinct is so powerful that you have to keep up with it or go under.'

Throughout the spring and summer of 1966 Fellini worked under an increasingly oppressive sense of doom. Liliana Betti fretted about 'a paralysing confusion which drove him to uncertain renunciation or useless, implacable stubbornness'. As Rome became hotter and the pressures more demanding, Fellini convinced himself that the project was under some malediction. Tullio Pinelli agrees that Fellini had 'a superstition' on the subject. Was he frightened of dying if he made it? 'I believe that, yes. All the times that he's spoken of it, he's upset himself. He says that the story brings him bad luck. He doesn't want to hear it spoken of.' The seers and clairvoyants concurred. Fellini was close-mouthed about the auspices, but a persistent rumour circulated that, after a visit to Rol, Fellini found a note in his pocket saying: 'Don't make this film.'

'In normal conditions,' says Betti, 'his vitality would have overcome all obstacles. He would have made the film he wanted to make, the way he wanted to and where he wanted to. But in a state of depression like the one he was suffering from, he could do nothing but defend himself, even at the price of complete immobility.'

He was troubled by nightmares, most of them marked by the central image of *Il viaggio*, an aeroplane. In one, which he saw as demonstrating his contrasting choices, he was first a parachutist in brilliant orange, then a diver plodding along the sea bottom in a lobster-red rubber suit. In a dream recorded on 7 March he saw himself piloting a plane that plunges towards a tunnel. It halts in time, but on each side of the entrance, standing guard, are old women whom he recognises as the Fates.

Fellini was alone at the production office at Vasca Navale when he experienced a startling hallucination. 'I was sitting on an old couch meant for resting on. Suddenly, in a flash, tons of stone crashed down on me, an inch away from my nose, something like the entire front of Milan or Cologne cathedral. I heard the wind it raised as it fell, then the terrifying crunch an inch from my feet. I leapt away like an acrobat. The wall covered everything – sky, space, and air; it was the size of Mont Blanc. I was an ant.' He lost consciousness, and woke to find he'd been thrown four metres during the experience.*

---

*Jung himself had a recurring dream in which an enormous turd descended on a cathedral, which he analysed as a psychic comment on the nature of creativity.

Bruised and terrified, Fellini began to plan how he might escape from what seemed the risk of certain death. The final entry in the diary he kept on *Il viaggio* ends with a rambling statement eloquent of confusion and despair. 'To try to give up the fight half-way through the film, as though the very idea of the story of Mastorna's voyage had the ill-omened and reasonable power to paralyse its author's creativity. Everything is blocked, everyone, even the public, is struck by this paralysis. Death is something so unknown that the sheer notion of speculating about it is senseless and wildly presumptuous. The wall of the eight-storey railroad car collapses on the platform of the station built in the studio. HALT! POSTPONED! TILL WHEN?'

Though he had, essentially, decided not to do the film, Fellini continued to go through the motions. With the 3 September deadline in sight and no star, he shot some tests of Mastroianni to see if he'd be physically credible as a cellist. Jungian analyst and cellist Peter Ammann, a friend of Ernst Bernhard, was called in to advise. The tests were convincing and the actor agreed to break his *Ciao Rudy!* contract, accepting the financial penalty, but still Fellini temporised.

The official first day of production came and went, with nothing shot. On the 14th, Fellini had another dream. He was at a railway station like the one in *Il viaggio*. Giulietta, wearing only a black slip, waits to see him off. Fellini is well in time to find a seat but the train leaves early. He runs after it, grabs a railing and is dragged along. The doors are locked and the train is going too fast for him to jump off. His record of the dream ends with an anguished 'Help!'

The same day he wrote to de Laurentiis:

'Dear Dino,

'I must tell you something that has been on my mind for a long time now and that has finally led to a decision.

'It's a question of a serious decision, one I don't want to over-dramatise but one which is the only honest answer, to my mind, to the constant and unnecessary efforts to gloss over deeper and more authentic feelings for reasons that stem only from a feeling of friendship.

'I can't start on the film – after everything that has happened, I wouldn't be able to finish it. Please don't misunderstand me. I have no doubts about the project, but a long series of contradictory and disruptive incidents which have nothing to do with the film itself created an atmosphere of resistance and hesitation from the beginning so that I have lost interest and no longer have the strength I need. Under these circumstances I can't make the film.

'In order to spare you and myself embarrassing situations and unnecessary external consequences, and because I really need a little peace and quiet and time to be alone, I would like to ask you, in all friendliness, to contact Giorgio de Michele, to whom I have entrusted everything.

'Given the friendship and respect that the long years of our relationship have brought with them, I hope that a way can be found to solve this problem.

'I am sorry, dear Dino, that things have gone this far, but I can't change it. I embrace you and wish you well.'

Why did Fellini write this letter? How seriously did he expect it to be taken? He'd tried a similar ploy before, on the eve of *Otto e mezzo*, but had wisely torn the letter up. As Daniel Toscan du Plantier says, Fellini would often 'officially' start shooting in order to draw more money from the budget, then continue casting and fine-tuning the script for another month. This letter looks like an attempt to wring similar concessions. Reassurances of not having lost interest, of needing a rest, of hoping to find 'a way to solve [the] problem' all hint at the possibility of compromise and renegotiation. Gideon Bachmann, to whom Fellini gave a guided tour of the sets shortly before his collapse, inclines to this view. 'I think he simply wasn't prepared.'

If he hoped to out-bluff the wily Dino, Fellini had miscalculated severely. Restrained by Luigi, Dino initially did nothing. For another ten days Fellini remained incommunicado at Fregene. Then, on 24 September, de Laurentiis announced to the press that *Assurdo universo* had been postponed until 3 October because of Fellini's ill-health. But at the same time he filed suit for breach of contract, demanding restitution of his investment of 1.1 billion lire, 600 million of which – about $500,000 – had already been paid out, including 45 per cent of Fellini's fee. He claimed seventy people had been thrown out of work by Fellini's refusal to start – omitting to mention they were the ones fired by him from the production the moment he decided to sue.

Almost everyone, including Luigi, felt Dino was over-reacting, but his legal rights were not in doubt and the courts authorised him to seize goods to the value of 300 million lire. Though most of what Fellini owned was in Giulietta's name, bailiffs did take between $5,000 and $50,000 worth, depending on which version you believe. (Since these included the Renoir, the latter figure seems more likely.) When it became clear these wouldn't cover even a fraction of the debt, Dino also attached Fellini's future earnings from *Otto e mezzo* and *Giulietta*, and launched another suit for damages over the second film of their deal. It was all eerily familiar. While giant towers rose for a science fiction film, a producer threatened his director with financial ruin if he didn't start shooting – the climax of *Otto e mezzo*.

The battle between Dino and Fellini was watched closely by everyone in the business. Richard Burton, making *Becket* at Dinocittà, wrote in his diary on 28 September: 'There is a huge set on the back lot which may now be unusable', adding: 'Dino will figure out a way to come out smiling. Betcha.' That afternoon, he noted: 'Fellini has found another backer. He will make the film at de L. studios but as an outsider. I betcha and I was righta!'

Fellini had indeed found new funds but Dino, busy with the première of *The Bible*, an all-star occasion which he'd arranged for 11 October in his native Naples, didn't feel particularly threatened. The new backer was Italnoleggio, a distribution organisation set up by the Socialist government to prime the pump for producers, and its resources were negligible. With hindsight, Fellini's announcement looks more like an attempt to accumulate bargaining chips against the inevitable renegotiation with de Laurentiis than a real attempt to relaunch the film. Fellini says he was convinced that if he could remove the project from Dinocittà, it might still be made, but it's not clear how he hoped to jettison Dino, whose credibility was inextricably engaged, or do without the giant sets.

After the *Bible* première, Italnoleggio and de Laurentiis got together and on 9 November details of a new and more credible deal were announced. *Il viaggio* would be made at Dinocittà, with de Laurentiis distributing through United Artists. Mastroianni would star. The one real difference was that Fellini would act as his own producer, having hurriedly formed a new company, Fulgor Films, specifically to do so. Such an arrangement might have worked had everyone been totally committed, but no sooner was the contract announced than cracks appeared. Mastroianni, kept waiting too long, announced he'd signed with Visconti to star in *Puccini*. Fellini replaced him with Enrico Maria Salerno, but United Artists, now with a pretext to bail out, did so.

By this time, the auspices for *Il viaggio di G. Mastorna* were so horrendous that only a man of peerless rationality would have dared start shooting it, and Fellini was anything but that. He'd already started negotiating to do another film, a version of Petronius' *Satyricon*, to be financed by Franco Cristaldi, with Claudia Cardinale, and Sordi as the pompous millionaire Trimalchio.

The impasse with Dino continued through Christmas. Fellini played out the game, representing himself to his friends as a penniless bankrupt harried by a malevolent producer, and to Dino as an international star of the cinema who might well make him a lot of money. In the former mode he was capable of extraordinary histrionics. Liliana Betti recalls him turning up at the office with a few gold trinkets which he proposed to sell to a jeweller in via del Tritone so he could buy lunch for the painter and the film-maker Hans Richter. As the tough bargainer, however, he continued, despite the producer's overwhelmingly superior resources, to defy de Laurentiis.

On a foggy morning in February the two met in the gardens of the Villa Borghese. Shouting and waving their arms, they walked back and forth under the trees that had seen so much intriguing over the centuries. After half an hour, they stopped, embraced, then returned to their limos, from where two high-priced teams of lawyers had watched the meeting, to announce, in effect, Fellini's unconditional surrender. He would complete *Il viaggio* with an international star chosen with Dino, who would withdraw his lawsuits. Shooting would begin between 20 April and 15 May.

Fellini and Dino haggled over a star. Fellini suggested Gregory Peck, Eli Wallach, Oskar Werner or Paul Newman, but all were busy. Omar Sharif's name came up, as did that of Danny Kaye, but Dino urged Fellini to use Ugo Tognazzi. Stocky and square-faced, Tognazzi, who would have his most enduring fame as the more masculine half of the homosexual couple in *La Cage aux folles*, was a far cry from Olivier and Mastroianni. He'd just starred in two misogynistically black comedies by Marco Ferreri, *L'ape regina*, where he's a new husband who expires from the sexual attentions of his randy wife, and *La donna scimmia*, playing an entrepreneur who marries a woman covered with hair in order to place her on show, then falls in love and, after she dies, tours with her embalmed body. Fellini agreed grudgingly to see him, and the highly flattered actor presented himself for his approval, only to be chilled by an obvious lack of interest. Fellini even sent him to a fortune-teller to review the omens, which Tognazzi took as a dire insult.

Still on the look-out for possible alternatives, Fellini went to London in February. Peter O'Toole, dining in a lunch club, saw Fellini and, anxious to introduce himself in a striking way, borrowed a waiter's coat and tried to serve him some lobster bisque. Having had too much to drink, O'Toole instead poured the soup over another diner. Fellini didn't miss any of this. He was moved by O'Toole's evident gaucherie, and the 'frail white hands' with which he tried to clean off his victim. O'Toole told Fellini of his admiration and eagerness to work with him, but he also was too busy to appear in *Il viaggio*. On 16 March, Fellini reluctantly signed the increasingly nervous Tognazzi.

After its invasion by bailiffs, Giulietta found the Fregene house unpleasant, and as the summer became more humid they moved to an apartment in the Residence Garden Hotel in EUR, from where Fellini commuted to Dinocittà.

However, as the revised start date approached, his anguish returned. He dreamed of railway level-crossings, customs barriers and executions by firing squad. On the evening of 10 April, alone in the apartment, he watched *La strada* on RAI. It was preceded by a critical commentary suggesting that the film, for all its merit, was so personal that it had little to say to a general audience. This reiteration of the old left-wing Neorealist line infuriated Fellini, who was already anxious about location trips to Bologna and Naples scheduled for the following week. Later that night, he had throat pains and called a doctor, who arrived in evening clothes from a reception downstairs to give him an injection for catarrh. Around ten, suffering from pains in his chest and back, he tried to call the doctor again, but collapsed on the floor. Convinced the omens were at last being realised, he could think only of putting a note on the door warning Giulietta: 'Don't come in alone', since he confidently expected she'd find him dead.

Fellini himself could scarcely have more effectively directed the incidents that followed. Finally discovered, he was carried through the reception downstairs and bundled into the doctor's car. Racing to the hospital, the doctor tried to run an amber light and narrowly avoided a collision. Dimly Fellini heard him shouting: 'I've got a dying man in here.' In the Salvator Mundi clinic, Fellini's problem, which had looked like a heart attack, was diagnosed as an acute anaphylactic inflammation, origin unknown. Drugged, he was plagued by hallucinations. The phone looked like a viper, the couch a puffy Rubens-esque face with buttons for eyes. He dreamed of eggs being swallowed by moist black walls.

The hospital staff, all nuns, prayed for him, dispensed water from Lourdes and summoned a priest in case he wanted to confess. News of his collapse travelled around the world, even making the front page of the London *Times*. His complaint was given as 'pneumonia' and it was assumed he'd contracted an allergic reaction of the bronchial tubes, perhaps from spores in the carpet on which he'd collapsed. There had seemed every chance the inflammation would clear up with antibiotics and Fellini announced he'd definitely start work the following week.

The hospital was swamped with telegrams, including one from Prime Minister Aldo Moro. Gustavo Rol sent magic ointments, and Fellini's room overflowed with flowers. The largest and best roses were from Angelo Rizzoli. Attached was a note of reconciliation. When he could talk, Fellini rang him back to say: 'Your note has made me better rather than the antibiotics.' A colleague in Milan took the phone from Rizzoli and said: 'Fellini, he's crying.' Not everyone was uncritically solicitous. Suspicious of another Fellini ploy, de Laurentiis sent his own doctors, who returned with a less optimistic second opinion. Fellini was not responding to drugs. He could no longer talk and was being helped to breathe. Five hundred X-rays (Fellini's estimate) had failed to locate the source of the problem, and there was every possibility that he might die. At the news, Dino burst into tears.

Friends came by the dozen to see Fellini. Even Ennio Flaiano turned up. When nurses told him that the writer was outside, Fellini said: 'Now I *really* know I'm dying.' His Riminese visitors brought typically abrasive good wishes. Titta Benzi made a fuss when he wasn't allowed into the room. 'But fuck it, why can't I see Federico?' Ercole Sega, his doctor friend from Rimini, also announced his imminent arrival.

It was Sega who made the diagnosis that saved Fellini's life. He recognised an effect observed in rabbits injected with cholera. If the animals were reinjected with the bacilli twenty-four hours later, a distinctive swelling, blue at the centre and red at the edges, appeared at the site of the first injection and blood vessels below it ruptured. This was accompanied by intestinal haemorrhaging and lesions on the internal organs. How a catarrh injection could have triggered this rare condition, known as the Sanarelli–Shwartzman Phenomenon, isn't clear, but Fellini's doctors stopped the antibiotics and started on cortisone. 'In twelve hours I could breathe,' he said, 'and in twenty-four I could talk.'

21   The Lady in Lace and Pearls: *Tre passi nel delirio*: *Toby Dammit*

'Fellini fears death. Fears death *so* much'
Magali Noël

Relieved though some may have been by his recovery, there was a widespread feeling about Fellini's breakdown that he'd had it coming. Perhaps, some muttered, it would impose a more tractable state of mind. Arriving in person at the hospital, Rizzoli told him: 'I hope this illness has sorted out your ideas. You mustn't make the sort of films you used to. It wears out your brain, you know. You must listen to me now and make the films I tell you to.'

To escape, Fellini moved to a *pensione* in Manzania. This brush with death, whatever its source, had freed him from *Il viaggio*, and he felt he could relax. He spent most of the time reading, though he did take time off to visit Rimini. American aid had restored the town more or less to its pre-war appearance, only for childhood haunts like Miramare to be engulfed by cheap motels and clubs. By the seventies Rimini had become Italy's trashiest beach resort, notorious throughout Europe as its sleaziest polysexual pick-up spot.

Critic and journalist Renzo Renzi had collected enough photographs of old Rimini for a book and asked Fellini to write an introduction. In 1964 *Cinema nuovo* published Renzi's essay 'The Ancestors of Fellini', which contended that the director, though born in the country of Mussolini, actually belonged to a more intellectual Romagnolo strain. Fellini had been flattered, so what began as a tape-recorded preface became a lengthy essay in autobiography, a rambling testimony to the power and value of memory which, since it was mostly dictated, has the chatty air of Fellini at his most engaging – and, it must be said, improvisatory.

Since the man speaking had just narrowly escaped death, there's also in much of the writing an almost erotic languor. As in Proust, sensations take an equal place with ideas. Fellini remembers the smell of the perfume squirted around the Fulgor, the feel of the fog that enveloped the terrace of the Grand Hotel in winter, the gaiety of the nightly promenade down corso d'Augusto. *La mia Rimini* was published in 1967, and Fellini's essay, 'Lo mio Rimini', became, despite its many evasions and distortions, the accepted version of his childhood.

By August, Fellini had recovered enough to try and salvage his career. Raoul Lévy, who five years before had wanted to make *Three Rooms in Manhattan* with him, was launching Kenneth Tynan's erotic stage revue *Oh! Calcutta!* and asked for a short film. Fellini expressed vague interest but nothing came of it. De Laurentiis also sent Paul Newman to see him at Manzania, hoping that he'd cast him in a revived *Il viaggio*, but though Fellini liked the actor and stayed in touch, he remained noncommittal.

At the end of the summer Fellini moved back to the Residence Garden and began meetings with Dino, who was understandably fretting at the potential loss of 500 million lire. The producer offered a deal. If Fellini genuinely couldn't finish *Il viaggio*, he'd accept three pictures to be made over the next five years in its stead. Fellini could reimburse him from their profits. Fellini knew that selling himself into slavery to Dino would merely compound the problems that had driven him to breakdown in the first place. On 21 August he recorded a dream of a series of babies being decapitated, symbols of his unborn films and their fate. At a late-night meeting with Luigi and Dino and their respective lawyers in the luxurious de Laurentiis office at Castel Romano, he refused.

For hours the old friends searched for a way out of the impasse and, not for the first time, failed. Liliana Betti remembers Dino leafing nervously through picture magazines with a bitter expression while Luigi paced the room, glaring at Fellini as he offered to refund de Laurentiis's investment out of his future earnings if Dino would transfer the rights of *Il viaggio* to him without strings. 'Look, Dino, it's as if you and I were at the bottom of a hole,' Fellini reasoned. 'Why shouldn't we give each other a hand to get out of it?' But the producer was unmoved. *Il viaggio di G. Mastorna* remained in limbo and Fellini with it.

Among the visitors that summer at the Residence Garden was Alberto Grimaldi, a Neapolitan lawyer who'd gone into films by forming Produzioni Europee Associate in 1961. Fellini initially avoided talking to him, but Grimaldi waited meekly in the lobby until summoned. Once in, he offered a startling proposal. Having made a fortune with westerns like *A Fistful of Dollars, For a Few Dollars More* and *The Good, the Bad and the Ugly*, and, in the process, turned failing TV actor Clint Eastwood into an international star, he wanted to put his profits to good use by backing a Fellini film. An astonished Fellini asked if that included *Il viaggio*. The producer said: 'Why not?'

Grimaldi's motives weren't as lofty as they seemed. He was negotiating for the same lucrative United Artists connection as de Laurentiis. Impressed by his track record, UA had agreed to put up 80 per cent of the budget of any PEA production and pay a $1 million producer's fee for each, plus a substantial allowance for overheads. Profits would be split 50/50, except for Italian rights, which Grimaldi retained. United Artists had one proviso. They wanted 'more complex, larger-scale pictures' than the Eastwood westerns. Grimaldi needed a prestige film and, Fellini being the one Italian director they might have heard of, he'd come to see the *maestro* in person.

Since Fellini would discuss only *Il viaggio*, Grimaldi asked his production manager to check its budget and the surviving sets. The manager was Enzo Provenzale, with whom Fellini had clashed on *Lo sceicco bianco*, but he decided the production could still be revived – for a price. De Laurentiis, stung that Grimaldi was trying to poach his project, set that price on 13 September: 435 million lire (about $725,000 at 1968 rates) for the rights, plus the money due to Tognazzi under his contract. And he insisted the deal be closed no later than the 25th. 'He might as well have asked me for the piazza di Spagna,' said Fellini glumly, but Grimaldi, with his Hollywood connection at stake, had no alternative. On the 25th he turned up at Dinocittà and handed a cheque to his fellow Neapolitan. An elated de Laurentiis was ready to believe in anything now, even the most famous of Naples miracles, the annual liquefaction of a vial of powder claimed to be the blood of its patron saint, Januarius. 'Santo Gennaro exists,' Dino said. 'I have him in front of me. His name is Alberto Grimaldi!' – and, according to Grimaldi, he fell to his knees before him.

European producers of omnibus films in the sixties raised the craft of making bricks without straw to high art. With a theme chosen because it was free of copyright, an impresario would approach Orson Welles, swearing that Visconti and Fellini had agreed to contribute an episode. If Welles signed, the producer would then hook Visconti and Fellini with Welles as the bait. In the summer of 1967, Fellini, perhaps less wary than usual after his illness, contracted with Raymond Eger of Marceau Film, the French co-producers of *Le notti di Cabiria*, to make one of seven Edgar Allan Poe adaptations for a film provisionally called *Tre passi nel delirio/Three Steps to Madness*. Welles and Bergman had already signed, Eger told Fellini, as had Joseph Losey and Jean Renoir.

With nothing yet decided about *Il viaggio*, Fellini started preliminary work on his contribution in the autumn, bringing in Grimaldi to co-produce with Marceau. It soon became clear that Bergman had never agreed and that Welles, burned before, had bowed out early. Renoir retired too when he found that Claude Chabrol replaced him. Chabrol wanted to do the same story as himself, and already had a script. Then Chabrol departed, to be replaced by the decidedly down-market Louis Malle and Roger Vadim.

Fellini could legally have vacated the contract, but since he hadn't worked in two years, he felt a short film might help him 'to find my own natural working rhythm again' and break in new collaborators. He consulted his psychic advisers, who included P. (for Patrizia) Norelli Bachelet, a pretty Chilean who was his personal astrologer, and the plumply effeminate Eugenio Mastropietro, who'd modestly adopted the pseudonym 'Genius' and claimed to be the Official Medium of Rome's police department, on call to track down murderers. Both advised him to make the film.

Spurning the first story suggested by Eger, the threadbare 'The Telltale Heart', Fellini, who'd never read Poe, set Liliana Betti scouring his works for a better one and began assembling a team. In the process he found a new writer. Bernardino Zapponi, though seven years younger, had worked for *Marc'Aurelio*, then gone on to make a career in fantasy and horror fiction. Fellini came across his book *Gobal* and was intrigued. When he discovered that Zapponi not only lived in Rome but had an apartment just opposite his office in via della Fortuna, he decided their collaboration was fated. 'We have similar tastes,' he told the astonished writer in an eight thirty am call. 'I feel we could be brothers.'

Zapponi was a far less distinguished writer than Pinelli, Flaiano or Rondi, which was probably why Fellini chose him. Short and meek, he trailed like an amiable mascot in the wake of the *maestro*. Fellini caricatured him maliciously in one of his sketches as a diminutive creature with wondering eyes and a crooked grin, one quizzical eyebrow permanently raised.

The pair began meeting, sometimes in cafés but more often on Rome's wintry streets. Fellini wanted to use a Zapponi story for his segment of *Tre passi nel delirio*, but Eger demanded there be some Poe connection, however tenuous. They toyed with doing 'The Premature Burial' as a farce, starring Sordi as a sacristan afraid of being buried alive. The producers, however, preferred drama. Eventually, Fellini tabled an obscure Poe fragment unearthed by Betti called 'Don't Bet the Devil Your Head'. Its hero, Toby Dammit, is a gambler from Poe's home state of Virginia, given to wild life-threatening wagers, but Fellini rewrote him as a self-destructive film star. A plot emerged during his walks with Zapponi, some of them on the empty beachfront at Ostia, desolate in midwinter. 'Such hopelessness,' says Zapponi, 'gave birth to the story of a mad, drug-addicted actor who comes to die in Rome', though it's more likely Fellini was remembering Broderick Crawford. He also recalled his dream about beheaded babies, which now seemed a premonition. Eger accepted the script, unaware or unconcerned that it bore little relationship to the story. (The credits call it 'a free cinematographic adaptation'.) At a post-production dinner with Betti and Nino Rota, Fellini would admit he hadn't read it until after the film wrapped.

Fellini's Toby Dammit is a movie star who arrives in Rome to make 'the first Catholic western' for a clerical production company. The airport arrival is a compressed version of the equivalent sequence in *Il viaggio*. A stoned Toby is escorted through a phantasmagoric terminal, past a group of wind-blown nuns carrying musical instrument cases, a cripple on crutches, Muslims praying to Mecca, a gaping black girl in mod clothing, and Americans in Stetsons sleeping amid sheaves of cellophane-wrapped flowers.

After a skirmish with *paparazzi*, he's driven into Rome while the producer, Father Spagna, describes the movie. 'The film will be "syntagmatic",' as my friend Roland Barthes would say, situated between Pasolini and Dreyer, with a *soupçon* of Ford.' Played fruitily by Salvo Randone, Spagna is a recognisable parody of Angelo Arpa. Toby is more interested in the scenes outside their limo: a truck filled with dangling carcases, a whore outside a lamp showroom blazing with light, a fashion shoot taking place in the midst of road works, hippies in Edwardian coats strumming guitars on a piece of waste ground. He also demands the new Ferrari promised him. Even the gypsy palmist who offers to read his future, then closes his hand in dismay, doesn't still his interest in the car.

Terence Stamp, twenty-seven years old and famously wild even in the uninhibited sixties, had been in Los Angeles, contemplating suicide after the collapse of his relationship with model Jean Shrimpton, when his agent called. 'Fellini's sent to London for the most decadent young actors we've got. He wants you to go to Rome. Can you travel today? I believe James Fox is going too.' Having been paid off by Antonioni when he decided he preferred David Hemmings as the photographer in *Blow-Up*, Stamp was cautious, but Fellini's name had sufficient magic to get him on the plane. They hit it off instantly. Even Bevilacqua, driving the actor to da Vinci for the flight back to Los Angeles, knew he had the job. Fox, he announced, had been too gentlemanly for Fellini. 'You, 'ee like,' he confided to Stamp. '*Decadente*, yes?'

Others had turned down the role. Visualising Toby, Fellini remembered his encounter with an alcoholic Peter O'Toole. Late in September, he rang London to confirm O'Toole was still interested in working with him. In October the actor received Zapponi's script, but refused it without explanation, supposedly because he found the character repellent.* Fellini immediately went to London and changed O'Toole's mind. Three days later, however, the actor rang and said he'd changed it back. Fellini demanded explanations, lost his temper, but it was useless. The call went out for dissolute Englishmen that brought Stamp to Rome.

On a make-up sketch, Fellini had noted: 'Important. Make Terence up like Poe (but without the moustache).' In baggy, crumpled rock gear, Stamp said he felt closer to Chuck Berry, but was delighted with the director's visual virtuosity. Life-like cutouts replaced some of the extras at the airport – a reflection, Fellini said, of the character's drugged state. The motif is picked up in Toby's whirl through the night just before his death. Some of the stiff, grinning waiters are cutouts, some actors.

In September 1967, Fellini moved into the PEA offices on largo Ponchielli. Provenzale had rented the Centro Sperimentale studio at Cinecittà. Rotunno, now established as di Venanzo's replacement, lit the film, but finding a designer to replace Gherardi was more difficult. Fellini's first choice was Fabrizio Clerici, an old friend with thirty years' experience in theatre whose surrealist canvases were enjoying a vogue, but Clerici couldn't keep up with the mercurial director, who filled notebook after notebook with his own ever-changing designs. He was replaced by yet another Visconti man, Piero Tosi, whom Fellini had tried unsuccessfully to lure on to *Il viaggio*. But Tosi didn't like

---

*Fellini was rumoured to have considered Richard Burton but rejected him because of his drinking. Had he genuinely been nervous about casting a drinker, he wouldn't have considered self-confessed substance-abuser Stamp or offered the role first to O'Toole, a legendary boozer. It's more likely that Burton, harried by *paparazzi* and given to drunkenly spouting Shakespeare, was another model for Toby.

either the Fellini court or the film. He moped through the production and didn't work with Fellini again for decades.

In the first script, Dammit tries to jump his Fiat 500 Innocenti over a metal barrier at the end of Ponte Milvio and is decapitated, but Fellini, returning home from Villa Florio one might after dining with Zapponi, saw that a span of Ponte Arriccia in the Alban Hills outside Rome had been demolished. A leap across *that* would be much more dramatic. When the experts decided it was too dangerous, he kept the idea but moved the location to a disused freeway.

Toby is haunted by death. At a TV studio he's quizzed by journalists. Asked if he believes in God, he says no, though he does believe in the devil, who takes the form for him of a little girl – a blonde with evil eyes, whom he glimpses at the airport, bouncing a large white ball. Having failed, after one of his now-familiar casting searches, to find a sufficiently devilish child, Fellini cast Russian actress Marina Yaru. The face of Yaru, twenty-two and fully grown, appears in close-ups, while she's doubled by a child in long shot.

Whisked to the presentation of the Golden Wolves, Italy's Oscars, Toby finds himself in a club where smoke swirls and cabaret tables cluster round a murky pool. Deal-makers, stage mothers, predatory starlets and fawning critics pass by as Dammit gets progressively drunker. A great comedian, tiny, decrepit and blind, is led on stage by his tall girlfriend to receive an award. Fellini coaxed Polidor out of retirement to play this parody of Toto in his dotage.

Just before he passes out, Toby is approached by a man with slicked-down hair and a thin moustache who introduces himself as 'Lombardi, associated with the production' and, mopping his sweaty face, suggests that Toby recite a little Shakespeare after he receives the award. In real life Lombardi was a Neapolitan piano-tuner named Campanella whom Fellini cast often because he had 'the knowing air of a Mafia man'. When Fellini called 'Action', Campanella sidled up to Stamp and, to his surprise, started slowly to count from one to ten. At 'eight', Stamp was directed to mumble to Campanella: 'Eight?' Campanella responded: 'Yessir, eight', then looked to where Fellini stood by the camera and said: 'Well, what do I do now?' Fellini said: 'Go ahead, count up to twenty-one, but a bit more gently.'

At the ceremony, a beautiful woman in furs and pearl earrings, sister to the Death figure Fellini described to de Vilallonga, sits down next to Toby. 'Don't be afraid any more,' she murmurs to the dazed actor. 'I'll take care of you always . . . Any time you reach out your hand it will be my hand you'll meet. No longer a runaway. No longer a castaway.'

Consoled by this apparition, Toby falls asleep, only to be hauled on stage to receive his Golden Wolf. He manages a few lines from Macbeth's 'Tomorrow and tomorrow' speech, rants at the audience, then runs outside. His Ferrari is waiting and he roars away in it. He races through a series of villages, a blur of sleeping streets, dead ends and squares glimpsed in the glare of his headlights. Bursting through barriers on to an unused portion of the *autostrada*, he barely escapes driving over a break in the roadway. Seeing the blonde girl with her ball on the other side, he tries to leap the gap. There's a close-up of a tight cable dripping blood and the devil child walks out of the darkness to pick up Toby's severed head.

On the day before shooting started, Fellini had a call from de Laurentiis. As if their battles had never taken place, Dino invited him to direct a new project – nothing less than *Waterloo*. If he agreed, he could have a blank cheque. Fellini was astonished. 'Between the two of us, Dino, it's you and not me who's the artist. By comparison I've got the good sense, the practicality and the taste for order of a bank clerk.' *Waterloo*, directed by Sergei Bondarchuk and released in 1970, would be the Waterloo of de Laurentiis, a failure so total it drove him out of Italian production for years.

On the set of *Toby Dammit* Fellini played up to his role as a convalescent. 'The door's open. There's a freezing draught. I'm just over a desperate illness and you want to kill me. Assassins!' But it was clear after the first few days that sickness and *Il viaggio*'s failure hadn't impaired his powers. If anything, they were enhanced. The ease of shooting, completed in twenty-six days, also convinced him he'd been right to shed his old collaborators. In doing so, he'd purged himself of the last vestiges of Neorealism. Zapponi, Rotunno and Tosi typified a new kind of cinema, more sensual, erotic, stylised. Fellini the carica-turist had given way to Fellini the painter.

The thirty-seven-minute *Toby Dammit* delighted both Eger and Grimaldi so much that they suggested Fellini shoot a second episode to make up a feature. Among Liliana Betti's Poe discoveries was a fragment of black comedy called 'How to Write a *Blackwood*'s Article' An elderly English tourist at an Italian carnival climbs a tower and sticks her head through a hole, only to find herself looking out through the face of a clock. Unable to escape, she's decapitated by the hands, though her eyes, popping out, get an excellent view.

Fellini decided that the Palio, Siena's baroque annual horse-race, would be the ideal setting. Jowly comedian Margaret Rutherford was in Rome, preparing to shoot what would be her last film, *Arabella*, and

Fellini met her for dinner at the Villa Hotel in Frascati. Unawed, Dame Margaret, then seventy-five, greeted him in a swimming-costume and floundered into the hotel pool for her evening swim. After this encounter a delighted Fellini was eager to work with her, but Grimaldi and Eger changed their minds and a promising collaboration never took place.

Tre passi nel delirio was accepted for Cannes but its screening was to be overshadowed by history. Henri Langlois's dismissal from the Cinémathèque Française in February 1968 triggered an extraordinary series of events that culminated in the 17 May invasion of Cannes by angry film-makers. The Poe film was the last to be shown that year. As the festival tried to screen the next feature, Carlos Saura's *Peppermint frappé*, Jean-Luc Godard clung to the curtains, preventing them from parting, while François Truffaut harangued the audience. Any critical coverage was engulfed in reports of the resulting riots and the film had a patchy release. It was retitled *Histoires extraordinaires* in France and *Spirits of the Dead* in America – where, to compete with Roger Corman's blood-boltered Poe adaptations, it was advertised as 'Edgar Allan Poe's Ultimate Orgy of Evil and Unbearable Horror'.

That spring, Ingmar Bergman visited Rome with Liv Ullmann. Bergman was typically diffident about meeting Fellini, who was himself embarrassed at having seen, among Bergman's films, only *Wild Strawberries* and *The Silence*, but a rendezvous was arranged and they immediately became friends, strolling round Rome with Ullmann until late at night, 'arms around each other' she recalled, 'Fellini wearing a dramatic black cape, Ingmar his little cap and an old winter coat'. Spontaneously, they decided to make a film together, a project that would haunt both for the next decade.

Shortly after Bergman's visit, Giulietta took her first film acting job since *Giulietta*, appearing in an adaptation of Jean Giraudoux's *The Madwoman of Chaillot*. Unexpectedly, Fellini accompanied her to France and sat silently on the set through all her scenes. Bryan Forbes, who'd taken over the project (and its cast, including Masina) with two weeks' notice from John Huston, says he wasn't resentful. '[Fellini's] presence on the set was a little disconcerting, for obvious reasons, though in fairness he never attempted to usurp my position where his wife was concerned.' Despite being interrupted by *les évènements de 1968*, it was a cheerful shoot. On location at Cap Ferrat the cast and crew, including the Fellinis, took over a local restaurant: 'Giulietta . . . used to make pasta in the kitchen,' says Forbes '[and] Danny Kaye used to make lemon chiffon pies.' Fellini and Kaye, whom Fellini admired in *The Secret Life of Walter Mitty*, the archetypal dream movie, became good friends.

Returning to Rome in the early summer, Fellini once more took up the reins of *Il viaggio*, now with Grimaldi in charge. Mario Chiari was refurbishing the sets. Provenzale had drawn up a new budget. Mastroianni was ready and available, though Fellini had also shown the screenplay to Terence Stamp, who said: 'I hadn't read such an inspired script before or since.' All seemed set for a successful relaunch. But the film would never be made.

During *Toby Dammit*, Stamp had been surprised to find himself provided with an attractive interpreter, though he protested he didn't need her. As they became more friendly, she admitted she was actually Patrizia Norelli Bachelet, Fellini's astrologer, for whom he'd shrewdly made a spot on the production. Through her, Stamp met the mystic Jiddu Krishnamurti at his villa outside Rome, and was surprised when Fellini, also with Bachelet, turned up too, supposedly to exchange ideas about the afterlife with the seventy-three-year-old sage, for whom he screened some rushes of *Toby Dammit*. The guru claimed to be impressed and presented Fellini, vain about his incipient baldness, with a bottle of hair-restorer.

Everyone noticed Fellini's growing coolness towards *Il viaggio*, which seemed fed by his psychic advisers. Late in the summer, he announced that he no longer wished to make the film. When Grimaldi pressed him for an explanation, he admitted that his superstitious fear of continuing was more powerful than his need to work. In the documentary *Block-notes di un regista*, which Fellini would make about the *Il viaggio* fiasco, Mastroianni attacks him for failing to complete this, the most personal and important project of his life. 'You are scared,' says the actor. Since the accusation rang true, Fellini left it in the film, his public confession of failure.

Grimaldi, who had too much at stake to break with Fellini (and who had never been enthusiastic about *Il viaggio* anyway), asked what he'd prefer to make. They discussed Boccaccio, Ariosto and a film about the Merovingian kings. Then Fellini suggested the *Satyricon*. After almost 2,000 years it was time to turn the cameras on Petronius. In May 1968 Fellini and Grimaldi signed a deal.

22   'A homosexual odyssey':
Fellini–Satyricon

'You do not know women and you do not know yourself.
You do not pursue women; you flee them. Loving that
many means that what you are seeking is probably a man'
Dialogue cut from the script of *Il Casanova di Federico Fellini*

The American première of *Satyricon* took place at New York's
Madison Square Garden on a snowy night in March 1970, following a
rock concert. The arena, normally used for boxing matches and
political conventions, was filled with an estimated 10,000, mostly
under twenty-five. They represented the target audience at which
United Artists, its US distributors, had decided to aim Fellini's breath-
taking improvisation on ancient Rome.

Fellini was exhilarated by the skyscrapers of Manhattan – like slabs
of light, he said, blazing in the cold – and no less delighted by the
audience that jammed the icy streets around the Garden on motor-
cycles and in garishly painted vans. Inside the arena, the crowd
manifested the tribal qualities that observers of the youth culture had
learned to recognise. Sex and drugs were in the air, to Fellini's ill-
concealed delight. 'You could smell the heroin and hashish through the
cigarette smoke,' he said gleefully, if improbably.

In 1968, Fellini had fallen in love with the hippies. During the
period of *Satyricon* he hung out with them in New York, Rome and
London. They featured in both *Toby Dammit* and *Block-notes di un
regista*, though in both cases they were actors, elaborately costumed,
playing Fellini's conception of hippies, the first in Edwardian gear, the
second in a designer's idea of drop-out *couture*. In *Roma*, drifters in an
equally immaculate degree of dishevelment strum guitars on the
crowded Spanish Steps while a sadhu stands with open arms absorb-
ing the noontide glare and girls bathe naked in the fountains – 'like
puppies,' murmurs Alghiero Noschese, Fellini's soundtrack persona.
As a couple embrace, he says: 'One can make love or not make love; it

doesn't matter', inaugurating a guilt-ridden sequence on the brothels of war-time Rome where Fellini probably bought his own sexual initiation.

It was the sexual, and specifically bisexual, element of the hippies that Fellini found most attractive. Aquarius, his astral advisers told him, was not only their sign and his but that of unisexuality. Visiting Electric Circus, the New York disco, he'd been less impressed with its décor in DayGlo lavender, violet and orange, the deafening music and the famous light-show pulsing through a moist fog of pot fumes than by a dance floor that was an undifferentiated mass of struggling, semi-nude bodies, and the holes in the wall from which jutted legs in every combination of gender and colour. In the way it ignored sexual categories, embraced grotesquerie, endorsed mysticism and placed style in the ascendant over sense, hippie culture came close to reflecting Fellini's interior world.

The *Satyricon* was the work of Titus Petronius Niger, a Roman courtier of the first century AD, famous for his taste. Young Nero made him Arbiter of Elegance at his court. 'Nero's jaded appetite,' says Tacitus, 'regarded nothing as enjoyable or refined unless Petronius had given his sanction to it.'

Nero fancied himself a poet and each night after dinner convened a circle to read and criticise members' works and listen to his own outpourings. Trained by Seneca, the emperor composed on classical themes – which, if they were wise, other members avoided. Shrewdly, Petronius wrote something that didn't threaten Nero, a series of erotic stories about Encolpio, his friend Ascylto and their shared lover Giton, told in high-flown prose made to seem ridiculous by the foul mouths and outrageous behaviour of the heroes. The *Satyricon* drew no obvious moral, a fact that ensured its survival. Copies were already circulating during the life of Petronius, and, though only fragments survive, they're enough to show the quality of the work.

Petronius' success was also his downfall. In AD 66 another courtier, Tigellinus, trumped up a charge of treason while Nero was away and imprisoned his family and friends. Having failed to reach Nero with his side of the story, Petronius held an elaborate party, at the beginning of which he slit his veins. Binding up the cuts and opening them as the mood took him, he bled slowly to death while friends feasted.

Thirteen years later, Vesuvius buried Pompeii and Herculaneum. They lay untouched until the middle of the eighteenth century, by which time the image of early Rome had been scrubbed out and aired.

In the popular imagination, Romans were men in togas white as beach towels who strolled along colonnades while at home wives in pastel muslin drowsed under grape arbours.

The first excavations of Pompeii in 1748 were a revelation. Instead of marble halls they found houses that were small, dirty, dark and badly built, decorated with wall-paintings of fat cupids, simpering nymphs and satyrs pronging everything in sight, all slapped on in crimson, green and blue. Faced with this fun-fair Rome, as vulgar as a Hamburg sex arcade, aesthetes went back to the Greeks, leaving the illusion of ancient Rome unsullied – until Fellini.

Fellini had studied the *Satyricon* at school, imagining what might have happened during the tantalising blackouts, then forgot it until 1942, when Marcello Marchesi thought it might make a musical for Fabrizi. Fellini read it once more during the days of the Funny Face Shops, when a publisher wanted a cover for a potted edition of the sexier bits, padded out with erotic illustrations, but Enrico de Seta got the job.

At the end of every film from *Le notti di Cabiria* onwards, he said, he'd felt the need to react against their realism with a pure fantasy. Each time, the pull of quotidian reality held him back. To film a fantasy, he needed to see some relevance, a connection with his own world. He came closest when he signed the deal in 1966 with Cristaldi for a version with Sordi and Cardinale, but still the topical hook evaded him. However, in the *pensione* at Manzania during his convalescence, Fellini picked up the book again and realised that the world of Petronius, amoral, bisexual and pleasure-seeking, now existed outside his window. As for the missing material, it offered a challenge that, given his mental state during his convalescence, was more seductive than daunting. 'Fellini selected Petronius,' Peter Bondanella believes, 'not as a substitute for a personal narrative of his own but as a challenge to his inventive powers, which, he feared, might be on the wane.'

Equally important, however, was the opportunity offered by *Satyricon* to discuss sex roles in a setting conveniently free of personal specifics. When a questioner in Los Angeles, perhaps having read Fellini's comment early in the production that the film was his 'first non-autobiographical work', implied the film wasn't as personal as *Otto e mezzo*, Fellini said: 'It is you who say *Satyricon* is not autobiographical. I think it is more autobiographical than $8\frac{1}{2}$. But it is not anecdotal.' While his approval of his heroes' homosexuality is obvious, he remains, as always, a voyeur, not a participant.

In August 1968 Grimaldi announced that shooting would start in November. Fellini, putting into practice the lessons learned from de Laurentiis, had already tossed out a few eccentric casting suggestions guaranteed to win headlines. His claim that he'd signed Mae West, who retired from films in 1943, was publicised around the world. Jimmy Durante (eighty-five years old) was up for a part, while Groucho Marx (seventy-eight) had once again been pencilled in, this time to play a philosophical pimp. Michael J. Pollard was cast, and the poet Eumolpo would be Van Heflin.

A pivotal scene of Petronius' satire is the banquet thrown by the pompous merchant Trimalchio at which guests gorge while their millionaire host brags of his wealth. Fellini's first choice had been Aldo Fabrizi, but his old mentor took the offer as an insult and the friendship, always troubled, fell apart at last, this time permanently. An admirer of the James Bond films, he thought about Gert (*Goldfinger*) Frobe as a replacement, or, failing him, Boris Karloff.

In March Danny Kaye had arrived in Rome, summoned by Fellini. 'I'm not sure why he invited me,' said Kaye, who hadn't made a film for four years. 'I presume he has some work to offer.' What Fellini offered was the role of Lichas, the imperial master of the revels, a character he and Zapponi had written as a murderous homosexual and transvestite. Kaye, who hid his own gayness throughout his career, prudently turned it down. Groucho Marx also passed, as did an ailing Karloff, who died the next year. Mae West declined on the pretext that Oenothea, written initially as a priestess who sexually initiates young men, had children. Still caking her face with make-up at seventy-six and boasting of her affairs, the original Diamond Lil was proud of never having played a mother in her life.

Discussion of this geriatric line-up ceased once United Artists told Grimaldi they saw *Satyricon* as a 'youth movie' for the eighteen to twenty-five age group. Fellini promptly replaced one fantasy cast with another. Terence Stamp and Pierre Clémenti were his new choices for Encolpio and Ascylto, he said, 'and I'd like Taylor, Burton, Bardot, O'Toole, [Louis] de Funès, Jerry Lewis, Brando, Lee Marvin, the Beatles, the Maharishi, Lyndon Johnson and de Gaulle, or else no one, not a known face, to increase the sense of foreign-ness'.

Fellini plucked this cast out of thin air. Henry Miller, who saw him on TV around this time, praised his interviews as pure creative acts. 'I like his honesty, his efforts to explain what is inexplicable. He was creating even as he talked.' Journalists ignorant of free association trumpeted the announcement, however, especially the bit about the

Beatles. 'We know nothing about this at all,' blustered a spokesman for the group. 'What's he talking about? There have not even been any negotiations between them and Mr Fellini about their taking part in the film or writing music for it.'

In September Zapponi started work on the script. The new writing relationship was settling down, with Fellini in unquestioned command. There were no arguments of the sort he'd had with Flaiano. Zapponi knew his place. People described the writer nervously haunting the set with the five-hundred-page script under his arm, a butt for Fellini's frustrations. Later Fellini referred jokingly to Zapponi's dogged approach to writing as 'somewhere between bureaucracy and fear of losing his job'.

Satyricon is 20 per cent Petronius and 80 per cent Fellini. Though Zapponi stuck as close as possible to the original, plugging the gaps with extracts from Suetonius and Apuleius, Fellini's imagination quickly carried them far from the text. Advice was sought from classical scholars, one of whom, the University of Pisa's Luca Canali, became the film's consultant on Latin, but, like all such approaches, these were mostly ritual. The experts anyway couldn't offer much help. Roman life in 66 AD was well documented, but Petronius had exercised the satirist's prerogative to invent an artificial world. The names of his characters are a clue. Encolpio, Ascylto, Giton, Lichas and Oenothea are Greek names, Trimalchio is Middle Eastern. Their story would make more sense if it took place not in Rome but in Egypt or Tunisia, both usefully distant and exotic. Fellini agreed. Even before the film was cast, he announced he'd shoot on the slopes of Vesuvius and in North Africa.

The vagueness of the original provided a useful excuse to ignore history. There's a poetic rightness in Fellini's suggested casting of West, Marx and Kaye. The free-wheeling action of the *Satyricon*, its changes of location, grotesque characters and fantastic humour are less like *Ben-Hur* and *Quo Vadis?* than *Hellzapoppin'* and *Duck Soup*. When he and Zapponi visited Pompeii and Herculaneum, Fellini dismissed the ruins with a crack Groucho might have made. 'I never knew exactly how much my fascination and enthusiasm were owing to the frescoes,' he said, 'and how much to a magnificent Swedish woman who was walking in front of me.'

As usual, Fellini took advice on the astral plane as well as the physical. His favourite psychic of the time was Penus, an old man who travelled in comfort with a chauffeur and a sullen young male assistant. With the always loyal Liliana Betti and a sceptical Zapponi,

Fellini set out with Penus at ten pm one night in October for a seance on the via Appia Antica. It went badly. Penus had trouble entering his trance and, once he did, the only communication he received was to do with lions. 'Ask me if the lions are here,' he directed in a trembling voice. 'Ask me: are the lions here?' Wondering if he'd made contact with some Christians about to be devoured, Fellini dutifully enquired: 'Are the lions here?' At this, Penus, suddenly calm and businesslike again, said: 'No.'

During pre-production, Fellini had an unexpected approach from NBC TV in New York. Burlington Industries, a carpet company, was' sponsoring a series of hour-long experimental documentaries in which artists would be given *carte blanche*. Producer Peter Goldfarb, says Fellini, told him that Picasso had already created a new work for the series and Stravinsky an original composition. From Fellini, he would be satisfied with a long interview. The contract disappeared into Fellini's files until Goldfarb turned up during shooting. When Fellini tried to bluff his way out by suggesting they stitch something together from a short interview and some *Satyricon* rushes, Goldfarb, he says: 'looked at me, half persuasive, half imperious. "We must do something more organic," he said.' The result was *Block-notes di un regista*, a dramatised documentary with a Zapponi script, Nino Rota music and guest appearances by Giulietta and Mastroianni.

It begins with a conducted tour of *Il viaggio*'s abandoned cathedral and airliner sets, now overgrown and occupied by a lone horse and a group of hippies, one of whom sings a lament he calls 'Mastorna Blues'. Fellini tours the warehouse where the props, designs and masks are stored, then embarks on another of his night-time forays around Rome, this time to the Colosseum, inhabited by a series of typically Fellinian grotesques. Explaining it was on such a nocturnal stroll that he met Mario Tirabassi, The Man with the Sack who appeared in the scene cut from *Cabiria*, Giulietta introduces a screening of it.

Fellini inserts a parody recreation of *Maciste all'inferno*, then travels to the via Appia Antica for a version of the abortive expedition with Penus, replaced here by Genius. After this, he tours the subways of Rome, the platforms of which abruptly fill with ancient Romans speaking in the dialects invented for *Satyricon*. He also visits Mastroianni at his new home, where the star takes time out from being fêted by photographers, publicists and fans to chat. The film ends in a 'Day in the Life' sequence, with Fellini conducting screen tests, wrangling with actors, choosing extras and visiting a slaughterhouse in search of suitably unsightly types. Finally, he begins shooting the new film.

Fellini enjoyed the effortlessness of filming for TV. 'That sketchiness, in the right sense of the word, that haste and lightness, made me feel very joyful. I felt I was walking faster, unhampered by luggage.' The new form he'd created, 'a conversational sort of programme that could be used with different subjects', would become the foundation of *Roma*, *I Clowns* and *Intervista*. Never having worked for television in Italy, however, let alone in the US, Fellini was unaware of its stricter morality. Burlington, the intended sponsors, recoiled from the whores, freaks and general eccentricity of *Block-notes* and refused to accept it, so NBC broadcast it as an unsponsored special in April 1960 as *Fellini: A Director's Notebook*, repeating it twice.

In mid-September Fellini was still casting *Satyricon*. Stamp and Clémenti had proved too pricy, so he elected to follow his second idea, a cast of unknowns. A cattle-call audition in Rome on 14 September for beautiful boys between fifteen and eighteen produced 250 candidates, but among the angelic choristers and sullen rough trade there were no serious possibilities for his three leads. The following day he flew to London, where he toured impresarios in search of cut-price talent. TV commercials were the mainstay of such performers and Fellini screened scores of them. He was impressed by their technical expertise. 'How can these people produce such little masterpieces lasting one minute?' he wondered aloud. It paved the way for his own entry into commercials some years later.

The first find of the trip was his Encolpio, a twenty-four-year-old Englishman named Martin Potter. He had little professional experience outside a spot in the series *The Caesars*, but his blond good looks reminded him, Fellini said, of Antinous, lover of the emperor Hadrian – the comparison drawn between Fellini and the young Dominique Delouche.

By chance, he also found his Giton, spotting seventeen-year-old Max Born, an authentic hippie, hanging out in Chelsea. Small, pale, pouting and androgynous, Born exhibited an authentic decadence. Bewitched by this 'little whore with an angel's face', Fellini took him, barefoot, bare-chested, wearing only leather breeches and a sheepskin waistcoat, to lunch at the Grill Room of the Savoy Hotel. 'I think I had my arm round the boy's shoulders as we came into the restaurant,' Fellini said. 'I only felt that something was wrong when I noticed that the ex-king of Italy, Umberto, was coming in at the same moment and was looking at me in astonishment. The *maître* came forward at this point and looked at us somewhat quizzically. I don't think he imagined I wanted to create a scandal or was trying to emulate Oscar Wilde. But the way in which he got out of it was so perfectly English that I couldn't really complain of being turned away. He simply said: "I'm sorry, sir, but the young man is not wearing a tie." The boy was practically naked!'

Also in London, Fellini chose Hylette Adolphe, a fashion model, to play a slave girl. From Paris, he took Magali Noël and Alain Cuny, both of whom had played in *La dolce vita*, and in Rome, Capucine and Salvo Randone. Other choices were more eccentric. The enormously tall Donyale Luna, a favourite model of Salvador Dali, became Oenothea, and as the young Caesar he cast Tanya Lopert, daughter of producer Ilya Lopert. Her sense of 'neurotic asexuality' fitted a film that was fast becoming a hymn to homophilia.

He went on to New York, where he located his ideal Ascylto in Hiram Keller, who'd spent nine months in the Broadway production of *Hair*. Fellini didn't see the show until after *Satyricon*, but Keller impressed him with his satyr-like leer. He gave him only one direction: 'You are evil and you lay everything in sight.' United Artists had no reason to complain about the cost of talent. At a time when Paul Newman got $750,000 a film plus 10 per cent of the gross and a share of the profits, Keller was paid $10,000, Potter $7,500.

This casting pushed homosexuality even closer to the heart of *Satyricon*. When students at a New York Lincoln Center seminar quizzed Fellini about his choices, he responded, only half-joking: 'I had to cast the English boy and the American because there are no homosexuals in Italy.' To another group at the American Film Institute in Los Angeles, he explained: 'They looked innocent. It is a film about homosexuality, but with no feeling of sin or shame. With Italians there is always a feeling of morality, but the Anglo-Saxon face has something detached, something crazy, something elegant.'

In the months following Fellini's walk around Rome with Ingmar Bergman and Liv Ullmann, news of a possible Fellini/Bergman film had reached independent producer Martin Poll, then riding the momentum of Sidney Lumet's *The Appointment*, which he'd just completed in Rome with Omar Sharif and Anouk Aimée. Poll offered to float the project, provisionally called *Three Stories of Women*, with episodes by Fellini, Bergman and Akira Kurosawa. Universal's production head, Jennings Lang, agreed to back the film with, in deference to their combined reputations, a minimum of artistic control. Kurosawa, who initially welcomed the collaboration and wrote to Fellini expressing keen anticipation, had since become embroiled in the finally catastrophic US/Japan Pearl Harbor film *Tora! Tora! Tora!* and pulled out. Poll was left with *Love Duet*, two films, each about an hour, to be shot in English in Stockholm and Rome by Bergman and Fellini.

On 5 January Poll, Bergman and Fellini held a press conference at the Excelsior. Fellini dispensed airy and ambiguous quotes to the press with his usual flair. 'Love in the north is sizzling hot,' he announced. 'Only in Italy is it cold.' Journalists certainly felt a chill. Bergman said little and, troubled by asthma, kept demanding mineral water. Also nobody seemed anxious to explain if these notorious independents would actually work in tandem. 'It will not be a poker game in which we hide aces up our sleeves,' Fellini insisted. 'The only person we may hide things from is the producer.' In the event, the boot would be on the other foot, with only Fellini ignorant of what his collaborators were up to.

Zapponi had planned *Satyricon* to begin with a scene in the arena. 'Gladiators fighting. Fans yelling "Jugula!"' Instead it starts more modestly with a tirade by a survivor of the games, Encolpio. Staring into the camera, he protests that his friend and lover Ascylto has run off with Giton, the boy they shared. Having rediscovered him in the theatrical troupe of the fat, farting actor Vernacchio, Encolpio spends the rest of the film bickering with Ascylto over who will sleep with the boy, until Giton, who has not a single word of dialogue, is carried off as part of the spoils of war and disappears from the story.

Fellini doesn't disguise the total venality of the three boys. Like many hippies, Encolpio claims to be a student and poet, but actually he's a stooge, easily bullied, while Ascylto is a crook. In the Rome of 1968, the two would have been snatching bags on a Lambretta, with Encolpio the nervous driver and Ascylto on the pillion with a flick-knife to cut the straps.

Kidnapped by Lichas, a roaming imperial pimp and homosexual pirate who enjoys wrestling his captives to death, Encolpio becomes his 'wife', going through a form of marriage, he the groom and Lichas, made even more grotesque by his height and one staring false eye, the simpering bride. In turn, Ascylto and Encolpio themselves snatch a sickly hermaphrodite psychic, who dies before they can collect from a prospective buyer.

'Fellini loves squalor,' Zapponi said. 'It never ages.' He'd hoped to satisfy this *nostalgie de la boue* by showing a Rome that was 'then, as now, full of bars and brothels, gaping provincials, paralysed traffic and speculative building'. The city, however, was to be so refracted through the multiple imaginations of Petronius, Fellini and designer Danilo Donati, among others, that it became unrecognisable, something between the contents of Fellini's dream books and Dante's vision of Hell.

There are no bars in Fellini's Rome, but there are brothels galore, all of them startlingly imagined. The whores loll in a bath or lie on a slab with flames underneath. One has a big metal mirror over the bed. Another squats to piss on the earth floor. Any beauty is betrayed by an awkward pose, sweaty, unhealthy skin, a tongue-wobbling grimace or a leer. When Encolpio, having been cursed by Priapus with impotence, seeks a cure in a bordello, its vast sand-floored room with a doleful elephant in the corner recalls the animal house at a zoo. Child prostitutes display skin decorated with henna in the Arabian manner. Another has the blue face affected by some North African women. They whip Encolpio with sticks in a vain attempt to tease out an erection, while Ascylto, under no such impediment, enjoys himself with half a dozen girls on a giant swing.

One of the newest and most valuable additions to the Fellini team was Pippo Spoletini, a casting director given responsibility for 'special people'. He satisfied Fellini's call for 'the most crippled cripple that existed' with Antonio Moro, a middle-aged man without arms or legs. As the military hero who is carried in to see the hermaphrodite seer, the limbless Moro gave a performance of dignity and aplomb.

Determined that *Satyricon* look unlike any other film. Fellini hired Parisian art and architecture photographer Gilles Ehrmann to advise on the colours of the larger scenes and the degree of smoke or mist in the air. Ehrmann was also responsible for positioning all the extras. Fellini wanted images so composed, so rich, that the eye would still be wandering in the middle distance when the shot changed. He was equally insistent that no costumes or props be hired. Donati conceived everything from scratch, even commissioning new fabrics dissimilar to anything in use in 1968. The evidence of his originality is the longevity of its influence. If *Otto e mezzo* was the *fons et origo* of sixties cinematographic chic, *Satyricon* is the cornucopia from which interior design fed for the next two decades, the source of every half-completed

Pompeiian mural in every post-modernist Italian restaurant, of the 'Rotted Cellar' décor of eighties New York bistros with their rough-cast walls blotched in orange and green, and the gnarled, angular *faux*-Roman utensils in yellow, ochre and verdigris green whose geometric handles still snag sleeves and handbags from Melrose Avenue to the Sixth *arrondissement*. If Fellini's aim was to show how long a shadow he could still cast, the film was a signal success.

Shooting was complicated by the presence on the set of a film crew led by Gideon Bachmann, who'd persuaded Fellini to let him shoot a documentary of the production. Few people were better placed to do so. Since 1965, Bachmann had worked on Fellini's biography, interviewing scores of friends and relatives, but with *Satyricon* he announced he was giving up. 'He's a hang-up,' he confessed to Eugene Walter. 'I have stack upon stack of tape-recorded interviews with everybody who's ever known Fellini, but the book just doesn't jell. No two people say the same thing about him, and he's completely contradictory about himself.'

Today, Bachmann admits his reasons for abandoning the book were, though related to the director's unreliability as a witness to his life, more dramatic. His tapes of many hours of conversation with Fellini fell into the hands of a third party, who demanded a large ransom for their return.

'I just laughed it off,' says Bachmann, 'I said: "Keep the bloody tapes. If you want to treat me like that I'll go and make new ones with Fellini." I told Fellini this story, quite gleefully, thinking he would take it all as a joke. No way! He was very upset by this. You know he never tells the same story twice – neither does any great artist – and I should have been smart enough to recognise that one story of his life told on a certain afternoon in via Archimede in a certain light on a certain rainy day would not be the same story as told in a tent at Ostia on a sunny afternoon in November.'

Ciao Federico!, the documentary Bachmann edited down from sixteen hours of film and twenty of sound, is the most revealing of all Fellini film portraits. In observance of *cinéma vérité* rules, he often shot from hiding or lied about whether or not the camera was turning. After a few days the director tried to talk Bachmann out of this approach. 'We'll sit down at a table and in a couple of days we'll jot down a script,' he cajoled, without success. 'Then I'll play it for you. I'd do it beautifully. I'll do whatever you want. I'll sing, dance, make jokes. But stop following me around all day with that thing!'

The relationship with Bachmann chilled after the film. 'Fellini was used to squeezing people like lemons, then throwing them away,' says Gerald Morin. 'This time, *he* was the one who was squeezed, and he didn't like it.' Fellini was not upset when his profanity and that of Hiram Keller denied *Ciao Federico!* the US TV release Bachmann had planned, and the *contretemps* over its theme song, with its unintended slur on Fellini's manhood, ended the relationship for a decade.

In April, another irritant appeared in the form of a second low-budget *Satyricon*, produced by Alfredo Bini with Gian Luigi Polidori directing. Ugo Tognazzi starred, with Rizzoli distributing. Grimaldi immediately started calling his film *Fellini–Satyricon* to distinguish it, an idea Fellini liked, and adopted as a trademark. *Fellini–Roma* and *Il Casanova di Federico Fellini* would follow.

Enough old adversaries were involved in Bini's film to suggest to Fellini they meant to torpedo his new career. Stung, he told the press he was accustomed to his work being imitated after release but it was something new to be aped before the film was even made. In July, Bini filed a suit for defamation, to which Fellini responded with a similar writ.

Meanwhile, costs were climbing, leaving the budget behind. Fellini complained that United Artists were too cheap. They'd only given him, he exaggerated to Hollis Alpert, enough money to make the credits. If more cash wasn't forthcoming, he joked, *Satyricon* would consist of nothing but these beautiful credits, after which the audience would be locked in the cinema and asked to imagine the film. 'It is very creative of them.' At less playful moments, Fellini offered another and more plausible theory. 'Our own industry hardly exists any more. So we make pictures with American money, and the one who takes the money has, in a sense, to prove that he is not a thief. We are good friends but I think [United Artists] are a little fearful. They don't trust us.' United Artists pointed out reasonably that they had already advanced 80% of the first budget to Grimaldi. It was up to him to find the extra money. As the cost passed $3 million and headed for $4 million, the producer began to regret his decision to back this elaborate fantasy.

Rome was soaked in spring rain when Fellini arrived at the setpiece of the film's first half, Trimalchio's banquet. As the host, he'd cast another amateur, the tall, glowering Mario Romagnoli, nicknamed 'Il Moro' (The Moor), whose restaurant, Al Moro, in vicolo delle Bollette, a narrow alley just behind the Trevi Fountain, was a favourite Fellini hangout. Romagnoli, then sixty-nine, was ideal casting. 'His eyes had a satiated look, as if no appetite went unsatisfied,' said an extra in the sequence.

The party begins at sunset at Trimalchio's private baths by the lake. The bank is littered with sedan chairs and tall candles. Guests recline on the grass, some being massaged, while a larger group stand waist-deep in steaming water. Extras were called to Cinecittà before dawn. One of them, an American amateur named Betsy Langman, noticed 'that the make-up was used to extend or exaggerate the features of the actors. The fat were made fatter, the thin thinner, the bald balder, long noses were made longer, big eyes bigger, wide mouths wider. Faces were coloured red, blue, green and yellow, sometimes simply to match a dress, sometimes to dramatise a characterisation – like the sick yellow-grey of the old men or the pale, translucent ivory of the young.'

'Baytsie', as Fellini christened her, was cast as a guest at the banquet. Muttering, *'Occhi grandi, occhi enormi'*, the make-up man plucked her eyebrows, then glued strings above each. By drawing the strings tight, he pulled her eyes so wide it was almost impossible to blink. They were enlarged even more with make-up, and the strings disguised under flat black curls and a wig.

The party moves inside Trimalchio's country villa, where the host lounges on a dais with his family and household, including the nymphomaniac Tryphaena, friend and lover of his wife, Fortunata. Guests, including Encolpio and Eumolpo, lie around a central well in which the main dishes are served. Fellini exercised all his flair in planning the dinner. Giant roast carcasses festooned with feathers and horns are succeeded by furred bundles from which a single eye stares. A fume-filled dome is offered from which guests sip or smoke with long straws. Startling and puzzling, the dishes are as much theatre as food.

As the party becomes wilder, Fortunata, wearing only string bra and briefs under a thin robe, dances. Magali Noël hadn't realised this would be required until Fellini sprang the idea during a lunch at Cinecittà. He even flew in a choreographer from New York to coach her. 'He made a big fuss over the professor,' says Noël, 'had his chauffeur take him back into Rome, gave him a dinner the day before he returned to New York, hugged him, put him in the car and waved goodbye. Then, on the set next morning, he said to me: "Magalotte, do what you like." But of course, though I improvised the dance, I used a lot of the movements the professor had taught me.'

Salvo Randone had trouble playing Eumolpo, who loses his temper with Trimalchio when the latter tries to pass off a verse by Lucretius as his own. Fellini based the scene on a real argument in the early fifties, when a critic accused Rossellini of making his films 'by accident'. When Eumolpo is dragged to Trimalchio's infernal kitchen with orders that he be thrown into the fire, Encolpio rescues him, just as Fellini loyally backed Rossellini in disputes over the roots of Neorealism. Eumolpo's speeches, some of them in Latin, taxed the actor's powers, so Fellini fell back on telling him to recite anything he liked. Randone did a scene from the play *Hadrian VII*, then simply mouthed numbers and colours. Romagnoli recited the menu from his restaurant.

For the last third of the film, Encolpio and Ascylto wander in a landscape of desert and swamp. They find a luxurious villa with its aristocratic owners dead by their own hand outside, and enjoy a cheerful orgy with a black slave girl overlooked in the exodus. Seeking a cure for his impotence, Encolpio is directed to the priestess Oenothea in the swamps. She manifests herself as an obese and randy black woman on whom his virility revives. He returns to the boat to find Ascylto murdered in a fight with the boatman. Walking to the sea, he discovers Eumolpo, also dead. The poet's will is read in which he bequeaths his wealth to his friends, provided they eat his body. The older men are prepared to do so, but the young, including Encolpio, laughingly refuse. Instead they embark on Eumolpo's boat and sail off, leaving the old men glumly chewing on the corpse. Encolpio explains that they had many wonderful adventures, and the film ends on the faded wall-paintings of a ruined villa in which many of the film's principals appear.

With the weather better, the crew moved to Fregene and the island of Ponza for the naval scenes. Petronius' Lichas was a rich merchant, but Fellini turned him into a rapacious homosexual general and cast Alain Cuny in the role. The dignified Cuny was required to wear a goggling false eye and to wrestle in a plainly sexual manner with two men. He co-operated but disliked the experience and has never seen the film.

The Lichas sequence is yet another statement of *Satyricon*'s homoerotic message, news of which spread in Rome's gay community. For one of the earliest scenes, and the only one which uses actual Roman ruins, Fellini took Potter and Born to the caverns under the Colosseum. A crowd quickly gathered, including two gay prostitutes, known, in homage to a popular cabaret sister act of the time, as the Kessler Twins. The 'twins' made approving comments and were immediately involved in an argument with the crowd. Afterwards, they stopped the director and said: 'Thank you, Fellini' – a common reaction among gays as the tenor of the new film became known.

Satyricon finished its twenty-six weeks in the studio with a flurry of shooting in the last week of July 1969, in expectation of a première at Venice in September. Fellini stood by his refusal to enter any film there, but once again agreed to let it be shown out of competition. Meanwhile, the Roman courts had formally condemned Bini's version on the grounds of obscenity and tending to the corruption of minors. Ironically, this decision helped Fellini, since censors compared his film favourably to Bini's catchpenny effort. In August, however, the court refused to rule that it was 'parallel' with Grimaldi's production and thus represented an act of plagiarism. Bini was therefore free to release it after censor cuts. Resignedly UA bought it for $1 million to keep it out of circulation.

In August Fellini showed his rough cut to critics like John Francis Lane, who called it in the London *Times* his 'greatest achievement as an author'. Though the director wasn't happy with the dubbing, the film had its première on 4 September at Venice. There was no hotter film that year. $3.20 tickets to the late-night public screening changed hands at 50,000 lire (about $100) and a line formed from three pm onwards. A special extra showing was arranged after midnight for the overflow. A five-minute ovation greeted the first screening and next day Fellini submitted to a press grilling marked mostly by confusion. The film was so startlingly new and, to many, so repellent in conception and appearance that nobody wished to be first in attacking it. Most critics took time to consider their reaction before writing their reviews, which were mostly cautiously approving, but the public, who flocked to the screenings, were less reticent. '*Brutto spettacolo*,' muttered one patron leaving a Venice cinema, though not with any animosity. Most Italian critics would rate it as more moral lesson than entertainment, excusing its excesses in the name of a higher truth. It wasn't the film that was a disgusting spectacle, but mankind.

Experts on ancient Rome jostled to list the film's historical errors. Romans didn't lie on their faces when they ate, nor did swimming pools exist at the time. The ships, cavernous within but hardly bigger than yachts outside, created an arrestingly sinister silhouette with their gondola prows, but the first breeze would have overturned them. Roman baths were white, clean and made of marble, unlike Fellini's, a deep pit lined in brown tile that might pass for a sewage farm or the cooling pool of a nuclear reactor. Nobody was too clear on the sound of Roman music, but it was almost certainly nothing like that which Rota confected. Fellini chose the basic sounds from a collection of African and Far Eastern tribal music. Rota distorted them further electronically and mixed them with new atonal passages. The effect was as far as possible from the pomp of the peplums, since Fellini demanded that the music have no conventional emotional associations of any sort.

Fellini brushed off the criticisms. He'd set out to make a film unlike any other and most agreed he'd succeeded beyond even his expectations.

United Artists struggled to build a following for the film among the American youth audience, but it was the outlaw cinema represented by *Easy Rider* that eventually captured this lucrative market. Fellini's film was a modest success, grossing 1.5 billion lire ($3 million) in Italy and $8 million worldwide. In Japan, where its excesses were especially to public taste, it ran for four years.

Critics have continued to puzzle over the subtext of *Satyricon*. There's no lack of seductive parallels between the film and Fellini's life. Fabrizi is the gross clown Vernacchio and Rossellini the self-pitying Eumolpo, while the cannibal oldsters would be the producers Fellini loathes. The incident of the dying hermaphrodite symbolises the death of his son. As for Encolpio and Ascylto, might they represent the two sides of Fellini's character, straight and gay? Asked by Jeremy Kagan if he cast Potter and Keller because they looked alike and were thus meant to represent 'two sides of one person', Fellini replied fliply: 'No – but I am very easily convinced.' With the killing of Ascylto, runs the theory, Fellini symbolically murdered the feminine aspect of his character.

Pressed about the gay element of *Satyricon*, Fellini could be evasive and irritable. 'Why don't you show the homosexuality more?' asked Charles Thomas Samuels in 1971. Clearly astonished that the academic missed the film's most prominent theme, Fellini said : 'I do.' 'All you see is one man kissing another's wrist,' Samuels complained, at which Fellini, irritated as usual by critical thick-headedness, demanded: 'What, do you want to see the prick going in? I wasn't making a film about homosexuality as seen by a prurient Catholic. I wanted everything to appear as if on a fresco.' Samuels tried to abandon what was obviously a sensitive subject but Fellini wouldn't have it. 'What did you want?' he exploded. 'Men kissing on the mouth?'

Other critics were not so obtuse. Rex Reed, then the ruling arbiter on the more flamboyant end of cinema, was lavish in his praise, finding the film 'an explosion of madness and perversion, designed like grand opera of the absurd – a homosexual odyssey in which the creatures of Fellini's mind writhe like sequined snakes towards some surrealistic damnation of the soul . . . ' More circumspectly, but no less accurately, Parker Tyler's history of gay films labels it 'the most profoundly homosexual movie in all history'.

23   'A little film for the tele': *I Clowns*

'I don't know how to ask questions, and even when I do
manage to ask an intelligent question, I find I am not
really interested in the answer'
Fellini on documentary

On 16 October 1969, Visconti's *La caduta degli dei/The Damned* had
its première in Milan. As the lights came up in the Teatro Barberini,
specially redecorated for the occasion, Fellini leapt to his feet in the
stalls and, turning to face Visconti and his stars, shouted: *'Il maestro! Il
maestro!'* The audience joined him in a standing ovation.

It was harder than usual for Fellini to celebrate the success of his
greatest rival, since he was having little luck himself. Though *Satyricon* was well into its release, money was still short. With no more films
in prospect after *The Madwoman of Chaillot*, Giulietta took parts in
TV serials like the 1973 *Eleanora*, began writing a column for the
daily *La stampa* that was to run more than a decade, and started
charity work for UNICEF.

She and Fellini had settled into a relationship more like brother and
sister than husband and wife. 'The word "marriage" is not appropriate in our case,' she said distantly. 'Federico and I haven't formed what
you could call a family. We haven't been parents, haven't raised
children. It would be better to speak of a couple, two people who stay
together by free choice.' Privately, Giulietta had emotional dominance,
but in public she was dutiful. In December 1969 they went to Paris for
Satyricon's French première. At the Hotel George V, Fellini held court.
Reporter France Roche asked what cinema was to him. 'The mirror of
my life,' he began expansively, 'the reflection of my researches . . . '
But Roche was watching Masina. 'She smiles,' she noted, 'always
impassive, next to her big adolescent of forty-nine years, full of
tempests.'

As *Satyricon* won bemused reviews in the French press, Fellini and Zapponi concentrated on their contribution to *Love Duet*. Martin Poll had meanwhile produced *The Lion in Winter*, the film that Peter O'Toole made instead of *Toby Dammit*. A considerable success, it inaugurated a new phase in the star's career.

For *Love Duet* Fellini chose *La città delle donne/City of Women*, a Zapponi fable about a philanderer who stumbles into a conference of feminists. Bergman's story, originally called *Adultery* but later *White Walls*, was more conventional, the account of an affair between a Swedish man and an American woman visiting Stockholm.

Fellini worked with misgivings. When Bergman returned to Rome for the press conference announcing the project, he'd watched a compilation of scenes from *Satyricon* – which, he told his host flatteringly, changed his way of looking at film. Despite this, and notwithstanding Fellini's assurances that he saw Bergman as a kindred soul and 'a milk brother', the spirit of the first stroll round Rome with Liv Ullmann proved hard to revive. Fellini and Liliana Betti took Bergman to dinner at Da Cesarino. Asked what he was then working on, Bergman said he was preparing a film about death, which he hoped to start shooting within three months. Death was a subject on which Fellini now felt expert. 'Six months ago I almost died myself,' he said, 'so I think . . . '

'Some years ago, I was very ill too,' Bergman interrupted. 'I thought *I* was going to die.'

'Yes, but me,' Fellini pressed on. 'I was *really* dying. For all practical purposes I was already dead. So on this subject I know it all.'

'Once I had an injection that provoked a sort of clinical death for five hours,' Bergman said. 'I came to the conclusion that death is simply non-existence.'

Fellini couldn't hide his scorn. '*Five hours* seems to me to be very little time for someone to formulate an opinion with such certainty.'

Ullmann's relationship with Bergman was also foundering, mostly on his inflexibility. When they travelled together, he'd send her ahead to establish the proper home-like atmosphere in their hotel. She suspected that Fellini shared some of Bergman's attitudes, an impression confirmed on a visit to Fregene. After dinner, with Fellini out of the room, Giulietta illustrated a point to Ullmann by starting to sing. Fellini came back and, standing in the doorway, said: 'I can't leave the room for a moment without my wife making a fool of herself.' For the rest of the evening, Giulietta remained silent, moving everywhere on tiptoe and with a fixed smile. What sort of films about feminism, Ullmann wondered, did these men think they were making?

In the autumn Fellini and Bergman delivered their screenplays to Poll, who passed them on to Universal. Jennings Lang liked *White Walls* and suggested casting Katharine Ross of *The Graduate*. He was less enthusiastic about *La città delle donne*, and his dislike intensified when Fellini nominated Mastroianni, who still spoke almost no English, to star. He'd been thinking of Warren Beatty. When Fellini refused to compromise, the studio rejected the script outright.

Poll had scheduled shooting for November. With that deadline looming, Fellini offered another Zapponi adaptation, *Una donna sconosciuta/An Unknown Woman*. This was one of Fellini's strangest projects, and intensely revealing of his sexual ambivalence. The main character is a wealthy middle-aged man who lives with his aristocratic mother outside a small Lombardy town and manages the family factory. At a press launch, he falls in love with a girl and marries her. After months of happiness, she tells him abruptly that she's leaving and forbids him to follow her. Obsessed, he discovers where she went to school, where she had her first job, but the woman herself has vanished. Abandoning the search, he retires to their house, where he begins to sample her perfumes, her lipstick, eventually to wear her clothes. 'In a climate of frozen horror, in drag,' Fellini wrote, 'he leaves the house, Frankenstein's monster, prey to a delirious love.'

Fellini sketched the character in detail. Zapponi, a devoted eroticist – his work includes the text for a collection of pictures of legendary forties S & M model Betty Page – visualised the man becoming a credible, even beautiful woman, but Fellini's vision is of rosebud lips, black wig, low-cut cocktail dress, limp wrist and the inevitable cigarette – something from an amateur drag night contest for Bette Davis lookalikes. He also set the film in 1928, in winter, in the foggy northern city of Mantua. It would comment, he said, on the moral malaise of early Fascism – a draft for the autobiographical *Amarcord*.

Not surprisingly, Universal turned the new story down as well. In November Poll visited Fellini at Chianciano, where he was resting, and told him that Universal were going to produce *White Walls* as a separate full-length feature. With *Love Duet* now a lost cause, he suggested that he and Fellini make *Una donna sconosciuta* as a feature too. Angry at Poll's failure to pull the deal together, Fellini refused, telling him that his next film was under option to Grimaldi.

The story became public on 17 December in a *Variety* piece headlined ' "Wha' Hoppen to 'Love Duet' Between Himself and Bergman?" '

Fellini Asks.' A pained Fellini claimed that Bergman had come to Rome several times for script conferences but that communication had then broken down. Poll was simply expunged from the story. Fellini said, improbably, he'd read about the plan for a separate Bergman film in a Stockholm paper. Bergman spent most of 1970 filming *White Walls* as *The Touch*. Its characters were reversed. The woman was now Swedish, played by Bibi Andersson, while Elliott Gould was the visitor, an American archaeologist. Despite Andersson's touching performance, it was one of his biggest flops.

Despite the problems with *Block-notes di un regista*, Peter Goldfarb now approached Fellini to make more NBC specials. The deal was attractive, the network financing travel and research, but leaving him free to decide after the trip if the film was worth making. They discussed a profile of Pope John XXIII, who had died in 1963. Fellini suspended his anti-clericalism for the chubby and amiable prelate who presided over the Church's partial and belated liberalisation. He'd once briefly been stuck in traffic next to the papal limo. The Pope recognised him and smiled. 'The innocence of his face! Like a baby. It was like an apparition in a fairy-tale.'

Other and more grandiose topics discussed included a Tibetan monastery, an American factory, the car giant Fiat and Mao Tse-tung. Fellini asked left-wing journalist friend Antonello Trombadori to explore the possibility of meeting Mao, though he soon realised that a formal interview would unacceptably limit his imagination. Gradually the idea of any sort of straight documentary was tacitly dropped.

Fellini was still suspicious of American TV – rightly, since he read in the small print of his contract that NBC reserved the right to shelve his films if they chose. Refusing to sign, he began courting European networks. Rossellini had been producing almost exclusively for the Italian national government network Radiotelevisione Italiana (RAI), which had also funded TV features by Bertolucci and Olmi. They welcomed the prospect of working with Fellini.

RAI already planned to make a live-action film of *Pinocchio*, restoring the violence and social comment of Carlo Collodi's fable, sugar-coated out of existence by Walt Disney. Fellini was interested, since Collodi had set his story in the Apennines of Romagna and both he and Gherardi loved Carlo Chiostri's sparse and spiky original illustrations. He'd also once compared the making of a film and its taking on of independent life to the carving of Pinocchio. 'For the first two weeks it's not me who directs a film but the film that directs me.

That's nothing new; it happened to Gepetto as well. He was still carving Pinocchio while the doll was taking its first steps.'

With Gherardi driving, the mountain-hating Fellini went searching for a location for the Country of Toys among the ravines inland from Rimini. Stuck there, they had to spend a night in the car – a bad omen.

As negotiations dragged on about *Pinocchio*, Fellini became impatient. It was to avoid cumbersome deal-making that he'd turned to TV. The fashion for lighter, more personal films pointed towards another quick sketch from his quirky imagination, a '*Block-notes II*' (his working title). RAI, which seldom invested more than half the budget of any film, introduced Fellini to Elio Scardamaglia of Leone Film and Ugo Guerra of Daima Film. Both had produced with RAI and were eager to work with Fellini if a sufficiently Italian theme could be found. Unexpectedly, he suggested a study of those 'ambassadors and forerunners of the film director's art', the circus clowns. Hooked, the producers set up Compagnia Cinematografazione Leone specifically to make the film, called simply *I clowns*.

Whatever his misgivings about TV, Fellini was as usual full of newsworthy casting ideas, even if some names were threadbare with use. He would be approaching Danny Kaye, he said, as well as Pablo Picasso and (again) Mae West. He hoped Chaplin would re-create the death of Corradini, who plunged on his horse from the peak of the big top after a stunt went wrong. Kaye, West and Picasso all passed, if indeed they were ever approached, and the Corradini episode, like the story of the Zacchinis, specialists in the human cannonball act, was dropped because he ostensibly 'didn't want to force [Chaplin] to refuse' (which, at eighty, he would very sensibly have done). He settled for Chaplin's youngest daughter Victoria, who'd gone into the circus in Paris, and, for celebrities, a cameo of Anita Ekberg shopping for a tiger cub.

A certain panic motivated his boosting, because Fellini had realised that, despite his affection for clowns, he actually knew little about their lives or the history and business of the circus. The travelling shows of his childhood had almost disappeared. Most of the great Italian clowns were retired or dead. 'Does this rough humour, this deafening slapstick I once found so funny, still exist?' he wailed. 'Can the things clowns did then still make people laugh? The world that brought them forth and of which they were an expression doesn't exist any more.'

Circus, however, did still flourish in France, where many clown dynasties were founded, so Fellini made a research trip to Paris with Zapponi late in 1969. An air of decay hung over the circus there. Of its famous permanent indoor circuses, the Cirque d'Hiver operated only three days a week, while the Cirque Medrano had become a Bavarian beer hall. They taped interviews with an old shoemaker who specialised in comic footwear for clowns and a theatrical photographer with a collection of ancient pictures. In boarding-houses they met venerable managers, still clinging to the dream of a last spectacular show. One of them, Jean Houcke, rambled about a scheme to hire an operatic tenor from La Scala, put him in a carriage and send him racing round the ring, singing at the top of his voice. Fellini pledged to include such a sequence in *I clowns*.

He left Paris more than content. Just as he preferred the low comics and lead-footed tap-dancers of vaudeville and the theatre of painted backcloths and ham acting, it wasn't clowning's courage and daring that attracted Fellini so much as its cheapness, cruelty and despair. All clowns were Pagliaccis to him, and the dismal atmosphere of the Cirque Medrano and Cirque d'Hiver echoed his own innate melancholy.

Scardamaglia and Guerra had negotiated a deal with RAI under which *I clowns* would be released simultaneously on TV and as a cinema feature. While they assembled funding, Fellini, with Giulietta and Grimaldi, went to the United States in January 1970 for the promotion of *Satyricon*, due to open nation-wide in April.

In Los Angeles, their first stop, Fellini at last saw *Hair*, though United Artists upstaged it with the *Satyricon* launch party. In a sound stage floored with plastic grass, waiters in togas served wine from carafes shaped like bunches of grapes, while others carved slices of roast sucking pig. A seminar held by the American Film Institute at Greystones, its Hollywood mansion headquarters, was no less stage-managed. Eager to make capital of the visit, Institute director George Stevens Jr faced Fellini and Giulietta, joined on the platform by Anthony Quinn, with an audience of the AFI's famously arrogant film-making students, leavened with celebrities like Billy Wilder, Jack Lemmon and Ray Bradbury.

Never comfortable in such company, Fellini found the tone of the event disagreeable. A student documentary crew falling over itself and noisily dropping equipment didn't help. The more he was pressed on specifics, the more Fellini temporised. Most of his audience had read articles in the American press, like Thomas Meehan's extensive profile in the *Saturday Evening Post* which quoted him as saying: 'If I first carefully wrote out a completed scenario, I'd feel that the thing had already been accomplished in the writing – I'd have no interest in trying to film it' and: 'I love to improvise while filming . . . I don't want to know where it is going or where it will end.' He startled them by insisting that improvisation was 'impossible' and the claim he enjoyed it 'stupid gossip'. He also said he worked from a full script and never saw rushes. He and Ray Bradbury indulged in some self-congratulatory cross-talk, comparing looking at rushes to letting people read a story only half-written. His audience was disconcerted by these evasions and half-truths, as the mischievous Fellini had hoped they'd be. (Stevens closed the event on an appropriately low note. 'OK, two more questions and we'll all go next door for the orgy.')

UA's American advertising campaign for *Satyricon*, with its arrogant, not to mention inaccurate slogan '*Rome. Before Christ. After Fellini*', grated with Hollywood's pietistic old guard. It awarded the film only one Academy Award nomination – for Best Director, which Fellini had no hope of winning. When the Oscars were handed out that year, Donati was honoured, but for his more conventional work on Zeffirelli's *Romeo and Juliet*.

On 8 February 1970 Fellini, back in Rome, wrote a long letter to Grimaldi. It began with a typical flourish. 'The moment to choose has come. I have before me three rough sketches for films, each of which pleases me for different reasons.' Dismissing *I clowns* as 'a little film for the tele' and knowing better than to suggest the ill-fated *Il viaggio*, he outlined *La città delle donne*, which he said misleadingly had been dropped from *Love Duet* 'when it was felt to be irreconcilable with the story chosen by Bergman'. He pushed hardest on *Una donna sconosciuta*. Fellini has few equals in 'pitching' a story. He described the ancient palace bathed in fog, the massive gas stations of the *autostrada* and the highway itself, 'a ring of Saturn which seems to unroll without end, a long streaked ribbon for the trucks, slow as elephants. In the fog all forms change perpetually; seen from a distance, a truck looks like a church.'

By comparison, he was almost perfunctory about the third project. For some time, he said, he'd been 'caressing' the idea of a portrait of Rome, 'a Rome anthropomorphised, seen like a woman whom one loves and hates at the same time; or like a universe which one believes one knows well because it has always been there, and which, all of a sudden, reveals itself completely unknown, like an unexplored jungle'.

Early in March Fellini got down to pre-production on *I clowns*. In America his concept of the film had changed radically as his imagination played with the clown persona. Most people, he decided, resemble clowns – either the White Clown, a symbol of authority, or Auguste, the victim and mischief-maker.

The personae of White Clown and Auguste superseded gender, he insisted. 'The clown is sexless. Has Grock a sex? Has Charlie Chaplin even?' He went on: 'Laurel and Hardy sleep together. They are a pair of innocent Augustes, absolutely lacking any sexual character at all.' As for Gelsomina and Cabiria, the most overtly clown-like of his own characters, they hadn't been women, he decided, but Augustes, sexually neutral. To publicise the film, Fellini had himself made up as a clown, one half of his face painted, the other untouched. To any disciple of Freud (a White Clown) rather than, like himself, of Jung (inevitably an Auguste), it was a powerful image of sexual ambivalence.

Once again, the myth was in control, with Fellini wrenching the exterior world into line with his own psyche. *I clowns* had become another self-examination in the form John Russell Taylor christened 'a fantasy documentary of the mind'. Chaplin's priapic personal life and the presence in Laurel and Hardy films of Jean Harlow in her step-ins were simply ignored. Fellini preferred the infantile image of sexual roles offered by the clown family, with its distant father (a White Clown), and naughty child and helpless, weeping mother (both Augustes), because it echoed his own experience.

Health-conscious America jolted Fellini into a physical reappraisal which, as usual, he embraced to excess. A New York doctor had taken him off the metabolisers he'd been using for years as an inadequate medication for his fainting spells and prescribed instead a regime of vitamins and mineral salts. 'He saved my life,' Fellini said. He also went on a diet and started exercising every morning with Bevilacqua. More sensitive than ever about his baldness, he began scalp treatments, a fact he disguised with a story, improbable but typical, of following a beautiful girl into a building and finding himself in the office of a trichologist. He also gave up smoking, pestering those around him to the extent that Giulietta, who refused to quit with him, further divided the via Margutta flat, giving herself a second 'smokers only' sitting-room. When they travelled now, she demanded a separate bedroom as well as the second sitting-room.

Early in 1970, driving to Riccione near Rimini to visit the Orfei family, Fellini almost ran down a boy on a motorcycle. Nobody was hurt but, in the altercation, Fellini abruptly decided to abandon driving altogether. A German tourist, overhearing his name as he gave it to the police, offered to buy his green two-door Mercedes convertible with the gold fleck as a souvenir. Fellini, as always superstitious, agreed immediately and never drove again. For long trips he was chauffeured, while journalists who arranged to meet him at the Conchiglia Hotel near his Fregene holiday house were taken aback to see the bulky Fellini wobble up on a bicycle.

On 23 March filming on *I clowns* began in Anzio. To inscribe his signature more clearly, Fellini employed the 'fake crew' format of *Block-notes* that was to become standard for his essay films. The enquiry into clowns and their history is conducted not by a dispassionate and neutral camera but by Fellini himself at the head of a scratch film crew. It's he who orders the action, poses the questions, speaks the commentary.

Fellini has always said the opening sequence, of a little boy woken at night by strange sounds and watching from his bedroom window as the circus tent is erected by firelight, rising like a bloated animal under the boy's startled gaze and that of prisoners in the local jail, was inspired by Winsor McCay's comic strip *Little Nemo*, an album of which he kept beside the bed during the filming, but one senses an evasion. Young Federico staring at the slowly swelling tent is almost certainly a reference to his first glimpse of the sexual act, the so-called 'primal scene', one which he has returned to often in his films. Fellini's erotic imagination remains essentially infantile, which is why he's never created a credible sex scene on film. Tongues wobble, faces grimace and sweat, voices hoot and squeal, bodies heave as if fighting, throwing enormous shadows on the wall – the memory of a toddler confronted by an act at once frightening and fascinating.

A maid warns little Federico to have nothing to do with 'those gypsies', but the boy is transfixed. In his sailor suit, he wanders through the chaos of the preparations for the show, seeing his first elephant, his first clown. That night, we experience the circus with him, a succession of acts in which an Indian mystic is buried in a glass coffin, a burly woman wrestles a man and a mermaid swallows live fish; all familiar Fellini fetishes or childhood memories. The clowns, often winking knowingly at the camera as they mock the strongman, the sword swallower and the pompous ringmaster, are the subversive, unruly, almost terrifying heroes of the night. His early circus experience, asserted Andrew Sarris, 'traumatised Fellini's childhood, plunging him into a nightmare of grotesquerie, vanity and death from which he has never awakened'.

A planned five-week shoot on *I clowns* lengthened to eleven, though only thirty days were spent filming. The rest went in chasing second thoughts and writing new sequences. However, since he was shooting on 35mm with a forty-person crew, the budget tripled. Through May and June, he shot in Paris, the first and only time he ever filmed outside Italy. Nothing went well. Money was short, he suffered attacks of phlebitis and gashed a finger on a hotel window. Above all, the mantle of dispassionate observer fitted him poorly. By the time Montmartre made him an honorary citizen on 8 June he was eager to escape.

Planned sequences on the shoemaker and photographer were abandoned. In a nod to a theory of social utility, Fellini re-creates a performance by the Fratellinis at a mental hospital, showing the brothers drifting over the heads of the distracted audience in butterfly costumes, but his heart isn't in it. As for the genealogy of clowning, he doesn't pursue this beyond an interview with the comedian Pierre Etaix and his wife, Annie Fratellini, a conversation with historian Tristan Rémy and some brief encounters with old clowns. Two of them, Bario and Loriot, have retired in comfort, but most are shown hunched in doorways, broke and rambling. Grabbing shots of mourning statuary, spiked park railings and the derelict Gare d'Orsay, he added a sequence which implied that Paris, once the cradle of the circus, had become its mausoleum, and hurried back to Rome.

Paris had given Fellini at least one good idea. While there, he'd experienced a waking dream in which he visualised people in the street as clowns. He dashed off a series of spidery sketches, reminiscent of Dix and Grosz, titling them 'The Clowns You See in Life'. They metamorphosed into a long sequence set in Rimini following the opening circus scenes. It begins with Fellini musing on the soundtrack: 'That night ended badly. The circus people with their twisted and crazy faces scared me. I was reminded of other clowns.' The 'other clowns' are Riminese who exhibit all the same distortions: a tireless midget nun, the pompous stationmaster, a crippled war veteran trundled round town in a wheelbarrow by a woman who knows all of Mussolini's speeches by heart, and a rogues' gallery of small-town seducers, crazies and Fascists. The picture of thirties Rimini is ribald, often almost obscene: a man gestures suggestively at the peasant women and young *vitelloni* lust after a glamorous German tourist who drops into the local bar, and are mocked in turn by 'Giudizio'.

Renzo Bronchi, an assistant-costumier on *Satyricon*, created a big-top interior at Cinecittà from artfully draped cloth. In it Fellini staged the last third of the film, a florid re-creation of a night at the circus in the golden age. As if to thumb his nose at those who would have preferred something more topical, he closes with a mock funeral for the clown Frou Frou, who has supposedly choked on an ostrich egg at the age of 200. Pantomime horses draw the cortège, the widow, a clown with enormous breasts, weeps crocodile tears and the oration abuses the deceased. As they try to nail down the coffin, it collapses to reveal nothing but a few rags. The tent fills with balloons, streamers and lights. It might not have been good but at least it was loud.

The problems of his Paris shoot encouraged Fellini even more to abandon the documentary form. Critics would complain that he stubbornly refused to shift the film's focus past 1925 and the forgotten names of pre-war circus. Instead of modern clowns from TV and films, he filled the cast with old friends from the Fabrizi days, like Fanfulla.

Its tone of funereal regret was to win *I clowns* many enemies in the circus community, though Liana Orfei at least was a supporter. 'Almost all circus people have contested that film,' she says, 'saying it foretold the end of their world and, above all, the end of clowns. They didn't understand that the film expressed Federico's love for that world, so fragile and yet so solid, which was drawing further and further away from the reality of everyday life, made up only of statistics and nights without dreams.'

During the autumn Fellini had another brush with Hollywood. Director Paul Mazursky, having almost completed *Alex in Wonderland*, a pastiche of *Otto e mezzo* in which Donald Sutherland plays a Fellini-obsessed Hollywood film-maker who can't decide on the subject of his next film and goes to Rome to ask Fellini's advice, bearded him on his home ground and, despite his resistance, persuaded him to play a cameo in the film. 'Oh, the ball-breaker! Get him out of here,' improvises Fellini as Sutherland tracks him to his Cinecittà cutting-room, where he's editing *I clowns*. The dialogue could well have represented his thoughts about Mazursky, though in fact the two became good friends and Sutherland, through a bizarre series of circumstances, would star in Fellini's *Casanova*.

I clowns was premièred in August at Venice, following a lavish private screening by RAI. The film was, as usual, out of competition, but no prizes were awarded that year anyway, the 'Events' of 1968 having briefly outlawed such bourgeois aspects of the festival system. Under new, politically correct selection procedures introduced by the panicky administration, many new young directors were admitted for

the first time. Most would prove to be firecracker talents, though Ken
Russell earned Fellini's interest with *The Devils*, a vision at least as
strident as anything he'd conceived. This invasion was the year's real
press story. Fellini and *I clowns* were pushed to the sidelines, relics of
an older, apparently moribund cinema. Daily, admirers and acolytes
like Gideon Bachmann and the handsome young Cuban Rafaele
Padilla, who played Choclit in *I clowns* (and, in a burst of revisionist
enthusiasm, had changed his first name to 'Rai'), loitered in the lobby
of the Excelsior, waiting for Federico. He never came.

24 'A city that calls itself eternal': *Fellini–Roma*

'You give me the impression of being a kind of King of Rome'

Charles Thomas Samuels to Fellini, 1971

After Venice, Fellini followed up his February letter to Grimaldi, but the producer was unresponsive. *Una donna sconosciuta*, with its fogs, Fascism and cross-dressing, hadn't ignited his interest, while *La città delle donne* (which, Fellini had warned, would demand thirty or more women characters, plus hundreds of extras) looked dangerously expensive.

They were closest on the Rome documentary – until Fellini explained the approach he had in mind. Hoping to recapture the playfulness and relaxation of *Block-notes*, he proposed to make it like a TV essay. Unlike a feature, it wouldn't be shot in sequence or within a definite period. Instead he'd film episodes throughout the year, one or two at a time, responding to the rhythm of Rome, its customs and seasons. One would deal with the *Ponentino*, the evening west wind that invaded the city, clearing the mephitic summer air. After that, filming might halt until the Feast of All Souls in November, when Romans laid flowers on their family graves. It would pick up again in winter for the football rivalry between Rome and Lazio. And when would such a film be finished? 'When the money ran out,' said Fellini. Tullio Kezich called this vision a 'Sunday film', in line with 'Sunday painting'. Grimaldi, however, wanted nothing to do with it. Leone–Daima, which produced *I clowns*, also passed.

Fellini estimated he made 200 phone calls in the autumn of 1970, looking for money. Since he seldom slept more than three hours, he was up most mornings at six, calculating who else would be awake at that hour and, more important, receptive. One who did not answer was Angelo Rizzoli. The publisher died on 24 September at eighty, ending a relationship that had become more and more distant since the collapse of Federiz. With his death Fellini lost the last of the old guard of producers – always excepting the demonic de Laurentiis, then struggling to keep his over-stretched empire intact. As a result, the world was looking exceedingly cold.

In October Fellini went ahead and formally unveiled his plans – more like hopes, and already widely leaked – to the press. *La città delle donne* wasn't mentioned but he did announce *Una donna sconosciuta*. The star would be an unknown English actor named Robert Wyghaham. He talked about the Rome documentary, and another on Alghiero Noschese, a Neapolitan comedian, mime and transformation artist who was also one of Rome's ace movie dubbing voices. Noschese spoke the gently insistent commentary to *Le tentazioni del Dottore Antonio* and the text to *Roma*, so effectively in the latter case, using a slightly more resonant version of Fellini's own light voice, that many critics mistook him for the director.

Almost immediately, a backer for *Roma* came forward. Turi Vasile had been a director in Giulietta's wartime university theatre group. Now he ran Ultra Film, a small company gasping in the vacuum left by the retreat of Hollywood's runaways. Ultra committed $2 million from the funds of sportsman banker Giuseppe Pasquale, backed by a distribution deal with United Artists for $1.25 million and a further $800,000 for the Italian rights from Italnoleggio. It wasn't enough to complete the film, but Fellini assured Vasile, as he had Grimaldi, that he'd stop shooting the moment there was no money to continue. On this basis, production was scheduled for November.

Though he'd lived in Rome for more than thirty years and was half-Roman on his mother's side, Fellini still, as his enemies never tired of pointing out, saw the city with the eyes of a country boy. He struggled to make *Roma* the film of a cosmopolite, but despite everything the city emerges as simply a large village, with a village's preoccupations: weather, food, scandal, sex. The imperial past appears as it does to peasants, something turned up by the plough, at best a curiosity, at worst an inconvenience. As for its pretensions as the national capital, he shows the city wearing them lightly, the way smart Romans (and Fellini) wore their overcoats, draped cape-like over the shoulders, easily shrugged off.

Above all, it's a friendly, welcoming Rome, a city where everyone knows everyone else and all of them know Fellini, the unofficial king of his adoptive city. He'd once compared Rome to an apartment – by now, it had become *his* apartment, and all Romans his guests. 'When I hear the word "Rome", he told Zapponi, 'I think of a ruddy face like that of Sordi, Fabrizi, *la* Magnani. An expression made thoughtful and pensive by gastro-sexual demands. I think of a brown sun, muddy; of a vast sky, zebra-striped, like an opera backcloth, with those same colours – violet, the blacks and silver; funereal colours. But all this combines to make a reassuring face.' And Fellini, as always, craved reassurance.

Fellini and Zapponi cruised on the Tiber, descended into the excavations for Rome's metro and explored the national archives. Plenty of cinematic possibilities came to light. One legend claimed that the catacombs under the Palace of Justice had become infested with rats so savage they devoured cats sent after them, so the city borrowed leopards from the zoo to scare them out. Fellini planned to re-create this incident. However, the authorities announced that the Palace was subsiding and abruptly – suspiciously so, Fellini thought – closed it.

As usual, the film's focus quickly shifted towards autobiography. Sketching to refine his vision, Fellini filled six books with drawings, each volume dealing with a major sequence. They became Danilo Donati's blueprints for the film. The first showed the view of Rome from the provinces as Fellini remembered it from his childhood. The second described what had, by now, become the official version of his arrival in the city, as a lone young journalist. In the third he detailed some visions of the roads into Rome, including a sequence in which the camera travels along the *autostrada*, snatching glimpses of ruins, crashes, whores.

The fourth and sixth books covered one of his most startling visions, an ecclesiastical fashion show in the palace of a Roman princess where models parade in fanciful religious regalia. The fifth, '*I casini*' ('The Houses'), contained his memories of Rome's wartime brothels.

Cementing these sequences and reinforcing the village atmosphere were other scenes in which Fellini wandered around Rome, chatting with old friends and arguing with students, followed everywhere by a German film crew. *Roma* would eventually become *Fellini–Roma*, and with the title change went all pretensions to objectivity. This was film-making as Fellini loved it, unfettered by dialogue, untroubled by character. There were no stars. Almost everyone in the film was an amateur or an unknown. Nobody would pester him about their lines because there were none – just curses, imprecations, greetings, few of them longer than half a dozen words, overridden everywhere by the commentary of Noschese-as-Fellini.

Production began officially on 2 November 1970, when Rotunno filmed the Verano Cemetery from a helicopter. One of Fellini's first visions of *Roma* had been a bird's-eye view of the city seen through swirling clouds. He had no intention of missing the experience simply because the scenes no longer fitted his new concept. He had ideas of combining this sequence with another of Rome mourning its dead, by following an old man, played by Mario Conocchia, as he visited family graves, but this was finally shelved.

Since he was well aware that $2 million wouldn't be enough to complete the film, Fellini set Donati to work on the most expensive sequence first. It was impossible to film on Rome's ring road, the Raccordo Anulare, so he constructed a section of four-lane highway at Cinecittà, complete with forty lights, fifty roadsigns, fifteen billboards and two restaurants. A note to Donati in the sketchbook says casually: 'Half a kilometre is sufficient.'

In addition to dozens of ordinary interiors, Donati, on Stage 2, re-created (as the Barafonda) the old Jovinelli vaudeville theatre. He also constructed a series of foyers for the brothel sequence, the interior of a sixteenth-century Roman mansion for the ecclesiastical fashion show and, most expensive of all, an entire block of via Albalonga, eighty metres long and twelve wide, complete with house fronts, a pavement restaurant to seat 200 and a working tramway.

Meanwhile, after a long wrangle over the relative importance of *I clowns*' theatrical and TV release, RAI and Leone Film had com-promised. RAI would broadcast it on Christmas night and Leone open the film in cinemas the following day. Spending Christmas in Rimini, Fellini watched the programme with Ida and the family, and was furious and embarrassed to find it transmitted in black and white. (Most Italian TVs were still monochrome.) Both ratings for the telecast and box office for the movie were poor and his meagre expectations of a television career evaporated. In January 1971 an angry Fellini told *Variety*: 'TV is not for me. It is a medium that sacrifices light, and light is vital to create images in all their nuances. Black and white programming practically decimated the substance and shape of my film.'

The experience underlined how little power he had over what he made for TV. He also sensed that, unlike Rossellini, he would always need the spectacle, the money, the expansiveness of real cinema, and its (relative) freedom. After *I clowns*, Fellini's public statements about television became increasingly jaundiced. By the eighties, he was the medium's sworn enemy – unless it suited him otherwise.

If Rome is the city that all roads lead to, those roads begin in backwaters like Rimini. *Roma*'s first image shows Romagnolo peasants trudging with their bicycles through the snow. A weathered block of stone announces: 'Roma 340 km'. On the background painting a threatening San Marino is clearly visible. 'He wrote from America,' says one woman. 'And?' asks another. 'Over there, all the food comes in cans.' They slog on out of the film, the ones who didn't manage to get away.

Fellini goes on to recall the echoes of Rome that littered his childhood. The most important of the many men to pass through en route to Rome, Julius Caesar, is evoked in the form of his statue in what had been, before the war, the piazza Giulio Cesare. The bearded and imperious school headmaster (Franco Magno) celebrates him as he leads his class across the Rubicone, chanting *'Alea jacta est!'* Fellini also recalls Achille Maieroni tottering through a performance as Caesar in the local theatre before pausing in the Caffè Commercio to sip a Mandarin Punch and, inevitably, move on.

In a scene celebrating Rome's most enduring lures, sex and antiquity, a slide show of Roman monuments presented by the local priest is interrupted when the image of a girl turning her backside to the camera pops up among the ruins. The schoolchildren go wild. Movies of Roman history produce a similar glee. A recollection of *Maciste all'inferno* triggers memories of the pharmacist's wife who haunted the Fulgor to be groped by young men. Fellini imagines her accommodating a queue of lovers in a twenties coupé parked on the windswept Lido. In a bar, a traveller praises the pleasures of the capital. 'What's good about Rome is, it's big. Nobody knows you. You're free to come and go.' 'And the Roman woman?' asks the barman. The traveller moulds ample hips in the air. 'She's got an arse like *this*.' It's clear why young Federico was so eager to live there.

I clowns had been a hermetic, almost stifling film about a closed world, and for the first few moments it seems *Roma* might suffer the same enervation. Movement is stiff and slow. It's often snowing or raining in Fellini's Rimini. Peasants plod through the slush, the schoolteacher steps painfully from rock to rock in the stony Rubicone, and the creaky old actor can barely manage a credible fall when Caesar is stabbed to death. The Riminese seem trapped, always looking out. They stare through windows or gape in disbelief at the cinema screen. Young Federico hangs mutely on the railway station gate as trains, teasingly labelled *'Internazionale'*, pull out. One of the film's most striking images is of Giudizio staring morosely through a bar window streaming with rain. It evokes exactly the boredom of a small town in winter.

Rome, by contrast, is turbulent, rowdy and above all alive. We're projected into weather, crowds, noise and appetite. Fires stream oily smoke in almost every outdoor scene, Fellini having prescribed his habitual mixture of naphthalene, magnesium and gunpowder to create a sulphurous atmosphere. Even the fashion show in Princess Domatilla's palace is wreathed in incense, and fumes eddy from beneath the catwalk, as if the shadowy palace and its gorgeously costumed guests float over the pit of hell.

While shooting *Satyricon*, Fellini had dreamed of being in prison. A voice said: 'On the other side of the wall there are Romans.' It was the germ of the underground sequence in *Roma*, one of the film's most effective. Guided by a melancholy archaeologist (played by London-based Marne Maitland, who spent most of his career as sinister Egyptians in mummy movies), Fellini's crew is led past a mammoth's tusk, a trophy of the excavation, into its dusty tunnels. As their little train rumbles into the earth and Maitland wearily describes the problems of digging in so ancient a city, the camera leaves the crew's point of view to weave like an historical ghost train through archives piled with files of the metro's century of construction and the bedroom of a terrified suburban couple whose whole house shakes.

The train passes workers coming off duty, posed on their travelling platform with the stiff formality of a monument, and debouches in a subterranean hall dominated by massive excavators. The Indicator, a milky dome like a psychic's crystal, has foretold an empty space ahead. While Maitland contemplates it as soberly as any clairvoyant, one of his men complains of feeling ill. There's an air of doom, of dangerous interference with the sacred past.

After a whining, almost anthropomorphic machine (in silhouette, like the mechanical penis to be featured in *Casanova*) is called in to grind away the last few metres of soil, the film crew burst into a pristine villa, partly flooded and decorated with vivid frescoes. But the air that billows after them is so polluted that the paintings blister and fade. Fellini and Rotunno so skilfully evoked the dream-like atmosphere and sense of doom that nobody queried how a Roman house got so far underground. Nor why a mosaic face stares up without hope from a pool too shallow for a well and too deep for swimming, or why, in an empty room, the statue of a matronly woman faces a blank wall as if in mourning.* As in all the best of Fellini, it hardly matters.

The sections of *Roma* showing young Federico's years in Rome are classic examples of fiction masquerading as biography. Played without much charisma by the flatteringly handsome young Mexican/American Peter Gonzales, Federico arrives at a crowded Termini station and checks in at the via Albalonga boarding-house. He's alone, rather than in the humiliating company of Ida and Maddalena, and overnight becomes a privileged if occasionally bemused spectator of the life of Rome.

Fellini lavished extraordinary amounts of time on the re-creation of the Jovinelli. Real music-hall artistes were interspersed with actors. Libero Frissi, star hoofer of the big production number, was a contortionist who performed at country fairs and weddings. The dogged Astaire imitator, Alvaro Vitale, had acted in a number of Fellini films but never danced before. Choreographer Giro Landi spent a month teaching him and other actors enough dancing to make them credibly inept.

Pursuing Rome's inextricable association with sex, Fellini shows his younger self taking cover in an air-raid shelter and picking up a lonely German singer. This is another of his fantasies, Fellini now admits, though a long-lived one. The girl, transmogrified into the French soubrette 'Jacqueline Bonbon', appears among Guido's harem in *Otto e mezzo*. Later, he's briefly seduced by the pleasures of the city's brothels. At a time when it was fashionable in films to show whorehouses as languorously middle class, with glamorous girls in black lingerie lounging on couches under the eye of a plump maiden-aunt-like madame, Fellini offered a vision of paid sex that's closer to the cattle market. Silent mobs of clients jam narrow underground corridors while the whores, mostly ugly, fat and old, tout for business, capering, urging, bullying the men, while the supervisors, tight-lipped harridans in strict suits, watch expressionlessly.

The luxury brothel, which Federico visits with a nervously giggling friend, is more plush, with marble floors, velvet couches and an elevator to the rooms upstairs, but even though the whores are more attractive they still parade and advertise themselves: 'I'm hot . . . I

*The equally anachronistic frescoes, reminiscent of twenties book illustrations, are by Rinaldo Geleng and his sons Antonello and Giuliano (who also did the Francis Bacon-like portraits of cardinals in Domatilla's palace, and would design the *Roma* and *Amarcord* posters).

want to make love but *I* choose . . . Come on! Come with the
Spaniard.' As the elevator lifts girls and clients to the upper rooms, one
woman calls scornfully to the loiterers downstairs: 'You're all queers!'

The only concession to cliché in this sequence is young Fellini's
crush on Dolores, queen of the luxury bordello, who wears the costume
of Messalina in *Maciste all'inferno* and bewitches him with her
smouldering stare. After a particularly satisfying blow job he asks her
for a date 'outside'. She seems to agree but we see no more of her. A
romantic adolescent fantasy? Or one of Mastroianni's tales?

The ecclesiastical fashion show is one of the great Fellinian set
pieces. In such sequences, Fellini exaggerates an incident to the very
edge of absurdity while retaining not only a foundation of reality but
also an element of pathos. His solemnity in the face of greed and
bombast is never a mask for derision. At the root of it is understanding,
even compassion. In an interview of the late sixties Fellini was already
discussing the 'religious choreography' of Catholicism and rhapsodis-
ing about its 'accessories – the most beautiful there can be: brocades,
golds, silks, plumes, mitres, sparkling capes, barbaric precious stones;
think of what Serge Diaghilev could have done as a director attached to
the Vatican'.

The show is held in the palazzo of ageing, lonely Princess Domatilla,
one of Rome's 'black aristocracy'. Out of respect for the family, which
has contributed countless Vatican bureaucrats to the Church, a cardinal (based on Ottaviani, a prominent supporter of the papal nobility)
has agreed to attend. Ancient portraits are dusted off and rehung, and
a ballroom fitted with bleachers and a catwalk. The guests assemble,
moving the Princess to tears with memories of the great parties of her
youth. 'The world should follow the Church, not vice versa,' says a
guest piously as two nuns at an antique pipe organ strike up one of
Nino Rota's sinister jigs and the show starts.

The costumes, mostly conceived by Fellini, are mockeries of Catholic regalia which, subtly at first, satirise the vanity and pomposity of
the Church. Almost sexy satin numbers for novices are succeeded by
elaborate bird-like coifs for mothers superior and white uniforms for
country priests, conveniently vented at the back for easier bicycling.
Fellini's spite becomes more visible as priests glide in on roller-skates
and sacristans preen amid layers of frothy white lace. Increasingly,
costumes overpower the models. Faces are often indistinct and, in the
case of fibreglass outfits for bishops and cardinals, festooned with
coloured light-bulbs or decorated with mirror plaques *à la* Paco

Rabanne, Fellini dispenses with people entirely: the clothes are empty shells.

Some of the last costumes are really *memento moris*, culminating in a tableau of death, with skeletons seeming to leap from a tomb, wreathed in veils, followed by a grey-faced figure in tulle, eerily like the desiccated corpses of saints on show in some Italian churches but inspired by Fellini's recurring dream of the enigmatic figure in rotting cloth who presents himself at an airport, offering no evidence of identity but demanding a decision on his fate.

After a parade of waddling priests in mirrored mitres and chasubles, the show ends in the *pièce de résistance* – the Pope, preceded by flunkeys with plumes and seated high on his ritual *sedia gestatoria* before a vast sunburst. The nuns and priests in the audience fall to their knees, but most of the aristocrats merely incline their heads. Pius XII, of which this figure is a parody, was, after all, a Roman prince by birth and Pope merely by appointment.*

Fellini was filming his encounter with students in the gardens of the Villa Borghese (they demand to know if his film will be socially relevant; he temporises) when he was visited unexpectedly by the comic-book artist Lee Falk, creator of *Mandrake*. Falk had been sent by de Laurentiis, who hoped he'd coax Fellini into directing a film with Mastroianni as the Fred Astaire of magicians. Fellini was sufficiently interested to incorporate a photo sequence of Mastroianni as Mandrake in a special Fellini issue of French *Vogue* at the end of 1972, an idea recycled years later in *Intervista*, but the film, like so many Fellini/de Laurentiis projects, came to nothing.

Fellini seems to have taken no psychic advice on the making of *Roma*. This may have been foolhardy, since the last half of its production was disastrous. In May 1971 the Swiss Val Lugarno bank collapsed, and with it the empire of Giuseppe Pasquale, backer of Ultra Film. United Artists refused to advance more money until it had seen the completed *Roma*. A desperate Turi Vasile demanded it be finished immediately and rushed into release. Fellini protested it was barely three-quarters complete. Donati was still building via Albalonga on

*Fellini irreverently chose a Spanish extra to play the role because of his resemblance to Eugenio Pacelli. The aura, a parody of the monstrance, a gilded sunburst used to display the host, was inspired by an advertising display for beer he'd seen in a bar in which back-lit plastic discs revolved slowly to create a shifting pattern. A cartoon in Paris's *Le canard enchaîné* showed Pope Paul VI ordering: 'Excommunicate *Fellini–Roma!*'

Cinecittà's Stage 5. But with Ultra Film broke and no other backer in sight, he reluctantly shut down production.

Then, on 8 June, Piero Gherardi died at sixty-two. Fellini hadn't worked with the designer since *Giulietta degli spiriti*.* In an ambiguous tribute, he called Gherardi 'an aristocratic hobo, an intellectual guest in the house of Trimalchio . . . as wise and detached as a bonze and as greedy, gluttonous and immature as a newborn babe'. Not what everyone would necessarily want on their tombstone, this obituary dramatised Fellini's competitiveness even with the dead.

By the summer, *Roma*'s problems were even more pressing. 'Word has somehow gotten around that my film on Rome will not show the city in the best light,' Fellini told *Variety*, 'so I am beginning to encounter mysterious obstacles.' In July he'd coaxed enough money out of Ultra, now negotiating with beer and oil millionaire Angelo Moratti for funding, to shoot the raucous Neo Antri Festival in Trastevere with its public boxing matches and boozy all-night parties. During one such scene, police descended with batons to break up a spontaneous hippie occupation of piazza Santa Maria. Fellini, who wrote such a sequence into the film, added his name to the accusations of police brutality delivered to the commissioner's office next day. Shortly after, they seized his film of the night's events, claiming to seek evidence of a murder. And in October, as shooting was about to restart, an actor who'd failed to get a part in the film incinerated a set.

If Fellini was distressed by this succession of disasters he showed no sign of it. Long lunches at the Grand continued, with *il maestro* taking over the dining room with his retinue, downing one of the fruity cocktails he loved, then diving into a typical five-course meal, interrupted by frequent passing visitors and the inevitable phone calls: his press officer, Mario Longardi, estimated an average eight per meal.

Fellini also took some satisfaction from the news that de Laurentiis, after battling to keep afloat, had been forced to sell Dinocittà to the government and relocate in Hollywood. The studio complex was left empty, picketed by unemployed technicians. Before he left, Dino approached Fellini for a favour. Out of friendship, would Fefé sign a deal with him, a sort of calling card to wave under Hollywood's collective nose? The opportunity to be magnanimous to his old antagonist was so novel that Fellini agreed. They concluded an open-ended contract for one film, title to be decided later.

*Ironically Gherardi's last film credit was for costumes on the TV version of *Pinocchio* he'd researched with Fellini but which Luigi Comencini directed.

On 24 June 1971 the court acquired a new member in Gerald Morin, a young Swiss critic who'd seen *Otto e mezzo* and decided he must work with Fellini. Seeking him out on Ponte Garibaldi, where he was shooting the motorcycle invasion sequence that ends *Roma*, Morin requested an interview for his Geneva paper. Fellini agreed, 'but later'. Morin returned each night. After ten days, Fellini asked Liliana Betti to remind him just who this long-haired observer was. When she discovered that his beard and shoulder-length hair disguised an ordained Jesuit, Fellini was delighted. Morin was jovially introduced to visitors as 'my private confessor'. Next day, Fellini handed him a letter from France asking for his autograph and said: 'Answer this for me, will you?' Morin obliged, eventually becoming Fellini's private secretary and assistant. He never did make the interview. Though Morin has long since left both the Church and the Fellini circle, for a successful career as a producer/director, Fellini still refers to him as 'The Priest'.

The Neo Antri sequence gave Fellini his chance to plant the message of *Roma*. He put it in the mouth of Gore Vidal, who's 'surprised' at a midnight supper with John Francis Lane and friends. 'Ciao, Gorino,' Fellini had said, meeting the writer in the foyer of the Grand weeks before. 'Come and be in my "Roma" film.' Vidal found himself reciting (as if it were his own dinner-party conversation) a speech about Rome as 'a city of illusions'. With creditable aplomb, he observes: 'It's not by chance that the Church, the government and the cinema are here – all sources of illusion.' Raising his glass, he toasts the end of the world. 'And where better to drink to the end of the world than in a city that calls itself "Eternal"?'

Both Alberto Sordi and Marcello Mastroianni also made guest appearances, though the most memorable celebrity sequence is the third, which would be the last screen role of Anna Magnani. She gives short shrift to Fellini, who (speaking in his own voice, not Noschese's) accosts her entering a house in a darkened street. She could be 'a symbol of the city', Fellini tells us. 'I'm *what*?' Magnani laughs. But Fellini is in full flight now. 'Whore and vestal virgin, aristocrat and beggar, sombre and buffoonish – I could go on until tomorrow . . .'*

'Federi', get some sleep,' Magnani says wearily.

'Just one question?' Fellini wheedles.

---

*Ironically, one provincial was celebrating another. Magnani wasn't born in Rome, or even in Italy, but in Alexandria, Egypt.

'No, I don't trust you,' she replies, closing her door on him, on us and her career.

Fellini couldn't resist the temptation to play a joke on his old rival for Rossellini's affections. A day of tests and close-ups for Magnani was scheduled at Cinecittà and, knowing her love of publicity, Fellini dressed three extras as *paparazzi* and told them to snap her at every opportunity. Then he introduced Gerald Morin as 'Monsieur Morin from *Cahiers du cinéma*'. But Morin went one better. 'Signorina Magnani,' he said, 'you are the only actress ever to have co-starred with Fellini. Tell me, how good an actor was he?' Fellini was indignant. 'I never told you to ask her *that*!' he protested.

Magnani was already fighting pancreatic cancer when she made *Roma*. She died in September 1973. Though the affair with Rossellini had long since cooled into friendship, she was buried, after a funeral attended by thousands, in his family mausoleum.

By the end of the summer, Fellini and his producer were locked in the sort of confrontation familiar from other films. Protesting he was broke, Vasile demanded that Fellini honour his agreement to stop shooting when the money ran out. Fellini refused, insisting Ultra adhere to their contract. When, at the end of the summer, Vasile's resources were exhausted, the Banco Nazionale di Lavoro agreed to advance the balance of the $3 million budget, but only on condition that Fellini make substantial cuts. He dropped the cemetery and football scenes. In October shooting restarted and, as quickly, ended.

The final scene of *Roma* was to become one of its most famous. As the last carousers of Neo Antri wander home, a group of motorcyclists roar into the city. Anonymous in leather jackets, faces masked by scarves, they flood through the deserted squares. Circling the monuments, their lights sending enormous shadows of horses and men sliding across the ancient façades, they race out of Rome into the night.

Intended, said Fellini, to show the city symbolically overrun by 'people I do not understand', the sequence, executed so smoothly that it seems effortless, was created during twenty-one exhausting night shoots. Since each of its shots was taken on a different location, Rotunno and his crew spent the first six hours of darkness lighting each vast space for a single image, shot between three am and dawn. The effort was worth it. Critics, especially the French, found the episode dazzling in its gratuitous visual drama. 'Nothing like it,' said director Alain Resnais, 'has ever been seen in the cinema.'

*

Fellini mimes, movement for movement, his memories of Rimini in *I clowns*, 1970.
BFI.
Young Fellini (Peter Gonzales) catches the eye of a prostitute in a part of the luxury-
bordello scene later cut from *Roma*, 1972. BFI.

Fellini directing the Messalina-like whore (Fiona Florence) for *Roma*, 1972. BFI.

Outside Fellini's recreation of the Fulgor Cinema, Gradisca (Magali Noel), watched by manager 'Ronald Colman' (Mario Liberati, on steps), accepts the admiration of Rimini's adolescents in *Amarcord*, 1973.

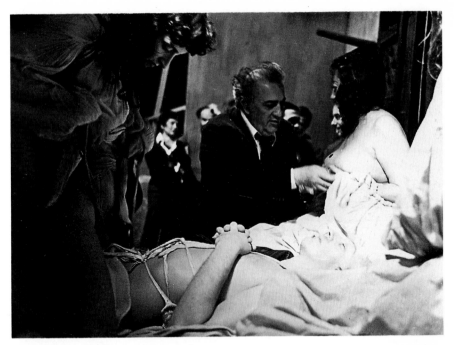

Fellini adjusts the bodice of Astrodi (Marika Rivera) on the set of *Casanova*, 1976.
Marika Rivera.

BELOW LEFT: Titta (Bruno Zanin) tries to guess the weight of the tobacconist's wife
(Mario Antonietta Beluzzi) in *Amarcord*, 1973. BFI.
BELOW RIGHT: Casanova (Donald Sutherland) dances with the clockwork woman
(Adele Angela Lojodice) in *Casanova*, 1976. BFI.

Fellini in full cry directing *La città delle donne*, 1980. Deborah Imogen Beer.

Directing Ettore Manni on *La città delle donne*, 1980, shortly before the actor's death. Deborah Imogen Beer.

Fellini flirting with some of his cast on *La città delle donne*, 1980. Deborah Imogen Beer.

ABOVE LEFT: Freddie Jones in *E la nave va*, 1983, BFI.
ABOVE RIGHT: Fellini with lighting cameraman Giuseppe Rotunno, 1983. Deborah Imogen Beer.

Fellini with Brunello Rondi, long-time confidant and script collaborator, 1983. Deborah Imogen Beer.

Michelangelo Antonioni (right) visits Fellini and production manager Pietro Notarianni on the set of *E la nave va*, 1983. Deborah Imogen Beer.

Fellini and Florenzo Serra, the amateur who played the Grand Duke of Harzock in *E la nave va*, 1983.

Giulietta with Fellini on *Ginger e Fred*, 1985. Parts of the film were reshot to disguise her wrinkles. Deborah Imogen Beer.

During the shut-down of *Roma*, Fellini opened negotiations on a new film with Franco Cristaldi. It would be autobiographical, building on the Rimini sections of *I clowns* and *Roma*, and exploring the regional roots of Fascism, the theme of the shelved *Una donna sconosciuta*. Cristaldi, who had a deal with Warner Brothers, felt confident enough of their backing to give the green light.

Fellini hurriedly dubbed *Roma*'s dialogue in the chilly Titanus studios over Christmas. He'd hoped to add a spoken prologue for the non-Italian market and to supervise the recording of the commentary, but Vasile was desperate to get the film into the cinemas. Gore Vidal says he demanded to dub his own words as a means of observing Fellini at work. In fact he was never offered an alternative. Strapped for cash, Fellini was reduced to re-recording the film with only three paid employees, including the inventive Noschese. All the celebrities speak in their own voices, even the less luminary John Francis Lane.

The December 1972/January 1973 French *Vogue* was designated as a Fellini number. Giulietta appeared on the cover in clown make-up, and there were three short memoirs of Rimini by Fellini himself, about the Grand Hotel, the Caffè Commercio and the annual ritual when husky young peasant girls would arrive on their bikes at Gambettola to have their pet chickens and rabbits blessed. All are recognisably drawn from the treatment for his film in preparation, *Amarcord*. A *fumetti* based on *Mandrake* with Mastroianni as the magician and Claudia Cardinale as his girlfriend Narda shows how credible the actor would have been as Falk's dapper hero. In the accompanying text, Mastroianni says he'd love to do the film, but with Catherine Deneuve (then his companion) as Narda and, as Lothar, his giant Nubian bodyguard, the English actor Oliver Reed in blackface.

Roma, now renamed *Fellini–Roma* – contrary to his wishes, Fellini says – was officially completed in February 1972 and publicly released on 16 March, two days after a screening at Cannes that provoked a scandal, though its focus was not the film but its poster. Ultra had accepted Geleng's design based on the image of Anna Maria Pescatori, a stern Roman bus-conductress, massively breasted, whom Fellini cast as a prostitute stoically patrolling waste ground littered with Roman ruins, a symbol of the city's eternal venality. Geleng posed her against a bloody sunset, summarising everything Fellini felt about the 'Roman face' and the sky that formed and reflected it. However, Artistes Associés, the French distributor, preferred an image of a nude girl on all fours, with three drooping breasts, a reference to Rome's she-wolf symbol. Feminists at Cannes, outraged, splattered with red paint every copy they could find, brushing aside Fellini's protest that he didn't like it either.

Fellini–Roma (as *Fellini's Roma*) wouldn't open in New York until October. In the interval, it lost nine minutes, though for once it was Fellini who made the cuts. Re-viewing the film in tranquillity, he decided Sordi's and Mastroianni's cameos were extraneous, as was the singing of the song 'Vierno' during the Barafonda sequence, the special nostalgia of which would be lost on non-Romans.

Romans were anything but enthusiastic about the film, which was greeted with derision. Audiences pelted the screen. On the first day of release, however, Fellini was spotted browsing in a Rome bookshop, leafing through a picture book on primitive painting. He could afford to be unconcerned. The critical reaction would be good, and though *Roma* returned only 882 million lire in Italy, it would become one of his most respected works. Even Luis Buñuel sent him a congratulatory telegram. Against all the odds, the film had turned out well. The king of Rome, exiled briefly to television, was back on the throne once more, and with a new film, destined to be one of his best, already in progress.

25　'Titta's gone away': *Amarcord*

'My cinema has always been the provinces; therefore childhood, and a whole lifetime that one dreams one is seeing again'
Fellini in a letter to Gian Luigi Rondi

Fellini's approach to *Roma* had been almost straightforward. By contrast, the production of his new film was, even for him, roundabout and secretive. Initially it was leaked as a science fiction story set in the year 2000, its hero a Swedish pollution expert named Hammarcord who no longer trusts his identity and those of the people around him. The doctor would reclaim this heritage by returning to the past.

People who knew Fellini were sceptical. His enthusiasm for science fiction went not very far beyond *Flash Gordon* and the folksy fantasies of Ray Bradbury. He seemed equally unacquainted with Sweden. 'Hammarcord' was supposed to be 'evocative of something between science fiction and Swedish geography', but sceptics wondered if he wasn't simply trading on a resemblance between the word and the name of the Swedish Secretary-General of the United Nations, Dag Hammarskjöld.

A more credible rumour gained currency in the spring. This held that the film was another chapter of autobiography in which Fellini would re-encounter his Riminese past. Didn't 'I remember' – '*Io mi ricordi*' – become in Romagnolo '*a m'arcord*'? Anyone who read the Fellini issue of French *Vogue*, where excerpts from the script were printed under the heading 'From the New Film', would have known this, but he continued to deny it. 'If I were supposed to make a film about the first things I can remember,' he said, 'then it would be a film about my beginnings at Cinecittà.' When critic Pietro Bianchi, an old friend, quoted him as saying the film would be called *Romagna*, he denied it.

Other titles tossed around were *Oscia della madonna*, a mild curse, *Viva Italia* and *Il borgo* – Romagnolo dialect for 'town'. He settled at last on a title less euphonic than any of them, *L'uomo invaso: The Invaded Man* or *Man Profaned*. This survived only until 'our American friends', as Fellini habitually referred to his US distributors (in this case Warner's, who'd advanced Cristaldi $2 million of the $3.5 million budget in return for world rights outside Italy), had a chance to think about it. They decided it sounded like a documentary and asked for another.

Resignedly he began calling the film *Amarcord*, but the smokescreen remained. Now he said 'Amarcord' was a nonsense word, chosen, like 'Mastorna', at random. He'd scribbled it on a napkin one day at lunch and his non-Italian companion had remarked that it sounded like the name of an aperitif – 'Drink Amarcord and Your Liver will be Strong.' If it would sell a drink, Fellini told journalists, it would sell a film. When this story become threadbare he dropped it in favour of a rambling explanation of 'Amarcord' as 'a word intended to be the synthesis, the reference point, the reflection almost of a mood, an attitude, a way of thinking at once ambiguous, controversial, contradictory, the fusion of two extremes, the marriage of two opposites, such as indifference and nostalgia, innocence and guilt, refusal and assent, tenderness and irony, irritation and torment . . . ' Fellini could extemporise like this until the eyes of even the most resilient reporter glazed over. Not for nothing had Pasolini nicknamed him 'The Great Mystifier'.

Why was he so diffident about identifying his subject as his Riminese childhood? In part, it was a strategy. 'Before *Satyricon*,' Gerald Morin explains, 'the press office issued so much information that, by the time people saw the film, they felt they already knew it. On *Amarcord*, Fellini decided to tell them nothing. And it worked.'

There were, however, other and more complex reasons. Most of the people Fellini knew in thirties Rimini were dead or had moved away. Even the town, rebuilt after the wartime bombing, no longer existed as he remembered it. He took this as a licence to remake the place and its people in the image of his own imagination. But the fact that his own mother, sister and certain originals of a few characters did still live there disinclined him to be seen as an autobiographer. Almost as much as their resentment, he feared their co-operation. Nothing stifles imagination more than a good memory, particularly someone else's. Once it got around that a film about his childhood was in prospect, he would be besieged by people anxious to help him 'get it right'. As he had avoided experts on ancient Rome while planning *Satyricon*, he shunned Rimini while writing *Amarcord*.

Even so, once the secret was out he was bombarded with advice. Liliana Betti overhead telephone conversations like:

Enquirer: 'And mosquitoes? Will there also be an invasion of mosquitoes in the film? I was talking to my sister last night and we were asking ourselves . . . '

Fellini (patiently): 'But of course! The one that took place in 1940 in the Agro Pontino will be a really terrifying sequence.'

To help put these memories on to film, Fellini went to a writer he'd never worked with before. 'Tonino' Guerra was born in the same year as he and in the village of Sant'arcangelo, almost within sight of Rimini, but any parallels ended there. During the war Guerra was deported to Germany, where he spent more than a year in a prison camp. He returned a poet, and it was as a poet, and in particular a poet in Romagnolo dialect, that he made his reputation before becoming a scriptwriter for, in particular, Antonioni. But Fellini knew from his fiction that, like Bernardino Zapponi, Guerra could write in a fantastic, dream-like and erotic style. He also had an intimate knowledge of Rimini's customs and dialects. The two went to extraordinary lengths to capture a Romagnolo tone in *Amarcord*. The script was written in dialect, then translated into standard Italian, retaining as much as possible the original accent and syntax.

Donati visited Rimini with Fellini and returned with photographs of every street and building of personal significance. He refined these into almost two kilometres of interlocking sets at Cinecittà. The town in the film is always 'Borgo', if it's referred to at all, but Donati's sources were obvious to every Riminese. Only one building defied his skill. The exterior of the Grand was too monumental to rebuild, even on Stage 5, but rather than use the real thing Fellini shot these scenes at a hotel in Anzio.

For his central figures, he chose not his own family but, as he had for some scenes in *Roma*, that of Titta Benzi. The Fellinis made dull subjects. Titta, in addition to a flamboyant anarchist father and a tough, unyielding mother, could also boast a lively collection of relatives: a younger brother, the amiable but forgetful grandfather whom he'd exhibited to Fellini, and layabout Uncle Lallo, a Fascist functionary who by day lounged round the house in robe and hair net, cosseted by his adoring older sister, and by night haunted the Grand in a white dinner jacket, pleasuring eager grass widows. In acknowledgement of his success, Lallo has the admiring nickname 'La Pataca' – The Cunt.

In *Amarcord*, Ferruccio Benzi's Anarchism singles him out for special attention by the Fascists. For his own good, his wife locks him in the house whenever there's a parade, but when the visit of the provincial director is interrupted by a blackout, during which a gramophone roars the *Internationale* from the bell-tower, he's arrested and tortured by being forced to swallow quantities of castor oil, then sent home slathered with his own excreta. It's a realistic sequence that sits oddly in the essentially fantastic film, a spectre at what is otherwise a feast of eccentricity and farce.

Fellini is more successful with the depiction of Titta's mother's death, which he wraps in mysticism. Based on memories of his grandmother's funeral, and presaged by a snowstorm during which a peacock, the symbol of death, escapes from the palace of the local prince to perch squawking on the fountain, the ceremony, with its silent gathering of black-dressed relatives and its solemn procession, captures, like the *fogharezza* sequence, the rituals that stubbornly survived Mussolini's modernisations.*

Fellini and Guerra are happier with the eccentrics they raked from their collective memory of Rimini. Some, like Zeus, the headmaster, and old Giudizio, had appeared in *I vitelloni*, *I clowns*, *Roma*, or all three. Newcomers include Zeus' tatterdemalion staff, the provoking hairdresser Ninola, known as 'Gradisca', the suave manager of the Fulgor and the Fascist 'Definite' (whose father announced, after his eleventh child, that this one was the last, and that was definite).

They also resurrected the town nymphomaniac, Volpina ('Vixen'), pretty but crazed, wandering the streets, treated by everyone with wary affection. 'How many have you had today?' someone yells. 'I bet you use one to stir your coffee.' Then there's Biscein, the town's ugliest man, a candy and cake vendor who casts himself as the hero of an unlikely tale involving a diminutive pasha and thirty frustrated concubines who smuggle him in to gratify their lust.

The setting for Biscein's harem fantasy, like those of Fellini and his schoolmates, is the Grand. In an atmospheric scene, Titta and his friends, who during the summer have crept through the shrubbery to spy on the guests, revisit the empty hotel in the fog to prowl its piazza, posing and preening in a fantasy of adult sophistication.

---

*Unable to find a trained peacock, Fellini used a mechanical bird. The white bull Titta's young brother encounters in the fog is also a painted cutout.

Because it reflects the imagination of a horny adolescent, *Amarcord* is preoccupied with sex, though as usual Fellini shies away from the act. It's played for comedy, as in a scene of group masturbation, with four boys jerking off in a stationary car while calling out the names of fantasy females. Titta also succumbs to the attractions of the tobacconist's massively breasted wife. A game of guessing her weight turns quickly into a sexual encounter. Re-creating Fellini's own early experience of being almost suffocated by heavy breasts, Titta is briefly allowed to browse on her enormous bosom, but since he's so ignorant that he blows rather than sucks, she thrusts him out unceremoniously into the night.

Borgo, like Fellini, revels in sexual gossip and innuendo. Though sex is freely available from Volpina and the town whorehouse, onanism, fantasy and suggestive banter are the norm. When mad Uncle Teo, taken on a picnic, climbs a tree and refuses to descend until he's provided with a woman, Titta's sensible suggestion that he fetch Volpina is shouted down. Teo's doleful and increasingly hoarse cries of 'I want a woman' echo over the fields until a midget nun arrives with his keepers to coax him back to earth and abstinence.

The unquestioned sexual ideal of everyone in the Italy of *Amarcord* is Mussolini. Il Duce's appeal to Italy was overtly erotic. He treated the crowd as a lover, wooing, bullying, consoling. His sexual strut during his speeches, the phallic thrust of his shaved head, imitated by Definite, his famous extra-marital liaisons, exaggerated in propaganda like everything else about him, contributed to an image of prodigious potency.*

The fantasy of a monstrously well-endowed Mussolini wasn't lost on young Federico. At the start of *Roma* Giudizio mocks the mutilated statue of Julius Caesar in the piazza Giulio Romano. 'Caesar crossed the Rubicon and lost his balls,' he jeers. A woman yells back from a window: 'Yes, and Mussolini's got them now.' In *Amarcord*, Lallo, trotting alongside the visiting party chief, assures the camera with an expansive gesture: 'I tell you just one thing – Mussolini has balls *this* large.' When Il Duce was shot by partisans in 1945, they hung his body by the heels in Milan's piazza le Loreto with that of his mistress,

---

*In the flesh, Mussolini was uninviting. He suffered chronically from venereal disease, seldom washed or shaved, preferring to douse himself in eau de Cologne, and generally coupled on the floor of his office, always at great speed and without removing either trousers or shoes.

Clara Petacci. 'To display him like that,' it was commented, 'the Italians must have loved him.'

Fascism dominated Fellini's public pronouncements about *Amarcord*. The Fascists, he said, conspired with the Church to keep his generation in a sort of moral and emotional slavery. 'Fascism is always waiting within us,' he warned, taking a high moral tone at odds with his usual indifference to politics. 'There is always the danger of an upbringing, a Catholic upbringing, that knows only one goal: to place a person in a situation of intellectual dependence, to limit his integrity, to take from him any sense of responsibility in order to keep him in a never-ending state of immaturity.'

These homilies need to be seen in the context of hindsight and the demands of publicity. If Fascism and its theatricality motivate the film's most striking scenes, it's more likely because they, as much as Gary Cooper at the Fulgor, were part of Fellini's most vivid childhood experiences. Except for Ferruccio Benzi's torture, *Amarcord*'s view of Fascism ranges from comic to affectionate. Titta imagines a lavish wedding where the class fatso, Ciccio, marries Aldina, its most prim and correct girl, before a giant face of Mussolini made from flowers, the lips of which move to articulate the blessing. The provincial director's visit provokes a display of patriotism which Fellini milks, a little too obviously, for laughs. The party arrive through an ornate railway entrance (actually the front gate of Cinecittà), only to be engulfed in smoke, and set off at a brisk trot through the streets, with breathless locals trying to keep up. Besotted like everyone else with the fantasy of power, Gradisca yells after the visiting supremo: 'I must touch him!'

Donati's skill was tested to the limit by one of *Amarcord*'s set pieces, the passing of the *Rex* on its maiden voyage. A flotilla of small boats puts out to await the liner. The Riminese bob for hours, yarning, eating, becoming increasingly bored until they drift into sleep. Only a child sees the ship approaching. He wakes them in time to watch it slide by, a cliff-like shape festooned with lights, as remote from their experience as the enthroned Pope in *Roma*. Donati created the effect of a rolling night-time sea with sheets of black polythene, while the boat is a flat model, ingeniously lit and shot. Fellini can't hide, nor does he try to, his delight in the theatricality of such occasions, a pleasure which, he no doubt realised, could only be made publicly acceptable by justifying them as political satire. But really *Amarcord* is less an attack on Fascism than an apologia.

Fifteen-year-old Titta is played by a blond and husky amateur named Bruno Zanin. Born near Venice, he'd been living as a fisherman on the Lipari Islands off Sicily for two years when Fellini spotted him at Cinecittà, which he was touring with a friend. For his mother, Fellini cast Neapolitan theatre actress Pupella Maggio from the company of playwright Eduardo de Filippo. As Ferruccio Benzi, he debated using footballer Nereo Rocco and then the real Titta Benzi, who'd remained in Rimini to practise law, but decided at last on another Neapolitan, Armando Brancia. 'Il Pataca' is Nandino Orfei, of the clown family. Mad Uncle Teo is Ciccio Ingrassia, one half of the famous movie comedy team of Franco and Ciccio. The rest of the cast Fellini found by auditioning amateur groups all over northern Italy.

In so far as *Amarcord* has a heroine it's Gradisca, around whom Fellini erected an elaborate structure of fantasy. If Mussolini did win the nation like a lover, then Gradisca – 'the archetype of femininity', Fellini called her – symbolises the acquiescing female Italy he conquered. Throughout the film Gradisca coasts on the momentum of the moment of glory that gave her her name. When a prince staying at the Grand languidly expressed a wish for some well-mannered female company, Ninola was persuaded by the town council to offer herself in the hope the prince would approve some much-needed civic improvements. After a coy strip-tease in which she removes only her dress, retaining her black lingerie and trademark red beret (Fellini shot a version with Noël bare-breasted, but deleted it), she snuggles into the prince's bed, murmuring with faultless deference and decorum: *'Principe, gradisca'* – roughly, 'May it please your highness' or 'Prince, please yourself.'*

Titta stalks Gradisca like a fabulous beast he could possess if only he had the courage. In a culminating fantasy he follows her into the empty Fulgor on a summer afternoon, switching seats until he's sitting beside her. As he reaches under her skirt she looks at him, without rancour and not entirely inhospitably, and asks: 'What are you looking for?' It's a question he finds impossible to answer and, even in fantasy, he retreats. Years later Fellini would confess to being 'traumatised by the memory' of this event that never happened, at least not to him.

To play Gradisca, Fellini tried to lure back Sandra Milo, who'd entered yet another retirement. After shooting tests, he believed he'd won her over, but as they parted he felt 'an air of melancholy'. 'I have something of a feeling we won't see each other any more,' he said. She

---

*There's no exact English equivalent. Some versions of the film translate *'gradisca'* as 'welcome', others as 'please do'. The American dubbed version renames her 'S'il Vous Plaît'.

replied: 'No, no', but later she told Fellini that her husband wanted her out of the movies. (Her last film was made in 1970.) Fellini hurriedly called on Magali Noël.

Noël was told nothing of the real Gradisca, the search for whom became a journalistic obsession after *Amarcord*'s release. Fellini had given his version of Ninola's subsequent history. Some years after 'his' rejection in the cinema, he said, 'I was passing near Commachio [a town between Rimini and Venice, on the Po delta] and searched out Gradisca. She had married around there, I'd heard, with a cousin who was a sailor. I wanted to see her. I drove in my Jaguar through the muddy delta. At the gates of a miserable town a little old lady worked in her vegetable garden.

'Excuse me, Madame,' I said to her. 'Where does Gradisca live?'

'Who's looking for her?' said the little old lady.

'An old acquaintance. Can you tell me where she lives?'

'It's me,' said the little old lady. It was her, Gradisca. She hadn't kept a trace of that triumphant brightness. She was sixty years old.'

Journalist Dario Zanelli also looked up Gradisca, and punctured yet another Fellini fable. In reality she still lived in Rimini, working as a dressmaker. Far from being decrepit, she was only five years older than Fellini, every one of whose inventions she rejected. 'Gradisca' was her given name, not a nickname. The day she was born, in 1915, her father was fighting at Gradiška in Bosnia. If she had any connection with Fellini, she'd forgotten it. 'Of all the boys who wanted to make time with me, how would I be able to remember which one was Fellini?' she told Zanelli. 'Of course, he would know *me*. In Rimini I was an institution. Moreover, his uncle had a store just a few steps from my father's store, so who knows how many times he would have seen me pass by? But I do remember something specific. I remember a skinny boy who stopped me once, and asked me if he could take a picture of me. I let him. He asked when he could see me to give me a copy of the picture. I said: "Let's not make plans." But later, this young fellow, in the ballroom of the Grand Hotel, asked me to dance, and he gave me the picture. I think that was Federico, but I wouldn't put my hand in the fire to prove it.' As for her carnal encounter with the prince, she denied it ever happened.

Magali Noël was pleased to be working again with Fellini, who'd been confident she'd drop everything to take Milo's part. 'If I say to her: "I'm hungry. Fry two eggs," she would do it,' he told a reporter complacently. 'She's a Goldoni actress, combining family and theatre.' Noël meekly put on ten kilos to bring her silhouette in line with

Fellini's opulent conception. The relationship Noël and her husband enjoyed with the Fellinis seemed reflected in the film, where the director gave her a generous amount of space. One scene in particular delighted her. Beginning at the end of a darkened street, it tracked towards a single light, gradually revealed as a street lamp focused on a poster of her idol, Gary Cooper. Next to it, filing her nails and staring adoringly at the image, is Gradisca.

Noël and her husband saw the completed film for the first time at a private showing for Carlo Ponti and Sophia Loren. By then, a number of scenes had been cut. They included a speech in which Pataca, lounging on the piazza at the Grand, explains that he always puts a dab of Vaseline behind his ear in case a woman shares his enthusiasm for anal sex (a hand run unobtrusively through the hair provides the necessary lubrication) and an episode in which the town's sewer man delves in a cesspit in search of a lost ring. But Noël was dashed to find that her moment with the poster had disappeared as well.

When Fellini asked her if she liked the film, Noël disguised her disappointment. 'But back home,' she says, 'I started to weep and complain. "How could he do it?" I said to my husband. "My best scene!" It was like this all night. And then, at two in the morning, the phone rang. I picked it up. It was Federico. "Well, Magalotte," he said, "have you finished crying yet?" He knew exactly how I felt. "This is not a film about Gradisca," he said. 'It is about *me*."'

Production on *Amarcord* technically began in January 1972, while Fellini was still finishing *Roma*. He shot on and off until June, interrupted by changes of mind but also by strikes. Under the new left-leaning coalition government, unions enjoyed greater power. A contract negotiated between the entertainment unions and the Producers Association just before *Amarcord* guaranteed a five-day rather than a six-day week, and a ten-hour day. Fellini was among its most vociferous opponents, partly because the profits of the film, an 'F. C. Production', would be shared between him and Cristaldi. 'Unionisation is destroying the artisan habits and instincts of the people in the unit,' he complained to *Variety*. 'In all of my films, almost every man in the unit participated, even the most humble worker. I do not feel any more the spontaneous urge of a set dresser, a grip or an electrician to become an integrated part of the set, enjoying and contributing at the same time.' In time, Fellini accepted the new system, even acknowledging that technicians deserved some protection after being ripped off by generations of rapacious producers. He edited on Saturday and spent Sunday resting – an option that, at his age, he found more and more welcome.

Released in Italy on 18 December at 123 minutes, *Amarcord* was instantly popular with both critics and the audience. Even the Riminese tentatively accepted the film, though most sneaked away to Cesena or Forli to see it. 'They came back after dark and slid into their homes on the sly,' recalled local journalist Sergio Zavoli. 'They never admitted they had something to say, good or bad.' When it opened at the Fulgor, Titta Benzi saw it three times in a row, retiring moist-eyed at each break to the foyer to receive the compliments of friends. He paid tribute to Fellini's recall of the feeling, even the dialogue of the Benzi household.

Out of competition, *Amarcord* opened the 1973 Cannes festival, a suitable curtain-raiser to world release. Fellini would never have such a commercial success again. Once the film was confirmed as a hit, he emerged from behind the smoke-screen and acknowledged it as at least a sort of autobiography. If asked about his schooldays, he'd reply: 'I have already told you about my time in grammar school in *Amarcord.*'

As much as *Otto e mezzo*, the film is a milestone in Fellini's career. With it, he closed the door definitively on a childhood for which he could no longer feel nostalgia, and which thereafter would exist only in the simplified, sanitised form dictated by the myth. All his films for the next decade would derive from his adult experience, and be blighted by his inability to come to terms with it. As the children play among the ruins of Gradisca's wedding, one calls for Titta to go with them to the harbour. 'Titta's gone away,' another replies. 'He went some time ago.'

26   'The worst film I ever made': *Il Casanova di Federico Fellini*

'Some people are afraid of God. I fear women'
Fellini

The ebullient mood of *Amarcord* didn't last. In 1973 Fellini turned fifty-three. At such times, one counts the cost of a life and assesses its future. The balance sheet looked bleak. He was in indifferent health, emotionally adrift. In November 1972 he had lost yet another old collaborator, Ennio Flaiano, who died with the rift between them unhealed.

The tax problems that had harried him since 1965 now become overwhelming. During the making of *Amarcord*, a claim for concessions was disallowed (at the instigation, suggests Gerald Morin, of a Revenue official alienated in earlier skirmishes) and with extreme reluctance the Fellinis sold the Fregene house, though they continued to rent in the area each summer. Without this bolt hole at the beach to retreat to, Giulietta and Fellini were forced together more and more. In response, the via Margutta apartment absorbed adjoining rooms as they fell vacant to become in effect two separate apartments, plus Fellini's office. For Fellini, accustomed to going where he pleased and spending as much money as he liked, his new life was stifling. 'Perhaps subconsciously I placed all my fears, the anxiety I can't face, in this film,' he said of his next project. 'Perhaps the film was fed by my fears.'

He continued to be a favoured target of the *paparazzi*. One of them snapped him embracing Capucine in a restaurant. Others noticed his intimacy with young actress Olimpia Carlisi, who has a small role in *Casanova*. Leo Janos, *Time*'s Rome correspondent, called Fellini 'her Svengali', and in December 1976 he would sue for libel a journalist who suggested he'd 'lost his head' over her. The relationship with Carlisi, dismissed by one insider as 'a minor actress, and a bad one', was, like most of Fellini's intimacies with women, more flirtation than affair, but he and Giulietta held a joint press conference to kill speculation about their marriage. 'Obviously,' Fellini told reporters, 'that kind of thing [the Carlisi and Capucine reports] has always been said about actresses with whom I have worked very closely, and it's easy to get pictures of us together.' Giulietta insisted Fellini had merely kissed Capucine when they met socially after a long separation, and that 'Olimpia Carlisi is part of our group.'

The distance between the couple was, however, all too visible. Giulietta's public appearances with Fellini now exhibited the disdain of a minor Royal opening a village fête. Watching her visit him on the set, Antonio Chemasi compared her to 'a candidate's wife, dutifully stumping. Her small face was almost hidden behind huge sunglasses; her reddish hair in a frozen seizure of waves. She took a chair and continued to smile at no one in particular.' Actress Marika Rivera defined the relationship as 'Cold . . . Cold. She kept to herself and talked only of money. The price of things.' (During their money troubles, Giulietta took over the finances, restraining Fellini's free spending and doling out weekly pocket-money.) Only close friends knew how the marriage worked. Fellini's flirtations could take place with Giulietta's chilling but also reassuring presence in the background. 'If Fellini were really in love,' says Bernardino Zapponi, 'I would think he would say: "How can I leave Giulietta?" My feeling is that Masina, along with the life they share, is a protection for him.'

Amid this emotional and professional turbulence, Fellini, in the summer of 1973, committed himself almost casually to the most complex project of his career – Casanova. Liliana Betti, remembering the impact of the announcement, was struck by the general reaction of agreeable surprise. '"Fellini Makes Casanova!" The information, once announced, had the reassuring and charismatic solidity of events destined to take place.'

A major Casanova movie was overdue. Though a stampede had been anticipated following the publication for the first time in 1960 of the full twelve volumes, unedited and uncensored, of his L'Histoire de ma vie jusqu'à l'an 1797, few producers had responded. Someone who did find Casanova an attractive subject was Dino de Laurentiis, who arrived back in Rome from Hollywood during the post-production of Amarcord to cash in on the contract signed two years before. There'd been a few nibbles at a Fellini film, but everyone demanded to know the subject. Pinelli's script of Casanova's Memoirs with Orson Welles had been one of the projects discussed before La dolce vita in 1957. Now Dino suggested it again, subtly offering as bait the promise that, should Fellini make Casanova, he might also revive Il viaggio.

Fellini had, like most boys, read those collections of salacious episodes that passed as his memoirs before 1960, but, while he had often talked about a Casanova film, it was, he admitted, 'one of those things I had been cunningly selling to my producers for years . . . one of three or four titles that I regularly used as bait'. This time, however, he succumbed. A name soon filled the blank on the contract – *Casanova's Dream*.

De Laurentiis may have suspected Fellini wasn't entirely committed but this didn't diminish his enthusiasm. The very name 'Casanova' was enough to interest an American distributor, and fortunately both that name and the incidents of Casanova's life were out of copyright. A costume comedy/romance, in English, with a Hollywood star and a heavy-breasted supporting cast might well repeat the success of *Tom Jones* ten years before. But Dino kept such hopes to himself, and Fellini was too busy with *Amarcord* to give the contract more than a passing thought. 'It could be said,' wrote Tullio Kezich disapprovingly, 'that this ambiguous and quite unique film . . . was born really from a signature placed without caution on a contract proposed without caution'.

The partnership of Fellini, de Laurentiis and Casanova made instant news in Italy. It was, wrote Liliana Betti: 'a quasi-mythical trinity, heavy with marvels [which] displayed the spectacular solemnity of a sung high mass'. As for Casanova himself, he was 'a prestigious and scandalous subject, and for that reason the object of speculation and of perplexed and fascinated forecasts'. Even she wondered what Fellini would make of him.

Jacques Jérôme (as he preferred to be called), or Giacomo Girolamo (as he was christened), Casanova was born in Venice in 1725. His mother, Zanetta, was an actress and thus, by definition in eighteenth-century Europe, a whore. She swept out of Casanova's life in infancy, bed-hopping to a career as the grandest of *grandes horizontales*, including a liaison in London with the Prince of Wales, later George II, who probably fathered Jacques's younger brother, the painter Francesco Casanova. The Paduan family with which she boarded the young Jacques brutalised and starved him, instilling an aversion to domesticity, but his life brightened when he moved to the house of a priest named Gozzi, who introduced him to art and literature and taught him the violin. Gozzi's younger sister, Bettina, also initiated him sexually when he was eleven. Casanova repaid their investment with an enthusiasm for the arts and for sex that lasted until his death in 1798 at Dux, in the chilly Bohemian castle of Charles Emmanuel, Count Waldstein, whose librarian he had become.

Casanova explored almost every experience the Enlightenment offered. He socialised and argued with Voltaire, Rousseau, Benjamin Franklin, Catherine the Great, George III, Frederick the Great and two popes, wrote plays and novels, even contributed to the libretto of Mozart's *Don Giovanni*. At the same time he was a well-paid international go-between and spy, a prodigious and successful gambler, the proprietor of a lucrative lottery scheme and an audacious swindler, especially of rich aristocrats with a taste for the occult. He also enjoyed inordinate amounts of sex with a wide range of companions: old women and girls, maids and countesses, giants and hunchbacks. He never specified the total number of women (and, occasionally, men) he bedded, but the memoirs mention 300.

Between 1789 and 1792, drawing on a retentive memory, he turned his life into a twelve-volume autobiography, remarkably accurate about dates and names as well as baldly descriptive of physical peculiarities and, inevitably, sexual acts. Casanova never saw it in print, but over the next century the memoirs were mistranslated, synopsised, pirated, plundered and bowdlerised by hundreds of publishers. Most discarded the political, social and cultural material, preferring to sieve out the sex, often embroidering where Casanova had been insufficiently explicit. In 1960 the copyright owners, Brockhaus, acquiesced to scholarly lobbying and published the first full and faithful translation. The breadth of Casanova's culture and his worth as a reporter became clear, but too late to save his reputation. His name had come to typify not the eighteenth century's archetypal sophisticate, cultured and cunning, but its great seducer, a dandy with an erect penis in his left hand and his pen in his right. In other words, as Fellini described him in notes scribbled on sketches for Casanova's mask-like make-up, a *stronzo*: a turd.

Early 1974 was a bad time for Fellini to begin a new film. Distractions were rife. Visitors in particular took up valuable time. One was Francis Ford Coppola, whose films were filled with homages to the *maestro*. When depressed, he'd screen *Otto e mezzo*. 'It was like an autobiography of Francis,' says his wife, Eleanor. In the spring, Coppola, who had transformed the old fish markets at Trieste into New York's Ellis Island, the immigration depot where young Vito Corleone in *The Godfather II* has his first glimpse of America, made a special trip to Rome to meet his idol, but the visit smacked to Fellini of condescension. 'You are so rich,' he told Coppola accusingly. Coppola, who'd suffered a bad press over his last film, *The Conversation*, retorted that money didn't solve all one's problems. Fellini stared at him incredulously. 'He *is* rich,' he said defiantly when Mike Sarne queried the quote in 1977. 'He has a whole building, so he does not have to pay the tax.' This was a particularly sore point. By centralising his American Zoëtrope company in one San Francisco building, he was able to write off most of his working expenses. 'And Spielberg is a tycoon, like Rockefeller.'

Fellini would have been happy to forget *Casanova*, but de Laurentiis was pressing for something on paper to tempt New York bankers and a Hollywood star, so the director got to work. To collaborate, he turned first to Tonino Guerra. They signed a contract, but personal problems forced Guerra to drop out, so Fellini returned to Zapponi – a better choice, since, as an enthusiast for erotica, he knew Casanova's work intimately. It was Zapponi who first showed Fellini the complete edition of the memoirs. The director was aghast. Six fat volumes, more than 2,000 annotated pages; the sheer flood of detail choked his imagination. Repeatedly during the weeks of writing he let his irritation boil over, even ripping pages out of the books in fury.

When Visconti began shooting *Gruppa di famiglia in un interno* on 8 April, Fellini bit on his resentment and courteously sent roses with a note felicitating him on starting work on 'a fine April day' – another day he would spend wrestling with the ghost of Casanova. By June, de Laurentiis had his script, though it promised anything but the modest romp he'd hoped for. Casanova's scheming, his chats with the great, the feats as a gambler, businessman and spy had disappeared. What remained was a sprawling synopsis of his sex life, suffused with a sense of Fellini's own frustration at the prolixity of the memoirs and with something even more disturbing: moral exhaustion and an existential despair.

During the writing, Fellini had come to see *Casanova* as a vehicle for his thoughts on age, on sex, on death. Thereafter, everything he wrote and said about him led away from the conventional vision, until Casanova's Casanova was replaced by the Casanova of Fellini. That Casanova is old and tired, dreamily reviewing his life in the castle at Dux. He fails to see that his pomposity earned him only the scorn of the great, while the pursuit of sensation stifled his ability to love. 'I never had the intention to recount complaisantly, amused and fascinated, the amorous adventures of Casanova,' Fellini says. 'A prisoner as in a nightmare, as immobilised as a puppet, he reflects continually on a series of seductive and disturbing faces which succeed only in incarnating each time a different aspect of himself.'

De Laurentiis's reaction to the script was unexpected. He'd wept when he read it, he said, with emotion and enthusiasm. Fellini and Betti were startled. Betti wrote: 'The unsuspected emotional vulnerability of the Neapolitan producer at reading a scenario about a refrigerated character in an overstuffed and repetitive pantomime surprised and amused Fellini. A week later we would understand that the aesthetic ecstasy of de Laurentiis was nothing but the rapture of financial erotism.'

Dino had been busy. A film by Fellini whose main character, however unsympathetic, appeared in every scene intrigued those stars who fancied themselves serious actors. Though he'd discussed it with both Marlon Brando and Al Pacino, Dino's final selection (and that of the financiers), he told Fellini when they met in Rome in the spring of 1974, was Robert Redford. As short as Casanova was tall, as blond as he was dark, as offhand in style as he was flamboyant, as archetypally American as he was Latin, Redford was so inappropriate a choice that Fellini couldn't believe Dino. For his part, the producer was incredulous that Fellini would spurn the star who'd made a hit with *The Sting* and was then filming *The Great Gatsby* in London. 'Not take Redford?' he blustered. 'But that's impossible!' He tried to cajole Fellini. 'Think of it, Fefé! He'll obey you like a puppy. "Here, Redford", and he'll come. "Down, Redford" – and he'll do it!'

When Fellini continued to resist, the suggestions became more bizarre. 'What does it matter to you? You take Redford and you put him in a mask, whoever you want – the face of Casanova.' As for love interest, why not write in an aerial bridge that disgorges cargoes of Hollywood stars at Cinecittà? Casanova's women! Fellini scorned this Ziegfeld Follies device as brusquely as he had Redford, and the men parted frostily. In time, de Laurentiis suggested two less bankable stars, Michael Caine and Jack Nicholson, but Fellini fancied neither. Though Zapponi disagreed with the choice, he'd written the script with only one actor in mind – Mastroianni. Mastroianni understood Fellini's methods and tolerated his excesses. Moreover, in real life he *was* Casanova, a notorious seducer with exactly the indolent sensuality and self-awareness the character demanded.

Back in Hollywood de Laurentiis reassessed the project in the light of losing Redford. Even excluding Redford's fee of $1 million, the film would cost $3 million, a sum unrecoverable without a major star. On 14 July *Variety* carried his face-saving announcement that a crowded schedule prevented him from giving *Casanova* the attention it deserved and he was therefore pulling out.

As for Fellini, he'd felt he could take a high hand because he was confident of finding money elsewhere. Angelo Rizzoli's empire belonged now to his son. At sixty, a survivor of two heart attacks, Andrea lived on the Côte d'Azur so as to be near the big casinos, where he regularly lost millions. In July he'd mortgaged everything to buy Milan's *Corriere della sera* and realise his father's dream of owning a major daily. Ironically, the gesture would ruin Rizzoli Editore, fulfilling Angelo's forecast when he toasted his family at the Christmas before his death: 'I built up this business like a jewel and in five years you will bring it to ruin.' Fellini knew the risk of doing business with Rizzoli, but on 15 August, in his Cap Ferrat villa, with occasional time out for a dip in his pool, Andrea agreed to back *Casanova*. Shooting was optimistically planned to begin on 30 October, with release exactly a year later.

Rotunno and Rota were signed to light and score the film and Donati began work on sets and costumes. From the start, Fellini took an obsessive interest in the look of the production. (For the first time he would get screen credit for original designs.) The scope was enormous, demanding the roofs and lagoons of Venice, a theatre in Dresden, *palazzi* in Rome, a Moorish harem, the streets of London and a fog-shrouded Thames, plus various inns, villas, prisons and whorehouses. To nobody's surprise, Fellini announced he'd shoot at Cinecittà, though his team were alarmed. The studios were more down at heel than ever. Roofs leaked, floors were uneven and cats still infested the grounds. Studio 5 might be the largest in continental Europe but it didn't have one interior toilet. Fellini, however, was adamant.

Clemente Fracassi, who'd joined Cineriz when Federiz collapsed and was now a vice-president, was assigned to keep the budget below $4 million. He persuaded Cinecittà to trim some of its costs and Donati to cut his seventy-two sets to fifty-four. He further reduced overheads by moving the costume department into Rome. Cinecittà's wardrobe area was anyway too small to accommodate *Casanova's* 3,000 costumes, each one hand-tailored, and 400 wigs. Fellini also stipulated only authentic eighteenth-century methods and materials, including silk stockings and underwear for everyone and fabrics hand-dyed with vegetable colours. Nobody talked any longer about a start in October 1974. February 1975 seemed more likely.

*

Even in the midst of preparations and with de Laurentiis out of the picture, Fellini had time to think about the promise to revive *Il viaggio*. In midsummer he called Guerra again and, under the pretext of commissioning a short poem for the Casanova project in Romagnolo dialect praising the '*mouna*' or vagina, asked if he was now free to revise the script written with Buzzati. For most of August, Fellini commuted each evening from Cinecittà to his office on via Sistina, where he and Guerra worked on a new, simpler version of *Il viaggio*.

After a few weeks Guerra, suffering from toothache, visited a dental surgeon. The subsequent meeting with Fellini is vivid in Guerra's memory. 'It was a summer afternoon around six-thirty. The shutters were almost closed in the room . . . Federico was stretched out on a divan of brown cloth in a white silk shirt. In front of him was a low glass table with roses whose petals were falling.' The heavy-smoking Guerra explained that he'd been diagnosed as having cancer of the gums. The disease could be contained, but clearly he wouldn't be able to work for some time.

To Fellini it was further confirmation that the hex on *Il viaggio* remained. 'I can still see Federico lift one hand to cool it in the window slightly open above him,' said Guerra. 'Then he touched his hair lightly with his fingers and whistled a tune, to hide the fact that he was deep in thought. He looked at the script and said: "You know . . . perhaps it would be better to postpone this story." He got up from the divan, scooped up in his hands all the fallen rose petals. "We'll put it on the shelf," he said. He placed the petals among the pages of the script, then put it in a little trunk . . . and he started to make *Casanova*.'

As the budget began its inexorable climb, Fellini grappled with casting. An office was opened near Termini and the usual notice inserted in the Rome papers. In August, with Paola Rolli and Guidarino Guidi, he went to London, setting up offices at the William Morris agency and in a second-floor suite at Claridge's Hotel. It was a leisurely visit. Fellini dined at the private White Elephant Club in Mayfair, a popular film hangout, caught the show of female impersonator Danny LaRue ('I like drag shows,' he explained) and the nude revue *Let My People Come*. He expressed interest in the waspish Ian Richardson and an unknown cabaret singer named Tom Deal, and on one occasion approached TV director John Scoffield in a restaurant, announcing dramatically: 'You are my Casanova!' Mastroianni, however, remained his ideal star.

Character performers were another matter. Fellini spoke to dozens, chosen mainly from portraits in casting directories, giving each, distinguished or not, just ten minutes. He liked the sang-froid of English actors, their habit of opening the interview with 'Nice weather today' and not asking lots of questions. 'They knew they were there to be seen. They didn't want a great discourse on the film or the character. At the ninth minute they got up with a bound, nodded and were gone.' One he chose almost immediately was Harold Innocent. He chatted with him for a few minutes, then said he definitely wanted him for the film. 'In what role?' asked the plump, balding stage actor diffidently. 'Well, you could play a pope who masturbates,' Fellini replied. 'Would you mind that?'

Dudley Sutton, who'd had small roles in films like *The Devils*, read in the press that Fellini was looking for eighteenth-century types. 'I didn't have any proper portraits so I sent a crumpled old black and white snapshot of me with my baby daughter.' Summoned for an interview, Sutton exerted himself to make an impression by wearing his most flamboyant outfit, a lime-green suit. Fellini commented on neither the clothes nor the photo, leaving Sutton unsure whether he'd intrigued the *maestro* or put him off. Months later, arriving in Rome to play the Duke of Württemberg, he found his snapshot pinned on Fellini's office wall.

Flamboyant and massively breasted, Marika Rivera, fiftyish illegitimate daughter of Mexican painter Diego Rivera, was then broke after a divorce and working part-time in cabaret. Flustered at being summoned to Claridge's, she gushed to Fellini: 'I love all your films' and was thrown when he asked her to name her favourite. '*Miracle in Milan*', she blurted. Fellini laughed and said disarmingly: 'I am a greater admirer of Vittorio de Sica too. For you to think I made one of his films – this is a compliment.'

Back at Cinecittà, Fellini moved into his usual first-floor suite, working for the moment at one small table in its large main room. In case a visitor should imagine the plump greying man behind it was not *il maestro* – in London, some actors had mistaken the fat, fluttering Guidi for Fellini – Liliana Betti placed a large arrow dramatically directing visitors to the man in charge.

From the desk Fellini filled in his 'landscape of faces', more important in this film than ever before. He gratified his taste for menacing horror-film actors by casting cadaverous Reggie Nalder and Paris-based Daniel Emilfork. Between interviews he sketched and doodled, refining the look of the film and of its protagonist. Most portraits show

Casanova in profile, posed to emphasise his arched nose, commanding chin and high forehead (made even higher by shaving the hairline). Fellini decided to film him that way. Casanova was already turning into Fellini's vision: 'a public figure striking attitudes . . . a braggart Fascist'.

At the end of August 1974 he flew to New York with Giulietta, Guerra and Franco Cristaldi for the US opening of *Amarcord*. They swept in to excellent reviews, but Fellini was offhand with the press. 'I am the author of the picture, not a salesman,' he said. 'But I am asked to help, so I try to help.' The trip also provided a new performer for *Casanova*, the stripper 'Chesty' Morgan, whose 200 centimetre breasts wallowed to her navel.

With shooting now rescheduled for February 1975, Fellini had more time to find a star. Plenty of Italians were interested. Even Sordi volunteered. Fellini didn't take him seriously but he did wonder if Gian Maria Volonte, cerebral star of politically engaged films for Francesco Rosi, might do if Mastroianni were unavailable. But Volonte, who had been known to work on films with a political theme for next to nothing, demanded $400,000 for *Casanova*. The snub was not lost on Fellini. Moreover, for that sort of money, one could have an international name. Donald Sutherland, for instance.

The Canadian actor was increasingly mentioned by the press as a candidate. Nobody knows who first had this idea. It may have been the actor himself. 'Sutherland's candidature seems to be born of rumour,' Liliana Betti wrote, 'and is built up from simple repetition of the rumour.' Sutherland saw Fellini when he visited Bernardo Bertolucci on the Parma set of *1900*, reminding him they'd met already on *Alex in Wonderland*. As rumours spread of his possible involvement in *Casanova*, the actor sent Fellini twenty roses, together with a letter Betti called scornfully 'a declaration of love'. Fellini remained unconvinced that he needed an English-speaking star, but Sutherland, anxious to make the film and demanding only a modest $180,000, began to look increasingly attractive.

Relations between Fellini and Cineriz were deteriorating. Fracassi hadn't been able to keep the budget below $4 million, nor was any American distributor prepared to invest serious money without a Hollywood star. The Rizzoli empire was haemorrhaging as Andrea struggled to service his 100 billion lire debt. Feeling himself and the film under threat, Fellini paid a visit to Gustavo Rol. Rol held a seance and made contact with Casanova, who, after snobbishly chiding Fellini for his impoliteness in addressing him in the familiar voice, called him 'Signor Goldoni' (after Carlo Goldoni, Casanova's play-wright contemporary). Rol then covered forty sheets of paper with crabbed writing which he claimed was Casanova's. Later, in his pocket, Fellini found what looked like the Great Fornicator's visiting card, on which he'd written some personal sexual advice for the Great Mystifier: 'Never standing up and never after a meal'. He returned from Turin depressed. This was not the sort of counsel he needed.

Meanwhile, the actors chosen in London had signed their contracts and were being flown to Rome for costume fittings. Not all of them got there. Marika Rivera, whom he had cast as a sluttish actress named Astrodi, was checking in at Heathrow when a message over the public address system told her not to come. With the budget at more than $5 million and still climbing, Cineriz's commercial director Fulvio Frizzi had decided just before Christmas to pull out. Fellini sued for breach of contract, protesting that he'd spent four months cutting the script to satisfy Rizzoli, but that the producer had refused to meet and discuss the project. Most people expected him to abandon the film, but through Christmas and the New Year he continued to court possible backers, among them the conglomerate Montedison and Gianni Agnelli, Fiat's playboy boss. He even lunched with executives of Giulietta's pet charity UNICEF, whose directors had claimed to be interested in investing. Over truffled risotto and beef in burgundy the UN bureaucrats talked millions, salting the conversation with statistics about world-wide famine, but no money was forthcoming.

These encounters drove Fellini as close to breakdown as he had been since *Il viaggio*. Over the simplest decisions – 'the choice of a restaur-ant or the idea of a walk' – he manifested, said Betti, 'a furious intolerance, unremitting, in which he wouldn't listen nor give his reasons'. The rage continued until 23 January, when Alberto Grimaldi, now enjoying a deal with Universal based on his success with *Last Tango in Paris*, rang from Hollywood with an offer. PEA would fund *Casanova* to $5.5 million, secured by a $3 million distribution guaran-tee from Universal.

Substantial strings dangled from the deal. Universal demanded a *Casanova* in English, ideally filmed in London, with an English-speaking star using his own voice. Fellini convinced Grimaldi that a move to London would cost more than it saved, but in most other respects he acquiesced. Rome-based actor and night-club performer Christopher Cruise, who'd worked on *Block-notes*, was hired as dialogue coach to train the supporting cast in the rudiments of English and, after a long and roundabout conversation, Fellini invited Gore

Vidal to rewrite the script. 'They love you at Universal,' he admitted, more with chagrin than enthusiasm. Vidal, though he knew there would be problems, agreed. Then, most humbling of all, Fellini relinquished Mastroianni and struck a deal with Donald Sutherland. *Variety* featured four pages of advertising for 'Fellini's First Film in English', and Universal predicted an enormous new audience for the director. Reassured, Gaumont agreed to distribute the film in France and Titanus in Italy.

Vidal read the Fellini/Zapponi screenplay and asked if he might rewrite certain sequences, especially Casanova's visit with Voltaire: 'I thought you owed something to the memory of a great man that he say something intelligent.' Zapponi acquiesced and Vidal got to work, always conscious of Fellini's cunning and determination to have his own way. He was right to be so. 'I wrote the script and Fellini showed it to Universal. They okayed it, and the money he needed came through. Then Freddie delicately lets me know that he will not be using my version, that he will not work in direct sound, as had been specified, that he would work in English when he felt like it, and in Italian when the actor was Italian. I don't think he used any of the script I wrote.' Vidal insists he wasn't bitter. 'To my mind Fellini is essentially a painter rather than a narrative artist, and with *Casanova* the painter took over again.' Fellini himself had come to the same view over the years. 'I do not like to find myself under pressure to narrate a story with all its successive developments,' he told Alain Resnais. 'I want to *show*. Film is an offspring not of literature but of painting.'

In February *Amarcord* was nominated for an Oscar as Best Foreign Film. Cristaldi had tried to persuade Fellini to accept some of the film's honours in person, but always received a scribbled excuse: 'Giulietta is ill. Go for both of us' or 'I have a sprained ankle; I swear it's the truth.' In this case Cristaldi demanded something more than a note. Fellini obliged with a telegram: 'Dear Franchino. Giulietta is fine. I don't have a sprained ankle, but I'm not going to Los Angeles anyway. You think up the excuse.' Cristaldi did so and, on the night of 9 April, rang with the news that he'd just accepted the Oscar on Fellini's behalf.

It was disquieting to wander through Cinecittà in the summer of 1975. Stage after stage was taken up with *Casanova*'s claustrophobic sets. Dark, low-ceilinged, painted purple, blue, black and ochre, they were choked with drapery and crowded with vast tables and armoires. In many rooms, open fires blazed. Everywhere, candles guttered, either singly to light a dinner table or crowded in vast chandeliers to illuminate a theatre.

On the studio lake, Donati had created an anthology of Venice. A shrunken Rialto bridge spanned a reduced Grand Canal, with the church of S. Maria Salute and the tower of St Mark's next door to one another and not, as in reality, a kilometre apart. This fantasy Venice would be the setting of the opening carnival, where a head of Venus as big as a tank is dredged from the canal, and of the melancholy conclusion, where the Grand Canal becomes a dance floor of grey ice for Casanova and his automaton lover.

Jostling in the corridors, crowding into the cafeteria for their morning cappuccino or dawdling under the pines during the ritual afternoon *pausa* was a cast strange even by Cinecittà standards. *Casanova* used more than 600 performers, 186 of them with dialogue. Dwarves and amputees socialised with victims of less visible afflictions, like Tina Aumont, daughter of Jean-Pierre Aumont and Maria Montez, a beautiful girl with a dissolute face who spooked everyone with her bizarre behaviour. Angelica Hansen, wearing a fake hunchback for her role as Astrodi's sex toy, shared the cafeteria with Diane Kurys, then an actress but later a successful director. Female giant Sandy Allen, 2.3 metres tall and 210 kilos, risked crushing tiny Italian ballerina Adele Angela Lojodice, whom make-up man Rino Carboni turned into a convincing automaton.

Performers were rotated as much as possible. Even those who lived outside Italy were flown in for their appearance, then sent home until needed again. As they arrived, most asked Fellini for a script, to receive the usual reply. 'I told him I didn't mind,' said Dudley Sutton. 'I'd worked with Ken Russell and done a lot of independent theatre where not much was written down. He said: "Ah, a professional!" After that, he always called me that – The Professional.' Sutherland didn't arrive until July, renting Roman Polanski's old villa for what would turn out to be a shoot of 150 gruelling days, since he appears in every scene. The actor had some inkling of what he was in for. In June he told *Time Out* magazine: 'I have to go to play Casanova for Fellini. There's no way I would play it for anyone else. I'm not playing Casanova. I'm playing Fellini's Casanova, and that's a whole different thing.' He couldn't know then just how different it would be.

A sense that Sutherland had been foisted on him poisoned Fellini's relationship with the actor at the source. The more he grappled with the role, the less Fellini sympathised. 'The poor guy,' he said derisively. 'He believed he was going to become – *him*, Sutherland! – the incarnation of the Latin lover. He had two tons of documentation under his arms. I told him: "Throw out the lot. Forget everything."' The Canadian had been chosen, Fellini told the press, 'because he is completely alien to the conventional idea of Casanova – the dark-eyed Italian, magnetic, raven locks, dark skin, the classic Latin lover. He reflects my thinking about Casanova, of estrangement.' Then why, some wondered, put such effort into his transformation? In a daily three-and-a-half-hour ordeal with special make-up man Gianetto di Rossi, his eyebrows were plucked, his hairline shaved back three inches and his eyes given a slant with clips at the corners. Di Rossi also built up the bridge of his nose and gave him a false chin. On top of all this went a smooth mask of make-up. In the course of the film Sutherland would have his false nose and chin applied 300 times, employ twenty-six variations on the basic make-up, run through forty changes of costume and ten wigs.

'Donald Sutherland was suffering a lot,' recalled Daniel Toscan du Plantier, brought in to oversee Gaumont's investment. 'The greatest role of his life had become a disease for him. I will never forget; Fellini was always calling him "The Canadian". "Where is 'The Canadian' this morning?" He mostly refused to speak to him. He never told him anything.' Every time Fellini approached him, the actor stiffened like an animal that couldn't escape. This evident panic brought out all Fellini's most disagreeable instincts. 'I wanted to laugh,' he said. 'Those fears were really comical. But if I laughed it would make everything even more menacing. When he thought I was making fun of him, his eyes would fill with tears and his nose, chin, eye clips, wig and false eyelashes came undone. Then he looked like Lionel Atwill in *The Mystery of the Wax Museum*, when his face melts during the fire sequence.'

The longer he worked on *Casanova*, the more Fellini realised it would be his most crucial film, not only to his career but also to his understanding of himself. His refrain that Casanova was a loathsome character had become tiresome, both to the press and to his team. Gore Vidal quoted him the old nostrum: you can't make a work of art about someone you despise. Fellini insisted he didn't really hate Casanova, but Vidal sensed a genuine antipathy which he feared would under-mine the film. Privately Fellini acknowledged the hatred, but he rationalised it. Casanova's destruction in the film would serve as a form of psychodrama. In disposing of this monstrous puppet, Fellini would also destroy those negative impulses in himself which Casanova typified. 'After this film, the moody and unreliable part of me, the undecided part of me that was constantly seduced by compromise — the part of me that didn't want to grow up – had to die. For me the film meant crossing the line, gliding into the last part of my life.' Each shot demanded his knife-edge decision. Images were judged not only for their value to the film but for their relevance to this private exorcism. 'I should never have made this film,' he lamented to friends. 'I should have let it go. This will be the worst film I have ever made.' To anyone who stood beside him on the set he would often remark: 'I forbid you to go to see this film if it ever makes it to the screen.'

At this point, when shooting was at its most difficult, Fellini had a curious dream. A year later, he confided it to Georges Simenon, who, since engineering the Palme d'Or for *La dolce vita* at Cannes, had become a friend. Fellini dreamed that he was asleep in a garden but was awakened by the sound of a typewriter coming from a tower. He tiptoed to a circular window and looked into a white-walled room as plain as a cell. A monk with his back to him was busy at something Fellini couldn't see. Children were seated round his feet, playing with his sandals and his cord. The monk turned. It was Simenon, though he wore a small and obviously false white beard. As he turned, a voice whispered: 'It's false.' 'What is he doing?' Fellini asked. The voice said: 'He's painting his new novel, it's about Neptune.' When Fellini woke, his depression had gone and he was ready to work again. Why? Perhaps Simenon's frank absorption in his work, his indifference to critics and acceptance of his aberrant sexual nature somehow reassured him. If the writer could behave as he did, why not Fellini also?

Critics who'd got their hands on a script of *Casanova* accused Fellini of following hundreds of earlier editors in discarding everything but the sex. But, having decided the real Casanova must occupy a back seat to Casanova-as-surrogate-Federico, Fellini felt free to take even more liberties. Material was added, little of it from the memoirs, and each addition placed like an explosive charge to demolish our (and Casanova's) conception of romantic love. At the dinner where Casanova introduces his new mistress Henriette (Tina Aumont) to his jaded friends, the wealthly homosexual Dubois (Daniel Emilfork), sumptuously dressed as a giant insect, performs, to a refrain by two white-faced *castrati*, a mini-opera in which he traps and devours a beautiful young man, a reminder that all lovers are either predators or prey.

Fellini also took particular care over a set-piece sequence in London. Cheated, infected with syphilis and abandoned in the fog by his latest lovers, a rapacious mother and daughter, Casanova decides to drown himself in the Thames. He's only up to his shoulders, however, when he sees a giant woman and her twin dwarf courtiers disappearing in the mist. He follows them to a sinister carnival, more freak show than circus, where a girl contorts herself, a man displays a belly painted with a woman's face and the giant wrestles men in a cage of rope, throwing them like toys through the mesh. To amplify the sense in this sequence of man's helplessness in the hands of woman, Fellini added an erotic lantern slide show designed by French artist Roland Topor. Monsters erupt and horrible faces gape from vaginas furnished with pointed teeth, the ultimate male nightmare. To view the show, men file in silhouette, mute and obedient, into the interior of a whale while the sideshow barker recites Guerra's verse 'The Great Mouna'.*

For the climax of the film, Fellini referred back to an earlier sequence in which Casanova, visiting the infantile Duke of Württemberg, is enchanted by one of his toys, a mechanical woman. Meticulously gowned, *coiffure* perfect, her face a porcelain mask, the tiny girl is the eighteenth-century equivalent of a sex doll. Unable to resist an experiment Casanova carries her to his room and couples with her, an experience that's perversely satisfying. At his death, it's this woman above all others that Casanova recalls. In his imagination they waltz over the frozen Grand Canal, a sexual encounter free for once of guilt and responsibility.

Shooting Casanova's sex scene with the automaton proved disturbing. 'The workers on a Roman film crew are the children of the people who went to the Circus to see lions eat Christians,' Fellini said. 'But when I shot this scene these hard types became silent, terribly concerned, even moved. I believe the scene materialised for them a childish dream of possessing such a woman and, at the same time, awakened a sort of remorse that was typically Italian; remorse at considering a woman as something dead, to be made love to or to be placed on the mantelpiece.' Whether the crew had such thoughts is debatable, but obviously Fellini did.

The disagreeable characterisation forced on Sutherland by Fellini's deconstruction of Casanova became increasingly galling. By making him the archetypal *Playboy* male, the lover who gulps fifty raw eggs a day for potency, knows every sexual position, can plot the borders of each erogenous zone but enjoys nothing except the conquest, Fellini

---

*Fellini had originally intended the figure to be that of a woman. His sketches show a beaming, Ekberg-like giant leaning back, knees raised, legs wide, while tiny men march into her inviting orifice.

left no room to introduce a sympathetic dimension. Even Casanova's performance in bed is mechanical, symbolised by his Portable Adam, a box like a reliquary containing a golden mechanical phallus disguised as a bird. As his erection rises, so does the bird, which chirps, twists its head and flaps its wings, all to one of Nino Rota's mocking circus tunes.

Casanova never removes more than his outer clothes, always making love in comic knickers and a frilled undershirt of the sort worn by small European children. The vest, known as a *brassière*, puzzled many people. When Simenon asked if such things existed in the eighteenth century, Fellini said: 'No. I wore something like it when I made love as a child. And now also.' Before Simenon could clarify if this was a joke or truly represented a Fellini fetish, the director laughed and continued: 'In fact, I wanted to invent a little garment to accentuate the infantile aspect of Casanova.'*

As usual, Fellini acted every role from his place beside the camera. Sutherland, who had a reputation as demanding and abrasive – producer Julia Phillips called him 'a top-ten brain fucker' – resisted, but Fellini won the test of wills with ease. 'I don't have problems with actors,' he said coldly. 'They have problems with me.' Cowed, the actor increasingly worked in a state of mental siege. During breaks in filming he took refuge in aimless activity, often tap-dancing with one of the film's children behind the scenes. Questioned on Fellini's stifling methods, he said resignedly: 'Why resist? The man's a genius.'

Marika Rivera, whom Fellini privately nicknamed '*La Porcona*' (Miss Piggy), was cast as one of the most odious of Casanova's women, the so-called 'false Astrodi'. Halting in Avignon in August 1760, Casanova noticed that an actress named Astrodi was playing in town. Assuming it was Rosalie Astrodi, whom he'd discovered in Paris to be a talented performer both on stage and in bed, he attended the show, only to discover Marguerite, her less able sister, trading on Rosalie's fame. To placate him, Marguerite invited Casanova to share a bed with her and a companion from the show, a hunchbacked girl whose deformity has forced her vagina into an unusual position. Inflamed as always by novelty, he enjoyed a lively night with the two women.

For this, the film's most libidinous scene, Casanova is locked in a vast shuttered wooden bed which shudders across the stone floor as the hunchback, tongue lolling lasciviously, crouches above him, riding

---

*Insiders assert that Fellini never removes his socks while making love – a habit shared with Mastroianni.

him tirelessly. Face whitened like a *kabuki onnagata*, the porcine
Astrodi fondles her own enormous breasts (which Fellini, attending
Rivera's costume-fitting, had exposed even more by demanding that
Donati cut the décolletage to the level of her nipples), and urges them
on. The rest of her troupe masturbate and fornicate around the walls,
dominated by the shadow of Casanova's clockwork bird-penis.

Rivera's memories of this sequence suggest it had more than narrative importance to Fellini. 'First, he wanted me to get into bed with
Nino, who was the chief electrician – a very nice, enormous man –
"just for the sound". Nino whispered to me: "It's always the same. He
always chooses me. He picks on me. Then he gets jealous." Fellini said:
"Now I want you to give me the noise when you are fucking together. I
want the breathing, the excitation, the whispering. And I want you
finally to get an orgasm, then another orgasm."' Rivera and the
electrician obliged – so enthusiastically that Fellini did, as the man
predicted, fly into a jealous fury, accusing them of actually making
love behind the bed's closed shutters.

When Sutherland came on the set tension was already high. 'I was
supposed to swing Donald around,' says Rivera. 'This big man. And he
was so nervous, sweating, afraid of the *maestro*. When he gave me his
hand it was absolutely cold and slimy; so frightened he was sweating
cold.' Fellini blocked out the scene, which began with Astrodi descend-
ing from the lavatory in the rough inn to recognise Casanova, angry
and alone after having been stood up by Olimpia Carlisi. 'Fellini said
to me: "I want you to be absolutely filthy. You've done piss, and when
you come down I want you to rub your cunt." I wasn't prepared for
that. I sat down on the stairs and I decided I was not coming out. He
came over and sat next to me. In the studio you could hear a fly. He told
me: "This woman is very bitter. She's been a prostitute all her life, and
she's become a lesbian, with this hunchback monster as a mistress."
And I said: "Why didn't you tell me this before? I would have been
prepared." Then he said: "How long is it since you last made love?"
And I said: "Four years" – because I was just divorced, and I had loved
my husband very much. And I'll never forget this. He left me on the
stairs and he shouted to all the studio: "She hasn't been fucked for four
years!" I came out of the door and I said: "You bastard! How dare
you!" He came up behind me and said: "You're going to do that scene
now with Donald." And he reaches round me and squeezes my breasts.
I told him: "Stop that, or I will squeeze your *fico fresco*."* When I did

*Fresh fig, i.e. genitals.

that, he said: "Yes. Now!" He pushes me to Donald and I grab him and pull him round. I could do it – then.'

While the scene was being shot, news arrived that Pier Paolo Pasolini had been found murdered at Ostia, where he had been lured by one of his Termini pick-ups. He'd been ambushed, beaten insensible, then run over repeatedly with his own car – by, it was assumed, thugs hired by his enemies on the right. Fellini left the set, and Rivera, following, found him weeping.

Harold Innocent hadn't been cast as a masturbating pope but as Count Saint-Germain, self-styled necromancer and alchemist. In the ten days it took to shoot his one scene, a dinner party at which he and Casanova compete for the patronage of the Marquise d'Urfé, a wealthy crackpot who dabbles in the occult and will pay a fortune to anyone who can grant her eternal life, he had ample time to observe Fellini's autocracy. Sitting for long periods in his heavy clothes made him sleepy. 'I asked: "Do you think I could get up, please, and move about?" Fellini said: "No!" So I actually did nod off occasionally. When I did, Fellini would pass behind me and punch me playfully to wake me up. He'd say: "If you are a naughty boy, I will put you in a spaghetti western." He also used to kiss the cameraman. When I saw this, I was absolutely riveted. He did it only to catch my eye. He said: "Are you shocked?" and I said: "Well, I'm a little surprised, yes", and he said: "Oh, no, I always kiss the cameraman in Italy."'

Fellini was under considerable pressure to finish shooting by 18 December, when all the artists' contracts except Sutherland's ran out. The approaching deadline did nothing for his temper. 'Like Jehovah,' complained another English actor working in the same scene as Innocent, 'he's an insufferable bully. One had expected genius to be all-demanding. But there's Fellini indulging in a childish tantrum, first with the wardrobe master, then with the extras. Giuseppe, a bearded Spanish nobleman in the film, is savaged for not sniffing a potato in quite the right way. After five takes and a stream of abuse he clearly couldn't place one foot in front of the other if told to walk. "You're mad, insane," screams Fellini. "Tell me what induced me to hire you." When it was my turn, Fellini rapidly demonstrated some hand gestures so Latin, so alien to my Anglo-Saxon nature, that I knew I wouldn't be able to reproduce them. "You're wooden," bellowed Fellini. "You look like a little queer. Be more virile." I lost count of the takes.'

Innocent recalled that another performer, cast often in Fellini films for his face but always so far silent, was given a line to deliver and fainted with the strain of getting it right.

On 27 August, in the middle of the summer holidays, portions of the negatives of three films, including *Casanova* and Pasolini's *Salo, or the 120 Days of Sodom*, disappeared from the refrigerated vaults of Technicolor's Rome laboratory. Missing from *Casanova* were seventy-four shots, comprising much of the first three weeks' shooting, including the sequence of Casanova rowing back at night from the island of San Bartolo, where he has been pleasuring a nun for the entertainment of her voyeur lover, the French ambassador. A ransom of half a billion lire was supposedly demanded by the kidnappers, which Grimaldi refused to pay. Donati, who had re-created Venice's lagoon with billowing black polythene as he'd remade the Adriatic off Rimini for *Amarcord*, didn't relish repeating the scene, so Fellini announced that, if the missing film didn't turn up, he'd rely on out-takes or, if they proved useless, simply insert into the film a card saying 'Scenes Stolen'. In May of the following year, just after *Casanova* finished shooting, most of Fellini's missing material turned up at Cinecittà. Some speculate that the disappearance was connected with labour troubles. During the last half of 1975, strikes repeatedly closed down *Casanova*, though in some cases the crew refused to stop work out of loyalty to Fellini. Others connect it with Pasolini's murder, implying the same right-wing forces blamed for his death may have tried to steal his film and taken the Fellini negative by mistake.

Such stoppages added to the cost of *Casanova*. Late in November Grimaldi pointed out that Fellini had spent $4.8 million but shot only 60 per cent of the film, with the costly editing and dubbing still to come. Two days before Christmas, he acted. Dudley Sutton, arriving in Rome, was met with news of a letter from Grimaldi firing everyone and closing down production as of 18 December.

Between December 1975 and March 1976 no camera turned. In public, Grimaldi and Fellini excused the hiatus as simply a holiday break. Elsewhere, never meeting in person, they carried on a paper war over the film's fate. Fellini acknowledged the budget blow-out and the delays, but blamed them on strikes, slowness in building sets, a week's sickness by Sutherland, general incompetence on the part of production staff and Grimaldi's own interference, under which *Casanova* had been, he said, 'disintegrating'. Furious, Grimaldi retaliated in the press that 'Fellini's regard for money brings to my mind Attila. Attila burned the earth. Fellini burns money.' He took Fellini to court for alleged wastage. Fellini responded with a writ for slander over the 'Attila' slur. Convinced the film would never be finished, Sutherland fled to Canada. 'Poor Donald,' Fellini said. 'He calls me every week from Canada to ask me: "What's happening?"'

Sutherland should have had more faith in the battle-scarred Fellini, veteran of a hundred wars with producers. To remind Grimaldi he was a film-maker of international standing, with plenty of other irons in the fire, he issued press releases announcing that both the Shah of Iran and the Emir of Kuwait had invited him to make films in their countries, the latter promising a fleet of helicopters and urging him: 'Think – if you've made what you've made with a setting like Rome, what could you do with Mesopotamia!'* Another release claimed that John Kelly of Warner Brothers wanted him to make *Erotikon*, a sketch film on pornography to be created with Ingmar Bergman and Luis Buñuel – a ghostly echo of *Love Duet*.

Fellini also signed a deal for his next film, this time with Franco Rossellini, Roberto's nephew, who enjoyed backing from *Penthouse* publisher Bob Guccione. Piqued by the entry into film production of his main competitor, Hugh Hefner, Guccione was dabbling in movies and had just launched in Rome a production of *Gore Vidal's Caligula* directed by Tinto Brass and designed by Donati. He'd also signed Ken Russell to make *Moll Flanders* and was in the market for more films of the kind his readers might patronise. Fellini predictably pushed *Il viaggio*, to star Mastroianni. At Christmas 1975 he signed a contract with Rossellini's Produzione Felix to reanimate the project yet again.

First, however, he had to complete *Casanova*. On 29 January the warring sides agreed on terms. Grimaldi would invest another $1 million, while Fellini guaranteed to finish shooting no later than May. Sandi von Normann was called in to take the load off by blocking out some sequences and the script was cut to speed completion.

Fellini, like most European film-makers, never fathomed the intricate system under which Academy Awards were given. In early 1975, he'd added his name to those of Coppola, Capra and Scorsese demanding – unsuccessfully – that the rules be bent to allow Ingmar Bergman's *Scenes from a Marriage*, barred from nomination on a technicality, to compete. Now, in February 1976, he was surprised to find himself again nominated for an Oscar as Best Director and Best Original Screenplay, with Guerra, for *Amarcord*. Steven Spielberg, who had expected to be nominated for *Jaws*, saw the choice of an

*For Persia, Fellini said fancifully, he contemplated an epic on Cyrus and Xerxes, while Kuwait would be an excellent setting for the Anabasis of Alexander.

Italian as a particular slur. 'I can't believe it!' he wailed to a film crew that was shooting him as he heard the news. 'They went for Fellini instead of me!' In the event it was the year of neither *Jaws* nor *Amarcord* but of *One Flew over the Cuckoo's Nest*.

On 17 March 1976 Luchino Visconti died. In more tranquil circumstances, Fellini might have felt a certain relief at the passing of his greatest rival, but *Casanova* gave him no time for such luxuries. On 23 March, after three months of inaction and the settlement of the interlocking court cases (the judge found no evidence of spendthrift behaviour; Fellini withdrew the slander claim), shooting recommenced with the scene of Casanova humiliating himself at the birthday party of the infantile Duke of Württemberg while six enormous organs thunder in the background.

Among the casualties of the hiatus was the film's framing dream. Though fragments remain, *Casanova*'s final version begins, not with the old man remembering past glories at Dux, but with a Venetian carnival that Fellini saved as the last major shoot of the production.

The set, as big as a football field, costing $500,000, was used for the film's opening and closing sequences, shot back to back. In the first, a carnival with fireworks, gondolas and 600 extras, the Doge cuts a ribbon which causes an angel to plunge into the water from a campanile. A gigantic head of Venus rises from the water, only to slump back and sink as the scaffolding crumples – the re-creation in yet another guise of Fellini's favourite dream.

For the second sequence shot on the huge set, the crowds have gone, the sky is black, the canal frozen. Casanova, close to death, remembers the automaton who, alone among his conquests, offered satisfaction free of all emotional demands. Black cloak fanning against the grey ice, he waltzes with her, the perfect woman. 'So this is what Fellini thinks it all comes to,' said Gerald Morin. 'A vacuous man dancing with a mechanical doll. Only a middle-aged man growing cynical could make such a statement. How sad. How honest.'

On 10 May Sutherland finished his role, not on a moment of triumph but of anticlimax. He'd intended to leave at one-thirty, after his final shot. Fellini planned a party on the set and bought an antique pocket watch as a parting gift. But rain interrupted shooting and the director realised that they would have to work through the afternoon. He went to Sutherland's trailer with the bad news and gave him the watch. Sutherland said: 'I love you', and embraced the director. ('But not too close,' Fellini said. 'It's difficult to hug and kiss someone with a false

nose and chin.') After his final take, Sutherland removed the pros-
thetics for the last time, took off his greatcoat and walked away over
the grassy field of the backlot, waving it like a flag in a final salute to
the crew. The coat was so heavy that it dragged him down on the field.
He got up, waved again and fell again. 'Accidents to the end,' Fellini
sighed.

With Sutherland off his mind, Fellini shot the big carnival scene and
some pick-ups. Dubbing and cutting occupied him for the next two
months. At three and a half hours, the film demanded severe editing.
Almost every supporting actor lost his or her major speech. Those that
remained were extensively rewritten for the English-language version
by novelist Anthony Burgess.* Some sequences disappeared altogether, including Chesty Morgan's entire role as the maid Barbarina,
and an Arabian Nights idyll in which Casanova is brought by gondola
to a Venetian seraglio, watched by adoring harem girls, then enjoys a
homosexual dalliance with a beautiful black man. Casanova admits to
a few homosexual acts in the memoirs but Fellini, typically, believed
that the great lover's compulsive womanising was, in part at least, a
flight from homosexuality. 'You do not know women and you do not
know yourself,' Casanova is lectured in the original screenplay. 'You
do not pursue women; you flee them. Loving that many means that
what you are seeking is probably a man.' The speech, like the
homosexual encounter in the harem, was cut.

Il Casanova di Federico Fellini, as it was officially titled, finally cost
$10 million, making it Fellini's most expensive film. Neither Grimaldi
nor Universal was happy with the result. Universal executives flew to
Rome from Hollywood in the hope of convincing Fellini to cut an hour.
The film was not erotic, they complained. 'Casanova is life!' one of
them chided. 'Is strength, courage, faith. He is the joy of living.
Understand, Fefé? Why have you made him a zombie?' Fellini had
already cut a number of major scenes to get the Italian running time
down to 165 minutes. Now Ruggero Mastroianni and his team went
through the Italian version and removed another fifteen minutes for
the French and English markets without deleting a single scene. But
the mass audience Universal had hoped to win for Fellini in America
never materialised. 'If the American audience wants to see a film
coming from Italy or France,' says Daniel Toscan du Plantier, 'they
want to see it in Italian or French. The tiny audience for foreign films

*Burgess was paid with a leather-bound book on Florentine antiquities, a Gucci
satchel and a cine camera. For an earlier film he'd accepted a Broadwood piano.

wants them in the original language, just as they want to drink Bordeaux from a real bottle.'

Today Fellini shrugs in resignation at the film's failure, hiding behind a studied unconcern. 'I have already said *ad nauseam* that I don't see my films again and therefore am in no position to make an objective detached judgement about them. *Casanova*, however, seems to me my most complete, expressive, courageous film.'

27 'The music saves us': *Prova d'orchestra*

'Politics I have never been able to follow. I look at it with
childish eyes. I am interested only in what makes a man
feel free'

Fellini on political commitment

In April of 1976, Fellini was in Venice when the actor James Coburn,
whom he knew slightly, stopped him in a hotel lobby to ask a favour.
Coburn was starring in *Cross of Iron*, a Second World War drama
being made in Yugoslavia by Sam Peckinpah. The shoot had been
disastrous from the start. The funding was unreliable, the weather
atrocious and Peckinpah was racked by the alcohol and cocaine abuse
that would shortly kill him. Coburn and Peckinpah's assistant, Katy
Haber, had brought him to Venice for a weekend's rest. Would Fellini
go up and say hello? Fellini, who had never seen a Peckinpah film,
obliged, though as a meeting of minds it was as unsuccessful as most of
his brushes with Hollywood.

When they entered his room, Peckinpah was drowsing. 'Who is it,
goddammit?' he snarled. 'We've got a surprise for you,' Coburn said.
To which Peckinpah replied: 'I *hate* surprises.' But when Coburn told
him it was Fellini, even 'Bloody Sam' was impressed. Climbing to his
feet, he took Fellini's hand and said awkwardly: 'Oh, Mr Fellini, thank
you for all the wonderful films you've given us.'

There was no shortage of Hollywood film-makers who acknowledged Fellini as a master, though their devotion was often selfish, or
seen as such by Fellini. Gene Wilder asked permission to base a film on
Lo sceicco bianco. Fellini agreed, but the result, *The World's Greatest
Lover*, released in 1977, was only distantly related to the original.
Wilder, who plays an inept silent-movie actor trying out as a replacement for Rudolph Valentino while his wife falls for the genuine article,
thanked Fellini in the credits 'for encouragement at the right time', a
tribute that hovers between obscure and perfunctory.

Woody Allen's admiration was equally ambivalent. Like many young film-makers, he adulated *Otto e mezzo*. In Allen's script for the 1967 *What's New Pussycat?*, harassed fashion editor Peter O'Toole in a black Stetson tries to calm his unruly women with a whip *à la* Guido Anselmi. Edra Gale also had a small role. Allen had asked Fellini to play a cameo in *Annie Hall*. Standing in line at a Manhattan cinema with Diane Keaton, Allen's Alvy Singer is enraged by a know-all discoursing to his girlfriend about Fellini. He'd planned to produce him from behind an advertising display as living refutation, but since Fellini was busy editing *Casanova* he approached Luis Buñuel, then made do with media ideologue Marshall McLuhan.

Despite these homages and the outright pastiche of *Otto e mezzo* in *Stardust Memories* and *Giulietta degli spiriti* in *Alice*, Allen's admiration has an edge of resentment. In 1969, he remarked: 'Fellini is an utter magician but he has no heart. I'm knocked out by his technique but his films bore me.' For his part, Fellini included an Allen lookalike among the phonies of *Ginger e Fred*.

Such rivalry exacerbated Fellini's competitiveness with other film-makers, and with his own collaborators. When Robert Altman wanted to meet him, Fellini told Gerald Morin to say he was leaving on a long train journey the following morning. Morin pointed out he'd chosen a day on which the Italian railways would be on strike, and the meeting went ahead, with Fellini, as always, charming. Once having accepted a homage, however, Fellini often became possessive of his new admirer. After *Casanova*, Tonino Guerra set up a dinner with Fellini and Russian director Andrei Tarkovsky, for whom he would write *Nostalghia*. Fellini agreed, but kept the fact from Morin, who had never disguised his admiration of the director of *Andrei Rublev* and *Solaris*. That day, Morin had his own meeting with Tarkovsky and Guerra, who suggested they all go to dine with Fellini. When Morin arrived with the guests, Fellini was visibly upset to see him. 'What are you doing here?' he demanded. When Morin explained he'd been invited by Tarkovsky, Fellini snapped: 'Why don't you go back to Moscow with him?'

Fellini had every reason to feel embattled. While he'd been immured in the eighteenth century with *Casanova*, the twentieth had turned on him. Until 1976 television in Italy was limited to a few national networks broadcasting by government licence. A gentlemen's agreement had existed with the cinema under which feature films were embargoed for TV until four years after cinema release. But that year the Constitutional Court ruled restriction of TV ownership illegal.

Immediately, tiny stations mushroomed all over the country, nourished on a diet of game shows, pornography and old movies. Not
feeling themselves bound by the deal with film producers, most
invested heavily in movie libraries, the cheapest programming of all.
By 1977 400 stations were showing 1,500 films a day. Cinema
audiences melted away. They'd dropped from 663 million in 1965 to
513 million in 1975. Now they plunged to 242 million by 1980 and
195 million in 1982, stabilising around 161 million throughout the
eighties.

Fellini could take some comfort in having found a producer for his next
film, but Guccione's behaviour looked anything but promising. As the
cost of *Gore Vidal's Caligula* rose to $15 million, he'd sacked Tinto
Brass and re-edited the film, adding new hard-core scenes. Brass sued.
Ken Russell and Guccione also fell out over *Moll Flanders*, spawning
another lawsuit.

Casanova opened in Paris in February 1977. To promote the film,
Gaumont arranged a meeting between Fellini and Simenon on 21
February. The two men, who'd carried on a lively correspondence
through the summer and autumn, met at Simenon's Lausanne home,
and an edited transcript of their conversation appeared in the weekly
L'Express. The interview became famous not for its insights into
Casanova but for an unexpected comment by Simenon, who, out of the
blue, volunteered: 'I did the sum a year or two ago and since the age of
thirteen and a half I have had 10,000 women.' The relevation was
publicised around the world. It passed into the mythology of his life
and of literature. In the fuss, the fact that it was said in the course of
promoting Fellini's film was forgotten.

Donati's costumes for *Casanova* won an Academy Award in April; it
had also been nominated for Best Screenplay from Another Medium.
Meanwhile, Guccione was having second thoughts, both about *I
viaggio* and about investing in Italy. Open war had broken out between
the coalition government and the radical left. Strikes and bombings
were commonplace and the Red Brigades seemed able to kill and
kidnap almost at will. Fellini revived his interest by offering to
substitute *La città delle donne*. With its sexual theme and almost
entirely female cast this was, superficially at least, the kind of film
Guccione wanted, especially with Mastroianni as Snaporaz. *Il viaggio*
was dropped and Franco Rossellini brokered a deal to make *La città
delle donne* with Guccione's money and distribution by Goffredo
Lombardo's Titanus.

Fellini moved into Cinecittà and shooting officially commenced in October. In reality, however, Fellini was still revising the script with Zapponi and Brunello Rondi. In the palmier sixties, one had been able to mark time with 'tests' and 'preparation' while writing and casting, but this leisurely approach was no longer tolerated. Guccione was impatient and Lombardo no less so as cinema attendance in Italy plunged. *La città delle donne* dragged on through Christmas 1977 with little to show except red ink. In January Titanus abruptly withdrew its distribution offer and Guccione suspended shooting.

Fellini was again in the position of personally seeking money to finish a film. In April he was in London and not in good humour as he searched for a rescuer. In this jaded state of mind he was waylaid in the fashionable Mr Chow's restaurant by director Mike Sarne, an enthusiast for his work, especially *Toby Dammit*, which he'd seen, he told Fellini, 'hundreds of times'. 'I am sure,' Fellini responded sceptically when Sarne told him, adding: 'When I finish a film I never see it again.' He told Sarne he was making some cuts in the film. 'Just a very few frames. I am going to reissue *Toby Dammit* in a programme together with *The Clowns*.'* Sarne confided that he'd succeeded in capturing Mae West (for *Myra Breckenridge*) where Fellini had failed. This further soured the encounter. Afterwards, photographer and mutual friend David Bailey, who'd arranged the meeting, explained that the word Fellini kept murmuring to his companion, which Sarne had taken as '*simpatico*', was in fact '*finocchio*' – Roman slang for 'faggot'. Sarne was not amused.

New finance for *La città delle donne* came in March 1978 from Gaumont, which contracted to distribute through Opera-Film. It was agreed that the film should be shot, as usual, in Italian, but just as the deal appeared set, Guccione announced he wanted it in English, and with a Hollywood star, ideally Dustin Hoffman. After some acrimonious confrontations, *La città delle donne* was closed down, this time apparently for good.

On 16 March the Red Brigades kidnapped Aldo Moro, leader of the Christian Democrats and broker of the historic coalition between his centrist party and the Communists. After fifty-five days, his corpse was found in the boot of a car which his kidnappers, with typical theatricality, had parked equidistant from the headquarters of the

---

*The feature combining *Toby Dammit* and *I clowns* emerged at the end of 1977. It was called *2 Fellini 2*, for which he slightly shortened both films and revoiced some characters, but it won no new friends for either and was soon forgotten.

Communists and the Christian Democrats. His murder numbed
Rome's cultural and social élite. Many retired to their houses in
Switzerland or France. Dinner-table conversation revolved around
kidnap insurance and bullet-proof limousines. Anyone who might
have considered reinvesting in the Italian film industry fled, and
Cinecittà once again fell dark.

Fellini knew Moro when he was Prime Minister. Returning from
Hollywood with his *Otto e mezzo* Oscar, he'd handed the statuette over
to the government so that Moro could re-present it at a lavish public
ceremony. While Fellini remained as apolitical (in the party sense) as
ever, the incident twitched his social conscience. Not the murder –
nobody seriously expected Moro to be spared. But 'what', he asked
himself, 'did the people who killed him really want? What had
happened to all of us living in this country? Why had things gone so far
here?'

The idea of a film on an orchestra had been with Fellini for some
years, since he watched the recording of one of Rota's scores. How well
musicians came together, he'd thought, even when they were obviously
of utterly different types and characters, and in some cases actual
enemies. What if these tensions were allowed to surface? Soon after the
Moro murder, Fellini told RAI he was interested in again making a film
for TV, and suggested such a piece. His ambitions initially went no
further than paying back the strikers who plagued the production of
Amarcord and *Casanova*. The topical subtext originated with RAI
producer Mimmo Scarano, who liked subjects with a political edge,
and Fellini, seeing that Scarano had already sold himself on the idea,
let him talk. RAI offered half of the film's $700,000 budget. For the
rest, Fellini went to Leo Pescarolo of Daima Film, who found backing
from Albatross Film in Germany.

Meanwhile, he started research by inviting a series of orchestral
musicians to lunch at Da Cesarino. His secretary took down their
conversation. In a fortnight he'd assembled some useful information
about musical life and its problems, from which he and Brunello Rondi
wrote a script.

Superficially, *Prova d'orchestra* is a documentary about a musical
rehearsal. By candle-light, an aged copyist distributes scores round the
music stands in an old chapel, explaining that, though three popes and
seven bishops are buried there, it's now been turned, because of its
acoustics, into a rehearsal hall. As the musicians arrive, Fellini himself
in voice-over puts questions to them. They brag about their skill, hand
round sexy pictures, listen to football on the radio, squabble over

who'll have which stand. Most of all, they inveigh against the conductor.

Dante Ferretti built the film's single set at Cinecittà. Religious pictures remain embedded high in one wall, and portraits of Mozart and Beethoven stare over the shoulder of the conductor while he labours to bring his dissident orchestra to heel. The sense of creation coffined in old ideas is palpable.

For the orchestra members, Fellini initially looked among professional musicians, but gave up and scoured Naples and Rome for interesting faces, leavened with a few familiar ones: for example, Angelica Hansen, the horny hunchback from *Casanova*, turns up as a violinist. Only fifteen real musicians appeared in the film, though Carlo Savina, Rota's musical director on all Fellini's films since *I clowns*, was brought in to conduct. He stood behind the podium as they played, and it was his beat they followed. Meanwhile, Rota, since most of *Prova d'orchestra* would be directed to one huge playback, was for the first time writing a score in advance of a production.

A ninety-three-year-old professor of music is carried in to be interviewed. He explains that the orchestra plays nowhere near as well as it once did. As much as the different factions within the orchestra distrust one another, they are unanimous in dislike of the man in charge. To play him, Fellini chose Balduin Baas, a minor Dutch actor picked from the photo collection. He had considered him for the Duke of Württemberg in *Casanova* but decided his face was too modern. For the neurasthenic German musical director, however, Baas was perfect, even if he understood only German and Dutch, and Fellini spoke neither.

A classic martinet, Baas stands on his dignity with the ramshackle orchestra. 'Where are we? On a soccer field?' he rages when they run out of control. 'All of you should be castrated!' In more lucid moments he sounds (appropriately to the chapel setting) more like a preacher quoting holy writ. 'A conductor is like a priest . . . Music is always sacred. Every concert is a mass.' But his congregation has lost faith. 'My musicians and I share only a lack of confidence . . . We play together but are united only in a common hatred, like a destroyed family.'

True to his worst expectations, the musicians soon become a mob. Mozart and Beethoven are pelted with mud. Graffiti is scrawled on the walls: 'Down with Beethoven', 'Hurray for phonographs'. A trumpet is used to inflate and explode a condom. A woman furtively eats a hamburger under cover of a music stand while beneath the piano two players make love. The union organiser demands that control of the orchestra be handed to the musicians. A huge metronome is installed on the podium in place of Baas, but even this is too potent a symbol of repression for some, who demand total autonomy.

Just as the chaos has reached a crescendo a wrecker's ball crashes through one wall of the chapel, killing the lady harpist. Dazed, the musicians forget their differences and the conductor briefly re-establishes control. 'The music saves us,' he says. 'Grab hold of the notes . . . Don't be afraid. The rehearsal continues.' And so it does, for a few moments, the musicians standing obediently, playing under his baton. The unity, however, doesn't last. Baas delivers another of his vituperative sermons, then yells: *'Da capo, signori'* – 'From the beginning.' The screen fades to black. From the darkness he lets fly a volley of imprecations in German, a hint, some thought, that the disorder in Italy could end only in a return to Hitlerian Fascism.

Filmed for the most part in emphatic close-ups, *Prova d'orchestra* develops a momentum far from typical of Fellini. Despite his well-earned reputation for prodigality and delay, he completed it in only sixteen shooting days, spread over two months. The connection between his fable and the political situation in Italy wasn't explicit during filming but it became more so during the dubbing. 'Not that I didn't see the particular importance of the film from the beginning,' Fellini said defensively. 'It had just not become clear to me why it was important for me to make this film at this particular time. Later on I knew; it was the assassination of Moro.' It's equally possible that the political theme was secondary, and that he visualised himself more as the musical director browbeating his recalcitrant musicians. Baas, after all, does and says nothing that Fellini hadn't done and said himself a hundred times.

Dubbing of the film, now running eighty minutes, took four weeks, since, to emphasise the political dimension, Fellini elected to turn the musicians into an anthology of national dialects. The percussionists became Neapolitans, naturally noisy. The union leader was Sardinian, perpetually aggrieved.

In the late summer, Fellini had been accosted on a late evening walk by a stranger who turned out to be the politician Alessandro Pertini. He'd just seen *La dolce vita* on TV and told him how much he liked it. When Fellini had a new film, Pertini asked, would he give him first look at it? Such was the pace of change in Italian politics that by the time *Prova d'orchestra* was finished Pertini was President of the Republic. As a result, the film had its first public screening on 19

October 1978, at Italy's presidential palace, the Quirinale, for the nation's most powerful politicians.

Fellini was nervous at the screening, and rightly so. What had seemed a useful publicity break backfired when most guests damned the film with faint praise. Some professed to find the language shocking. Others accused Fellini of boosting one faction or another. Enrico Berlinguer, head of the Communist Party, who happened to be from Sardinia, took the character of the organiser as a personal insult. In vain Fellini protested that the actor, Claudio Ciocca, *was* really Sardinian. RAI had scheduled the film for November but in the light of the furore they withdrew it for further 'preview' screenings. Italy's countless political and social splinter groups were given an opportunity to pick their particular nits. Fellini broke the impasse by taking the film to Gaumont. The French company owned 600 theatres and was expanding. Daniel Toscan du Plantier was now in charge and agreed to release *Prova d'orchestra* theatrically. The film opened in February 1979 to modest business and finally reached Italian TV in December, by which time the issues it raised seemed remote. As for Fellini, he was deep in the disastrous complexities of *La città delle donne*, which Toscan du Plantier, in a gesture of generosity and admiration he would come to regret, had agreed to fund.

28   Ten Thousand Women: *La città delle donne*

'It's very sad – all the women we will never make love to'
Fellini to Freddie Jones, 1983

As Fellini entered his sixties, his reliance on his fantasy life became increasingly obtrusive. The self-psychoanalysis of *Casanova* had dissipated some fears of encroaching age, but the residue of a lifetime's anxiety – about his public image, about relationships and above all about sexuality – remained. Much of it was conserved in his dream diaries. Fellini was not the first artist to record his dreams and draw on their imagery in his work, but few have interwoven them quite so completely with real life.

On *Casanova*, an odd ceremony had taken place. Lunching a group of money-men at Cinecittà, Fellini invited Tina Aumont and Marika Rivera to join them. As the food was served, he asked Rivera to 'bless the meal' by opening her dress at the head of the table and spilling out her ample breasts. With some misgivings, she did so. So many odd things had been demanded of her that one more hardly counted. For Fellini, the occasion was literally the realisation of a dream – specifically one of 1 April 1975, in which 'The Great Fabricator and Dissolver of Clouds' sits on a cloud which Fellini propels with his breath. As he orders her to 'fertilize what lies below', she holds out her breasts and rain falls.

The diaries could even, in a sense, substitute for him in his relationship with a woman. American journalist Charlotte Chandler interviewed Fellini, an experience more intimate than she'd expected. 'He grips your arms, squeezes your hand, wraps his arm around your shoulders. Physical contact seems to count for a lot with him.' Obviously attracted, Fellini spent days squiring Chandler around Rome. Their conversation, as she later recounted it, dealt almost entirely with sex. Fellini took her to his office in corso d'Italia and showed her some volumes of the dream diary. Clearly he was aware of the erotic effect of the drawings, even counting on them to draw Chandler emotionally closer, just as his hugs and squeezes invited a greater physical intimacy.

'I have a wonderful life at night in my dreams,' he told her. 'I'll show you, except the pictures are often obscene. Do you want to see them in spite of that?'

'Please,' said Chandler.

'But my drawings are *very* obscene,' he pressed. 'You don't care?'

Would Fellini have capitalised on such an intimacy? Probably not. Chandler was not the first female journalist to be the target of sexual innuendo, and the others had escaped unscathed. 'Do you like beans?' he'd enquired of the *Observer*'s Anna Coote over lunch in 1970. 'They are very aphrodisiac. Are you sure you still want some?'

In *Ciao Federico!* Gideon Bachmann filmed another such encounter during *Satyricon*. On Lichas' boat moored near Fregene, Fellini chats with three girls who appear in the scene:

Fellini: 'Did you make love last night?'

Girl (puzzled): 'Love? Love?'

Fellini (in English): 'Have you make love tonight?'

Girl: 'No . . .'

Fellini (in English): 'So you have lost a night . . .'

Magali Noël insists righteously: 'Federico is *not* Casanova!', but the sense of him manipulating such encounters for sexual satisfaction remains.

Fellini's triumphal return to Cinecittà in the spring of 1979 after *La città delle donne*'s shut-down seemed an affirmation of his standing. With Visconti dead, he was, in the eyes of most people, Italy's undoubted king of cinema. It was an idea Fellini did nothing to dispel. The studio accommodated itself as usual to his methods. Beside each sound stage a small dining-room was provided for those indispensable lunches for colleagues and distinguished visitors. Daniel Toscan du Plantier had a chance to watch Fellini close up when he entertained the Minister for Arts and Tourism. After a jovial meal, Fellini conducted the politician to his car, wrung his hand, then, as he drove off, murmured: 'Don't worry, we won't be seeing him again.' Toscan du Plantier wrote later: 'I laughed, too quickly, not realising I wasn't being treated any better.' Some time later, when the producer was supplanted as head of Gaumont, Fellini was heard to laugh gleefully at his fall, and trumpet to friends: 'Toscan's gone. That's the end of him.'

*

La città delle donne is the dream diaries turned into film. *Casanova* had been conceived as a sustained reminiscence, tinted with nostalgic sexuality, but here the whole story, except for brief framing passages, is a sexual fantasy – or, more correctly, a nightmare.

It begins with an image that Hitchcock's ironic use in *The Thirty-Nine Steps* and *North by Northwest* has made the most familiar sexual joke in cinema – a train plunging into a tunnel. In the wildly rocking train is Snaporaz, a suited, spectacled but still attractive male chauvinist. Drowsing, he's stimulated by the arrival of a voluptuous and well-dressed *bourgeoise*. Their fingers touch as both grab for a mineral water bottle rolling on the table between them, and Snaporaz senses an unspoken invitation.

The woman is Bernice Stegers, an unknown Fellini spotted in London, and only one of many odd casting choices. With such a large cast, Liliana Betti was forced to shunt women through Cinecittà almost daily. French composer Yves Simon, visiting the set well into production, was surprised to see Fellini stop work while a group trooped on to the set for his inspection.

When the stranger leaves the compartment, Snaporaz follows, waylaying her in the toilet. She accepts his kiss and seems to offer something more – if he's audacious enough to take it. But before he can act, the train stops in the middle of the countryside. She gets out. Snaporaz, importuning her constantly, follows as she crosses a meadow and enters a wood. She doesn't drive him away, and even offers to kiss him again if he'll stand against a tree with his eyes closed. But when he does so, she slips away. He glimpses her entering an isolated hotel, the Miramare, and follows. The place is filled with women. It's a conference of feminists, of which Snaporaz becomes a baffled observer. In the lobby is a large poster of an egg with eyes – Fellini's favourite image of the half-submerged head, given added relevance because the eyes are his own.

Snaporaz wanders the hotel, eavesdropping on lectures on the similarity between the vagina and the shapes of shells and flowers, on masturbation and lesbian love-making, and on how to subdue a man with a kick to the balls. At another seminar, a woman introduces her six husbands who file in and shyly take their bows. In the audience is Stegers. She points out Snaporaz lurking behind a pillar and warns the others that here is a typical man, not to be trusted. As she does so, slides appear on the screen: Snaporaz pursuing her from the train, and standing against a tree, eyes closed, lips pursed.

He is rescued by an amiable girl named Donatella (Donatella Damiani). She takes him into another part of the hotel and fits him with a pair of roller-skates. As Snaporaz totters about the floor, a gang of women appear, all expert skaters, and, forming a ring, whirl around him. He finally takes refuge in the furnace room. The stoker, a husky and very plain lady with a heavy Triesteno accent, offers to get him out of the place and to the nearest railway station. However, she takes him to a farm where, on the pretext of having him examine some plants in an improvised plastic greenhouse, she tries to rape him. Her mother appears to rescue Snaporaz, who runs off as she berates her daughter.

Shooting continued through the summer at a leaden pace, to the growing frustration of Toscan du Plantier. '[Fellini] likes to stop during the shooting,' he says, 'so he takes some rests. Usually something happens which obliges him to stop. But obviously he's so happy with what's happening that it's difficult to think he's not involved.' The first delays could hardly have been engineered. The mothers of both Brunello Rondi and Marcello Mastroianni died, as did his old friend, chauffeur and masseur Ettore Bevilacqua. On 9 April Fellini met Nino Rota at a gallery on via Condotti where Fabrizio Clerici, the artist who'd briefly tried to design *Toby Dammit*, had his new show. The next day Fellini took a call on the set and was heard to say: 'Oh, no!' Rota, sixty-eight, had died of a heart attack.

Production halted, to recommence on 1 May with a flurry of visitors. Germaine Greer, Susan Sontag, Danny Kaye, Ingrid Bergman, Paul Newman, Chaplin and Mazursky would all drop by in the next few weeks. On 10 April the guest was Henry Balthus, whom Fellini had met through Alain Cuny while the painter was resident at the Villa de Médicis, France's cultural embassy in Rome. Balthus's dream-like, erotic tableaux of adolescent girls impressed Fellini, and he wrote an essay for the Villa's magazine extolling them. Minister of Culture Jack Lang reciprocated by commissioning a Balthus portrait of Fellini.

Snaporaz, fleeing at night from the randy horticulturist, is picked up by two cars filled with wild-looking girls who dress bizarrely, groove to rock music, speak a meaningless slang and play chicken along the narrow dirt road. He barely escapes a car crash and finds himself in the grounds of a mansion protected by savage Great Danes. Fortuitously, however, the house belongs to an old friend, Dr Sante Katzone, a famous seducer. (In other versions of the film, he's called Xavier Zübercock.)

On 13 June Fellini started shooting in Katzone's villa. Ettore Manni was a controversial choice to play the doctor. Once a bare-chested star of peplums and a famous ladies' man, he was now balding, overweight and drinking heavily – problems which Fellini's abrasive direction accentuated. Complaints by Manni's agent to Toscan du Plantier about Fellini's public mockery of his client's drinking and womanising did nothing to relieve the tension. Nobody seemed able to shield Manni from an increasingly humiliating experience.

Katzone, in a sideways nod from Fellini to Simenon, is holding a party to celebrate his ten-thousandth conquest. Most of the guests are as old and tired as he. Among them is Snaporaz's wife, Elena, drunk and bitter in her dissatisfaction with marriage. Anouk Aimée was considered for Elena but the role was offered finally to Glenda Jackson. When she was too busy, Fellini chose the Paris-based Polish singer Anna Prucnal who had starred in Dušan Makavejev's erotic *Sweet Movie*.

Snaporaz explores the mansion and stumbles on an enormous museum of Katzone's women, each represented (in classic cinema front-of-house style) by a large transparency. A switch beside each one lights up the picture and runs a record of the woman's gratified moans. When he returns, Katzone is ready to cut a huge cake, its tiers decorated with 10,000 candles. He blows out some and pisses on the rest.

The party is entertained by Donatella and her sister, reincarnated in skimpy outfits as a popular song and dance team of Snaporaz's childhood. They dance with him, Mastroianni doing a credible Fred Astaire routine in top hat and tails, then show him to bed. They refuse to join him, however, putting an onion under his pillow and three apples under the bed to help him sleep. Elena appears, drunk, to almost rape him (a grotesque imitation of male sexual practice) before herself dropping off.

Waking as a storm rages outside, Snaporaz hears sounds from under the bed. Exploring, he finds a magic entrance to a huge carnival-like area, where three old men in evening dress, gliding down a long slide, remind Snaporaz of his pre-pubescent sexual history. (Since Fellini was delivered during a storm it's inviting to see this scene as a symbolic rebirth.) At this point, Snaporaz was to have been joined by Katzone and together they would explore their sexual past. But on 27 July the actor was found dead in his apartment. A bullet from a .45 Magnum revolver, part of the cowboy outfit he was wearing, had passed through his genitals and severed the femoral artery. Fellini's comment to Toscan du Plantier on hearing the news – that it was a tragedy but it proved the script worked – may well have disguised distress, though it is worth comparing it to his obviously genuine dismay at Rota's death.

In practical terms, however, Manni's death was more damaging to *La città delle donne* than Rota's. The composer could be replaced, and was, by Nicola Piovani and Luis Bacalov, whereas the script called for Katzone to accompany Snaporaz through the rest of the film. Manni was buried on 31 July, by which time production had been suspended once again while Fellini, Zapponi and Rondi rewrote.

Shooting recommenced on 24 September with the childhood fantasy scenes, now adapted to include only Snaporaz. Introduced by spotlights, like acts in a circus, eight incidents of adolescent sexuality from Fellini's childhood are recalled: his early fascination with a maid, with a fishmonger girl who lasciviously handles some eels, then leatherjacketed girls in a circus, a masseuse at a spa, a woman in a thirties swimming costume undressing in a beach tent, and a whore with big buttocks. Most striking of all, and an image as archetypal as any in Fellini's work, is a fantasy in which a score of men and boys sleep in an enormous bed, masturbating as they watch movies: *Maciste all'inferno*, Garbo, Mae West.

Snaporaz reaches the foot of the slide to find himself in a basement, being judged by a tribunal of hard-eyed women, watched by others in ski masks. From time to time, other older men are called to fight in a nearby arena. Shortly after, they're brought back on stretchers, dead. The tribunal accuses Snaporaz of a score of 'crimes', from not understanding women to pissing standing up. He finally enters the arena to find the bleachers filled with women and the ring itself occupied by a black monolith. He climbs a ladder to the top; meanwhile, the women leave. On top, Snaporaz finds himself in the basket hanging under a balloon in the shape of the huge near-naked Donatella – 'The Great Fabricator and Dissolver of Clouds' made real. As it lifts into the dark, the real Donatella machine-guns him from the ground, and the basket breaks loose and starts to fall. At this point, Snaporaz wakes up in the railway compartment, with Elena opposite him. But his glasses are broken as they were in his dream, and a moment later Bernice Stegers enters the compartment. Before Snaporaz can react, the train plunges into another tunnel.

On 6 October shooting halted briefly once more so that Fellini could be a witness at the wedding of Renzo Rossellini. Four days later Fellini broke his right arm and shooting halted for a week. On 29 November he shot the Donatella balloon floating away and *La città delle donne* was finished after shooting for eight months and spending 7 billion lire.

In a sense the film had actually taken ten years to complete. Had Fellini made it at the height of his reputation and powers, critics might well have jostled to praise it and revel in its implications, as they had with *Otto e mezzo*. Instead, the reaction was lukewarm. Most agreed that, notwithstanding Manni's death, the script *didn't* work. The project had been on the shelf too long, and that particular caravan had passed by.

Critics taking it seriously tended to be those who, like Fellini, saw it as an exploration of the myth. Some read it in classic Freudian terms, as a symbolic tour of Fellini's sexuality. In such a reading the 'city of women' is the unconscious of Snaporaz/Fellini. It's filled with images of erection, most obviously the Donatella balloon, which are attacked by militant females. Skating, like many physical skills, can be equated with sexual performance but Snaporaz/Fellini 'hasn't skated in years'. The women skate skilfully, but only by themselves; thus Snaporaz/ Fellini fears sexual inadequacy. Images of sight in the film (the egg with Fellini's eyes and Snaporaz's broken spectacles) play on the association of blindness with castration. It's hard not to believe that the armchair analysts had seen something of the truth.

La città delle donne was shown at Cannes in May 1980 to less than wild enthusiasm. Its release coincided with another ambiguous homage from Woody Allen. *Stardust Memories*, with its chalky black and white photography, melancholy dream sequences and overall air of despair, harked back to *Otto e mezzo*, the point at which appreciation of his work seemed to have jammed, at least in the United States.

Dominique Delouche called on Fellini in Rome and found him depressed. 'We talked for two hours, in a very concentrated way. He was saddened by the death of Nino Rota, and by the position of the cinema in Italy, sour about the government. His career was shipwrecked, he said. He was tired, and bitter about some of the people in his entourage. It was sad to think that the greatest living film-maker was in this position.' The same tone of self-pity permeated a letter he wrote to Daniel Toscan du Plantier in response to an article in *L'Express* about the producer's experiences with him. '*Caro* Toscanino,' he wrote, 'My work has obliged me to hate producers and I have suffered a great deal with you, since I never did come to despise you. You know that my life is painful, a business of so many failures, alone in the face of fame. Explain to me what the world wants, why they ask me incomprehensible things on the decline of Western civilization that they tell me I depict in my films. How can I explain that I only wanted to amuse myself a little?' '*Fellinisimo,*' commented Toscan du Plantier dryly.

29   The Soprano, the Journalist and the Rhinoceros: *E la nave va*

'How beautiful! It looks painted'
Actress of a sunset in *E la nave va*

The eighties should have been the high noon of Fellini's career. Instead, he spent them in a premature sunset – though at least he enjoyed the warmth. Almost every major film museum in the world presented retrospectives of his work. Exhibitions of his caricatures and sketches were held in London, Paris and Berlin, and lavish albums were published. In 1985 he received an honorary Golden Lion at Venice and the prestigious accolade of the Film Society of Lincoln Center in New York, a train of honours that would culminate in his honorary Academy Award in 1993.

Numerous critical studies and two biographies were published. In 1980 he even produced his own book, *Fare un film/Making a Film*. Actually Liliana Betti compiled it from interviews and pieces he'd signed (though not necessarily written) over the years. Fellini then, despite her protests, rewrote everything, putting himself in a more favourable light. 'It's all lies,' she says ruefully. But in Fellini's career that was nothing new.

His work was often adapted to the stage. In 1959 Bob Fosse, then an up and coming Broadway director/choreographer, had been planning to make *I soliti ignoti* into a musical when he saw *Le notti di Cabiria*. It so captivated him that he turned it into *Sweet Charity*, with a book by Neil Simon that laundered Cabiria into Charity Hope Valentine, a 'dance hostess'. Later the show made a successful film. There had been a short-lived sixties Broadway version of *La strada*, and an eighties ballet which never got out of Italy. Stephen Sondheim also acknowledges *Giulietta degli spiriti* as one inspiration of *Follies*. In 1982 Maury Yetson and Arthur Kopit transformed *Otto e mezzo* into *Nine*, the figure signifying the number of women in the life of its director hero Guido Contini. It won twelve Tony Awards.

*

La città delle donne opened in the United States in April 1981 as *City of Women*. Gaumont distributed it through a small independent, New Yorker Films. Fellini and Giulietta came to New York for the première but no amount of promotion could sell a film widely recognised as a dud. It did only mediocre business, almost entirely on the east coast.

On his return, Fellini began looking for finance again, and complaining about his lack of success. 'The truth is, I'm out of work,' he said. 'I have four screenplays ready but I can't find a backer to put up the money for them.' His problem was publicised as a national scandal, and Italian newspapers demanded that Cinecittà offer him a project. It was hardly the studio's task to find films for directors and they rightly pointed out that, if they gave Fellini some special concession, Francesco Rosi and a dozen other distinguished but expensive film-makers would expect the same.

Instead, Fellini found himself playing 'the pivot role in a game performed by producers, speculators, Arab investors and strange middlemen'. Critically, *Satyricon* had come into its own as its influence trickled down through interior design, so the projects most often mentioned were the *Iliad*, Dante's *Inferno* and the Greek myths, usually with scripts by Anthony Burgess and funding from CBS and Gaumont. He was also said to be preparing a film about a newspaper editor with Mastroianni, and RAI invited him to consider a series of made-for-TV police thrillers called *Poliziotto*, to be shot in different Italian cities, in imitation of the successful French *Inspector Lavardin* films. Fellini toured Rome with an ex-detective looking for locations, but, as producer Serge Sevilloni admitted, getting Fellini to make even one film was hard enough; a series was next to impossible. The project passed to independent producer Giorgio Salvani, who in February 1982 announced that shooting would begin in July on the $7 million series. It was never heard of again, though Fellini did propose filming some stories of Dashiell Hammett. Alberto Grimaldi, however, had already bought them and sold them to a US company.

Offers to work in the United States came with increasingly regularity. During the New York trip, a *Fellini–New York* had been proposed, on the lines of *Fellini–Roma*. Sherry Lansing, boss of Twentieth Century–Fox, also invited him to visit the US for three months to find a project. De Laurentiis, whose empire was then at the limits of its expansion, never stopped offering him films, dismissing his claim that he didn't know enough about the people to work there. In truth, this argument, which had been valid during his Neorealist period, made no sense for a Fellini who had created an almost entirely artificial world, using performers who were as often English and French as Italian.

Fellini periodically threatened to relocate, but always to stampede public opinion or shame a producer. He never seriously contemplated abandoning Italy.

With *Poliziotto* dead, Fellini revived a film he'd been incubating for years, *The Assassination of Archduke Ferdinand*. The source was a newspaper report about the theory of a Jesuit priest on the origins of the First World War. The priest had corresponded with a retired Hungarian ambassador who supplied some obscure information that contradicted the history books. Fellini kept the clipping. 'Maybe I cut it out because I was moved by the realisation that we have to consider carefully what we think of as historic fact before we pass it on to others.' He also told a press conference a few days before shooting started that he'd been intrigued by reports of ships disappearing in the Bermuda Triangle. There was, too, in the main incident of the film, a clear reference to the scattering of Maria Callas's ashes off Greece in 1977. But to most people all this seemed remote from his usual concerns.

In 1979/80, Fellini and Tonino Guerra had written a quick treatment on the theme, hoping to sell it to Gaumont in the honeymoon between the end of shooting on *La città delle donne* and the bad news from the box office. He'd outlined the plot to Renzo Rossellini, head of Gaumont's Italian subsidiary Opera-Film, who was enthusiastic, so 'without much conviction' they started work on an outline and 'after two or three days of idle chatter . . . got the plot and continuity ready in only three weeks'. But Gaumont wanted changes and the project foundered on mutual inflexibility. In the next two years Fellini offered the script to Vides, Franco Cristaldi's company, then to de Laurentiis, to Aldo Nemmi, a film-struck Milanese industrialist, and to RAI. In the end Nemmi and Vides persuaded RAI to contribute 35 per cent of the $5 million budget, raising the rest themselves. Cristaldi produced the film, now relaunched as *E la nave va/And the Ship Sails On*.

In July 1914, the ship *Gloria N. . .* is about to sail from Naples. A movie cameraman is filming the preparations, and for a few minutes the clatter of his hand-wound camera is the only sound we hear. Passengers gather; an elegant crowd, with an artistic look. Most are musicians, assembled for the funeral voyage of the greatest of all sopranos, Edmea Tetua, who's asked that her ashes be thrown in the sea off her native island, Erime. Our guide is the diffident journalist Orlando, who offers an apologetic on-camera commentary throughout the film. His position as a hack on a ship of snobs is unenviable. 'They tell me: "Get the news. Tell them what's going on",' he mutters. 'But does anybody know?'

Fellini took over nine Cinecittà stages for the shooting of *E la nave va*, which began on 19 May 1982. Studio 5 was filled with an enormous duplication of the ship's deck, supported on hydraulic jacks that allowed it to rock realistically. The sea itself was created by Dante Ferretti in imitation of Donati from polythene and glitter. Grips underneath moved it to simulate waves. Fellini had come a long way from the first shots of *Lo sceicco bianco*, when the sea refused to behave. However, the exterior of the ship wasn't created in the studio. Fellini preferred to paint the wall of a Rome pasta factory in imitation of a black iron hull, then move the camera as if it were pulling out. The factory was the same one where Urbano Fellini met Ida Barbiani in 1918.

At dinner on the first night, Orlando, after being politely moved out of the waiters' way when he tries to do his stand-up to camera, introduces us to the main passengers: Ildebranda Cuffari, now the greatest living soprano, Sir Reginald Dongby, pompous director of the Covent Garden Opera House, and his flighty wife, Violet, Aureliano Fuciletto and Sabatino Lepori, rivals for the title of world's greatest tenor, and so many child prodigies, elderly voice coaches, conductors, ballerinas and opera administrators that Orlando loses track. Also on board is the elephantine Grand Duke of Herzog, his blind sister the Princess Lherimia and their retinue, including her lover, Prime Minister Hupperback with whom she's probably plotting a coup.

Fellini chose his cast almost entirely in England. Freddie Jones plays Orlando, Barbara Jefford is Ildebranda Cuffari and Janet Suzman appears as Edmea Tetua in old home movies. He remembered Norma West from his *Casanova* casting visit to London. He'd short-listed her for Volpina in *Amarcord* but decided she looked too well bred. Needing someone to play the randy Violet, he recalled her nostrils, 'moving, and slightly vibrating'. Her professionalism awed him. 'Think that Norma West arrived and said she was perfectly documented on nymphomaniacs. She had interrogated many of them. And where did she find them, these nymphomaniacs? In the telephone book under "Professions"?'

For the Italian performers, he dug through his picture files. Fred Williams, the Indian godson from *Giulietta degli spiriti*, put on an Edwardian moustache to play Lepori. Fiorenza Serra, the plump, blond, capon-like boy cast as the Grand Duke, was a Neapolitan amateur who had struck Fellini as 'at once vacant and corrupt'. The most improbable member of the cast is Pina Bausch. Fellini had

glimpsed the eminent German choreographer backstage after a performance, swathed in white, and asked her on the spot to be the blind
Princess Lherimia. 'She never stopped smoking,' recalled Freddie
Jones. '*Never*. Thin as a rake. She had no idea what to do. Never acted
before.'

E la nave va is self-consciously artificial, as if Fellini was determined
to wall himself off from the outside world. A passenger admires a
backdrop sunset and says: 'How beautiful! It looks painted.' When
Jones pointed out that the night sky had no stars, Fellini climbed up
and poked holes in the cyclorama to create some. At the end of the film,
he has the camera pull back to show the vast construction on its jacks,
with the crew and the onlookers, tracking in at last on the dark lens of
the camera; as he had observed on *Giulietta degli spiriti*, 'everything is
false, just like in life'.

Rivalries among the passengers – animal passions, as Fellini sees
them – are never far below the surface. Peter Cellier's Dongby,
sexually aroused by his wife's promiscuity, is forever prowling the ship
in hope of catching her *in flagrante*. Dinner is disturbed when a seagull
flies in, there's a lovesick rhinoceros in the hold en route to an
Amsterdam zoo, and a bass later uses his voice to hypnotise a chicken
(and also Orlando, who nods off). The Princess describes a dream
(recycled from *Il viaggio*) where the Grand Duke is carried away by an
eagle, and as the ship is sinking, two butterflies flutter down a flooded
corridor.

When the passengers visit the ship's boiler-room, the opera-loving
stokers request a song from Cuffari, but before she can open her mouth
Fulciletto bursts into an aria, leading to a cutting contest on 'La donna
è mobile' for the highest and longest sustained note. Thereafter,
passengers harmonise periodically on extracts from Verdi's *La forza
del destino*, *Aïda*, *Nabucco* and *La traviata*, with libretti rewritten by
Andrea Zanzotto to fit the plot. This operatic subtext is one of the
film's most unexpected features. For decades, Fellini insisted he
disliked all music, excepting only Nino Rota's compositions in his own
films.* In the eighties, however, he abruptly announced a conversion to
opera. There was, as usual, an accompanying rationalisation. Growing
up, he explained, he had never been far from opera. Productions at the
Teatro Bonci in nearby Cesena were advertised all over Rimini and half
the town went there for performances, returning drunkenly in the early

---

*He is supposed to have sometimes given Rota musical ideas, e.g. the title theme of *La
dolce vita*, but neither ever confirmed this.

hours to harmonise under the Fellinis' windows. 'I have always felt like an outsider,' he said, 'carrying a vague sense of guilt because of not wanting to participate in this warm, enveloping, impassioned, collective Italian ritual.' Rota, the year before he died, is said to have persuaded Fellini to visit a Verdi opera. Fellini prefers a story in which, watching a TV production of *La traviata*, he found himself unexpectedly moved to tears. While it's undoubted that in the eighties Fellini became a lover of opera on records and TV, he seems to have shunned live performances, which belies his tale about a late discovery of a shared ritual.

Hearing of his change of heart, impresarios badgered him to direct. A Sicilian entrepreneur entertained him repeatedly at La Scala, taking him through its subterranean corridors to the elaborate lighting console in the hope of tempting him with its sophistication. A British conductor visited via Margutta and, on the piano given to Fellini by Rota, played through almost the entire score of *Il trovatore* in the hope of persuading him to work at Covent Garden (as both Visconti and Zeffirelli had done). Fellini always refused, for reasons that might have been clarified with a documentary on opera he first proposed in 1987 at the time of *Intervista* but which he has never got around to making. It's clear, however, from *E la nave va*, with its scenic artificiality, broad playing and ensemble musical sequences, that Fellini would have made a superb producer for the operatic stage.

For Orlando, Fellini needed 'the face of an old clown, at the same time noble and miserable', and he considered Tognazzi, Michel Serrault and Paolo Villaggio before choosing Freddie Jones. A classically trained actor who'd worked for years with the Royal Shakespeare Company, Jones, who had recently enjoyed a triumph on stage as the ageing actor-manager in *The Dresser*, thinks Peter O'Toole had something to do with recommending him. He had a call requesting him to come to Fellini's London hotel, which, since O'Toole's name was associated with it, he at first assumed was an alcoholic practical joke.

Fellini explained he was looking for someone like Charlie Chaplin or Groucho Marx. Not entirely helpfully, Jones pointed out: 'But they're both dead.' An uncertain Fellini left for Rome, with the parting comment: 'We're both called Fred, so perhaps the fates are with us.' A few days later he summoned Jones for tests. They went to a restaurant at Fregene, where Fellini had him try on hats while some stills were shot. Afterwards Jones left for London to fulfil a prior commitment. ('They still talk about it at Broadcasting House. Me leaving Fellini in Rome to do a play for BBC Radio.') On the way back from the airport,

Fellini saw a bus bearing a large sign for an ice-cream called 'Orlando' and took it for an omen.

Accustomed to detailed direction, the British actors were disconcerted to find Fellini more interested in costumes and make-up than character. Since his impatience with writers was at its most intense with *E la nave va*, nobody was given a script, and when Fellini noticed that a girl in the cast had one, he snatched it away from her. At a Christmas party at via Margutta for the foreign performers, he presented Norma West with a specially bound screenplay as a gift. It was the first copy she or anyone else had seen.

Forced to rationalise Orlando, Jones decided: 'He's a journalist, a class Fellini despises. So he has no character, no beliefs, just a job, which he pursues indefatigably.' Trying to humanise him, Jones played the role, in line with the film's antique look, as silent comedy. At his costume fitting he was given a coat which Fellini told designer Maurizio Millenotti to make 'from the same material as umbrellas'. This also suggested slapstick, an impression Fellini reinforced by having the outfit resewn with more visible stitches. Fellini also asked Jones to lose weight. It contributed to a hangdog look, not unlike Stan Laurel.

Jones found Fellini's control 'Chaplinesque', the director miming every gesture and movement. 'It was like having a hand shoved in your back.' Occasionally, he revolted. For a scene of a filmed interview with the captain, Orlando, seeing Dongby, a more important interviewee, pass the door, had to leave hurriedly, apologising to the audience. Asking Rotunno to mark exactly where the frame ended, Jones stepped out of shot, then leaned his head back in to make his excuses. Fellini wasn't pleased, but the effect was too funny to cut.

The topical subtext of *E la nave va* surfaces two-thirds of the way through the story. The night before the ship arrives off Erime, its captain rescues a group of Serbian refugees. Almost immediately a battleship appears and demands their surrender. The captain negotiates a truce to dispose of Tetua's ashes, but after the ceremony the Serbians are handed over. One of them tosses a bomb into the warship, which fires on the *Gloria N. . .*, sinking it before itself exploding. Ironically, Orlando survives, finding himself in a lifeboat with the rhinoceros – which, he's happy to discover, gives good milk.

Does *E la nave va* have a political message? At times, Orlando does seem to be playing the role of a politically aware and committed investigator, notably when he cons his way into the Grand Duke's morning fencing practice in search of an interview. Since every answer is filtered through a series of interpreters, however, he confuses the

Duke's words and begins to harangue him about the deficiencies of the Austro-Hungarian empire. The idea of a world war being sparked by a trivial international incident had resonances for Cold War Europe, and Fellini did his best to bolster this interpretation, lamenting: 'We are filled with such a cold, rigid, soporific and impenetrable indifference that the absurd desire for a catastrophe secretly arises within us, for a catastrophe that could shake us out of our lethargy so that we can gain a new sense of reality and experience other possibilities. A misfortune that can make rebirth possible.' Like all his political pronouncements, however, this one sounds like little more than post-hoc philosophising.

Despite a sixteen-week shoot adhered to 'with Germanic efficiency', *E la nave va* cost $7 million, which it had no hope of recouping. It was at once the most accessible of all Fellini's films and the one which critics found hardest to analyse. For the first time he had set a film outside Italy. It was also, as well as being free of overt autobiography, innocent of sexual ambivalence. Stripped of the myth, Fellini's world looked curiously calm and explicable. Without finding any specific parallels, critics in America tended to compare the film with Katharine Anne Porter's metaphor for the events of the Second World War, *Ship of Fools*, but the French and Italians loyally searched for deeper significance. A few decided it was *Il viaggio di G. Mastorna* sailing under false colours, with the ship replacing the airliner and Orlando standing in for Mastorna. There is the same sense of people on an enigmatic voyage during which they discover themselves, and a climax at which the protagonist comes to self-acceptance. Even Fellini, however, while always willing to endorse any theory that reflected well on a film, was stretched by the French critic who suggested the rhinoceros was a metaphor for the sexuality and primal emotion that always sustains his characters; that it represented, in his words, 'twenty brothel whores and ten Roman matrons'. 'Poor rhinoceros,' Fellini responded wearily. 'What hasn't been said of it?' before rallying to assure him: 'It represents the unknown part of us that can save us if we know how to accept it. That's the sense of the last image.' As for the voyage itself and the ship, '*Gloria*, well, that's glory . . . With the N and the dots, I wanted to suggest an idea of mystery, of something not achieved, a certain disquiet.' *E la nave va* means 'And the Ship Sails On', he said, but its real significance is 'Life goes on', the implicit motto of all his films. It seemed a limp summation of an appealing but essentially trivial film. Fellini was going on, agreed most people. But in what direction? And why?

30   Face the Music and Dance:
Ginger e Fred and *Intervista*

'What can you possibly have to say to others, you who
have never been able to tell the truth to the person closest
to you, to the woman who's grown old by your side?'
Otto e mezzo

Since the *Love Duet* débâcle, Fellini had stayed at arm's length from
Ingmar Bergman. He was not pleased to learn that the 1983 Venice
Festival, at which he'd agreed to show *E la nave va* out of competition,
was giving red-carpet treatment to *Fanny and Alexander*, Bergman's
most ambitious film in years. It was also awarding him an Honorary
Golden Lion. Fellini wrote to Festival director Gian Luigi Rondi that
he couldn't get to Venice until after Bergman had left, claiming he was
working on 'the English version' of his film, but this smells of pretext.
For his part, Bergman, who, playing up to his reclusive image, claimed
to be nervous of crowds and insisted on being shuttled from his hotel to
the cinema by armoured car, showed no sign of wanting to meet
Fellini. While the rest of the festival watched his film, he screened
Fellini's in private and left for Sweden soon after. His reaction isn't
recorded.*

The public screening of *E la nave va* on 10 September, at the climax
of the Festival, was wildly successful, with an emotional audience
welcoming Fellini back with fifteen minutes of applause. But he was
deeply depressed by the contrast between this enthusiasm and the
blank ignorance of the Italian film-going public who would have the
final say on its fate. 'The other day I went to the cinema,' he told Daniel
Toscan du Plantier. 'A character comes in, a big blond kid with
chewing gum and a Walkman. He sits down near me and during the
whole of the film he doesn't take off the Walkman! That's the spectator

*Fellini also saw *Fanny and Alexander*, apparently in the French version, since he
specified that the same team under Michel Drach dub *E la nave va*.

of today.' After the fuss died down, he realised that the film, at 150 minutes, was unlikely to attract even his most devoted admirers, let alone the Walkman set, and cut it first to 137 minutes, then to 120.

At the end of September, Fellini and Giulietta went to Rimini. In a moment of fantasy he'd told a journalist he could almost see himself spending more time there if he owned a tiny cottage by the old port on the Marecchia. Encouraged by the young Socialist mayor, Massimo Conti, a committee led by Titta Benzi presented him with such a house, though Fellini insists he bought it himself. His visit to take possession became the occasion of a week-long festival of all his films, culminating in the first public screening of *E la nave va*.

Fellini has always seen television in apocalyptic terms, as what Jean Douchet called a 'technocratic power that feeds on the cinema and bleeds it white'. Throughout the eighties he continued to fight the guerrilla war begun after the botched transmission of *I clowns*, though his quarrel was increasingly not with RAI but with the commercial channels that dominated the field. Periodically he signed a truce and accepted TV money to make a film, only to go well over his budget and spend the next year sniping at the medium for its parsimony and lack of vision. Like his rejection of Hollywood, it was a disastrous strategy, cutting him off from a major source of funding. He'd courageously but wrong-headedly chained himself to the wheel of the art cinema, which was going down with all hands.

To Fellini, television's devil incarnate was media magnate Silvio Berlusconi, whose empire included Canale 5, Italy's most successful commercial channel. Under him, Italian TV had become a wallow of cheap titillation and relentless salesmanship. Movies, invariably dubbed if they were foreign and riddled with commercials, vied with game shows, mindless variety spectaculars and, later at night, soft-core porn and hit shows like *Tutti-Frutti* in which a succession of pretty young Italian housewives stripped for the camera.

Berlusconi owned the rights to many of Fellini's early movies in perpetuity. He also bought his Cineriz films from the bankrupt Rizzoli empire. When these played on TV with commercials, Fellini went to court to block the screenings. Three cases were thrown out, since directors had no legal control over their work and the concept of intellectual property was not then sufficiently well established. He fought most vigorously on TV itself. He had sympathetic hearing on RAI's *Viaggio intorno all'uomo*, but was incensed by Canale 5's *Tivu Tivu*, whose presenter Arrigo Levi, after interviewing him, 'hand-picked', according to *Variety*, 'the least damning of three magazine poll stats on spot breaks during film features to mitigate Fellini's complaints'. The polls ignored by Levi showed that 53 per cent of Italian viewers found commercials in movies 'annoying' and 30 per cent 'intolerable'. Fifty per cent favoured a law completely banning their use during films. The battle continued until 1989, when the son of Pietro Germi won a decision that each insertion of advertising 'represents a change in the fundamental nature of the work'. Fellini said: 'In the long run, the very long run, there is a little justice in the world after all.' By then, however, he was making *La voce della luna/ Voices of the Moon*, which was financed almost entirely by TV. Whatever he said in public, privately Fellini had accepted the inevitable.

His first concession took place surreptitiously as early as 1984. In June the 'secret project' on which he was working at Cinecittà was revealed as a series of TV ads for Campari vermouth. He followed with others for Barilla pasta. He'd been persuaded by advertisers who hoped to win for Italian commercials the same high artistic reputation they enjoyed in Britain, where the best new feature directors, men like Alan Parker and Ridley Scott, emerged from advertising. Antonioni and Zeffirelli also agreed, having been promised a more or less free hand. Visibly humiliated by the revelation of his volte-face, Fellini initially dismissed the rumour as ridiculous, then admitted jokingly that he might have shot the thirty- and sixty-second Campari promos, but only 'in a trance'.

The first Campari ad featured a bored woman looking at a window in which her friend provides a series of exotic and dream-like views by remote control. She perks up when, asked if she wouldn't prefer an Italian landscape, she's offered an image of a Campari bottle, tilted and floodlit like the Tower of Pisa. For Barilla pasta, Fellini showed lovers in a smart restaurant overawed by the succession of French dishes until 'Rigatoni' is mentioned, at which everyone, even the waiters, relax. In another, the woman coos with erotic delight at the thought of this particular noodle.* He followed the Campari and Barilla campaigns with commercials for other sponsors and even, in February 1992, for the Italian Republican Party. 'Cinecittà is the fabricator of dreams,' says party secretary Giorgio La Malfa, strolling

---

*Peter Bondanella claims that 'rigatoni' in Riminese slang signified fellatio, which, if true, gives added piquancy to the final comment: 'Barilla always makes you feel *al dente*', i.e. hard.

round the studio, 'and I dream of a cleaner Italy.' For a 1992 Banco di Roma compaign, he employed the dream image again with a model train gliding out of a tunnel from under a mountain shaped like a giant fist, and a passenger waking to the idea that a loan from the bank can make dreams come true.

The commercials divided Fellini's admirers. The more loyal preferred to see them as snide attacks on the form rather than simply crass money-makers. The Campari ad could, they suggest, be an implicit criticism of mindless channel-jumping. Fellini, on the other hand, has said the image of sitting in a moving train staring out of the window is an old one for him, and a metaphor for his creative life. 'When I'm not making a film, I'm preparing one,' he says. 'If I'm not preparing one, I think about the next. When I'm at rest, it seems to me – pardon the romantic image – that I'm leaning on my elbow and looking out the window of a train that's about to leave, free of all obligation, of all responsibility. Then the train leaves, and the vibration puts me in my preferred situation, that of movement, and of images passing behind the glass, ceaselessly. It's the attitude of someone who has an alibi, a justification for his lack of responsibility in life, [who] has the role of watching everything around him, but a rather vague relationship with reality.'

After *E la nave va*, Fellini flirted again with the spirit world. An admirer of the work of Mexican novelist Carlos Castaneda, he met the author of *Voyage to Ixtlan* through an actress who'd worked as his assistant on *La città delle donne*. Fascinated by his tales of strange happenings in the hinterland, Fellini interrupted plans for a new film at the end of 1984 and flew to Los Angeles, where he rendezvous'd with Castaneda.

Up to this point, the record is relatively straightforward. Alberto Grimaldi was living in Los Angeles and there was talk of him backing Fellini's new film, a satire on television. Seeing that the director was enthusiastic about Castaneda's work and apparently interested in filming it, Grimaldi also bought the rights to his novels. It's less clear whether Fellini and Castaneda then travelled together to the Yucatán to visit ancient Mayan sites. With a group that included Grimaldi's son Maurizio but also a medium, an actor, a parapsychologist and a beautiful girl named Sybil who attracted paranormal phenomena, they are supposed to have gone to Mexico where, despite losing touch with Castaneda, they went on to Chichen Itzá and the ruined Mayan city of Tulum, where certain puzzling manifestations took place. Did this happen? There's no circumstantial evidence of the trip; only a script treatment called *Voyage to Tulum* which Fellini never filmed but allowed to be published as a serial in *Corriere della sera* in May 1986. Later, comic-book artist Milo Manara freely adapted it into a graphic novel, a stylish visual improvisation on an event that may itself be nothing more than a Fellini invention.

Whether he returned from Yucatán in the winter of 1984/5 with insights achieved in Mayan ruins or simply from Beverly Hills with nothing more than a promise of money from Alberto Grimaldi, Fellini immediately pitched into the new project, now called *Ginger e Fred*.

'It was me who was the origin of the project,' insists Giulietta. 'I wanted to make for television a series of six episodes where I would interpret each time a contemporary personality, anchored in today's society. Some great directors – Antonioni, Carlo Lizzani, Zeffirelli, Fellini – had given their OK, but the project was judged too dear and abandoned. That's how the one episode to be made, the history of Ginger, an old-time music-hall dancer, came to be made as a feature.' Not only did Grimaldi come up with $7 million; he also optioned the other specials in the series, though none was ever produced.

The Ginger episode was to have been Fellini's contribution to this anthology, and to write it he'd returned to his oldest and most reliable collaborator. Tullio Pinelli was astonished when Fellini appeared on his doorstep, though the habit of picking up old acquaintances when he needed them was typical. Fellini offered two projects. One was Franz Kafka's fragmentary and uncompleted novel *Amerika*. The other was the notion of two old partners in a dance team from the thirties being briefly reunited for a TV Christmas show. Not one to hold a grudge, Pinelli ignored the fact that, except for the odd social occasions and phone calls, he'd heard nothing from Fellini in twenty years, and got to work on the plot of what would become *Ginger e Fred*. Once they had an outline, Tonino Guerra came in to provide the sceptical critical voice once supplied by Flaiano.

Masina plays Amelia Bonetti, a trim and prosperous grandmother in her sixties, who comes to Rome for a reunion on the TV show *Ed ecco a voi/It's for you* with Pippo Botticella (Mastroianni), the dancer with whom she made up the duo of Ginger and Fred four decades before. Though they were lovers then, she hasn't seen him in years.

She arrives at a jammed Termini station. A promotion for pork sausage is in full swing – literally – with a gigantic *zampano di maiale* dangling above the crowd while peasant musicians play and a chef hands out samples. Also poised above the crowd, equally inflated, is a

TV screen which bombards it with commercials for turd-like sausages and every imaginable form of pasta, including one that supposedly makes you slim. On a tiny TV in the van which takes them to their hotel through piles of rotting garbage, the driver watches a puppet Dante advertising Beatrix watches. The hotel staff are too busy watching a football telecast to check Amelia in, and the bellboy who takes her to her room also puts on the TV, not to demonstrate that it works but to keep watching the game. That night, she takes a walk outside the hotel, only to run into the new Rome: a menacing mugger and a bike gang gathering outside a garish disco – yet more reminders of Fellini's apocalyptic vision of the motel in *Il viaggio*. Unable to sleep because of someone snoring in the next room, she pounds on the door, to find the snorer is Pippo. Unlike Amelia, he's aged badly. A near derelict, he earns a little money selling encyclopedias.

Next morning the hotel is bulging with a freak show of guests for *Ed ecco a voi*. They include a cow with eighteen teats, accompanied by its owners in picturesque regional costume, and a troupe of midget flamenco dancers called 'Los Lilliputs'. They join an aged admiral, a transvestite who wants to bring sex to men in prison, a terrorist hostage whose finger was severed during ransom negotiations, a priest who's left the Church and married – he'll be badgered into kissing his new bride on camera – and another, played in an odd cameo by photographer Jean-Henri Lartigue, who believes he can fly, and has cured the sick simply by handling a photo of them.

Everyone is parked in the huge, noisy and overcrowded studio cafeteria. Pippo gets into conversation with a writer who's signing copies of his new book. Pippo boasts that he himself composes epigrams, which he says have been compared to those of Martial. He quotes one – roughly: 'When you're horny for a midget/The girl's as long as your digit' – to the scorn of the writer and his girlfriends, and the embarrassment of Amelia.

Even inside the network's own headquarters TVs blare everywhere, omnipresent but unwatched, gushing commercials and game shows, mostly to do with food. Fellini saw a compelling comparison between TV and eating. In a 1985 article for *L'europeo* headed 'This Kind of Television Doesn't Deserve to Survive', where he vented his loathing of Berlusconi, he wrote: 'The viewer is a taster who always has his mouth full but can't taste anything any more because he can't distinguish between one flavour and another.' He enjoyed making some fake commercials, which he dropped randomly into *Ginger e Fred*, hoping to undermine the real commercials which he knew would interrupt it.

In one, a baby from Mars discovers a new snack food, and in another a liqueur is so delicious it raises a man from the dead.

The sexiest of the channel's presentation announcers is identified significantly as 'a good friend of the company president'. They meet the president (Narcisso Vicario) when he drops in to greet the guests. Ginger has been growing increasingly jaded with the show and especially with Pippo, who's fallen back into his old ways, drinking, bragging and bossing her about. She's ready to quit when the president, confessing shyly that he's an Astaire fan, partners her in a few steps. (Berlusconi is proud of having started as a band singer, and often breaks into song.) The applause ignites her show-business instincts and she finishes putting on her make-up and wig.

The shooting of *Ginger e Fred* had its ironic and finally disastrous parallels with real life. From the start, Giulietta insisted this was her vehicle. After watching the first rushes, she complained that Fellini and cameraman Tonino delli Colli were showing her in the worst possible light, and in particular doing nothing to disguise her wrinkles. Some scenes were reshot, but not to her satisfaction. Delli Colli baulked at putting even more gauze over his lenses, and Fellini closed down the film. When it started up again six weeks later Ennio Guarnieri was behind the camera, and the photography more flattering.

Ed ecco a voi, presided over by an unctuous Franco Fabrizi in a lamé jacket, is Berlusconi TV at its glitziest, with leggy dancers, a studio audience of 500 and a full orchestra. Guests are fed in like sausage meat, given a few minutes, then ejected. From the audience Fabrizi introduces a woman who's achieved the significant feat of giving up TV for a month. The experience has unhinged her, since she bursts into song. Fellini lets his imagination loose on the rest of the night's attractions, which include doubles of Clark Gable, Bette Davis, Proust, Kafka and Woody Allen, a man who's invented edible panties, a group of muscle-pumping bodybuilders and a girl training for a media career who has a sheet of glass the size of a TV screen fixed in front of her face through which she makes announcements.

As Amelia and Pippo come on stage, the electricity fails and they're left for five minutes in the dark. Pippo, drunk and frightened, is all for sneaking away, but Amelia persuades him to stay, and when the lights go on they perform creditably enough to a medley of thirties oldies like 'Let's Face the Music and Dance'. At Termini that night, Amelia boards her train, half hoping that Pippo will follow her, even though she knows any life together would be hell, but he takes a seat among the other drifters who haunt the station, while overhead the *zampano* hangs in the dark and the enormous TV flickers.

The atmosphere on *Ginger e Fred* degenerated as shooting progressed. Masina's demands for more flattering treatment and Fellini's ill-humour drained the crew of will and energy. 'Towards the end,' said stills photographer Deborah Beer, 'the atmosphere had really deteriorated. We were shooting on a railway platform. I went down to street level for a moment, and when I came back the place was empty. Everyone had disappeared. Finally someone told me: "That's it. The film's finished. Everyone's gone home." No farewells, no party. It just ended.'

In June Fellini was honoured by the Film Society of New York's Lincoln Center, a group of wealthy arts enthusiasts who periodically paid tribute to a major film-maker (though never before a foreigner) with a $150 a plate dinner and a gala presentation of a pot-pourri of his works. Though he claimed still to have four more days' shooting, Fellini attended with Giulietta, Mastroianni and Anouk Aimée. The *New Yorker* published a tongue-in-cheek account of a lunch at the Darien, Connecticut, house of wealthy socialite Dorothy Cullinan, the Society's chairperson, apparently more interested in showing off her Senufo sculptures and heated swimming-pool than in anything Fellini might have had to say.

The Rome première of *Ginger e Fred* in February 1986 raised few temperatures. It had become routine in Italy to fob off Fellini films with perfunctory first releases. Exhibitors wary of a hostile public reaction sometimes screened them for a day or two in their larger theatre, then shunted them into a smaller one. The new film fulfilled the worst fears of its crew: 125 minutes was too long to endure Giulietta's relentlessly perky persona and Fellini's bilious view of TV, and most audiences stayed away. On 13 March, as Fellini was getting ready to go to New York for the US première, then on to Hollywood for the Oscars, where he'd agreed to join Akira Kurosawa and Billy Wilder in presenting that year's Best Picture award, Ginger Rogers issued a statement from retirement claiming she found the film (which she hadn't seen) 'offensive to her reputation and personality', and sued for $8 million. In public, Fellini shrugged off the threat, suspecting – probably correctly – an exercise in publicity-seeking from the chronically crotchety Ginger, but it disinclined him to appear in Hollywood just then. *Variety* published his face-saving excuse that he'd 'fractured a leg last week while shopping with his wife Giulietta Masina on via Marguetta [*sic*] in Rome'. John Huston took his place.

*

That summer Fellini announced a new film, to be produced by the little-known Produzione Aliosha. He was vague about the theme, the performers – about everything, in fact, except that it would be a semi-documentary, set at Cinecittà and partly financed by RAI. For once, his customary evasiveness was justified, since he had little or no idea about its content. A brainwave of actors' agent turned producer Ibrahim Moussa (whom he calls '*vitelloni*-esque'), the film was prompted by the fact that Cinecittà would celebrate its fiftieth anniversary in 1987. Francesco Barilli was making the studio's own slick commemorative documentary, *Fifty Years of Cinecittà*, but there was room for one more, especially with the Fellini name attached and aimed at television. At least Moussa thought so, to the extent of investing 5 billion lire – $1 million at 1987 rates.

Unveiling the deal, with a deadline of January 1987, Moussa said this would be the first of three productions with Fellini. The second was to be about his life-long love–hate relationship with opera. The third, announced as a film about the Fulgor Cinema, would, Fellini admitted later, have dealt also with Hollywood, re-creating his trips there in the fifties, in particular his meetings with Hecht, Hill and Lancaster and their mysterious envoy Serenella, and his first visit to Disneyland. 'A film of a day in the life of Disneyland,' he's said. '*That* would be the real film.'

Everyone was studiedly vague about what was being celebrated. When a journalist at Cannes mentioned that the project was 'commissioned by RAI for the Cinecittà anniversary', Fellini said: 'Not at all. I ignored that', and claimed he'd been inspired by finding himself alone in the empty studios during the summer holidays. Nobody wanted to be seen raking up the ghost of Mussolini.

On the other hand, in his present state of mind there could hardly have been a more reassuring or appropriate subject for Fellini than Cinecittà. After the disaster of *Ginger e Fred*, it had become for him less a workplace than a Never-Never-Land of lost content. 'I feel myself comforted by the idea that Cinecittà exists,' he mused. 'Let's say it's like a fortress, an alibi if you like. That's it, it's perhaps an alibi.'

Over the half-century, Cinecittà hadn't worn well. Though it had been refurbished and modernised during the great days of *Cleopatra*, those were long past and the place was visibly down at heel. A government grant in the eighties had been spent almost entirely on a new coat of paint. Once a long tram ride from Rome, the studio was now in the city's outer suburbs, and a ring of slab-like apartment buildings stared down on the weedy backlot. Asked whether Cinecittà made an impression on him, actor Harold Innocent said: 'Yes, and not a very good one. It's rather shabby, a bit like an old aircraft hangar. And there are a lot of cats around.' Freddie Jones was even less enthusiastic. The power habitually shut down on *E la nave va* (the inspiration for the blackout of *Ginger e Fred*) – once because a rat had gnawed through a cable. The wooden floors were also rotted and uneven. 'I wonder that some international star hasn't broken her ankle,' he says.

RAI, as usual, was prepared to invest only half of the budget and Moussa had problems in raising the rest. As Fellini tells it, he came to him on his knees and, metaphorically clutching his children to him, appealed for him to turn the documentary into a theatrical feature. Fellini agreed, but only if they dropped the other two films, though since he has never, with the exception of Rizzoli, worked for any producer on two consecutive projects, the concession was simply a *de facto* acceptance of the inevitable.

Faced with a film of twice the planned length and a deadline less than six months away, Fellini turned to Gianfranco Angelucci, the assistant who helped make the TV special *E il Casanova di Fellini?* Angelucci suggested they simply conflate the formats of *Block-notes, I clowns* and *Roma*: that is, a director shooting a documentary investigates Cinecittà. Fellini himself, if he wasn't the documentarist, would appear in a few scenes, as would old friends in flippant cameos. There would also be a dramatised flashback to his childhood. Fellini preferred this time to be subject rather than reporter, so a Japanese TV crew filming him became the pretext for the film. After being announced as *Block-notes di un regista II* and *Appunti di Federico Fellini/Federico Fellini's Notes*, the film was released simply as *Intervista*.

Intervista opens with one of the most evocative scenes in all of Fellini's later work. The darkened grounds of Cinecittà, plunged in the soft Roman night, are aroused by a convoy of cars. Headlights swerve across the familiar ochre walls. The full invasion of a film crew follows, led by lighting cameraman Tonino delli Colli and Menicuccio, his chief electrician. An enormous cherry-picker crane is unlimbered. Banks of movie lights flare and smoke machines belch clouds of silver fog through the old pines that have already seen so much fantasy. The ingredients are familiar from almost every Fellini film, those components of which he never seems to become weary – night, mist and the moon.

At the height of this drama Fellini himself arrives, with a retinue that includes the inquisitive Japanese. To them, and to us, he explains he's come here to his spiritual home to shoot a scene for a new film. For the *Viaggio* of *Block-notes* he substitutes another unrealised project, *Amerika*.

Kafka, who never went to the United States, wrote *Amerika* between 1911 and 1914, but the novel remained unfinished and wasn't published until 1927. It's a classic European's view of the New World, refracted, like Fellini's own vision, through the prism of cheap fiction, the movies and hand-me-down immigrant tales. Kafka had aimed for something like a novel by Dickens, a tragicomic fantasy peopled with expansive benefactors and plausible rogues who bully and cajole his naïve hero, sixteen-year-old Karl Rossman. Fellini had been a Kafka admirer ever since Marchesi introduced him to *Metamorphosis* on *Marc'Aurelio*. 'Kafka moved me profoundly,' he says. 'I was struck by the way he confronted the mystery of things, their unknown quality, the sense of being in a labyrinth, and daily life turned magical.' Though the book's episodic structure appealed to him as a vehicle for some speculations about the United States, he probably never seriously intended filming it. The idea of doing so had come to him when a German producer asked him to direct a version of *War and Peace*. He'd never read Tolstoy but the approach set him toying with the idea of literary adaptation, a form he'd avoided all his life.

For *Intervista*, he chose one of *Amerika*'s more baroque scenes. Karl, having fallen in with Robinson and Delamarche, two rogues who manage to lose him his job as a lift-boy and the patronage of his rich uncle, is taken to the apartment of Delamarche's mistress, an overweight and sluttish opera singer named Brunelda. Ordered to lie down on a heap of curtains, he goes to sleep, but is woken by the sounds of Delamarche and Brunelda making love. Claiming she needs to take a bath to cool down, Brunelda orders Karl and Robinson out on to the balcony, where the two find some food, including a tin of sardines. Sharing this improvised meal, Robinson fantasises about their remaining in the apartment as Brunelda's servants, but nothing is ever settled, and this section ends with Karl, still puzzled and unsure, dropping off to sleep while Brunelda mutters over her bad dreams.

The one scene Fellini shoots in *Intervista* would have startled the dour Kafka with its eroticism. Set in a sumptuous Edwardian apartment it shows two men (supposedly the actors trying out for the role of Delamarche) eating sardines with relish and licking oil from their fingers, all the time being directed by Fellini in his typical detailed monologue. The two then roll Brunelda to a large bath in a wheeled armchair, help her in and bathe her, after which she's placed back in the chair and trundled out of the studio, heading for a sequence even more remote from Kafka, to judge from a conversation between assistant-director Maurizio Mein and Nadia Ottaviani, the girl whom Fellini has cast as Cinecittà's Vestal Virgin, a sort of studio emblem. 'And now what's going to happen?' she asks. Mein replies: 'We continue to the end of the screen-test, if you don't mind. That's on the street, where Karl will accompany Brunelda in the wheelchair to the brothel.'

Like the film essays that preceded it, *Intervista* interweaves three strands. One is the reconstructed tests for *Amerika*, with their dramatised search for talent, the make-up and costuming of the candidates and some sideways glances at Fellini collaborators like Danilo Donati and Maurizio Mein at work. A harassed Mein is besieged by people convinced they're 'the Fellini type'. His confusion is contrasted with the sang-froid of Donati, who's shown contending coolly with everything from Fellini's expensive demands to a bomb hoax. When the threat is phoned through, he simply tells everyone he's forgotten an appointment, shoos them out to an early lunch and waits for the bomb squad to arrive. The second strand is a visual poem about Cinecittà itself, the camera prowling its corridors, glancing into its rooms. On this level, it celebrates old-fashioned film-making and the studio which emblematises that tradition and is under threat, like the tradition itself.

Watching Fellini prepare the *Amerika* shot, the Japanese interviewer asks him when he first came to the studio. The question triggers a flashback into the third strand of the film in which 'Sergio Rubini', his 1937 surrogate, takes the long tram ride to Cinecittà and has his initial encounter with big-budget film-making in the form of a bloated Indian epic starring the seductive Greta Gonda-like actress who receives him in her all-pink caravan. We already know that most of this, like the bulk of Fellini's filmed memoirs, is fantasy, but the realisation doesn't diminish the sense of discovery he conveys in the scenes of Sergio travelling through sunny green countryside on a tram and chatting up a pretty girl. The trip has the casual illogic of a dream. Sergio sees Red Indians, waterfalls and elephants on a seashore, which turn his journey into something out of a Hollywood romance.

Returning to the production strand, Fellini is shown searching downtown Rome for the Casa del Passagero, the depot from which he started that journey and, finding it a ruin, creating another by refurbishing the company's workshop. A tram, vintage 1939, is built in two sections and mounted on a truck to shoot the journey.

By the middle of *Intervista* the strands have become inextricably entwined, with Rubini, after having played the younger Fellini, being caught in the preparations for the *Amerika* tests. He ends up trying out for a role, as does the girl he meets on the tram. Another candidate is a pretty girl in male drag. There's a surreal ecumenicalism about *Intervista* that gives it an irresistible charm. For no particular reason, Fellini tosses in a tribute to his best-known performers. Mastroianni appears outside his office window on a crane, dressed in top hat, white tie and tails, and supposedly on his way to play *Mandrake*. Both of them, with the inevitable retinue and the Japanese TV crew, then pay a surprise visit to Anita Ekberg at her country house. They watch some extracts from *La dolce vita* – the Caracalla sequence and, inevitably, the wade in the Fontana di Trevi – inadequately projected on a sheet spread across the room. The greying Mastroianni and a bloated Ekberg, diplomatically enveloped in a sheet, watch with bleary amusement. Fellini, however, never shows his own reaction.

Intervista ends untidily on the muddy backlot. Interrupted by a rainstorm, the cast shelter under sheets of polythene, huddled in cheery companionability – a scene taken from a real-life incident on *E la nave va*, when rain interrupted shooting at the Panetone pasta factory. As if stumbling in from another film, a tribe of mounted Indians sweep over the hill, but the lances they brandish are TV antennae. Victorious in the film as they never were in real life, they are driven away by the movie people.

Back in the studio, Fellini's own voice tells us the film is over, but 'it seems to me I hear the voice of an old producer. "What, that's how you finish? Without a thread of hope, a ray of sunshine. Give me at least a ray of sunshine," he would beg me at the first screenings of all my films. A ray of sunshine? Oh, I don't know. We'll try . . . .' The lights go down except for a small patch of light framed by a camera. An assistant steps into shot with a clapperboard, says: 'Take one!' and snaps the board. The image freezes – not here, as it is so often, a cliché, but a touching assurance of endurance.

Fellini has always spoken ambivalently about *Intervista*, calling it a *'filmetto'*, even though it runs for 112 minutes. At the same time, however, it was the film he defiantly included in his list of the top ten films of all time for the *Sight and Sound* survey in 1992. Though not shown in the US or UK until 1993, it won a reputation as one of the most distinctive of all his retakes on autobiography, showing him, as

Robin Buss says, in the role of a 'friend and patron, treating Cinecittà as his private estate, commanding a world of fantasy and fun'. Fellini was still the King of Cinecittà, and of Rome. Why, one can see him wondering, did people not bow any more?

31   Just a Little Silence: *La voce della luna*

'You tell me that once *Fellini* was put in an insane
asylum, that he was mad for a while. I hope he is still
"mad" in the best sense of the word; mad as poets and
creators should be. Mad in a world of idiots and
murderers, of slaves and dope addicts'
Henry Miller in a letter, May 1970

Intervista was awarded a Special Prize at the 1987 Cannes Festival
and both the Audience Prize and Grand Prize at Moscow, but its
distribution was sparse. Whatever Moussa may have intended for the
film, it was perceived everywhere as a TV documentary masquerading
as a feature, and dismissed accordingly. Perhaps for this reason, Fellini
was more than usually vehement in its defence. When the channel
transmitting it in Italy admitted it proposed to interrupt it with two
commercial breaks and a news broadcast, he complained so bitterly
that it was shown intact. The concession infuriated Franco Zeffirelli,
who hadn't become any less strident since he disrupted the Venice
award ceremony for *La strada*. He declared that in his opinion
Intervista would have benefited from 'a little pause', and accused
Fellini of allowing his other films to be shown by Berlusconi without
the same stipulation. Fellini called his remarks 'in bad faith, unin-
formed and liable to be misconstrued'. When Zeffirelli refused to
withdraw them, he sued for slander.

Also in 1987, in Brussels, a panel of thirty professionals from
eighteen European countries named *Otto e mezzo* as the best European
film of all time and Fellini the best director. Typical of the honours
heaped on Fellini, it was cold comfort, since money was as scarce as it
had been for a decade.

For years Fellini had planned a film about insanity. In the years
since *La libere donne di Magliano* his belief that madness wasn't a

disease so much as a self-protective adjustment to unbearable circumstances – 'learning to tolerate the intolerable', as he put it – had become widely accepted, partly through the work of the British psychiatrist R. D. Laing. When Fellini published an album of portraits from his photo collection in 1986, Laing wrote the introduction.

Of Italy's new young comedians, Fellini had been most interested by Roberto Benigni, a balding, pale and intense man with a Woody Allen air of distraction who would eventually achieve international exposure as Peter Sellers' replacement in the *Pink Panther* films. They'd flirted for years with the idea of working together. Fellini tested him for *La città della donne* and *Ginger e Fred*, asking him in the latter to read for a character of sixty. He also gave him a girl's lines for *Intervista*, presumably thinking of him for the drag role of the actor trying out for Karl. Each time, Benigni sensed Fellini wasn't serious, that it was part of a game, a 'love affair that might eventually bear fruit', but when they met in 1988 to discuss a new film there was, Benigni said, a difference in the way Fellini looked at him, something in the eyes and lips that told him they were on another plane.

Fellini gave Benigni six pages he'd written with Pinelli, distantly based on *Il poema dei lunatici/The Poem of Lunatics*, a first novel of the young Bolognese academic Ermanno Cavazzoni. It was the story of Ivo, recently discharged from a mental hospital, uncured but harmless. A sort of Pierrot Lunaire, second cousin to Gelsomina and Osvaldo, the mute autistic child of *La strada*, he wanders the foggy fields of an unnamed countryside in northern Italy with other outcasts, listening to the voices that speak to him from the wells, and obsessed always by the white face of the moon.

The treatment was extensively revised with Cavazzoni's friendly but increasingly remote assistance. Fellini had believed for years that he could do without writers, and with the new film he tried to put the belief into practice. He poured more of himself into the script than he had into anything he'd worked on for a decade, finding most of his material, not surprisingly, in his Gambettola childhood. However, the tunnel between conception and filming was longer and darker than for many years. He finished the script in 1987, but it wasn't until the middle of 1989 that Mario and Vittorio Cecchi Gori coaxed a downpayment from RAI and assembled enough French and German TV pre-sales to fund *La voce della luna*.

The first sequence is a companion piece to the opening of *Intervista* in the moon-drenched grounds of Cinecittà or the scene in *Casanova* where Casanova encounters in the moonlit garden a willing virgin made almost ghostly by repeated bleeding to cure her erotic swoons. Under the moon, Ivo wanders the misty fields, and sees half a dozen other men sneaking towards a lone house. They're chanting: 'We're going to see the cunt', and offer to let him share their recreation, that of watching the house owner do an amateur strip-tease to the TV (a gibe at *Tutti-Frutti*). He declines – she is, after all, his aunt – and starts quoting them the legend of Juno and Zeus, but they're more interested in the middle-aged and overweight lady prancing around in her corset and stockings.

Pigafetta, supervisor of the local cemetery, interrupts them, and Ivo walks with him to the cemetery. Though it's late, the place is busy with the village's more unconventional residents. One of them, an oboist, describes how, during his practice, he stumbled on a group of notes with the diabolical power to move furniture, and to summon up a greedy creature who, describing himself as 'The Great Eater', empties his refrigerator.

Ivo climbs up on the roof of the columbarium to get closer to the moon. In memory he drifts back to his childhood, and the young grandmother who used to call him 'Pinocchino'. She carries him out of a storm, dries him in front of a roaring fire and places him lovingly in her big bed, warmed by a *prete*. Relaxed, he describes how sounds manifest themselves to him visually. The autobiographical link here is explicit. A Gambettola boy had suffered from a similar neurological dysfunction. The bellow of an ox was like 'a huge piece of red lasagna [coming] out of the wall, a sort of very long carpet floating in the air that would cross his head under his left eye and vanish, little by little, in the sun's reflection'.

The town in *La voce della luna* isn't identified. Fellini said only that he meant it to be in the Podana, the waterlogged area of the Po delta where Rossellini shot the last sequence of *Paisà* and where Gradisca was supposed to have settled. Caricaturist Nino Za had also retired there, to Reggiolo, and the fact that Fellini called on him to congratulate him on his eighty-sixth birthday shortly before he began shooting convinced people that this was his model. However, from the recreation of his grandmother's house, like a scaled-down version of the farm in *Otto e mezzo*, it's clear that he had Gambettola in mind.

To play opposite Benigni as the bewildered Prefect Gonnella, a high official who's cracked under the strain and who believes, like Fellini at his more depressed times, that 'everything is false', he chose Paolo Villaggio, a fat, grey, middle-aged actor with a major reputation in Italian comedy. Physically the two men resemble Laurel and Hardy, but the effect of their ensemble playing is closer to Beckett, as is the film's dream-like style.

Ivo is fascinated by Aldina, a pale blonde with curly silver hair whom he first glimpses asleep in a shaft of moonlight. 'She's like the moon,' he whispers, and the effect is genuinely romantic, a hint at the softer Fellini of which his work allows only occasional glimpses. His erotic preoccupations are more obtrusively on show in the story of Nestore, who marries Marisa, the town's flirtatious manicurist, only to find her sexually insatiable. She drives him so relentlessly that he calls her 'The Locomotive' and feels as if he is strapped to a steam engine of fornication. Inspired by this metaphor, Fellini fills their bedroom with steam and flying leaves, shakes the pictures and sends giant shadows spilling across the walls.

Giacomo Leopardi, whose distant, moonstruck poems Fellini had used as an excuse for his adolescent moodiness, is Ivo's *alter ego*. He quotes him often, and a picture of Leopardi hangs in the room in the family home where, his sister reminds him, his madness began. Below it is a Pinocchio puppet designed in imitation of Chiostri's illustrations. When Ivo visits the house, which now belongs to his sister, she puts him to bed. That night, he wakes to the moon and wanders out into a silvery landscape of madness.

Benigni found working with Fellini as confusing an experience as had Freddie Jones. Unconcerned with nuances of performance, Fellini told him that only his appearance mattered. He should think of himself, he suggested, as Ava Gardner. When a shot was done he wouldn't tell him to do it again but turn to the cameraman and ask if he was good-looking. Benigni was given three make-up people whose job it was to protect him every minute. 'I couldn't go to the toilet without someone going along with me to make sure I didn't trip.' One senses his scepticism about such idiosyncratic methods. The cinema had changed a great deal in the eighties, but Fellini showed no signs of changing with it. His casting suggestions for *La voce della luna* show how badly he was out of touch. A letter to producer Pietro Notarianni about performers is filled with names from a decade before, or even earlier. 'Do you remember the famous Raimu?' he asks. Another character brings Buster Keaton to mind, and also Daniel Emilfork, from *Casanova*. Many of the others he mentions are French, including a clown from Paris's Crazy Horse strip club. They reflect a world which, for Fellini, had contracted to a few shows a year and almost no films at all.

The first half of *La voce della luna* is suffused with lunar calm, and a kindness far from typical of Fellini's work, but once the stage has been set he can't help trotting out his hobby-horses. He excoriates the degrading effects of the mass media and encroaching youth culture (which, in promoting the film, he called 'one of the most repugnant forms of lowness of our time'). The town is taken over by the annual Gnocchi Festival, presided over by a Gnocchi King and Queen in grotesque inflated outfits. A bumptious midget entrepreneur announces he's launching the town's own TV station. When his beloved Aldina is elected 'Miss Farina' in a shower of flour, Ivo dumps a plate of gnocchi bolognese over the head of the man dancing with her and flees to the countryside. He tries once more to follow his voices down a well, in hopes of a better world. Instead, Gonnella shows him another contemporary hell – a monstrous disco in a factory, with hundreds of kids dancing to Michael Jackson from a giant ghetto blaster hanging from the ceiling. Appalled, he breaks into the DJ's cage and demands over the PA system if anyone there has ever heard the sound of a violin. He's tossed out.

Soon after, the town fills with TV crews who hang huge screens around the main square to show the latest sensation: the burly Micheluzzi brothers, the town's working-class technocrats, have managed to trap the moon with their giant harvesting machine. They're offhand about their feat. 'The moon is a woman. A little smile, you blow in her ear and she falls into your hand.' Peasants kneel to worship the moon, roped down in a barn, blazing hard white light into the countryside, while in town intellectuals wrangle over what questions they should ask of it. A cardinal shrugs off the query: 'What do we have to ask? We know everything.'

With the piazza quiet again, ownership of the town reverts to its outcasts. Ivo stares up at the moon, now restored to the sky. It begins to talk to him in Aldina's voice, telling him he's fortunate to hear the voices of the moon, even if they do give him a headache. As a crestfallen Ivo tries to understand, she says: 'Oh, I almost forgot the most important thing.' Aldina's face briefly appears on the surface and she giggles *'Publicità'* – time for a commercial break. Hopeless, Ivo wanders back to the well in the foggy fields and bends over, listening. 'If only we could have some silence,' he says, 'if things were a little quieter, we might understand something.'

Ironically, Cinecittà's backlot was now so cluttered with junk and overlooked by apartment buildings that there was no room to build the large exterior sets, so the film was shot on via Pontina in the Dinocittà studios de Laurentiis had built and abandoned. Maybe Fellini took some ironic pleasure from the fact that, as he made *La voce della luna*, Dino had filed for Chapter 11 bankruptcy protection in the United States with losses in the hundreds of millions of dollars. But in 1992 Dino fought back with the old flair, announcing that he was about to make *The Bible* again, this time for TV, though with a venerable Angelo Arpa once more as his adviser.

La voce della luna was shown at Cannes in 1990, out of competition, but to less than rapturous acclaim. The French critic Bernard Genin spoke for many when he wrote of 'the eclipse of the *maestro*'. This was Fellini's most assured film in years, and certainly the most personal, but the very recognisability of his concerns and the familiarity of the ingredients made it seem negligible. Andrew Sarris had remarked as early as 1961: 'There is more to a great film than a great conception, and Fellini has enlarged his material without expanding his ideas.' Fellini never learned to look beyond his childhood, and, no matter how flamboyant, inventive and original his improvisations might be, he would inevitably exhaust its possibilities. Like Gatsby, he paid the price of living too long with the same dream.

But Fellini remained as lordly as ever, still the king of Rome. When the 1992 Taormina Festival put together a season of sponsored movies by Italy's best directors, including his commercials, he declined to attend. 'I'm not coming to Taormina, not even in a coffin,' he said. 'It would be like accompanying myself to a party I don't want to go to.' All the same, he did make available some of his work-prints, complete with their legendary guide tracks. For the first time people outside his circle became aware of just how indelible had been his mark on films like *Satyricon* and how rigorous his control.

Since 1990 and the failure of *La voce della luna*, Fellini has seldom been out of the trade papers. In 1991 he announced that he was about to start work for Ibrahim Moussa on the documentary, now called *Cinema*, that they'd planned at the time of *Intervista*. 'My film will be composed of four sections. The first speaks of producers, the problems I've had with them and that they, sometimes, have had with me. The second throws a personal spotlight on the actors that I particularly love – Giulietta Masina, the indispensable Marcello Mastroianni, the comics Paolo Villaggio and Roberto Benigni, the beautiful Francesca Dellera. In the third, I tackle the art of singing. I'm not a specialist, but that domain has always fascinated me. The fourth . . . well, we'll see about that later.' But after this confident announcement in August 1991, nothing more was heard of *Cinema*. Not even his honorary Academy

Award in 1993, presented by a dutiful Mastroianni, could persuade his many Hollywood admirers to invest in a new Fellini film.

Fellini told Ennio Cavalli in 1992: 'There are no films lying unmade in the drawer', but in private he talked to Benigni about the possibility of making *Il viaggio*, the old ghost rising up as it had before to taunt him. In other respects, however, Fellini seemed to have come to an accommodation with the world. He still dreams of himself, he says wonderingly, as a young man, dark-haired, slim and energetic. 'I feel as if my years have passed suddenly, have betrayed me. I'm not really certain what I was doing when I was fifty-one, thirty-eight or sixty-three, or how many years have actually passed. I feel somewhat bewildered, stunned, and I find myself forced to admit – with wonder if not astonishment – that fifty years of work have slipped away inside a film studio, moving a person a little closer, asking for lights, putting the right lines into the mouths of others. I feel as if I had lived through one long single year.'

32 Postscript

Fellini: 'How are you going to show me? Young? Old?'
Fayolles: 'Immortal.'
Conversation with photographer Eric Fayolles, 1990

In June of 1993, in secrecy, Fellini entered a Zurich clinic for sixteen hours of bypass heart surgery. Rather than brave the paparazzi in Rome, he elected to convalesce in Rimini, behind the black steel security gates of the Grand Hotel. Given the bad luck Fellini always associated with Rimini, his decision was puzzling and, finally, fateful. On 8 August, he collapsed with a stroke and was rushed to the local hospital, his left arm, left leg, and the left half of his face paralyzed.

Once out of danger, he transferred to a Ferrara clinic specialising in stroke therapy. It immediately became the focus of media attention. Messages of goodwill arrived from all over the world. Even Madonna, whom Fellini had never met, sent flowers and a note saying she hoped to work with him someday. Ruefully, since he must have known his career was over, Fellini said, 'Why not? She's a beautiful girl.'

Masina, constantly at his side, was joined by other members of the court. As Roberto Benigni left the clinic, the actor made some ambiguous remarks to the press, suggesting that the collapse was nothing but a Fellini stunt, then switching tone to announce that the *maestro* was near death. The following week, Fellini's long-time secretary Fiametta Profili issued a tight-lipped 'clarification.' His mind was alert. He could talk and even draw a little. Doctors hoped to restore partial use of his arm, though they suspected his leg would never recover. She shrugged off Benigni's remarks. 'You know actors. They are always playing about.'

On 9 October Fellini was transferred to the Umberto I Hospital in Rome. Allowed out for the first time on Sunday, 17 October, to spend the day with Giulietta, he returned that night and, while eating dinner, suffered another, more massive stroke. His brain was so badly damaged that doctors offered little hope of recovery.

A tasteless but archetypally Roman death-watch began in front of the hospital. To entertain the crowd, music from Fellini's films were played over the public address system. He was given the last rites. Friends mounted a guard to exclude the paparazzi, but at least one got through. In an unexpected display of respect, almost nobody bought the pictures of Fellini enmeshed in cables and tubes, not even in Italy, where his condition was a matter of national interest. Only his old antagonist Silvio Berlusconi ignored the call by Guilietta and Maddalena not to use the shots. 'He doesn't deserve any more respect than anyone else,' said a Canale 5 spokesman. 'Each day, newspapers publish much more dramatic pictures.'

Fellini lingered. On 23 October a tracheotomy was performed to help his breathing but at the same time doctors declared his brain dead. He died the following Sunday, 30 October, late in the morning. It was his fiftieth wedding anniversary, almost to the hour.

Fellini's gradual slipping away gave ample time to prepare obituaries and tributes. The flops were forgotten, and his triumphs recalled with enthusiasm. Both church and government declared themselves ready to reverse a half-century of disapproval. Cardinal Achille Silvestrini, Vatican Prefect of the Congregation for the Oriental Churches, announced that, as a 'friend of the family,' he would officiate at the funeral. President Oscar Luigi Scalfaro, who, thirty-three years before, had denounced *La Dolce Vita* in the Vatican's *L'Osservatore Romano* for its 'scenes of perversion, prostitution, and orgiastic eroticism', confirmed he would lead the mourners.

On Tuesday, 2 November, the body lay in state at Cinecitta on Stage 5. National guardsmen flanked the coffin displayed on a dais against a cyclorama of blue sky. Thousands of ordinary Romans as well as scores of filmmakers filed past. The low-key event was in contrast to the funeral the next day at Michelangelo's Church of Santa Maria degli Angeli. Among the *pezzi grossi*—bigwigs—who swept up in limousines and were ushered into a private enclosure were Franco Zeffirelli, his feud with Fellini forgotten; Michelangelo Antonioni, himself mute, livid, and tottering from brain damage; Francesco Rosi; Costa-Gavras; Lina Wertmuller; Vittorio Gassman; Angelo Arpa; and Sandra Milo. Hollywood, however, was notably absent. Clutching a rosary, Giulietta appeared from the sacristy leaning on her brother Mario. She wore white. 'Federico hated mourning,' she explained.

The doors closed thirty minutes before the service, leaving ten-thousand people jammed into piazza della Republica. Inside, Mozart's *Requiem* was interrupted by the twitter of mobile phones and the 'Pronto? Pronto?' of mourners too self-important to turn them off even for a funeral. Silvestrini told the congregation that Fellini's work was 'poetry, which enters the hearts of the people. We should put our questions to the poets, listen to them for the knowledge they have of the suffering world.' True, Fellini had denounced the Church, but 'with irony and love.' A solo trumpet played Gelsomina's song from *La Strada* and Silvestrini descended from the altar to kiss Giulietta's hand. It was an event to the obsequiousness, dishonesty, and sentiment of which only Fellini himself might have done justice.

Many editorials and obituaries, especially in Italy, remarked that Fellini's death ended an era. For once the generalisations had merit. It was more than apt that he should die just as Italy was convulsed by scandals and purges that expunged within a few months a generation of power-brokers and opinion-makers. No filmmaker more accurately mirrored the nation they created, nor with such enthusiasm. The indignation of *La Dolce Vita*, like that which suffused his vision of imperial Rome in *Satyricon* and of fascism in *Amarcord*, had the lubriciousness of someone who relished a scandal or a celebrity. Even the replacement of his own past with something more befitting his status accorded with the ethics of their world. 'Why not?' he must have asked himself. In an Italy of industrial robber barons and Vatican-created marquesses and princes, where every journalist and pimp was at least a *dottore* or *professore*, a little biographical enhancement was excused—even expected.

After his posthumous and unwilling welcome back into the Church, Fellini was even more humiliatingly repatriated to Rimini, to be interred next to Urbano and Ida rather than in his beloved Rome. He could have taken comfort, however, from the obituaries that dusted off the fantasies he'd spent so much time confecting. His fictional circus days, the imaginary months spent with the Salesians, his phantom redrawing of Flash Gordon in Florence and going on the road with Aldo Fabrizi all lived again, achieving a reality they never had in life. The myth had won, as he always intended it to.

Nobody who met Fellini ever forgot the experience. The power of his personality was like sunlight, surrounding him with an air of good humour and calm. He behaved like the guru of some radical sect whose central tenet of faith was his own infallibility. What if messiahs have acolytes and worshippers but few friends? It was a price Fellini was more than prepared to pay for immortality.

Once, over coffee at Caffe Canova, I mentioned Magali Noel's lament that he'd cut her best scene from *Amarcord*. 'A poster? Gary Cooper?' He looked out over piazza del Popolo as if he saw Broderick Crawford and his daughter walking towards him from forty years ago. 'I don't recall a scene with a poster.' And immediately one felt one's belief begin to falter. Might Noel have invented that detail? How could one find out? I realised in that instant that it was time to pay the bill and move on. The spell had begun to work on me as it had on thousands of others. I never saw him again.

But before I forget—from all your friends: *'Ciao, maestro.'*

—John Baxter
Paris, 1993

Acknowledgements

Given a subject who systematically destroys his papers and who has admitted proudly that he lies to everyone, I decided that the most sensible way to approach Fellini's life was through the written record and the reminiscences of colleagues and friends.

Signor Fellini was cordial in talking to me, placed no barriers in the way of the book's writing and responded amiably to everything requested of him, but he has not read the book and did not ask to do so.

For sharing their experiences of Fellini and for giving me access to their files and records I'm grateful to Gideon Bachmann, Liliana Betti, Deborah Beer, Alain Cuny, Dominique Delouche, Catherine Deneuve, Maddalena Fellini Fabbri, Eric Fayolles, Bryan Forbes, Harold Innocent, Freddie Jones, Madeleine Lebeau, Gerald Morin, Magali Noël, Silvia Pinal, Tullio Pinelli, Daniel Toscan du Plantier, Marika Rivera, Yves Simon, Dudley Sutton, Bernardino Zapponi, and to Fabio Diottalevi and his many friends at Cinecittà, as well as to the people of Rimini.

In my researches, Brian and Mary Troath, and the staff of the Australian Embassy in Rome, especially Clelia March, were invaluable. My thanks also to Rebecca Levin, Pat McGilligan, the Bibliothèque André Malraux, the British Film Institute, the staff of the American Library in Paris, Laurène L'Allinec, Patrick Marnham. Bill Warren, Silvia dal Mastri, Florent LeClerc and Eric Joseph of the Villa des Médicis. My wife, Marie-Dominique Montel, was, as ever, an unfailing source of support and shrewd criticism, and an indefatigable translator.

Like all Fellini scholars, I owe a great debt to my senior colleague in the field, Tullio Kezich, whose admirably researched *Fellini* (Biblioteca Universale Rizzoli, Milan, 1987) was a valuable guide to Fellini's career. Hollis Alpert's *Fellini: A Life* (Paragon, New York, 1988) and Peter Bondanella's critical study *The Cinema of Federico Fellini* (Princeton University Press, Princeton, 1992), as well as the latter's many other books of Fellini scholarship, were never less than stimulating.

Index